SOUL ON FIRE

SOUL ON FIRE
A Life of Thomas Russell

James Quinn

IRISH ACADEMIC PRESS

DUBLIN • PORTLAND, OR

First published in 2002 by
IRISH ACADEMIC PRESS
44, Northumberland Road, Dublin 4, Ireland
and in the United States America by
IRISH ACADEMIC PRESS
c/o ISBS, 5824 NE Hassalo Street, Portland,
OR 97213 3644

Website: www.iap.ie

British Library Cataloguing in Publication Data
Quinn, James
Soul on fire: a life of Thomas Russell, 1767–1803
1. Russell, Thomas, 1767–1803 2. United Irishmen – History
3. Revolutionaries – Ireland – Biography 4. Ireland – I. Title
941.5′07′092

Library of Congress Cataloguing-in-Publication Data
Quinn, James, 1961 –
Soul on fire: a life of Thomas Russell, 1767–1803/James Quinn.
p.cm.
Includes bibliographical references and index.
ISBN 0-7165-2732-4 (alk paper)
1. Russell, Thomas 1767–1803. 2. Revolutionaries–Ulster (Northern Ireland
and Ireland) – Biography. 3. Nationalists–Ulster (Northern Ireland and Ireland –
Biography. 4. Nationalism – Ireland – History 18th century. 5. Ireland–Politics
and government – 1760–1820. 6. United Irishmen–Biography. I. Title.

DA948.6.R87 Q56 2001
941.607′092–dc21
[B]   2001039176
ISBN 0-7165-2732-4

Typeset in 11pt on 13pt Sabon
by FiSH Books, London.
Printed by MPG Books Ltd., Bodmin, Cornwall

To my parents, Joseph and Helen

Every motive exists to stimulate the generous mind — the widows and orphans of my friends, the memory of the heroes who fell, and the sufferings of the heroes who survive. My very soul is on fire; I can say no more.

(Thomas Russell, Fort George, to John Templeton, 5 June 1802
(TCD, Madden papers, 873/638.)

Contents

List of Illustrations

List of Abbreviations

B.L.	British Library
Bartlett, *Life of Tone*	Thomas Bartlett (ed.), *Life of Theobald Wolfe Tone* (Dublin, 1998)
Beresford corre.	William Beresford (ed.), *The correspondence of the Rt. Hon. John Beresford*, 2 vols (London, 1854)
Byrne, *Memoirs*	*Memoirs of Miles Byrne, ed. by his widow*, 3 vols (Paris, 1863)
Camden papers	Kent County Record Office (Maidstone), Pratt (Camden) papers
Castlereagh corr.	*Robert Stewart, 2nd marquess of Londonderry (Viscount Castlereagh), memoirs and correspondence*, 12 vols (London, 1848–54)
Charlemont MS	Historical Manuscripts Commission, *The manuscripts and correspondence of James, first earl of Charlemont*, 2 vols (London, 1891–4)
Colchester corr.	Lord Charles Abbot Colchester (ed.), *Diary and correspondence of Charles Abbot, Lord Colchester*, 3 vols (London, 1861)
Commons jn. Ire.	*Journal of the house of commons of the kingdom of Ireland*
Cornwallis corr.	Charles Ross, *Correspondence of Charles 1st Marquis Cornwallis*, 3 vols (London, 1849)
Curtin, 'Transformation of U.I.'	Nancy J. Curtin, 'The transformation of the Society of United Irishmen into a mass-based organisation, 1794–6' in *Irish Historical Studies*, xxiv, no. 96 (Nov. 1985), pp. 463–92
Curtin, *United Irishmen*	Nancy J. Curtin, *The United Irishmen, popular politics in Ulster and Dublin 1791–8* (Oxford, 1994)

DNB	*Dictionary of national biography*, 22 vols (London, 1908-9)
Dickson, *Narrative*	William Steel Dickson, *Narrative of confinement and exile* (Dublin, 1814)
Dickson, Keogh and Whelan (eds), *United Irishmen*	David Dickson, Dáire Keogh and Kevin Whelan (eds), *The United Irishmen: republicanism, radicalism and rebellion* (Dublin, 1993)
Drennan letters	D. A. Chart (ed.), *The Drennan letters, 1776–1819* (Belfast, 1931)
Drennan papers	Public Record Office of Northern Ireland, Drennan papers
Elliott, 'Despard conspiracy'	Marianne Elliott, 'The "Despard conspiracy" reconsidered' in *Past and Present*, 75 (1977), pp. 46–61
Elliott, *Partners*	Marianne Elliott, *Partners in revolution: the United Irishmen and France* (New Haven and London, 1982)
Elliott, *Tone*	Marianne Elliott, *Wolfe Tone: prophet of Irish independence* (New Haven and London, 1989)
Emmet memoir	T. A. Emmet (ed.), *Memoir of Thomas Addis and Robert Emmet*, 2 vols (New York, 1915)
Frazer MS	National Archives, Frazer manuscripts
Fruchtman, 'Apocalyptic politics'	Jack Fruchtman jun., 'The apocalyptic politics of Richard Price and Joseph Priestley: a study of late eighteenth century millennialism' in *Transactions of the American Philosophical Society*, lxxiii, pt. 4 (Philadelphia, 1983)
Gough and Dickson (eds), *Ire. and Fr.Rev.*	Hugh Gough and David Dickson (eds), *Ireland and the French revolution* (Dublin, 1990)
Hope papers	Trinity College Dublin, Hope manuscripts
I. H. S.	*Irish Historical Studies* (Dublin, 1938–)
Journals	C. J. Woods (ed.), *Journals and memoirs of Thomas Russell, 1791–5* (Dublin, 1991)
Lecky, *Ireland*	W. E. H. Lecky, *A history of Ireland in the eighteenth century*, 5 vols (London, 1892)

Lion of old Eng.	*Review of the lion of old England* (Belfast, 1794)
MacDonagh, *Viceroy's postbag*	Michael MacDonagh (ed.), *The viceroy's postbag* (London, 1904)
Mac Giolla Easpaig, *Ruiséil*	Séamus N. Mac Giolla Easpaig, *Tomás Ruiséil* (Dublin, 1957)
MacNeven, *Pieces*	W. J. MacNeven, *Pieces of Irish history* (New York, 1807)
McSkimin, 'Insurrection of 1803'	Samuel McSkimin, 'Secret history of the Irish insurrection of 1803' in *Frazer's Magazine,* xiv (July–Dec. 1836), pp. 546–67
Madden papers	Trinity College Dublin, Madden papers
Madden, *United Irishmen*	R. R. Madden, *The United Irishmen, their lives and times,* 3rd ser., 3 vols (Dublin, 1846)
Madden, *Antrim and Down in '98*	R. R. Madden, *Antrim and Down in '98* (Glasgow, 1888)
Belfast Soc. minute books	Linen Hall library, Belfast, The Minute Books of the Society for Promoting Knowledge
Morgan, 'Sketch of Russell'	James Morgan, 'Sketch of the life of Thomas Russell' in *Ulster Magazine,* i (1830), pp. 39–60
N.L.I.	National Library of Ireland
Paddy's resource	*Paddy's resource: being a select collection of modern and patriotic songs for the use of the people of Ireland* (Belfast, 1795 and 1798) and (Dublin, 1803)
Parl. reg. Ire.	*The parliamentary register: or, history and debates of the House of Commons of Ireland, 1781–97,* 17 vols (Dublin, 1782–1801)
P.R.O., HO	Public Record Office, (Kew), Home Office papers
P.R.O., P.C.	Public Record Office, (Kew), Privy Council papers
P.R.O.N.I.	Public Record Office, Northern Ireland
1798 rebellion in County Down	Myrtle Hill, Brian Turner, Kenneth Dawson (eds), *1798 rebellion in County Down* (Newtownards, 1998)

Reb. papers — National Archives of Ireland, Rebellion papers

Rep. comm. sec. — *Reports of the committees of secrecy of the House of Commons and House of Lords of Ireland, with appendices* (Dublin, 1798)

Russell, *Letter to the people* — Thomas Russell, *A letter to the people of Ireland on the present situation of the country* (Belfast, 1796)

S.O.C. — National Archives of Ireland, State of the country papers

Sirr papers — Trinity College, Dublin, Sirr papers

Smyth, *Men of no property* — Jim Smyth, *The men of no property: Irish radicals and popular politics in the late eighteenth century* (Dublin, 1992)

Thuente, *Harp re-strung* — Mary Helen Thuente, *The harp re-strung: the United Irishmen and the rise of Irish literary nationalism* (New York, 1994)

Tone, *Writings* — T. W. Moody, R. B. McDowell and C. J. Woods (eds), *The writings of Theobald Wolfe Tone 1973–98: volume I: Tone's career in Ireland to June 1795* (Oxford, 1998)

Woods, 'Place of Thomas Russell' — C. J. Woods, 'The place of Thomas Russell in the United Irish movement', in Hugh Gough and David Dickson (eds), *Ireland and the French revolution* (Dublin, 1990), pp. 83–108

Acknowledgements

In acknowledging the assistance I received with this book I must first mention the contribution of James McGuire of University College Dublin, who supervised the doctoral thesis on which it was based; I am deeply indebted to him for his constructive criticism, sound advice and constant encouragement. I would also like to thank those members of the UCD history department who stimulated my interest in late eighteenth-century radicalism and assisted me in various ways, notably Professor Thomas Bartlett, Dr Maurice Bric, Professor Mary Daly, Professor Fergus D'Arcy and Dr Eamon O'Flaherty; the advice and encouragement of Professor Louis Cullen of Trinity College, Dublin, and Professor Kevin Whelan of the University of Notre Dame are also much appreciated. I owe a great debt to my colleague Dr C. J. Woods: firstly, for his painstaking work in editing and publishing Russell's journals, which greatly eased my task; secondly, for the way in which he generously made available to me his research materials on Russell; and thirdly, for his comments and corrections to my text. I would also like to acknowledge the assistance of the staff in the various libraries and archives in which I worked, especially Siobhán O'Rafferty, Bernadette Cunningham and Marcus Browne in the library of the Royal Irish Academy.

For their helpful comments on the text or general assistance I wish to thank Kate Bateman, Jeremy Chapman, Catherine Conway, Richard Hawkins, Avril Hoare, John Killen, Dr Linde Lunney, Dr Ian McBride, Dr Eoin Magennis, Dr Breandán MacSuibhne, Dr Éamonn Ó Ciardha and Paul Quinn. I would also like to thank my grandmother, Mrs Margaret Reilly, for pointing out to me some of the landmarks of eighteenth-century Dublin, and to thank Dr Manuela Ceretta for her philosophic insights, general supportiveness and for taking my mind off Thomas Russell.

Finally I owe a great debt to my mother and father for their encouragement and support over the years, and it is to them that I dedicate this book.

Introduction

'A lovable creature, a devoted friend, a sincere patriot, he might for all that never have been recorded if it were not for Tone's admiration for him — teasing, mocking, but always affectionate.'[1] So says Sean O'Faolain of Thomas Russell in his edition of Tone's journals. This has long been the traditional view of Russell: a genial and faithful companion to Tone, accorded his place in Irish history as a mere supporting character to his more celebrated friend. Patrick Pearse, for example, shared this impression, declaring that he had 'always loved the very name of Thomas Russell because Tone loved him so'.[2] Such a view, however, seriously undervalues Russell's historical importance. Of late, modern historians have recognised this and have begun to treat him as a notable figure in his own right. For Christopher Woods, Thomas Russell was the 'most dedicated and determined of the United Irishmen'; Marianne Elliott has noted that his 'contribution to the development of Irish republican nationalism has been grossly underestimated'; while Mary Helen Thuente regards him as the 'quintessential' United Irishman.[3]

Russell's career as a United Irishman is unique, spanning the foundation of the society in 1791 to its last stand in 1803. During these twelve years probably no other member was as indefatigable in promoting the aims of the movement. In the latter part of 1791 he was a key figure in the preparations for the founding of both the Belfast and Dublin United Irish societies. Thereafter, he was closely involved in the movement's constitutional agitation for parliamentary reform and Catholic emancipation, particularly as one of the United Irishmen's leading propagandists. When in 1794–5 the political climate changed, and the United Irishmen were reconstituted as a popular secret society with avowedly republican aims, Russell was in the vanguard of this transformation. He was among the United Irish leaders who swore the celebrated oath on Cave Hill not to desist from agitation until Ireland had achieved her independence, and he remained committed to this solemn pledge until his death.

During 1795–6 Russell travelled tirelessly throughout Ulster building up the new United Irish movement. He was in the forefront of attempts to incorporate the Defenders into the republican movement and he assumed a key command when the United Irishmen

1

began to organise themselves on a military footing. Until the time of his imprisonment, perhaps no other United Irishman had such direct involvement in the organisation of the underground republican movement. This was done with as much secrecy as possible, and the fact that so much of his radical and revolutionary activism was carried out behind the scenes has contributed to the underestimation of Russell's influence on militant Irish republicanism. His activities, however, did come to the attention of the authorities and he was arrested on a charge of high treason in September 1796.

Held in custody for an uninterrupted term of almost six years — longer than any other United Irish leader — Russell still continued his revolutionary activism from prison. After the rising of 1798 he proved far more reluctant than most of his fellow United Irishmen to open negotiations with the government. Although he eventually acquiesced in his colleagues' decision to give information to the Castle in return for the ending of executions, he continued to plot and was one of the chief organisers of plans for insurrection in the early part of 1799. Even after he was packed off to the remote Fort George in Scotland by a nervous Irish government, his resolve remained unshaken. His letters from these years reveal no weakening in his revolutionary ardour, but bristle with a firm determination to take up the struggle again at the first available opportunity.

Released from prison in June 1802, he spent some time in Paris before being summoned back to Ireland by Robert Emmet in the spring of 1803 to assist in his plans for insurrection. Russell was given the task of raising the North but, although he attempted this with all the energy and eloquence at his disposal, much had changed in Ulster in the past six years and the province refused to rise. Soon afterwards, he was arrested, convicted on a charge of high treason and hanged in Downpatrick on 21 October 1803.

Russell's political development is an instructive example of the impact of the polarising forces which operated on Irish politics in the 1790s. At the beginning of the decade he was an admirer of the parliamentary Whigs and he appears to have aspired to nothing more than moderate political and social reform. However, the rapidly changing events of these years soon worked a powerful influence on his outlook. The latter half of 1792 and the early part of 1793 was a key period. These months saw the elections for and the summoning of the Catholic Convention, the spread of a more politicised form of Defenderism, a strong Protestant backlash against this novel level of politicisation and assertiveness in the Catholic community, and eventually the grudging abolition of most, but not all, of the penal laws. There was also the continuing controversy between supporters and opponents of a rapidly radicalising French revolution, the outbreak of war with France, and the subsequent enactment of a range of repressive legislation by the Irish parliament with the acquiescence of the opposition Whigs. Appalled by what he saw as the opposition's capitulation to a tyrannical government, by 1793 Russell had shed his whiggish sympathies and become one of Grattan's most scathing critics. The next couple of years saw his position harden even further and by the middle of the decade he had committed himself to the overthrow of British rule in Ireland.

In terms of both his political and social outlook, Russell was among the most radical of all the United Irishmen. No other prominent member proclaimed the rights of the common man so forcefully: in an age suspicious of democracy Russell expressed the forthright opinion that 'it is not only the right but the *essential duty* of every man to interest himself in the conduct of the government'.[4] Moreover, his democratic instincts extended into the social as well as the political sphere. He accepted that a thorough reform of the existing system of property-holding was needed to alleviate the plight of the poor; he encouraged artisans and labourers to form combinations to protect their interests; and although he took a keen interest in the new industrial technology, he was appalled by harsh conditions that the factory system inflicted on its employees. An inveterate rambler, he often came into contact with ordinary working people on his travels and regularly extolled their virtues, praising their warmth and generosity, as well as their understanding of political matters. His attitude contrasts sharply with that of Tone, who in the early 1790s at least, showed little sympathy with the poor and dismissed the Defenders as rabble. Russell, however, reserved his most scathing criticism for the wealthy and privileged, and the moral superiority of the poor to the rich is a recurrent theme in his writings.

Russell's social radicalism was largely a product of his religious beliefs. His sense of Christian ethics filled him with a sincere and genuine outrage at the injustices of the day. He believed that these injustices were an affront to God, the work of self-interested minorities who had used their powers and privileges to frustrate the divine plan of liberty and justice for all, and he sympathised with all those who suffered oppression. In particular, he viewed the slave trade as an abomination and seldom missed the opportunity to rail against it in his writings.

An essential element of Russell's Christianity was his belief in the doctrine of the millennium — the thousand years of justice and harmony that scripture had foretold would precede the end of the world. Russell's millennialist beliefs have largely been ignored by his previous biographers, although they have been examined in a brief but insightful article by John Gray.[5] This work contends that understanding Russell's millennialism is the key to understanding his career. It was the conviction that his efforts to establish a world of peace and justice marched in step with a providentially-ordered plan which convinced him of the righteousness of his cause, and gave him complete confidence in its eventual success. He believed that the turmoil of the 1790s and early 1800s represented the time of troubles that the book of Revelations had foretold would precede the thousand years of Christ's reign on earth, and that it was the duty of Christians to prepare the way for Christ's kingdom by liberating humanity from the political, social and intellectual shackles that held them in thrall. Millennialism, offering as it did the prospect of far-reaching change, held a particular appeal for the poor or for those who wanted a fundamental improvement in the position of the poor, and could easily be transmuted into a revolutionary doctrine for the transformation of society. Thus Russell's religious, political and social views were all closely intertwined in his millennialist vision. His commitment to establishing the millennium does much to explain his steadfast adherence to United Irish ideals while many of his colleagues fell by the wayside. This was particularly so during the last months of his life when, failing to appreciate the dramatic change of mood that had taken place in Ulster during his exile, he remained confident that he could effect a rebellion in the province, in spite of overwhelming evidence to the contrary.

On a personal as well as a political level, Russell is an intriguing man. He had an extensive range of interests: his personal papers covered such diverse topics as literature, biblical scholarship, anthropology, political economy, manufacturing and agricultural processes and techniques, chemistry, physics, biology and geology. Similarly, his restlessness led him to embark on a number of different careers. In his youth he had strongly considered becoming a clergyman and before his imprisonment in 1796 at the age of twenty-eight, he had served as a soldier in both India and Ireland, as a magistrate, a journalist and a librarian, in addition to performing a host of tasks as a United Irish emissary and organiser. His clerical and military training were important formative influences: throughout his life he combined the bearing of a soldier with the manner of an earnest young clergyman. He did not , however, lead the life of an earnest young clergyman. He drank heavily and was sexually promiscuous, and was afflicted by bouts of deep anguish and remorse in the wake of his debauches. Prone to brooding and self-doubt, he regarded himself as an abject sinner and often lapsed into prolonged bouts of morbid despair. To a great extent he regarded his political activities as a form of atonement for his moral failings, and this was one of the crucial motivations behind his resolute commitment to the ideals of the United Irishmen.

His bouts of brooding and despair were simply one facet of a complex and enigmatic personality. Russell also had many attractive personal qualities and excited strong feelings of admiration and devotion in his colleagues. A charming and strikingly handsome man, he frequently crops up in the letters and memoirs of contemporaries as a fascinating and charismatic figure. His personal charm helped to ease his way into aristocratic circles and polite Belfast society, while his radically egalitarian views and personal poverty ensured that he felt equally at home among artisans and labourers. Once they became a mass movement, the United Irishmen contained men of all classes and creeds, and the strains often showed. Russell, with his rare mobility between social classes, acted as a bridge between the lower orders and wealthier elements within the movement. In addition to spanning the social divide, he often performed the same function between Belfast and Dublin, and between Catholic and Protestant. A restless individual, through either choice or circumstance Russell was almost constantly on the move throughout the northern half of the country. This gave him something of a rootless, mysterious quality — evoked in the well-known ballad written about him, 'The man from God-knows-where'.[6]

As a rootless *déclassé* Russell was well qualified to bridge social and geographical divides, and in a similar way his religious views enabled him to reach out to people of all faiths. Baptised into the Church of Ireland, he played the role of Catholic advocate during the foundation of the United Irishmen and he also came to feel a deep kinship with Belfast Presbyterians. Russell remained a devout Christian throughout his life — he strongly disapproved of the deism fashionable in some republican circles and was deeply offended by

Paine's *Age of reason*. He respected all forms of Christianity and the establishment of religious fraternity in Ireland was one of the great objectives of his life. He viewed this as not simply a tactical alliance to help achieve parliamentary reform or national independence, as it undoubtedly was for some United Irish colleagues, but as a cherished goal in itself. This absence of class or sectarian prejudice put him in an ideal position to make overtures to the Catholic peasantry and he was among the most committed of the United Irishmen in attempt-ing to forge an alliance with the Defenders. He also made an effort to bridge the gap between English and Gaelic cultural traditions, showing a genuine interest in Gaelic culture. Lastly, he forms a junc-ture between those who, seeking constitutional reforms, were present at the birth of the United Irishmen in 1791 and the small group willing to resort to arms in 1803.

In his pivotal position within the organisation, Russell numbered among his close friends the most celebrated of the United Irishmen: Theobald Wolfe Tone, Robert Emmet and Henry Joy McCracken. He exerted considerable influence on all three, particularly on Tone. Russell's intervention at particular points in Tone's career would prove critical, most notably in drawing him into the founding of the United Irishmen and in encouraging him to seek a French invasion. Tone himself, on his own admission, relied heavily on Russell's advice and assistance in his work, and one of his chief motivations in all he did was to impress his beloved friend. Theirs was a friend-ship of considerable importance in Irish history and it was, moreover, a friendship of equals.

NOTES

1   Sean O'Faolain (ed.), *The autobiography of Theobald Wolfe Tone* (London, 1937), p. 28n.
2   P. H. Pearse, *How does she stand?* (2nd ed, Dublin, 1915), p. 5.
3   Woods, 'Place of Thomas Russell', p. 96; Elliott, *Tone*, p. 95; Thuente, *Harp re-strung*, p. 18.
4   Russell, *Letter to the people*, p. 14.
5   John Gray, 'Millennial vision…Thomas Russell re-assessed' in *Linen Hall Review*, vi, no. 1 (spring, 1989), pp. 5–9.
6   Florence Mary Wilson, *The coming of the earls* (Dublin, 1918), pp. 9–12.

CHAPTER ONE

Ensign Russell

In July 1790 war was in the air. Spanish ships had seized the cargoes of two British vessels off Nootka Sound on the north-west coast of America, and the Irish parliament reconvened for a short time to vote funds and to prepare the country for war. Few at College Green doubted the righteousness of Britain's cause: even the normally fractious Whigs were ostentatiously playing the role of loyal opposition, with Henry Grattan pledging that Ireland would 'rise or fall with Great Britain'.[1]

Parliamentary debates were one of the great spectacles of the day and on such important occasions the House of Commons' public gallery was packed to capacity. Among those present on 2 July were Thomas Russell, a 22-year-old army officer, and Theobald Wolfe Tone, a 27-year-old barrister. Both men had little better to do: Tone was attracting little legal business while Russell had not been assigned to a regiment for several years. Although they did not know each other they became embroiled in a friendly political argument: Russell was a supporter of the Whigs, whereas Tone was already disillusioned with them and had written a pamphlet on the proposed war with Spain that was implicitly critical of their position.[2] Ironically, for two men drawn together by a disagreement they soon discovered that they had much in common. Nor was it the first time that Russell's path had crossed that of a member of the Tone family: while travelling to India in 1783 he met Tone's uncle Jonathan, an ensign in the 22nd regiment. Russell lent him £5 and Tone's father had settled the debt. It is also likely that Russell and Tone discovered that they were both acquainted with the Knox family of Tyrone: while completing his legal training at the Middle Temple in London, Tone had formed a close friendship with George Knox, the younger brother of Colonel John Knox, who had fought alongside Russell in India.[3]

Tone and Russell were immediately taken with each other. They were both intelligent, witty men but with differing personalities that

complemented each other. Tone was the more assured and self-confi-
dent of the two, Russell quieter and more reflective. They agreed to
meet on the following day to continue their discussions. Some years
later Tone recalled his meeting with Russell. He described it as:

> a circumstance which I look upon as one of the most fortunate of my
> life. He is a man whom I love as a brother . . . to an excellent under-
> standing, he joins the purest principles and the best of hearts. I wish I
> had ability to delineate his character, with justice to his talents and
> virtues. He well knows how much I esteem and love him, and I think
> there is no sacrifice that friendship could exact that we would not
> with cheerfulness make for each other, to the utmost hazard of life or
> fortune. There cannot be imagined a more perfect harmony, I may say
> identity of sentiment, than exists between us; our regard for each
> other has never suffered a moment's relaxation from the hour of our
> first acquaintance, and I am sure it will continue to the end of our
> lives. I think the better of myself for being the object of the esteem of
> such a man as Russell. I love him and I honour him.[4]

Tone was to come to rely greatly on Russell's friendship. When
deprived of his company, he invariably bemoaned the fact, and he
usually mentioned Russell in the same breath as his wife when talking of those he most loved. Russell was not generally so expressive
about his feelings towards Tone but he seems to have been as devoted
to Tone as Tone was to him. He certainly had a high opinion of his
friend's abilities and 'always foretold great things' for him.[5]

This chance meeting was perhaps the most significant encounter
of Russell's life. He had met someone who had political contacts,
firm political views, and a strong desire to act on them, who would
help him harness and channel his hitherto inchoate idealism. His
meeting with Tone in College Green effectively marked the beginning of Russell's political career, a career that was to end twelve
years later on a scaffold in Downpatrick.

Thomas Russell was born on 21 November 1767 at Betsborough, a
large two-storey farmhouse in the townland of Drommahane in
Kilshannig parish, three miles south-west of Mallow, Co. Cork. His
father, John Russell, was an army lieutenant then stationed at
Mallow. The Russells had come to Ireland from Taunton in Somerset
in the seventeenth century and settled near Kilkenny city. John
Russell's father was a once prosperous tailor but had fallen on hard
times in later life. John Russell, born c.1720, had originally intended

to become a Church of Ireland clergyman and entered Trinity College, Dublin but left before taking his degree — apparently when pressurised to give information against his fellow students following a disturbance in the college.[6] He joined the British army and had a military career of some distinction. He was present at the Battle of Dettingen in 1743 where his conduct was noticed with approval by King George II, and at the bloody battle of Fontenoy in 1745 when the charge of the Irish Brigade turned the tide for the French. He also served in Portugal during the early 1760s. Letters he wrote while serving in Portugal, where he seems to have been in charge of sick troops, give the impression of a kindly man doing his best in difficult circumstances. In his old age he was described by Tone as having 'the courage of a hero, the serenity of a philosopher and the piety of a saint'.[7]

Less is known of Thomas's mother. She was an O'Kennedy from a Co. Tipperary family that was probably Catholic, and her first name may have been Margaret. According to Thomas 'she was the best mother and wife and we all tenderly loved her'. She died on 8 April 1786.[8] John Russell also had Catholic antecedents: his mother was one of the O'Clears, a Catholic gentry family from Ballyragget, Co. Kilkenny. Most of her family's property was confiscated during the Williamite wars, and she and her siblings converted to Protestantism.[9]

Thomas was the youngest child and had three brothers: John (c.1748–c.1815), Ambrose (c.1756–93) and William (d. *ante* 1803); and a sister, Margaret (1752–1834).[10] Because of changes in their father's postings, the family was often on the move. They may have settled near Kilkenny in the late 1750s, and during Thomas's childhood they lived for a time at Durrow in Queen's County. In the early 1770s they moved to Dublin after Lieutenant Russell was appointed Captain of Invalids at the Royal Hospital, Kilmainham, a splendid building on the outskirts of Dublin built to house retired soldiers.[11]

Though John Russell would have been regarded as a gentleman because of his position and commissioned rank, the Russells were a relatively poor family: a lieutenant's pay would have stretched thinly over the rearing of five children and made it difficult to provide them with any real start in life. Money matters were a pressing concern in almost all family correspondence and genteel poverty or worse was to be the lot of most of the Russells. The failure of the authorities to promote his father beyond the rank of lieutenant seems to have been a cause of deep resentment to Thomas in later life.[12] Probably because of family circumstances Thomas was educated entirely at home by his father, who apparently was an accomplished classical scholar, and by his sister Margaret. He was given a good grounding in mathematics, Latin and Greek. John Russell was a devout man who held sincere and broad-minded Christian beliefs which he passed on to his son. Like his father it seems that Thomas was intended for the church, but at the age of fifteen he put his studies aside and enlisted in the army. This may also have been due to family hardship, but whatever the reason, soldiering was in the Russell blood. All of Thomas's brothers followed in their father's footsteps and served in the army. Ambrose became a captain in the 52nd regiment and fought in the American War of Independence. An account of his courage at the storming of Fort Montgomery, in which he was wounded, so impressed George III that he had assured the young officer 'his welfare would be attended to by him'. William Russell was an ensign in the 32nd regiment during the American wars, and later received various other commissions, while John served as an officer in the West London militia.[13]

In March 1783 Ambrose's regiment was sent to India and Thomas sailed with it as a volunteer. This was a course taken by many young men at the time who sought fortune and adventure, particularly those without money or connections. Commissions were granted more easily in the East Indies and there were opportunities for officers who survived the Indian climate, the threat of disease and the hazards of war to amass sizeable sums of money from bounties, plunder, gifts from native rulers and private trading. Russell was commissioned ensign in the 100th regiment of foot on 9 July 1783, but soon afterwards attached to Ambrose's 52nd regiment. He probably received his commission on account of his family's military background, rather than, as Madden maintained, in recognition of any particular act of heroism.[14]

Since 1780 the British East India Company had been at war with the state of Mysore in southern India. Taking advantage of Britain's preoccupation with America, the Mysore prince Haidar Ali had swept into the Carnatic, putting British possessions at risk. Hyder died in December 1782 but the fight was ably carried on by his son, Tipu Sultan, who, assisted by landings of French troops in 1782 and 1783, won several notable victories against British forces. By the summer of 1783 the military situation along the Malabar coast had reached stalemate: the British had taken the strategic port of Mangalore, Mysore's main outlet to the sea, but was now besieged by a large force led by Tipu. In November 1783 Russell's regiment, under the command of Colonel Norman MacLeod, later to be a prominent Scottish radical, took part in an unsuccessful attempt to relieve British forces besieged at Mangalore. After this action they were marched south on a punitive expedition to the small state of Cannanore. The local queen, Ali Rajah Biby, an ally of Tipu, had imprisoned about 200 of the Company's sepoys after they had been shipwrecked off the coast, and the British were determined to punish the queen and free the captured troops. McLeod's troops attacked Cannanore on 10 December 1783 and it fell after four days of stiff fighting. The attackers rescued the sepoys from the queen's dungeons, where they lay naked and starving in chains, and then sacked the town and divided up the plunder.[15]

The British force had four officers and fifty-three men killed or wounded in the attack; one of those wounded was the acting commander of Russell's regiment, Colonel Henry Barry. It seems that young Ensign Russell performed well in this engagement: family lore had it that he carried Barry to safety after he had been wounded and such is the tone of studied modesty that Russell used to describe this incident in a letter to his parents, it is likely that he did indeed distinguish himself. His letter mentioned briefly that Colonel Barry was wounded and that Ambrose 'will give a fuller account, so I shall say no more on this head'. Whatever happened, Russell must have impressed his superior officers because he was soon afterwards appointed aide-de-camp to Colonel Barry.[16] One of those officers he impressed was Colonel John Knox, who commanded the 36th infantry regiment in the attack on Cannanore.[17] Knox was the second son of the first Viscount Northland, who had considerable estates and influence in Co. Tyrone, and his patronage later proved important for Russell.

The attack on Cannanore is Russell's only action in India which is reasonably well documented; he may have been wounded later in fighting at Bangalore, but details of this are vague.[18] By all accounts the campaign against Tipu was a difficult one, with long sieges and marches and counter-marches over difficult terrain.[19] In March 1784 the East India Company and Tipu agreed peace terms and signed the Treaty of Mangalore, which restored the territorial status quo in the region. One of the articles of the treaty stipulated that the fort and district of Cannanore should be evacuated and restored to its former ruler, and accordingly the occupying force returned to the coast of the Coromandel. Russell's regiment then returned to Madras.[20]

We know little of how he spent the rest of his time in India. After the campaign on the Malabar coast it appears that he served with the 52nd regiment mostly in or around the presidency of Madras at such places as Pondicherry, Poonamallee and Arcot. He wrote few letters during this period and of these only a single one to his parents survives. Years later he recalled that 'when in India I could not find either words or ideas to write a letter home to my father and was in great distress at my want of capacity'.[21] He seems to have recorded his Indian experiences in a journal, but this is now lost.[22] The only journal entry that sheds any light on his time in India was written several years later: it reminisced about his 'walks in India from the camp at Cannanore down to Tellicherry. Fifteen miles in that burning climate and for what? To get a wench!'.[23] He may also have spent some of his time in a slightly more edifying manner. Years later his commanding officer, Colonel Barry, wrote in a Dublin newspaper of a 'most agreeable' tour to the spectacular caves on Elephanta Island, near Bombay, around this time.[24] Although he did not mention Russell by name, it is quite possible that he would have been accompanied on this tour by his young aide-de-camp.

Some biographers of Russell maintained that while in India he attempted to protect the native population from acts of oppression perpetrated by the British authorities and that disillusionment with colonial rule was the main reason why he left the sub-continent.[25] Certainly, the rule of the East India Company was far from benevolent in the 1780s: to defray the costs of war it had engaged in several questionable expedients to raise money.[26] Examples of injustices perpetrated by the Company's agents were eagerly seized on by Edmund Burke in 1786 when he called for the impeachment of Warren Hastings, the governor general of British India. Such a sympathy with the oppressed would be in keeping with Russell's later views, but there is no hard evidence to prove the claim one way or the other. A snippet from his one surviving letter of this period suggests that, in his early days in India at least, Russell's concern for the native population was no more than might be expected of the average sixteen-year-old officer: he wrote to his parents to 'tell my sister that I will pluck the ornaments off some black princess to adorn her with at my return'.[27]

As the campaign continued, however, he would undoubtedly have seen many deeply distressing scenes. A report of the war by a British officer painted a grim picture of the misery and hardship endured by the native people in and around Madras:

the infant dying on the breast of the mother, the old and the young, the parents the children mingling their last groans and expiring... whole families in human shape digging in the entrails of dead carrion; and when these means have failed surrendering themselves with a truly Asiatic apathy to the wild dogs and vultures that waited to devour their carcasses.[28]

Russell would have been deeply affected by such scenes. However, those sources which cite his uneasiness with British rule in India claim that it was injuries done to certain members of the Indian aristocracy rather than the misery of the masses that finally disillusioned him, namely his failure 'to protect from indignity and gross injustice the wife and family of one of the petty rajahs' and his 'disgust . . . after witnessing the unjust and rapacious conduct pursued by the authorities in the case of two native women of exalted rank'.[29] The latter may well have been a reference to the celebrated case of the persecution of the elderly princesses of Oude, from whom Hastings had seized lands and treasure in particularly brutal circumstances. This case formed the core of the famous speech made by Richard Brinsley Sheridan in the British House of Commons in February 1787 which led to Hasting's impeachment.[30] However, the actual events occurred in the early 1780s before Russell's arrival in India, and by the time of Sheridan's exposure of Hasting's behaviour in 1787, it is likely that Russell was already returning to Ireland and so these claims seem dubious.

Whether disillusioned with British rule in India or not, Russell's reasons for leaving were probably more mundane: in 1785 his regiment was disbanded.[31] The following year Lord Cornwallis was appointed governor-general of India and landed at Madras on 24 August 1786 with instructions to rationalise the Company's civil and military services and to root out irregular practices. With the region at peace, there were few opportunities open to a young officer and it is likely that Russell had little choice but to return to Ireland, which he did probably in early 1787.[32] If his intention in going to India had been to return with a large sum of money, as it was with most young volunteers, then he was to be disappointed. It seems that he lent most of his savings to a fellow officer who did not repay him. Several years later his brother John was still pursuing the debt in London.[33]

On his return to Ireland it seems that Russell intended to enter the church and he renewed his studies with this in mind. According to

Madden, certain difficulties with ordination regulations arose but it
may be that Russell simply changed his mind. Whatever happened,
he did not become a clergyman.[34] It may be that he took a similar
view to his contemporary Jonah Barrington, who declined a clerical
career on the grounds that 'I could not in conscience take charge of
the morals of a flock of men, women and children when I should
have quite enough to do to manage my own.'[35] We know little about
how Russell spent the next three years or so of his life. He resided
with his father at the Royal Hospital, Kilmainham, living on his
ensign's half pay of £28 a year. It was probably during these years of
leisure that he read widely and laid the foundations of his wide-ranging academic interests. During this time his political interests seem to
have been muted and he seems to have been far more interested in
literary matters. Later, when speaking of this period to a Belfast
friend, he claimed that during these years 'Burke's *Sublime and beautiful* had more charms for him than all the speculations of Mr Paine
on the rights of man'.[36]

These years were a period of marked economic, cultural and
social vitality in Dublin. After the granting of 'free trade' in 1780
and legislative independence to Ireland in 1782 there was a sense
that the country had been freed from its economic and legislative
shackles, and the capital was imbued with a new optimism: agricultural production was on the rise and new industries were springing
up.[37] The buoyant economy generated considerable tax surpluses
which the Irish parliament used for improvements in roads and
canals, and for new buildings. The Irish élite were anxious to make
Dublin a worthy capital of an 'independent' nation and the decade
saw the construction of many of Dublin's grandest architectural
achievements: the Custom House, the Four Courts, the west front of
Trinity College and alterations to Parliament House; impressive
town houses were springing up in North Great George's Street,
Dame Street and Harcourt Street, and the Wide Streets' Commission
was active in broadening and improving the city's main thorough-
fares. Visitors from abroad regularly commented on the city's
growing splendour: one reported that anyone who had left Dublin
even for a short time 'would scarcely know the city, so much is it
improved, so rapidly is it continuing to improve ... I cannot but feel
daily astonishment at the nobleness of the new buildings and the
spacious improvements hourly making in the streets ... there never
was so splendid a metropolis for so poor a country'.[38]

Visitors to the city also often commented on the conviviality and relative openness of Dublin's social life, observing that politicians, soldiers, clergymen and lawyers all mixed together in the great houses. Lord Moira's house on the south quays was the scene of much entertaining and, as Moira was a strong advocate of parliamentary reform and Catholic emancipation, his home was a magnet for a wide spectrum of liberals and radicals — Lord Edward Fitzgerald, Henry Grattan and Charles James Fox were all regular visitors. Lady Moira, a daughter of the earl of Huntingdon, was renowned as a woman of great charm and intelligence, and gathered around her a coterie of interesting young men; in the early 1790s Tone and Russell were among the visitors to her home.[39]

Like other great urban centres at the time, the city also exhibited a strong sense of intellectual curiosity. It had an active scientific community and scientific advances attracted great popular attention, such as Richard Crosbie's first successful balloon flight from Ranelagh gardens in 1785. The burgeoning interest in the sciences and antiquarianism was also indicated by the foundation of the Royal Irish Academy in May 1785, which became one of the main forums for Irish scholarship. This lively intellectual scene forms the backdrop to Russell's life in Dublin and it may have been at this stage that he made the acquaintance of Dublin's most famous scientist, Richard Kirwan. Kirwan had returned to Dublin from London in 1787 and set up house at 6 Cavendish Row, where he regularly hosted soirées for the Dublin intelligentsia. Known to Dubliners more for his eccentricities than his advances in chemistry (he had a dread of flies, would never remove his hat for fear of catching cold and kept a menagerie of pets including several fierce dogs and an eagle), Kirwan was however a much respected chemist and corresponded with many of the leading scientists of the day.[40]

At this time in his life Russell's politics appear to have been moderately liberal. In the summer of 1790 he was still a staunch supporter of the Whigs.[41] This is hardly surprising: the Whigs were the natural focus for the loyalties of an idealistic young man who, as yet, was far from alienated from the established order. He considered himself 'a loyal subject, entertaining strong theoretical opinions of the advantages of republican institutions united with monarchical government and, above all, of the truth of the axiom that the end of good government was the happiness of the great body of the people'.[42] Russell was probably using the word 'republican' in the sense of popular or representative institutions, implying no particular hostility to monarchy as such, and his statement sits squarely in the Real Whig tradition of belief in mixed government. Indeed the British Constitution was often cited by political commentators as a republic in all but name, in which monarchy and representative institutions co-existed harmoniously, and exercised a restraining influence on each other.[43] However, in the 1790s the French Revolution and in particular the widespread dissemination of the anti-monarchical writings of Thomas Paine were to imbue the term 'republican' with a more precise and extreme meaning.

As a teenager Russell lived through some of the most remarkable years in Irish history. He witnessed the growth of the Volunteer movement, the independent militia founded in the late 1770s to protect Ireland from foreign invasion after France and Spain had allied themselves with the American colonists and declared war on Britain. In Dublin the Phoenix Park, a stone's throw from the Royal Hospital, was a favourite place for massive Volunteer reviews. As more and more regular troops left Ireland to fight in America, civic-minded Protestant gentlemen stepped in to fill the breech by forming local Volunteer corps. Since it was a relatively painless way of demonstrating patriotism and enjoying the pleasures of soldiering, volunteering became all the rage and spread rapidly throughout the country. Because Volunteers usually had to supply their own uniforms and equipment, membership was largely composed of the gentry and middle-class, and with Catholics forbidden to carry arms, it was almost exclusively Protestant. The recreational and social functions of volunteering accounted for much of its attraction and Volunteer corps soon became informal political clubs which voiced the grievances of the Protestant middle-class, most notably the restrictions on Ireland's overseas trade and the subordination of the Irish parliament to Westminster.

This citizen army, around 30,000 strong by 1779, effectively became the military wing of the parliamentary 'Patriots', with most of the leading popular politicians — Charlemont, Leinster, Grattan, Flood — holding Volunteer commissions, and lent considerable weight to the Patriot campaign to assert Ireland's independence. Emboldened by the example of the American colonists, they realised that there would never be a better time to press their claims. The combined efforts of Patriot spokesmen in parliament and Volunteer sabre-rattling in the country at large brought about the removal of commercial disabilities in 1780, allowing Ireland greater freedom to trade with Britain and the Empire. The Volunteers continued to press home their advantage and at a convention in Dungannon in February 1782 adopted resolutions in favour of legislative and judicial independence and relaxation of the penal laws, while Patriots turned up the pressure in parliament. When Lord North's government collapsed in March 1782 and was replaced by a Rockingham Whig ministry, formed of politicians who had in the past been sympathetic to Patriot demands, the tide turned in the Patriots' favour. During the summer of 1782 legislation was passed in Westminster and College Green removing the British parliament's right to legislate for Ireland and establishing the independence of the Irish parliament. It was, however, a tightly circumscribed form of independence, as the link with Great Britain was still maintained through the Crown, but Ireland could now at least claim to be an autonomous sister kingdom, governed by the king, lords and commons *of Ireland*.

It is impossible to know how much of an interest the young Russell took in these events but, if he left Ireland in 1783 with hopes that this constitutional settlement heralded a new era of Irish independence, he was likely to be disappointed on his return. He would have found that despite the achievement of legislative independence, the Irish parliament was still open to easy manipulation by an Irish government appointed from London. Most of the Irish parliament's 300 MPs were elected from parliamentary boroughs with small electorates usually controlled by aristocratic patrons. Thus, the key to managing parliament was to placate this handful of powerful aristocrats, who could deliver the necessary parliamentary votes to the government, and by judiciously dispensing the broad range of patronage at his disposal, the viceroy and his agents in Dublin Castle found that they could generally command sufficient support in parliament to have their way.[44] For the parliamentary opposition the only way to counter undue executive influence was to reform parliament, to make it an assembly representative of the public will, rather than one dominated by borough mongers and the pensioners and placemen of Dublin Castle.

Realising that the victory won in 1782 was still far from complete, middle-class Protestants, who had formed the rank and file of the Volunteers, soon began agitating for a reform of parliament that would give them a real say in the country's political life. In November 1783 a National Volunteer convention met at the Rotunda in Dublin. It produced a plan of reform that called for the enlargement of small boroughs, the granting of the franchise to all

Protestant freeholders and thirty-one-year leaseholders, the duration
of parliament to be limited to three years and the virtual exclusion
of government pensioners from parliament. It was presented to the
House of Commons by Henry Flood in his Volunteer uniform on 29
November 1783, but was overwhelmingly defeated by a majority
unwilling to 'receive propositions at the point of the bayonet'. This,
however, did not mark the end of the reform agitation. Radicals such
as James Napper Tandy, William Drennan and Joseph Pollock
continued to press for change and a series of radical reform
congresses were held in Dublin between October 1784 and April
1785. These adopted the Volunteer plan of reform but a divisive
issue soon arose: extending the franchise begged the question of
whether or not it should be given to the Catholics. Some reformers
believed it to be hypocritical and contradictory to propose the limi-
tation of political rights to Protestants, while others still feared
Catholics and believed them to be incapable of exercising such rights
responsibly. The more this argument dragged on, the more it sapped
the vitality of the reform movement. Divided on the Catholic question, and facing an unyielding administration in Dublin Castle, by
the time of the last reform congress in April 1785 many reformers
had grown demoralised by their lack of progress and all but the radical fringe had ceased their agitation. When Russell returned to
Ireland he would have found a fairly calm political scene and considerable public apathy towards the question of parliamentary reform.

Parliamentary reform was not the only major political issue that
had stalled. The year 1782 had seen some progress on the dismantling
of Catholic disabilities: acts passed in this year allowed Catholics to
acquire land, to open schools and to act as guardians. However, the
Irish parliament, believing that enough had been done for Catholics,
was not prepared to go beyond these measures and in the intervening
period no further relief had been granted. With little likelihood of
extracting further concessions, the movement for Catholic relief also
became moribund. Thus, the same issues of parliamentary reform and
Catholic emancipation that were on the political agenda when Russell
left for India were still on it when he returned.

The relative calm of Irish politics in the late 1780s was shaken by
the onset of George III's insanity in November 1788. At Westminster
the Whig opposition led by Charles James Fox demanded the granting of full regency powers to the Prince of Wales in the expectation
that this would lead to the appointment of a Whig ministry. Prime
Minister Pitt resisted these demands and the debate was still raging in

London when the Irish parliament convened in January 1789. Allies of the Foxites at College Green, notably the Ponsonby faction, were anxious to assert the right of the Irish parliament to determine the powers of the regent in relation to Ireland. They were supported by a number of parliamentary factions, who for one reason or another had cause to be dissatisfied with the existing government and hoped for more from an incoming administration. The anomalous nature of 'the Constitution of 1782' was revealed when the Irish parliament, stressing its independence from Westminster, presented the lord lieutenant with an address to the Prince of Wales requesting him to assume the powers of regent. The Lord Lieutenant refused to accept the address and an awkward constitutional controversy was only averted by the recovery of the king in March 1789.

This 'regency crisis' was to have important implications for Irish political life. A large and diverse group of Irish politicians had acted together in opposition to the government and many continued to co-operate after the crisis had passed. This grouping, consisting of Patriots, the Ponsonby and Leinster factions, and others who had opposed the government, amounting to roughly one-third of the members of the house, called themselves the Irish Whigs and soon formed an effective parliamentary opposition. In June 1789 they formed a Whig Club in Dublin to co-ordinate the activities of the opposition and to enlist the support of public opinion outside parliament in the cause of reform. The cause of reform received another boost in July when news came from France that the Estates General had constituted itself into a National Assembly and the people of Paris had seized the Bastille, a hated symbol of royal despotism. Reaction to this news from Irish Whigs was mainly favourable, the actions of the French at this stage generally being seen as an attempt to excise the worst excesses of royal despotism and establish a constitutional monarchy, similar to that established in Britain by the Glorious Revolution of 1689. There were also lessons for Irish reformers, as a Dublin newspaper noted in September 1789: 'Let those who ridicule the French Assembly consider they have abolished game laws, tithes, unmerited pensions and religious bars to office.'[45] By the following year Volunteers began to drill again, some of them sporting French-style national cockades, and in September 1790 a Volunteer committee called for constitutional reform and the abolition of tithes.[46]

At the first parliamentary session of 1790, an opposition bloc of about ninety members, ably led by Henry Grattan and George Ponsonby, introduced a number of bills to secure a more independent legislature. These consisted of a place bill (to prevent government appointed office-holders sitting in parliament), a pension bill (to curb the executive's powers of patronage by freezing the amount of crown pensions charged to the Irish exchequer) and a responsibility bill (to establish an Irish Treasury Board that would monitor and sanction the use of all public monies).[47] Grattan, in particular, was the darling of Whig supporters, and in speech after speech, he castigated the corruption and hypocrisy of the Irish government. On 2 February 1790, for example, he charged the Crown's ministers:

> with making corrupt agreements for the sale of peerages...to purchase for the servants of the Castle, seats in the assembly of the people...with committing these offences, not in one, not in two, but in many instances, for which complication of offences we say they are impeachable, guilty of a systematic endeavour to undermine the Constitution in violation of the laws of the land.[48]

Faced with a solid phalanx of government supporters, the Irish Whigs failed to enact any significant legislation. Russell, who probably witnessed these proceedings, several years later wrote a pamphlet which referred to these debates, admitting that given the 'first rate' abilities of the opposition 'all the argument was on their side; but the dead majority who did not come to argue but to vote, was on the side of the government. They exhausted themselves therefore without producing any effect, except that of detaining the government members...from their festivity till a late hour'.[49] But although the reforming efforts of the Irish Whigs had failed, their rhetoric had raised the political temperature and opened many eyes to the hollowness of the independence won in 1782.

After their argument in the public gallery, Russell and Tone began to see more of each other and their friendship blossomed. In the summer of 1790 Russell became a regular visitor to the small house that the Tones had rented in the Dublin seaside suburb of Irishtown. He was often joined by other members of his family — his father, his brother John and his sister Margaret — and during these months the two men and their families grew close to each other. When the Tone's second child, William, was born on 29 April 1791, John Russell senior was one of the godfathers.[50] Years later, Tone recalled this summer with heartfelt nostalgia:

Russell and I were inseparable, and, as our discussions were mostly political, and our sentiments agreed exactly, we extended our views, and fortified each other in the opinions to the propagation and establishment of which we have ever since been devoted. I recall with transport the happy days we spent together during that period; the delicious dinners, in the preparation of which my wife, Russell, and myself were all engaged; the afternoon walks, the discussions we had, as we lay stretched on the grass. It was delightful! Sometimes Russell's venerable father... used to visit our little mansion and that day was a fête. My wife doted on the old man, and he loved her like one of his children... Russell's brother John, too, used to visit us, a man of a most warm and affectionate heart, and, incontestably of the most companionable talents I ever met. His humour, which was pure and natural, flowed in an inexhaustible stream. He had not the strength of character of my friend Tom, but for the charms of conversation he excelled him and all the world. Sometimes, too, my brother William used to join us for a week,... when the two Russells, my brother and I were assembled, it is impossible to conceive of a happier society... These were delicious days. The rich and great, who sit down every day to the monotony of a splendid entertainment, can form no idea of the happiness of our frugal meal, nor of the infinite pleasure we found in taking each his part in the preparation and attendance. My wife was the centre and soul of all... She loved Russell as well as I did. In short, a more interesting society of individuals, connected by purer motives, and animated by a more ardent attachment and friendship for each other, cannot be imagined.[51]

Matilda Tone too was to remember these days fondly and years later reminisced with Margaret Russell about 'Tom's coming down to Irishtown and eating a herring with us after *swearing* he would not come. We have no such friend now.'[52]

With time on their hands, Russell and Tone worked on a plan, which Tone had devised some years earlier, to establish a military colony to thwart Spanish expansion in the South Pacific. Since there was still a possibility of war between Britain and Spain, they believed that the time was favourable and sent a detailed memorial to the government. This came to the attention of the Duke of Richmond, master-general of the ordinance, and the foreign secretary, Lord Grenville. Tone received a polite reply, praising the plan but stating that it was not required in the current circumstances. While waiting to sail with Hoche in 1796 he mused that, had his memorial been accepted, he and Russell might have been South Sea privateers — for which he felt they both had the required romantic spirit, instead of revolutionaries seeking to overthrow British rule in Ireland. He claimed that they both swore they would make the government regret its decision to reject their services.[53] If this was the case, then these vows were probably made with more youthful bravado than serious intent, as several years were to elapse before the two became irrevocably alienated from British rule.

These lazy summer days came to an end in late August when Russell was unexpectedly assigned to a full-time ensigncy with the 64th infantry regiment, then stationed in Belfast. Before leaving, he dined once more with the Tones in Irishtown, arriving at their cottage in a splendid new uniform. To bring him back down to earth, his hosts immediately packed him off to the kitchen to prepare the dinner. Having said his farewells, he set off for Belfast early in September 1790 to take up his new post.[54]

NOTES

1   *Parliamentary reg. Ire.*, xi (1791), pp. 2–3; *Dublin Chronicle*, 3 July 1790.
2   Hibernicus, *Spanish war: an enquiry how far Ireland is bound, of right, to embark in the impending contest on the side of Great Britain* (Dublin, 1790).
3   Bartlett, *Life of Tone*, pp. 24, 32; J. F. Fuller, 'The Tones, father and son' in *Journal of the Cork Historical and Archaeological Society* (1924), p. 96.
4   Bartlett, *Life of Tone*, p. 32.
5   Ibid., pp. 482, 569.
6   A John Russell entered the college as a pensioner on 6 June 1735, but he does not appear to have taken a degree (G. D. Burtchaell and T. U. Sadleir (eds), *Alumni Dublinenses* (Dublin, 1935), p. 721).
7   Notes by J. A. Russell, n.d. (Madden papers, 873/674, f. 1); Russell's journal, 30 July 1793 (*Journals*, p. 89); Bartlett, *Life of Tone*, p. 33; John Russell to – , 15 to 25 Nov. 1762 (B.L., Add. MS 44076, ff 97, 114, 141, 230).
8   Russell's journal, June 1792 (*Journals*, p. 62); notes by J. A. Russell, n.d. (Madden papers, 873/674, f. 1v); her name is given as Margaret in F. J. Bigger, *Four shots from Down* (Ballynahinch, 1982), p. 47, and Cathal O'Byrne, *As I roved out in Belfast and district* (Dublin, 1946), p. 391, but neither of these cites a source.
9   Russell's journal, 30 July 1793 (*Journals*, pp 89–90).
10 *Journals*, p. 15; examination of John Russell, 1 Nov. 1803 (P.R.O., P.C. 1/3583).
11 *Journals*, p. 16; John Russell jun. attended school in Kilkenny in the late 1750s, see T.U. Sadleir, 'The register of Kilkenny School' in *Journal of the Royal Society of Antiquaries of Ireland*, xiv (1924), p. 163.
12 McNally's report of a conversation with Russell, 24 Sept. 1803 (P.R.O., HO 100/113/195–8).
13 Mac Giolla Easpaig, *Ruiséil*, p. 19; notes by J. A. Russell, n.d. (Madden papers, 873/674, ff 1-2); Madden papers, 873/674, f.1v; Sirr papers, 868/2 f. 125; Reb. papers 620/25/136; examination of John Russell, 4 Nov. 1803 (P.R.O., P.C. 1/3583); *Army list* (1779), p. 102.
14 G. J. Bryant, 'Officers of the East India Company's army in the days of Clive and Hastings' in *Journal of Imperial and Commonwealth History*, vi, no. 3

(May 1978), pp. 204, 210; Patrick Cadell, 'Irish soldiers in India' in *Irish Sword*, i (1949–53), p. 77; Mac Giolla Easpaig, *Ruiséil*, p. 19; Madden, *United Irishmen*, 3rd ser., ii, 142; *Army list* (1785), p. 138.

15 W. S. Moorsom, *Historical record of the fifty-second regiment* (2nd edn, London, 1860), pp. 27–8; Denys Forrest, *Tiger of Mysore: the life and death of Tipu Sultan* (London, 1979), pp. 43–57, 82–3.

16 Notes by J. A. Russell, n.d. (Madden papers, 873/674, f. 2); Russell to his parents, Cannanore, 12 Feb. 1784 (Sirr papers, 868/1, ff 262–3); examination of John Russell, 4 Nov. 1803 (P.R.O., P.C. 1/3583).

17 Richard Cannon, *Historical record of the thirty-sixth or Herefordshire regiment of foot* (London, 1853), p. 39; J. W. Fortescue, *History of the British army* (London, 1902), iii, 498–9.

18 Examination of John Russell, 4 Nov. 1803 (P.R.O., P.C. 1/3583).

19 William Fullarton to Lord McCartney, Jan. 1785 (India Office Records, Home misc. series 84/17, pp. 255–441).

20 W. S. Moorsom, *Historical record of the fifty-second regiment* (2nd edn, London, 1860), pp. 29–30; H. H. Dodwell (ed.), *The Cambridge shorter history of India* (New Delhi, 1979), p. 592; notes by J. A. Russell, n.d. (Madden papers, 873/674, f. 2); Bombay general consultations, 4 May 1784 (India Office Records, Home misc. series 84/15, p. 231).

21 Russell's journal, Nov. 1794 [?] (*Journals*, p. 179).

22 In December 1822 Margaret Russell applied to Dublin Castle to have his Indian journal and other papers returned to her, though she appears to have had no success (National Archives, Official Papers II, 583/540); see also Mary Ann McCracken to Madden, 19 July 1842 (Madden papers, 873/692) and Madden, *United Irishmen*, 3rd ser., ii, 174, 273.

23 Russell's journal, 30 Sept. 1793 (*Journals*, p. 126).

24 *Dublin Chronicle*, 22 Dec. 1787.

25 Morgan, 'Sketch of Russell', p. 41; Madden, *United Irishmen*, 3rd ser., ii, 143.

26 H. H. Dodwell (ed.), *The Cambridge shorter history of India* (New Delhi, 1979), p. 592.

27 Russell to his parents, 12 Feb. 1784, Cannanore (Sirr papers, 868/1, f. 263).

28 William Fullarton to Lord McCartney, Jan. 1785 (India Office Records, Home misc. series 84/17, f. 411).

29 Morgan, 'Sketch of Russell', pp. 41–2; Madden, *United Irishmen*, 3rd ser., ii, 143–5.

30 'Debate on the articles against Mr Hastings, 2 Feb. 1787' (*The parliamentary history of England…15 May 1786 to 8 Feb 1788*, xxvi, (London, 1816), pp. 282–3; for the impact of this speech see Fintan O'Toole, *A traitor's kiss: the life of Richard Brinsley Sheridan* (London, 1997), pp. 210–20; an article in the 'Chinese journal' series (of which Russell may have been the author) appeared in the *Northern Star* of 26 Feb. 1795 which strongly condemned the East India Company in general and its persecution of the princesses of Oude and the nabob of Arcot in particular.

31 J. W. Fortescue, *History of the British army* (London, 1902), iii, 498–9; Russell is listed as being on half pay with the rest of the officers of the 100th regiment in the *Army list* (1786), p. 339.

32 Mac Giolla Easpaig, *Ruiséil*, p. 23.

33 John Russell to Thomas Russell, 4 Mar., 17 Oct. 1796 (Sirr papers, 868/2, ff 118, 112).

34 Notes by J. A. Russell, n.d. (Madden papers, 873/674, f. 2).

35 Jonah Barrington, *Personal sketches and recollections of his own time*, 2 vols (London, 1830), i, 93–4.

36 Bartlett, *Life of Tone*, p. 35; Madden, *United Irishmen*, 3rd ser., ii, 149.
37 *Dublin Chronicle*, 14 July 1787, 6 Oct. 1787, 2 Aug. 1788, 28 April. 1789.
38 — to Lord Auckland, 1785 (cited in Constantia Maxwell, *Dublin under the Georges* (2nd ed., London, 1956), p. 89).
39 J. T. Gilbert, *A history of the city of Dublin* (Dublin, 1861), i, 393–6.
40 See Michael Donovan, 'Biographical account of the late Richard Kirwan, Esq.' in *Proceedings of the Royal Irish Academy*, iv (1847–50), lxxxi–cxviii; F. E. Dixon, 'Richard Kirwan, the Dublin philosopher' in *Dublin Historical Record*, xxiv (1971), pp. 52–64; P. J. McLaughlin, 'Richard Kirwan' in *Studies: an Irish quarterly review*, xxviii (1939), pp. 461–74, 593–605, xxix (1940), pp. 71–83, 281-300.
41 Bartlett, *Life of Tone*, p. 32.
42 Madden, *United Irishmen*, 3rd ser., ii, 149.
43 For the influence of the Real Whig tradition on Ireland, see Caroline Robbins, *The eighteenth-century commonwealthman* (Cambridge, MA, 1959), pp. 134–76.
44 There were 300 members in the Irish parliament: two members were elected from each of the thirty-two counties by the forty-shilling freeholders of the county; two members were also elected from each of 117 boroughs, only about eight of which had a broad electorate; most of the others were in the gift of local landowners.
45 *Dublin Chronicle*, 3 Sept. 1789.
46 *Freeman's Journal*, 22 July 1790; National Archives, Westmorland papers, 1, f.8.
47 Lecky, *Ireland*, iii, 1–3; R. B. McDowell, *Ireland in the age of imperialism and revolution, 1760–1801* (Oxford, 1979), pp. 342–3; David Dickson, *New foundations: Irish history 1660–1800* (Dublin, 1987), pp. 170–1.
48 Cited in Francis Plowden, *An historical review of the state of Ireland...* (London, 1803), ii, 296–7.
49 Russell, *Letter to the people*, p. 6.
50 Elliott, *Tone*, p. 164.
51 Bartlett, *Life of Tone*, p. 33.
52 Matilda Tone to Margaret Russell, 5 Sept. 1792 (Sirr papers, 868/1, f. 264), Tone, *Writings*, i, 270.
53 Bartlett, *Life of Tone*, p. 35.
54 *Dublin Chronicle*, 28 Sept. 1790; Bartlett, *Life of Tone*, p. 35.

CHAPTER TWO

The Cradle of Politics

Belfast in 1790 was a thriving medium-sized town with a population of just over 18,000. Although it was only the fifth most populous town in Ireland, its inhabitants reckoned it Ireland's third town in terms of trade and importance. It was a neat, handsome place, with wide, straight streets and solid brick houses. Belfast's linen and cotton industries were thriving and made fortunes for many local manufacturers and merchants. The town's wealth was widely spread and it had an active and varied social life, with frequent balls and *soirées* held in the town exchange's superb Assembly Room.[1]

Most of the town's inhabitants were Presbyterians and, although formal disabilities against Irish Dissenters had been abolished in 1780, they still found much to resent in the privileges and inefficiencies of the Anglican establishment. They had, for instance, no say in choosing their parliamentary representatives: although Belfast was a parliamentary borough, its MPs were elected by the sovereign (the equivalent of the town mayor) and twelve burgesses of the corporation, a self-elected body, controlled by the Earl of Donegall, the local landowner.

Since the corporation's powers were strictly limited, and the town's inhabitants had so little involvement in municipal government, it was left to the public-spirited citizens of Belfast themselves to fill the vacuum and provide effective local government, and when the need arose they created committees and established institutions to cater for the town's educational, social and charitable needs. Local initiative had led to the founding of a poor house, a dispensary and a Chamber of Commerce in the 1770s and 1780s, the Belfast Academy in 1785 and the Belfast Reading Society in 1788. The citizens themselves built the impressive new White Linen Hall in 1783 by subscription and, in the absence of any official police force, they formed a voluntary association for policing.

25

The prosperity and religious independence of the town's citizens bolstered their confidence and spirit of self-reliance, and Ulster's close links with Glasgow University meant that much of Belfast's élite had imbibed the progressive notions of the Scottish enlightenment. It was not surprising therefore that as in growing industrial towns elsewhere, Belfast's bourgeoisie clamoured for a political say commensurate with their commercial interests. One reformer claimed that despite 'residence of numerous wealthy and spirited inhabitants' the town remained 'in abject slavery to the absentee Earl of Donegall'.[2] Belfast had been to the forefront of the Volunteer movement and its Volunteer corps had participated prominently in the agitation for legislative independence and the campaign for reform of the Irish parliament in the early 1780s. Such experiences encouraged the growth of a self-consciously liberal political class in the town, and whereas Volunteer corps elsewhere generally stood down after the war, those in Belfast continued to meet and drill. These gatherings of armed citizens acted as a focal point for reformist sentiment and in the early 1790s they were given fresh encouragement by events in France, which provided an example to the Belfast middle classes of their French counterparts effectively challenging aristocratic and clerical privilege, and infused political debate in the town with a new urgency and militancy. Some years later, describing the impact of the French Revolution on Ulster Dissenters, Thomas Addis Emmet claimed that it:

> paved the way for the entire accomplishment of what the Volunteer institution had begun. A Catholic country had, by its conduct, contradicted the frequently repeated dogma that Catholics are unfit for liberty, and the waning glory of the British Constitution seemed to fade before the regenerated government of France. These things sunk deep into the minds of the Dissenters, who likewise saw another law of liberality enforced by their new teachers: that no religious opinions should be punished by civil disenfranchisement.[3]

A Northern Whig Club was founded in Belfast in March 1790, but advanced reformers soon grew disillusioned with its moderate stance and general lack of vigour. By the summer of 1790 there was already talk of new clubs and alliances. In the autumn the Irish government had become alarmed at new signs of radicalism among Belfast's Volunteers, who passed resolutions advocating the abolition of tithes, the enfranchisement of Catholics and a thorough reform of parliament, and praised 'the glorious spirit of the citizens of France in forming and adopting the wise system of republican government', exhorting the Irish people to imitate France's 'bright example'. Even more worrying for the administration was the fact that the Volunteers advocated co-operation with Catholics to achieve these aims and called on Irishmen throughout the land to arm to assert their rights.[4]

Russell, therefore, arrived into a place that was already a political hotbed and found its industrious, progressive and disputatious community very much to his liking. The attraction was mutual: a charming and strikingly handsome man, Russell was warmly received by fashionable Belfast society. Martha McTier, sister of William Drennan and the matriarch of radical Belfast, remembered him as an 'agreeable, improving, fascinating visitor...I never heard a sentence or word from him that did not do him honour as a religious, moral man, a polite, finished gentleman (where he chose), and an entertaining improving companion'.[5] Another prominent Belfast woman, Mary Ann McCracken, recalled in detail the impression made by Russell:

A model of manly beauty, he was one of those favoured individuals whom one cannot pass in the street without being guilty of the rudeness of staring in the face while passing, and turning round to look at the receding figure. Though more than six feet high, his majestic stature was scarcely observed owing to the exquisite symmetry of his form. Martial in gait and demeanour, his appearance was not altogether that of a soldier. His dark and steady eye, compressed lip, and somewhat haughty bearing, were occasionally strongly indicative of the camp; but in general, the classic contour of his finely formed head, the expression of almost infantine [sic] sweetness which characterised his smile, and the benevolence that beamed in his fine countenance, seemed to mark him out as one who was destined to be the ornament, grace and blessing of private life. His voice was deep-toned and melodious, and though his conversational powers were not of the first order, yet when roused to enthusiasm he was sometimes more than eloquent. His manners were those of the finished gentleman, combined with that native grace which nothing but superiority of intellect can give. There was a reserved and somewhat haughty stateliness in his mien, which, to those who did not know him, had at first the appearance of pride; but as it gave way before the warmth and benevolence of his disposition, it soon became evident that the defect, if it were one, was caused by the too sensitive delicacy of a noble soul; and those who knew him loved him the more for his reserve and thought they saw something attractive in the very repulsiveness of his manner.[6]

Russell's liberal outlook was well in tune with reformist sentiment in the town and led to invitations to join several political clubs. In these he met Belfast's politically progressive Presbyterian merchants and manufacturers — men such as Samuel Neilson, William and Robert Simms, William Sinclair, Henry Haslett, William Tennent, Samuel McTier and Thomas McCabe — and under their influence his theoretical republican principles became more steadfast and practical.[7] Russell also found the religious temper of liberal Belfast congenial: his religious beliefs having much in common with the progressive and undogmatic beliefs of New Light Presbyterianism. Moreover, he was at home with the town's artistic and scientific communities. His interest in music brought him into contact with the musician Edward Bunting and the McCracken family, who had adopted Bunting as a child. In turn, the McCrackens introduced Russell to their friends — people such as John Templeton, the botanist, and Dr James McDonnell, a physician and an important figure in the town's social and cultural life.[8]

Another significant acquaintance made by Russell soon after his arrival in Belfast was that of Thomas Attwood Digges, an American Catholic. Digges, then thirty-eight years old, had a colourful past. Disowned by his family at the age of twenty-five, he went to live in Portugal, where he wrote a picaresque novel, *The adventures of Alonso*. During the war of Independence he lived in London, from where he sent intelligence reports to the Benjamin Franklin and John Adams, smuggled war supplies to America via Spain and acted as an intermediary for abortive peace negotiations. He also served an American agent for the exchange of prisoners, and in this capacity he was accused of misappropriating funds intended for prisoners, and was denounced by Benjamin Franklin as 'the greatest villain I have ever met'. After the war he moved to Dublin and clearly had serious financial troubles for in 1785 he was imprisoned as a debtor in the Four Courts Marshalsea in Dublin.[9] Although Digges would later prove to be a very false friend indeed, the young Russell was deeply impressed by his knowledge and experience. Nor was he alone in having a high regard for the American. In Belfast Digges was regarded as 'a man of extensive information, of specious address, particularly neat in his attire, of conversational powers that seemed to belong to a vigorous understanding... [he] was received into the houses of all persons of note in the town; his society was courted and his opinions received with respect.'[10] Russell was so impressed by his abilities that he wrote to Tone asking him to allow Digges to review his South Seas project. In his reply Digges encouraged Tone to expand his plans to include the emancipation of Spanish America, which he believed was ripe for revolution. Tone took Digges's suggestions on board and sent an expanded memorial to the government. In December he received another polite refusal from Grenville. After this Tone sent no more memorials, though he kept all the relevant papers and never quite gave up hope on this, his pet project.[11]

Towards the end of the year Tone turned his energies to founding a small political club to be made up of members of Dublin's liberal élite. It included Whitley Stokes and John Stack, both fellows of Trinity College; the physician William Drennan and the lawyers Thomas Addis Emmet, Peter Burrowes, Joseph Pollock and William Johnson. Russell became a corresponding member. Tone expected great things from this distinguished membership but the club lasted just three or four months and managed to produce only about a dozen mediocre essays.[12] It fell to Russell to write essays on religious toleration and Catholic emancipation, though he came up with nothing more than some rough notes. In these he attempted to assuage traditional Protestant fears that a relaxation of the penal laws would result in a reversal of the seventeenth-century land settlement and the establishment of an intolerant Catholic ascendancy:

> The great sums of money lent on mortgages by Roman Catholicks to Protestants would be another strong and insuperable bar to any violent revolution in property and is a better security to estates than ten thousand declarations and abjurations... That a state should interfere with the religious belief of any one where it does not affect the gover[n]ment and morals of the country is manifestly absurd and unjust... I would not... have myself the smallest doubt of the loyalty of the Catholicks... Their loyalty has been established too well to need any panegerrick, but I wish to take away from the zealots of intolerance, civil and religious, every shadow of argument. I am sure the measure would produce this effect and, if so, it would wrest from the hands of this proflagate gover[n]men[t] their strongest weapon — the distrust that the two religions have of each other. I know of no good results from these laws, either political or religious, but many evils.[13]

These rough jottings anticipated several of the key points that Tone was to employ in his *Argument on behalf of the Catholics of Ireland*, published in August 1791.

Russell's notes were included in a journal that he began in February 1791. He claimed that he decided to keep a journal because 'should I live to old age they will be a pleasant mode of renovating the scores and ideas of youth, and I hope though hitherto it has not been the case, they may show a progression in virtue'. His journals were written in an almost illegible hand with very idiosyncratic spelling and punctuation: Russell may have been dyslexic and some entries were probably written when he was under the influence of drink. His appalling handwriting and erratic spelling was a source of amusement to his family and friends: he produced so many variants on 'Enniskillen' that his niece asked him bluntly 'why you can't contrive to spell Enniskillen 'Enniskillen'.[14] Tone, for one, was certainly not overly impressed with his friend's efforts — '[Russell] is writing a journal, but mine is worth fifty of it'.[15] Nevertheless, these jottings form an important historical document and provide valuable information on Russell's activities, opinions and private thoughts. Russell often committed his innermost personal feelings to paper without reserve and his journals give an intimate insight into his emotions and psyche. They also show him to have a lively enquiring mind that ranged over a host of subjects: politics, religion, trade and manufacturing, agriculture, social institutions, scientific and geological observations, the position of the poor and the general state of the country, and they contain important information on his travels through the North and of the development of radicalism in the early 1790s.

An entry from March shows him to be speculating on the possibility of Ireland breaking its political ties with Britain. He concluded that the people were, for the time being, unwilling to take the risks involved.[16] He may have been considering this issue because of his growing concern at what he saw as the unenlightened attitude of the Irish parliament towards the development of domestic manufacturing, which he attributed to fear of offending British interests. In the outline of an essay, probably written for the club founded by Tone, he wrote:

> As the pro[s]perity of my native country has always been the great object of my wishes, I (as I think every honest Irishman ought) have endeavour[ed] to procure information on such subjects as may

improve its trade and manufactures and to find the causes of the decay
of some branches of them, and the reason why others for which this
kingdom seem eminently qualify[d] are either not attempted or remain
in a state of sickly infancy. Ireland of all countrys of Europe seems the
best qualify'd for trade and manufactures, as from its southern ports
you are instantly in the Atlantic Ocean, and the northern and eastern
connect it immediately with England and the northern powers of
Europe. This situation and the cheapness of the provisions on which
the common people live should enable them to undersell other countrys in manufacture, yet with all these advantages we are so far from
striking out that some of our former ones are decaying.[17]

Russell's journals and papers contain numerous references to new
industrial technology and manufacturing processes, interests probably stimulated by meeting the merchants and manufacturers of
Belfast. He shared the contemporary enthusiasm for applied science
and was strongly interested in discoveries that might have industrial
or agricultural uses. In roughly-made notes he considered whether
the prism might be of use to colour makers, the best new ways of
fertilising with lime and how new chemical techniques might be
applied to bleaching and dyeing.[18] He took a keen interest in the
industrial controversies of his day. In an essay written for Tone's club,
he dealt in detail with the state of the Irish leather tanning industry,
then in serious difficulties. He considered the export of raw hides to
England as a 'nefarious practice' which 'should excite the most serious attention of the legislature'. He maintained that the dwindling
supply and rising cost of English oak bark (needed for the tanning
process) were making the production of leather uncompetitive in
Ireland and that the Irish exchequer should pay a bounty on its
import from America, where the product could be bought cheaply.
His essay bore a close similarity to the petition presented to the Irish
House of Commons by a delegation of Belfast tanners and he felt so
strongly about this issue that he argued the case for an import bounty
on oak bark to Henry Grattan, who was heading a Commons
committee on the tanning industry in February and March 1791.
Apparently, Grattan was impressed with Russell's suggestion but
informed him that it had already been dismissed by the Chancellor of
the Irish Exchequer, Sir John Parnell, on the grounds that it might
offend English commercial interests. Russell concluded with obvious
irony that Ireland had a 'good government' and had 'a precious
rascal for Chancellor of the Exchequer'.[19] He was not alone in

holding a poor opinion of Parnell, who was generally regarded as an indolent and ineffective chancellor — Jonah Barrington, for example, described him as 'a sloven and a gentleman'.[20]

Some time later Russell was equally unimpressed with the treatment given by a Commons committee to a new two-webbed loom developed by William Pearce, then in business with the Belfast watchmaker, Thomas McCabe. Pearce was a talented inventor, regarded by Digges as 'a second Archimedes'.[21] The two partners petitioned the Irish parliament for financial assistance to help develop their new machine and a House of Commons committee was set up in February to inquire into the matter. Russell was one of those who gave evidence to the committee of the superiority of Pearce's new loom over existing machines. The committee published a report which admitted the efficiency of the invention but took no further action and Pearce went unrewarded. Soon afterwards he emigrated to America with the encouragement and assistance of Digges.[22] This example of the unimaginative treatment of domestic technical innovation was cited by Tone in his *Argument on behalf of the Catholics* as evidence that a subservient Irish parliament would always be unwilling to promote Irish prosperity for fear of meeting with a hostile response from Britain. Russell, too, was amazed that someone as talented as Pearce should be treated in such a shabby manner. He found it unbelievable that Ireland could 'slight such a man', and he noted that Pearce swore 'against ever benefiting it by his labours'. Months later, the issue still rankled sufficiently to be a major topic of conversation among the founders of the United Irishmen in Belfast.[23]

It may well have been the representations of Russell and his friends that prompted an exasperated member of parliament in March 1791 to complain of the manner in which 'soldiers and lawyers and churchmen all talked upon commerce, some merely for the sake of talking, others from a motive somewhat worse, to agitate and exasperate the public mind'.[24] Ireland's economic subordination to Britain and her undeveloped potential were among the most frequently voiced complaints from the administration's critics. Unlike vague constitutional concepts that were often of limited public interest, British interference with Irish commerce — whether stemming from legislation enacted at Westminster, or through the neglect of a quiescent domestic parliament — was a tangible grievance that could arouse public opinion. Liberals frequently claimed that once Ireland had a truly independent legislature which could foster and encourage Irish agriculture and manufacturing, and once the remaining mercantilist legislation restricting Irish commerce with the wider world was abolished, the country could not fail to prosper. As Digges put it to some of the founders of the United Irishmen in Belfast in October 1791: 'if Ireland were free and well governed... she would in arts, commerce and manufactures spring up like an air balloon and leave England behind her at an immense distance. There is no computing the rapidity with which she would rise'.[25] The prevalence of this belief among the Irish commercial classes was one of the main reasons why the programme of the United Irishmen proved so attractive to the merchants and manu-facturers of Dublin and Belfast in the early 1790s.[26]

Russell's journal also gives us an insight into his more general polit-ical views. It indicates that he had read Joseph Priestley's *Letters to Edmund Burke* and Thomas Paine's *Rights of man, part I,* a work which had first appeared in Dublin in March 1791, and was to have an electrifying effect on Irish popular opinion. In April 1791 it was published in a subsidised cheap edition by the Whigs of the Capital, a group of radical guild politicians led by the veteran Dublin radical James Napper Tandy, and within eight months it had sold 40,000 copies, more than twice its sales in England, and several Dublin news-papers printed lengthy extracts.[27] Intended as a riposte to Edmund Burke's *Reflections on the revolutions in France*, the *Rights of man* brought a new immediacy into the debate about the French revolution in Ireland. Paine's clear and logical arguments about the folly of hered-itary government and the advantages of republicanism and democracy hit home to businessmen and tradesmen who saw themselves excluded from politics, and the book became the radical gospel of the age. But it seems that at this stage Russell was not yet completely convinced by its arguments. He admitted to some strong reservations about Paine's principles and praised the British Constitution for according a measure of real security to the individual, particularly in relation to property. He believed that 'in England the whole power of the king, lords and commons would be ineffectual to crush any individual however obscure... the nation at large would take up his cause'. In contrast he noted that in revolutionary France 'absolute power is supposed in the nation. That must be exercised by some body. An individual may be obnoxious to them and what is his security? Does it much signify, if a despotism does exist, by whom it is exercised?'. He was still sceptical about the wisdom of violent revolution, reflecting:

if the happiness of a society (faulty in some respect[s]) is more promoted by dissolving the whole and forming it anew, leaving out the exceptionable parts, or by applying slow remedies [and] partial alterations? The present race are, according to Paine, the only ones to be consider'd. Why then not leave posterity to take care of themselves and enjoy as much of life as we can? In a violent revolution thousands are reduced to beggary. It is not so certain whether thousands are relieved from it, but supposing they were, it remains to be shown whether the whole society are happyer by it.[28]

At this time Russell was far from being a doctrinaire radical, still less a revolutionary. Although Tone maintained that Russell 'did not remain long under the delusion' of supporting the Whigs, in a letter written in July 1791 Tone appears to be still attempting to wean his friend from his whiggish sympathies. According to Tone, Grattan and his allies:

are not sincere friends to the popular cause. They dread the people as much as the Castle does... If they do not join you in supporting a reform in parl[iamen]t they do not deserve support themselves. Apply the touchstone. If they stand the trial, well, if they fail, they are false and hollow and the sooner they are detected the better... To be candid I dare say that my Lord Charlemont, and I am pretty sure that Mr Grattan would hesitate very much at the resolutions which I send, but I only beg you will dismiss your respect for great names... and then determine impartially between us.[29]

But while Russell's politics appear fairly moderate in the summer of 1791, some of the seeds that later developed into his social radicalism are discernible even at this stage. A number of journal entries exhibit a greater interest in the welfare of the lower orders and a stronger sympathy with their plight than was usual in mainstream whiggism. Having spent most of the previous four years in Dublin, he was well aware of the city's serious social problems. Despite the relative prosperity of the late 1780s, and the impressive grandeur of Dublin's public buildings and fashionable residential districts, the city was plagued by serious poverty. All eighteenth-century cities were places of sharp contrast between rich and poor, but in Dublin the disparity was more jarring than in most, and was often commented on by visitors. The French traveller, the Chevalier de Latocnaye, observed that 'the splendid carriages and the apparent wealth of the principal houses render the more displeasing the sight of the beggars, whose abject poverty is horrible... they may be seen hanging on for hours to the railings of basements, forcing charity by depriving those who live in these places of light and air'.[30] Dublin's rudimentary social services were completely unable to cope with the hordes of the city's poor, and in February and March 1791 parliamentary committees reported on the working of the city's main charitable institutions, the House of Industry near Oxmantown Green and the Foundling Hospital in James St. The regime in the House of Industry, to which any able-bodied person found begging could be brought, was a particularly harsh one: the inmates were worked hard and offences could be punished by flogging and imprisonment on bread and water. Even then, it was vastly overcrowded. In 1796 the infant ward, containing sixty-one beds, housed eighty-nine women and 109 children. Statistics from the Foundling Hospital were even more disturbing. Between 1781 and 1790, 19,368 children were entered on its books — of these 10,428 died, 4,395 of these from venereal diseases — a great many of these children were born to Dublin's large population of prostitutes.[31] Probably prompted by the findings of the parliamentary committees, Russell made some brief comments on the workings of these foundations. He suggested that paying premiums to foster parents for rearing unwanted children rather than bringing them to a foundling hospital would be a more effective way to prevent infanticide, and that a system of badging paupers might be better than arbitrarily committing them to workhouses. He was appalled by the harsh treatment which these institutions meted out to the poor. The committal of women to such places for petty offences and the shaving of their heads struck him as particularly barbaric. He noted that 'the laws do not afford their protection to the lower orders'.[32]

Russell's sympathy for the poor and his political outlook generally were based largely on his religious beliefs. He found an inspiration for his ideal state in the communities set up by the Jesuits in South America. At a time when the Jesuits had been disbanded throughout Europe, and their name was a by-word in Protestant and liberal circles for intolerance and deception, this liberal Irish Protestant was fulsome in their praise. He noted of Jesuit rule that 'it is the only government ever set up by a priesthood — those supposed to be the most ambitious race in the world — and yet the government is beyond compare the best, the happiest that ever has been instituted'.[33] For Russell the basic principles of Christianity were more important than sectarian dogma. He himself, though born into the

Church of Ireland, attended Presbyterian services while living in Belfast and took communion with a Jansenist congregation in France in 1802.[34] He saw all varieties of Christianity as contributing to morality and thus, he believed, to true happiness and liberty. He dismissed the notion, held by many of advanced opinions at the time, that Christianity facilitated the establishment of tyranny; instead he claimed that tyrannical governments had simply perverted and exploited Christianity for their own ends.[35]

Russell's journals also give some insight into the private life of a young army officer. His military duties appear to have been light — he makes little reference to them besides noting that he was 'at church with the men' on Sunday 10 April.[36] This allowed him considerable leisure for other diversions: he dined at the mess, played billiards and indulged in the heavy drinking and whoring that were common among young army officers. He also picked up a facility for swearing from his army days. Mary Ann McCracken considered it his one flaw and she was tempted to speak to him about it but 'the stateliness of his manner' prevented her.[37]

Much to the consternation of its more respectable citizens, Belfast offered many distractions to the licentious young army officer, having a number of brothels and a public house or tavern to every seventeen houses.[38] Normally of a sombre demeanour, Russell tended to shed his reserve when relaxing with friends, especially after a couple of bottles of wine. On most evenings he records himself as ending up in varying states of inebriation ranging from 'half drunk' through to 'drunk' or 'very drunk'. A typical night was that of Tuesday 12 April, when after dinner with two fellow officers his drunkenness was such that he fell in the gutter, ruined his coat and bent his sword; on another occasion he threw himself on his knees before a group of women in the street. On 25 April he described how he and a fellow officer had gone walking around the town 'in quest of game' after dinner. He met a servant girl of Victor Coates, one of Belfast's leading hairdressers, who brought him back to her master's house in Castle Street, where he stayed until near eleven o'clock at night, only narrowly avoiding detection. He returned to the barracks (falling over a heap of dirt on the way) to find a drinking party still going and he stayed up with them until the early hours of the morning.[39] Visits to prostitutes usually followed these drinking sessions. After such debauches Russell was usually stricken by bouts of anguish and remorse. Throughout his life he was painfully aware of the glaring discrepancy between his Christian principles and his dissolute behaviour. After one such occasion he noted: 'drank too much last night with Neilson, which often leads me into other vices, as it did then. I must amend, for which I beg the grace of God, my strength daily declining'.[40]

There was nothing out of the ordinary in a young army officer regularly visiting brothels, but the evidence suggests that Russell felt a particularly strong sexual attraction towards women. Tone often joked with him about this proclivity and Russell was well aware of it himself and often chided himself for 'thinking too much on women'.[41] His journals and papers frequently contain comments about women, their physical appearance and their sexual habits. The notes he regularly took on native peoples often contain observations such as 'North American Indian women chaste after marriage but not before, nor thought worse of for having whor'd — offer their wives to strangers which they think a mark of high respect — this more prevalent before they knew Europeans'.[42] But Russell combined his strong sexual passion for women with a deeply chivalrous attitude to them (at least towards those of his own class). Most women who knew him seem to have fallen under the spell of his gallantry: 'if all men knew how to treat women as Tom does . . . we would be much better than we are', observed Matilda Tone.[43] In the one great love affair of his life he idealised the woman to such an extent that he was almost stricken by paralysis in her presence. He could never bring himself to express his true feelings to her and their relationship proved the cause of much anxiety and anguish to him. He first saw Eliza Goddard, daughter of John Goddard, port surveyor of Newry and a justice of the peace for Co. Down, in Belfast on 21 April 1791, and was taken aback by her beauty.[44] Some days later he managed to secure an introduction to her at the Belfast coterie and attempted to monopolise her company to the extent that his friend Dr James McDonnell gently chided him for being 'a robber' in taking her away from her dancing partner. With 'great warmth' Russell replied 'who would not be a robber in such a case?'. Afterwards he danced with Eliza and became 'extravagantly delighted with her beauty and simplicity. Almost drunk when the set is over. Talk very loud, as McDonnell afterwards told me, in praise of her to some of the people and express my abhorrence of any villain who attempts to invade the peace of such a creature. I little thought then of what was to follow'. Later that evening Russell was 'quite mad' at failing to gain a place near her at dinner and quietly cursed McDonnell, who was soon to be married, for sitting next to her.[45]

Russell would soon have other personal matters to concern him. His friend Digges was threatened with imprisonment, and appealed to Russell for help. According to Madden, he was arrested for failing to return a pair of silver spurs to Samuel Neilson, but it seems more likely that he was again in financial difficulties and was being threatened with debtors' prison. Russell agreed to put up security for him of £200. He was advised by William Brown, a local merchant, to be wary, but Russell was completely taken in by Digges. To raise the money it appears that he was forced to sell the only asset of real value he possessed — his ensigncy in the 64th. On 30 June 1791 he sold his commission and quit the army.[46] Russell's behaviour in this instance seems incredibly naive but it has to be borne in mind that Digges was a particularly convincing charlatan. Writing to the archbishop of Dublin to caution him against dealing with Digges, Archbishop John Carroll of Baltimore warned that he 'has sufficient dexterity, by shifting his scenes of action and displaying extraordinary abilities, to gain confidence for a time'. No less a man than George Washington was willing to defend Digges against his detractors (Digges was one of the few people invited by Merthe Washington to her husband's funeral), and Tone, usually such a shrewd judge of character, was genuinely impressed by the American when he met him.[47]

The following year Digges's real nature was revealed. In July 1792 he joined a group from Belfast on a shopping trip to Glasgow where, as well as stealing some muslin neckcloths from shops, he took several items from his travelling companions. His thefts were discovered and he was arrested again. It seems that he escaped after spending a few days in prison and absconded without repaying his debt to Russell. Russell wrote an account of these events to Tone, who was genuinely surprised and saddened, noting 'Digges, the hero of my last journal, a shoplifter!'. The American did not go on to mend his ways. He was back in England during the mid–1790s, unsuccessfully pursuing a claim to Chilham Castle Manor, his family's ancestral English seat. During this time John Russell, serving as a militia officer in London, was forced to detain him. He wrote to Thomas, who was still apparently concerned about the American's welfare, that 'as to Digges . . . he swindled everyone here that he could, so say no more of him'. Digges also managed to extricate himself from this scrape and returned to America in 1798, where he became a strong supporter of Thomas Jeffereson and James Madison. He died in Washington D.C. in 1821, his obituary

in the *National Intelligencer* praising him as an 'undeviating republican and patriot'.[48]

NOTES

1 *Walker's Hibernian Magazine* (Sept. 1792), p. 193; George Benn, *History of the town of Belfast* (London, 1877), i, 86; R. B. McDowell, 'The late eighteenth century' in J. C. Beckett and R. E. Glasscock (eds), *Belfast: the origin and growth of an industrial city* (Belfast, 1967), p. 56.
2 W. H. Crawford, 'The Belfast middle classes in the late eighteenth century' in Dickson, Keogh and Whelan (eds), *United Irishmen*, pp. 62–5; R. B. McDowell, 'The late eighteenth century' in J. C. Beckett and R. E. Glasscock (eds), *Belfast: the origin and growth of an industrial city* (Belfast, 1967), p. 59.
3 T. A. Emmet, 'Towards the history of Ireland' in W. J. McNeven, *Pieces*, p. 12.
4 Westmorland to Grenville, 5, 17 Oct. 1790 (Lecky, *Ireland*, iii, 8–9); National Archives, Westmorland correspondence 1, f. 8.
5 Martha McTier to Sarah Drennan, Sept. 1803 (*Drennan letters*, p. 328).
6 Morgan, 'Sketch of Russell', pp. 44–5.
7 Bartlett, *Life of Tone*, p. 45; Madden, *United Irishmen*, 3rd ser., ii, 147.
8 Mary McNeill, *The life and times of Mary Ann McCracken: a Belfast panorama* (Dublin, 1960), pp. 71–2.
9 L. H. Parsons, 'The mysterious Mr Digges' in *William and Mary Quarterly*, 3rd ser., xxii (1965), p. 486.
10 Madden, *United Irishmen*, ii, 3rd ser., 152.
11 Tone, *Writings*, i, 10–16, 68–89; Elliott, *Tone*, pp. 100–101.
12 Bartlett, *Life of Tone*, pp. 35–6.
13 Russell's journal, early 1791 (*Journals*, pp. 54–6); in line with C. J. Woods's edition of Russell's journals, I have retained Russell's erratic spelling in quotations from his journals.
14 Margaret Russell to Thomas Russell, 29 June 1793 (Sirr papers, 868/2, f. 25).
15 Russell's journal, 3 Nov. 1794 (*Journals*, p. 171); Elliott, *Tone*, p. 95; Tone to Matilda Tone, 20 Oct. 1791 (Tone, *Writings*, i, 144).
16 Russell's journal, *c*. Mar. 1791 (*Journals*, p. 39).
17 Russell's journal, *c*. Mar. 1791 (*Journals*, p. 44).
18 Russell's journal, Feb.–Mar. 1791, 9 July 1793 (*Journals*, pp. 44–6, 83–4); and notes in his hand (Sirr papers, 868/1, ff 72, 111, 246–8, 318 and 868/2, f. 168).
19 Russell's journal, *c*. Mar. 1791 (*Journals*, pp. 44–6); *Commons jn. Ire.*, xiv, 189–90; 227, 318–19.
20 Jonah Barrington, *Historical anecdotes and secret memoirs of the legislative union between Great Britain and Ireland* (London, 1809), p. 19.
21 C. W. Pursell jun., 'Thomas Digges and William Pearce: an example of the transit of technology' in *William and Mary Quarterly*, 3rd ser., xxi (1964), p. 555.
22 *Journals*, p. 39n; Pursell, 'Digges and Pearce', p. 556; for McCabe and Pearce's petition, the committee's report and Russell's appearance before the committee, see *Commons jn. Ire.*, xiv, 65-6, 126, ccxlii.
23 T. W. Tone, *An argument on behalf of the Catholics of Ireland* (Dublin, 1791), p. 8; Russell's journal, c. Mar. 1791 (*Journals*, p. 40); Tone, *Writings*, i, 136–7.
24 Richard Archdall, 7 Mar. 1791 (*Parl. reg. Ire.*, xi, 292).
25 Bartlett, *Life of Tone*, p. 121; Tone, *Writings*, i, 136.
26 R. B. McDowell, 'The personnel of the Dublin Society of United Irishmen 1791–4' in *I. H. S.*, ii, no. 5 (Mar. 1940), pp. 12–53.

27 Russell's journal, 9 Apr. 1791 (*Journals*, p. 49); David Dickson, 'Paine and Ireland' in Dickson, Keogh and Whelan (eds), *United Irishmen*, p. 135, 137.
28 Russell's journal, c. Mar. 1791 (*Journals*, pp. 42–3).
29 Tone to Russell, 9 July 1791 (R.I.A., Burrowes MS 23 K 53); Bartlett, *Life of Tone*, p. 32.
30 Chevalier de Laṭocnaye, *A Frenchman's walk through Ireland*, translated by John Stevenson (Belfast, 1917), p. 17.
31 J. D. H. Widdess, 'The Dublin House of Industry (1772–1838)' in William Doolin and Oliver Fitzgerald (eds), *'What's past is prologue': a retrospect of Irish medicine* (Dublin, 1952), pp. 40–55; *Commons Jn Ire.*, xiv, cci–ccii, ccxcix–cccx; Charles A. Cameron, *History of the Royal College of Surgeons in Ireland* (Dublin, 1886), p. 319.
32 Russell's journal, c. Feb. 1791 (*Journals*, pp. 35–6).
33 *Journals*, p. 37n; Dr Woods points out that these musings may have come about after Russell had read the Jesuit Pierre-Francois-Xavier de Charlevoix's *The history of Paraguay containing . . . a full and authentic account of the establishments formed there by the Jesuits from among the savage natives in the very centre of barbarism*; a Dublin edition was published in 1769; Russell's journal, c. Feb. 1791 (*Journals*, p. 37).
34 Madden, *United Irishmen*, 3rd ser., ii, 268; Revd. Forster Archer to –, 3 Oct. 1803 (Reb. papers 620/50/21).
35 Russell's journal, c. Feb. 1791 (*Journals*, p. 37).
36 Russell's journal, 10 Apr. 1791 (*Journals*, p. 50).
37 Mary Ann McCracken to Madden, 21 June 1859 (Madden papers, 873/89).
38 John J. Monaghan, 'A social and economic history of Belfast, 1790–1800' (MA thesis, Queen's University Belfast, 1936), pp. 67–8, 74.
39 Russell's journal, Apr. 1791, 25 Apr. 1791 (*Journals*, p. 50, p. 51).
40 Russell's journal, 21 Aug. 1793 (*Journals*, p. 108).
41 Russell's journal, 5 June [1797/8?] (Sirr papers, 868/1, f. 6); Bartlett, *Life of Tone*, p. 516.
42 Sirr papers, 868/2, ff 190–91; for similar observations see Sirr papers, 868/1, ff 85–9, 165, 239–40, 323, 334v and *Journals*, pp. 112, 119, 166–7.
43 Matilda Tone to Margaret Russell, 5 Sept. 1792 (Sirr papers, 868/1, f. 264).
44 *Journals*, p. 154n.
45 Russell's journal, 26 Apr. 1791 (*Journals*, p. 52).
46 Madden, *United Irishmen*, 3rd ser., ii, 142–3; Morgan, 'Sketch of Russell', p. 46; P.R.O., HO 100/31/211–12, 227.
47 Archbishop John Carroll, Baltimore to Archbishop Troy, Dublin, 16 Apr. 1792 (F. P. Moran (ed.), *Spicilegium Ossoriense . . .*, 3rd ser. (Dublin, 1884), pp. 511–12; L. H. Parsons, 'The mysterious Mr Digges' in *William and Mary Quarterly*, 3rd. ser., xxii (1965), p. 486; Bartlett, *Life of Tone*, p. 861.
48 Tone, *Writings*, i, 209; Madden, *United Irishmen*, 3rd ser., ii, 144; John Russell to Thomas Russell, London, 18/21 Sept. 1795 (Sirr papers, 868/2, ff 119–20).

CHAPTER THREE

The Dawning of Liberty

By the spring of 1791 many Irish reformers were becoming deeply disillusioned with the passivity of the Whigs, particularly on the Catholic question. Drennan complained that the Whig club was simply 'an eating and drinking aristocratical society without any fellow-feeling with the commonality', and noted that sectarian suspicions would have to be confronted if the cause of reform was to advance.[1] In Belfast similar thoughts were being aired. In his journal for March Russell noted a new openness among northern Presbyterians to the prospect of the repeal of the penal laws, while he himself believed that if the Catholics were given the franchise they would become 'good citizens'. He believed that the best way to gather momentum for the abolition of Catholic disabilities was to begin by agitating for parliamentary reform.[2] He and his friends were critical of the political timidity of leading Ulster Whig members of parliament, such as John O'Neill and William Brownlow, and lamented the way in which religious suspicions had immobilised the people.[3]

A general dissatisfaction with the status quo was generating an impetus for a new political initiative. Because of his exasperation at the caution of the Whigs Russell, anticipating his later democratic tendencies, was considering establishing a tradesmen's 'Whig club' in Belfast.[4] This came to nothing but by the early summer of 1791 it seems that plans were brewing, north and south, for something more ambitious — plans that would lead to the foundation of the Society of the United Irishmen. These plans, however, took some time to bear fruit and the precise roles played by particular individuals in the months leading up to the formation of the society are difficult to disentangle.[5] The starting point seems to have been the letter sent by William Drennan, a Belfast physician who had moved to Dublin and played a central role in the radical agitations of the 1780s, to his brother-in-law Samuel McTier in Belfast on 21 May 1791. Drennan outlined his plan to create a masonic style secret society in Dublin which would be:

> A benevolent conspiracy — a plot for the people — no Whig club — no party title — the brotherhood its name — the rights of man and the greatest happiness of the greatest number its end — its general end real independence to Ireland, and republicanism its particular purpose — its business every means to accomplish these ends as speedily as the prejudices and bigotry of the land we live in would permit.[6]

In June a document written by Drennan, spelling out his plans in more detail, circulated in Dublin. It called for the creation of an 'Irish Brotherhood', which would seek to overcome 'the distinctions of rank, of property, and of religious persuasion' by a programme of public education and communication with like-minded societies throughout Ireland, Britain and France.[7]

A copy of this document was sent to McTier in Belfast, where it met with the approval of the town's radicals. McTier wrote to Drennan that 'if your club brotherhood takes place we will immediately follow your example'.[8] It may have been Drennan's letter to Belfast that prompted Samuel Neilson to consider the creation of a new society — McTier was a close friend of his — or it is equally possible that, in the prevailing atmosphere of dissatisfaction with the Whig clubs, northern and southern reformers were already thinking along the same lines. A secret committee of Belfast Volunteers had been founded in the spring of 1791, by either Neilson or William Sinclair, and Russell may have been a member.[9] It was probably at a meeting of this committee, in the summer of 1791, that Neilson discussed plans with Russell, Henry Joy McCracken and other reformers to found a society that would pursue the parallel aims of parliamentary reform and Catholic relief. All were strongly in favour and the proposal began to gather real momentum.[10] The day set for the inauguration of the new society was 14 July 1791, when the Belfast Volunteers were to assemble to commemorate the second anniversary of the fall of the Bastille.

A declaration written by Drennan was to be read on this occasion but when McTier asked him to draw up resolutions for the new society as well, Drennan claimed he did not have time and advised him to contact Tone, who he was sure would 'be able to throw off some addresses to the people or to mould his resolutions into that shape — he has a ready and excellent pen'.[11] It was most probably at this stage that Russell, who was close to the radical element within the Volunteers, was asked to write to Tone to request him to compose the resolutions.[12] Tone responded with a document that contained three proposals: the first stated that since 'the Constitution of Ireland exists only in theory... a more general extension of the elective franchise is indispensably necessary'; the second that undue English influence could only be countered by 'a cordial union among the people... which is essential to the preservation of our liberties and the extension of our commerce'; the third lamented the disunity among the people of Ireland and declared that 'we shall heartily co-operate in all measures tending to the abolition of distinctions between Irishmen'.[13] The document was a relatively cautious one and made no explicit mention of the removal of Catholic disabilities. Tone, aware of this, sent a covering letter to Russell that went considerably further. He admitted that the resolutions:

> fall short of the truth, but truth itself must sometimes condescend to temporise. I hope you and the gentlemen with whom you communicate will find them so temperate as not to require much lopping or pruning... My unalterable opinion is that the bane of Irish prosperity in [sic] the influence of England. I believe that influence will ever be exerted while the connexion between the countries continues. Nevertheless, as I know that opinion is, *for the present*, too hardy, tho' a very little time may establish it universally, I have not made it part of the resolutions. I have only proposed to set up a reformed parliament as a barrier against that mischief which every honest man, that will open his eyes, must see in every instance overbears the interest of Ireland. I have not said a word that looks like a wish for *separation*, though I give it to you and to your friends that such an event would be a *regeneration* for this country.[14]

These documents almost immediately found their way into the hands of the authorities. When this became known to Russell two years later he instantly suspected Digges as the culprit, since he had given him the letter to copy; Drennan also believed that Digges was responsible. But as Marianne Elliott has pointed out, the documents were transcribed by a clerk in Dublin Castle and forwarded by Westmorland to Dundas on 11 July 1791, which probably would not have given them time to make the journey to and from Belfast, and the government may have received its information from a source other than Digges, possibly from an agent in the post office.[15] Not surprisingly, Tone's letter caused quite a stir in Dublin Castle. John

Fitzgibbon, the Lord Chancellor, produced it on a number of occasions in the House of Lords as evidence that Tone and his associates had been intent on the destruction of the British connection since the summer of 1791, despite the reformist sentiments they expressed in public. It was one of his trump cards in forcing through the Convention Act of 1793 and he even sent a copy of the letter to Pitt in an effort to discredit Tone and his then employers, the Catholic Committee.[16]

When Tone's resolutions came before the Belfast Volunteers on 14 July 1791 they received a mixed reception. Those criticising English influence and advocating parliamentary reform were readily accepted but the third resolution calling for the abolition of all distinctions between Irishmen met with stiff resistance. It was narrowly defeated in the supervising committee itself and, when put to the Volunteer gathering at large, it went down by a majority of about ten to one.[17] The resolutions were finally accepted only by withdrawing the third. Russell wrote an account of these events to Tone which led Tone to apply himself to thinking more seriously on the Catholic question than he had done hitherto. Since it seemed to him that northern reformers wanted 'rather a monopoly than an extension of liberty...contrary to all justice and expediency', Tone resolved to become 'a red-hot Catholic', and immediately set about writing his *Argument on behalf of the Catholics of Ireland*. Aimed primarily at northern Dissenters, it sought to convince them that 'they and the Catholics had but one common interest and one common enemy; that the depression and slavery of Ireland was produced and perpetuated by the divisions existing between them...and...it was necessary for the future to form but one people'.[18] Tone argued that a unified drive for Catholic emancipation and parliamentary reform would prove irresistible and presented Dissenters with a stark choice between 'reform and the Catholics, justice and liberty' or 'unconditional submission to the present and every future administration'.[19] It was a bravura performance: well-written, beautifully structured and highly persuasive, and stands as one of the finest pieces of political propaganda of the day. It found a wide and appreciative readership, among Catholics as well as Dissenters, and proved to be enormously influential in helping to erode sectarian suspicions and in encouraging a spirit of fraternity between the sects. One of Connacht's leading Catholic activists wrote of it:

A better pamphlet...I never read. It is from beginning to end a chain of close arguments, linked together by strong facts and forcible deductions. It speaks to the heart as well as to the head, and like a well conducted play, it rises by an imperceptible gradation, from the first page to the last, both in action and in interest. It may be called (as Russell says) the manual of the North. But surely it should become the manual of every person who is worthy of being an Irishman.[20]

Russell's biographer Mac Giolla Easpaig credits him with a considerable influence on Tone's *Argument*: he cites Russell's presence in Dublin in late July when Tone was writing the pamphlet; the similarity between a number of Tone's arguments and the draft essay in Russell's journal; and the fact that Tone was, at that time, unacquainted with either northern Dissenters or Catholics, whereas Russell had lived for almost a year among the former and had recently begun to correspond with the latter.[21] It is likely that Tone consulted him on particular points and drew on their discussions in his writing, but it took Tone's literary skill to shape and structure Russell's ideas. In the introduction to his draft essay on Catholic emancipation Russell noted that his effort would be of some use 'if it excites men of more ability or information to establish or refute my principles', and since he tended to avoid writing whenever possible and had a high opinion of Tone's literary talents, he was probably delighted to leave the work to his friend.[22]

The success of Tone's pamphlet in easing sectarian suspicions was a stark demonstration of the power of the printing press to mould public opinion and was probably an important factor in encouraging the radicals of Dublin and Belfast to set up their own newspapers. In September 1791 preparations for both publications began. The Dublin newspaper was to be called the *National Journal* and to be published three times a week. Drennan believed that Russell was most likely to be appointed as editor.[23] The paper's prospectus proclaimed its intention to 'abolish those unjust, invidious and ruinous distinctions, which bigotry in religion and in politics have raised among us...To accomplish this purpose, little more need be done than to make the great sects which divide this country... *know each other*'.[24] The first issue did not appear until the end of March 1792 and publication ceased after only a few weeks. Its paper and print were of poor quality and there were difficulties in finding a suitable editor. Russell did not, after all, secure the position, since by the time of publication he was employed as a magistrate in Tyrone.[25] The Belfast paper, the *Northern Star,* fared better. It was adequately financed by the town's radical Presbyterian merchants, particularly by Samuel Neilson, who acted as editor until his arrest in September 1796. Dedicated to the twin credos of unity and reform it proved a popular and influential paper, with a circulation in its first year averaging 4,200 copies per issue. For over five years the *Star*'s unashamedly radical perspective on events in Ireland and abroad aroused considerable disquiet in government circles and Russell would, in time, become one of its chief contributors.[26]

In the meantime the auguries for an alliance of Catholics and Presbyterians had never been better. Although Tone's resolution calling for a union of Irishmen of all creeds had been overwhelmingly rejected by the Volunteer gathering of 14 July, it was accepted by the radical first Belfast company.[27] Moreover, the assembly as a whole had approved a declaration which included the aspiration that 'all civil and religious intolerance [be] annihilated in this land' and late in the evening after the wine had flowed drank a toast to 'an abolition of the popery laws and an extension of privileges to the Roman Catholics'.[28]

The desire of some Dissenters to reach out to Catholics was reciprocated by liberal Catholics. Since the 1760s Catholics had petitioned for relief from the penal laws through the Catholic Committee. Dominated by conservative gentry and prelates, the Committee was anxious not to endanger the *de facto* toleration won in recent times, and its petitions were characterised by deference and at times near abject declarations of loyalty to the king. Reassured about their loyalty, the government pushed through significant relief acts in 1778 and 1782 which removed restrictions on Catholics owning and inheriting land. After the passing of the 1782 act the Committee had refrained from pressing for further instalments of relief and had avoided associating itself with the parliamentary reformers, although individual Catholic activists had lent their support to the reform movement. For the next few years the Catholic question receded into the background but by the end of the decade Catholics were again ready to press for relief, inspired by the agitation of their co-religionists in England and the establishment of religious equality in France. In the Catholic Committee radical veterans of the campaigns of the 1780s, such as the businessmen John Keogh and Richard McCormick, came to the fore and began to challenge the Committee's aristocratic leadership and advocate the adoption of a more vigorous style of campaigning.

Recognising the advantages involved in an alliance with northern Presbyterians, the Catholics of Elphin, Co. Roscommon, probably prompted by local activists such as Owen O'Connor and James Plunkett, sent their thanks to the Belfast Volunteers for their pro-emancipation declaration of 14 July. On 4 October a meeting of Belfast Volunteers, their suspicions probably eased by Tone's *Argument,* replied warmly to the Catholic address. The meeting, chaired by William Sinclair, resolved to set up a committee to open correspondence with the Catholics and endorsed a declaration that pledged 'to restore to *Irishmen* — their long lost rights', and to achieve them through a united drive for reform by all the Irish people. The declaration's tone towards the Catholics was warm and fraternal:

> We have said that our great object was to effectuate an adequate representation of the people in parliament . . . to conduct the community by the impulse of its own will. Of this will, you form a great part. If to be free a nation has only to will it, let us will it — let all out enmities rest with the bones of our ancestors. Differing in our religion as we differ in our faces, but resembling each other in the great features of humanity, let us unite to vindicate the rights of our common nature; let the decisive and unanimous voice of the society at large, of the body of the people, the mighty and irresistible whole — be heard, it will — it must be obeyed.[29]

According to one of Russell's Catholic contacts (probably Charles O'Conor (1736–1808), a leading Catholic gentleman of Belanagar, Co. Roscommon, and later representative for Co. Sligo at the Catholic Convention of 1792) the Catholics of Connacht were 'intoxicated' by this reply, which was circulated throughout the province.[30] Russell was also playing his part. He spent the months from July to September in Dublin but stayed closely in touch with developments in Belfast and kept up a correspondence with Sinclair to orchestrate the movement of the sects towards common ground.[31] Sinclair notified Russell of the friendly response of the Belfast Volunteers to the Elphin address, but greeted with some caution his suggestion that a deputation should be dispatched immediately to the Catholics to capitalise on the prevailing atmosphere of goodwill. Sinclair believed that it might 'be better to defer it a little until a correspondence is opened with some people in that quarter who might assist in such a business'.[32] Russell, however, was overjoyed at the moves towards union and was anxious to consolidate them. He was particularly concerned that sectarian rioting, then going on between Defenders and Peep o'Day Boys in Co. Armagh, should not be allowed wreck these stirrings of religious fraternity. He wrote to a northern activist, possibly Sinclair:

> I lose no time in sending you what I am sure will give you as much pleasure as it gave me — a copy of the answers to the letters from Elphin. It really has given me more pleasure than almost any event of my life. I think a coalition is now inevitable if matters are prudently managed and we may hear a great noise from the C[atholic]s next summer. THJ will set off for Belfast tomorrow where I hope and believe he will be of use. I will then be able to see what is to be done at Armagh. I think at present an end may be put to those dissensions — for heaven sake write to all your useful people and make them work tooth and nail at disseminating the papers...The south of Ireland is the place I fear that will hang heavy on hand — but we must only work the harder.[33]

The pieces of the jigsaw leading to the foundation of the United Irishmen were gradually falling into place. In September, Tone, on the strength of his authorship of the *Argument,* had been elected an honorary member of the first company of Belfast Volunteers and was invited north to assist the town's leading radicals in establishing a new political club. On 11 October he and Russell arrived in Belfast. The remaining preliminaries for the founding of the new society were to be carried out by a secret committee of Volunteers. Its leading members were all men with whom Russell was closely acquainted — Samuel Neilson, William Sinclair, Samuel McTier, Thomas McCabe, William and Robert Simms. Tone was amazed at how the mood in Belfast had changed within three months. Those passages relating to the Catholics in the resolutions he had written in July, which had proved so contentious then, had now to be rewritten because they were considered too bland. On 14 October, at a meeting of the secret committee, Tone's resolutions were adopted unanimously and the Society of the United Irishmen was formally established.[34]

Russell was delighted at what had been accomplished. Soon after the foundation of the United Irishmen he wrote to a Catholic friend to inform him of recent events. The new society was:

> daily increasing; they declare their full and unequivocal disapprobation of the unjust and impolitic restraints under which you labour and

for a parliamentary reform on the most tolerant plan including *all sects*. The first corporate act of this society was to decree a republication of 2000 of T[one]'s book to be distributed all throughout the North...The title page will set forth in capitals reprinted by order of the Society of United Irishmen of Belfast... your people...may see by the title page that the people of Belfast have taken up their cause seriously and firmly. I hope you will write to the same effect to some of your people in Dublin...I confess I am quite proud of this club — it is the first ever instituted in this kingdom for the removal of religious and political prejudices. I think it is an event in the history of the country. It if [*sic*] properly managed is the dawning of liberty.[35]

Russell's role in the creation of the society had been pivotal: most notably in drawing Tone into the preparations and in attempting to effect the union of sects to which the society aspired. Maureen Wall singled out Drennan and Russell as the key activists who had worked for several months on the project before it came to fruition in October 1791.[36] Although it was Drennan who had first suggested the name of Tone to compose the society's resolutions, in July 1791 Tone was almost completely unknown to the Belfast Volunteers, and it was his friendship with Russell that opened the way for his involvement in the founding of the society. Although a relative latecomer to the preparations, Tone was then able to forge a number of half-formed ideas into shape, and also came up with the society's name and clearly proclaimed its principles.[37]

Russell's other important contribution was his part in encouraging the tentative *rapprochement* of Catholics and Presbyterians. During the preliminaries to the founding of the society in Belfast in October 1791, Russell, to a far greater extent than Tone, played the role of spokesman for the Catholic interest. He had negotiated and corresponded with leading Catholics in the preceding months and was obviously well-informed about their activities and opinions. On his arrival in Belfast he delivered to the secret committee 'a mighty pretty history of the Roman Catholic Committee and his own negotiations'.[38] At the time he was in touch with Charles O'Conor of Belanagare, and he repeatedly used O'Conor's sensible and enlightened correspondence to counter traditional Presbyterian prejudices against the Catholics. It also seems that Russell had a number of other Catholic correspondents throughout northern Connacht. He had, for example, discussed the merits of Tone's *Argument* with Dr Hugh MacDermot, a leading Catholic activist from Coolavin, Co. Roscommon, who became a United Irishman and was elected to the

Catholic Convention as a representative for Co. Sligo.[39] Significantly, it was the Catholics of north Connacht who had played the leading role in establishing amicable relations with the Belfast Volunteers in the previous months.

Despite the tentative communications between the two groups, Belfast Presbyterians were still ignorant of Catholic politics and Russell's information was greeted with surprise and pleasure by members of the secret committee. It became clear, however, that even Tone's cogently-argued pamphlet had failed to convince everybody in Belfast of the wisdom of granting complete and immediate relief to the Catholics. On several occasions, notably an evening at the Northern Whig Club, Russell and Tone were confronted with the traditional Protestant arguments against entrusting Catholics with liberty, namely that they would use their new found freedom to repossess their confiscated estates and would eventually seize political power and deny civil and religious liberty to Protestants. There were also those who believed in the principle of abolishing the penal laws, but were only prepared to admit the Catholics to full civil and political rights in a cautious, step-by-step manner, once Catholics had proved themselves worthy. Tone and Russell confronted these objections and reservations head-on. Russell proved particularly adept at fighting the Catholic corner, leading one opponent, James Williamson, 'into palpable absurdity by a string of artful questions', and earning the nickname 'the Socratic' from the same adversary. In order to counter the arguments of Dr William Bruce, one of the most extreme opponents of immediate relief, Russell threatened at one stage to write a pamphlet, but like many of his planned literary ventures it came to nothing.[40]

There were several factors which would have disposed Russell to take such a pro-Catholic stance: his inclusive Christianity; his instinctive hatred of all forms of injustice and the probable presence of Catholic ancestry on both sides of his family. His father, who had overseen his education and for whom he had the deepest respect, was an important influence in this regard. John Russell retained a strong sympathy for Catholics to the end of his days. On his deathbed in December 1792 he expressed his approval of his son's involvement with the Catholic Committee and a deep admiration for 'the Catholic gentlemen who were the good old inhabitants of Ireland'.[41] These sympathies probably lay behind Russell's efforts to open communications with leading Catholics in mid-1791. Although the precise nature and extent of Russell's communications with the

Catholic Committee remain vague, they must have been substantial for him to have adopted such an authoritative position on the Catholic question. His activities in this regard even came to the attention of the Lord Lieutenant, Westmorland, who noted that 'Russell has certainly commenced a correspondence in Galway, Mayo and Roscommon, and, I think, Leitrim.'[42] While in Belfast Russell promised to send Sinclair details of the debates among the Catholics in 1791 'with notes', and he was sufficiently informed on the structures of the Catholic Committee to propose that northern Dissenters should organise themselves in a similar manner.[43]

With his strong pro-Catholic sympathies, Russell was far more wary of offending Catholic sensibilities than were most of his colleagues. Liberal Protestants such as Tone and Drennan could combine calls for the admission of Catholics to full civil rights with a hostility to Catholicism as a creed — Tone's *Argument*, for example, contained passages that were undoubtedly offensive to many Catholics, notably his description of Irish priests as 'men of low birth, low feelings, low habits, and no education'. Russell, in contrast, tended to adopt a far more conciliatory tone towards the Catholic religion. Writing to a Catholic correspondent Russell informed him that the new version of the *Argument* to be published by the United Irishmen of Belfast was 'much improved' since 'that part reflecting on your clergy is expunged'. In an effort to distance the society from ascendancy triumphalism he also noted that the revised edition made 'a serious swipe at the memory of William of Orange'.[44]

During his time in Belfast Tone began to keep a regular journal, possibly in imitation of Russell. He intended that it should be read by Russell and immediate members of Tone's family at a later date.[45] Whereas Russell's journals consist largely of introspective musings and assorted observations thrown together in no particular order, Tone's is written with greater facility and is a much racier and more coherent work. It relates in some detail their activities and discussions during their stay in Belfast. Many of the matters discussed were highly speculative: for example, Ireland's prospects of success in an uprising against British rule — Russell and Sinclair were particularly confident of victory, convinced that the army would be wiped out in days.[46] Besides its accounts of political matters, Tone's journal gives additional insights into Russell's character and the nature of the friendship between the two men. The two friends had their own particular form of discourse, regularly indulging in 'strained quotations, absurd phrases and extravagant sallies'. Tone's proclivity for studding his journals with literary quotations seems to have come about as a game he played with Russell to see who could produce the most apposite quotation for any particular occasion. Some of Tone's most commonly used quotations were ones he had borrowed from Russell, particularly his "Tis in vain for soldiers to complain' which he used to console himself repeatedly throughout his journals. Russell, it seems was particularly fond of the phrases 'That is manly and decided!' and 'God bless all here!', and also regularly used certain quotations from Mr Vellum, a character in Joseph Addison's *The drummer*, namely 'The gift is two fold', and 'A thundering dog!'. It may be that Russell did not quite have his friend's facility in quoting, for Tone often made fun of his tendency to mangle quotations.[47]

Tone's journal also catalogued their consumption of alcohol, which was copious. Of the two, Russell was usually the worse for wear, Tone recording him as being in various phases of intoxication such as 'drunk', 'very drunk' and the finely judged 'pretty well on for it, but not quite gone'. He also detailed his morning-after suffering, describing him as being in such states as 'the horrors', which he put down to his excessive smoking, and 'in the blue devils — thinks he is losing his faculties; glad he had any to lose'. Russell's dissolute behaviour often elicited stern lectures from Tone, who tended to adopt an older brother role to his younger friend, regularly berating him about his heavy drinking and late hours. There was a jocular, bantering note to most of this lecturing, and Tone would often laugh himself into good humour at Russell's expense. Tone enjoyed the role and, on his return to Belfast the following year without Russell, complained 'want [Russell] in order to advise him; just in a humour to give advice'. There were times when Tone's lecturing would prove too much for Russell, who would take his friend to task for harrying him with advice, but for the most part Russell took these reprimands to heart and on occasion even made an effort to mend his ways: To Matilda Tone he wrote: 'I am at present composing a pretty moral treatise on temperance, and will dedicate it to myself, for I don't know who is likely to profit so much by it.' For the most part, however, these attempts at moral reformation appear to have been rather short-lived and after a visit to a Dublin alehouse in November Tone noted 'Left [Russell] getting very drunk, after all his fine resolutions. Bad! Bad!'.[48]

It was on this trip that Tone christened Russell 'P.P.', after a fictional character in a work entitled *Memoirs of P.P., clerk of this parish* possibly written by Alexander Pope. This was the story of a young cleric who 'was determined to reform the manifold corruptions and abuses which had crept into the church', but despite his sincere intentions to live a pious life, he was occasionally 'overtaken with liquor' and was also a 'follower of venereal fantasies'.[49] The nickname was particularly apt and Russell recognised as much by applying it to himself in his own journals. Something of the aura of the serious young clergyman clung to Russell throughout his life. He tended to adopt a tone of immense gravity when speaking of religious matters and was liable to become deeply offended if anyone spoke flippantly of Christianity.[50]

The manner in which Russell was portrayed in Tone's memoirs was a matter of some controversy in later years. Russell's nephew claimed that Tone had deliberately set out to blacken his friend's character so that he could monopolise credit for the founding of the United Irishmen, and he completely denied that Russell was a womaniser or a heavy drinker.[51] Madden, writing for a Victorian readership that had little tolerance for drunkenness, claimed that Tone tended to tax his friends with faults that were the 'very opposite of their most prominent virtues and estimable qualities', and therefore 'Russell's well-known gravity of deportment and demeanour, his strong sense of the importance and value of religion, his habitual decorum and propriety in social intercourse, were made the subject of ironical jocularity in Tone's diaries.'[52] But Tone was simply telling the truth, and the picture of Russell that emerges from his journals, far from being an attempt at character assassination or ironic caricature, captures much of the complexity of his personality. Tone credits Russell with being a confident and effective public speaker, but relates how he could be indecisive and unsure of himself in his personal life — on one occasion he had to make several journeys to and from the Belfast Assembly Rooms and summon 'a council of waiters at which the chambermaid assisted' before working up the courage to go in. At times he could be gripped by a deep anguish for the most apparently trivial of reasons. Returning from church after what Tone termed 'a vile sermon...against smuggling and about loyalty and all that', he describes Russell as being 'in great sorrow and distress of mind'. Walking along the Mall, Russell's distress was aggravated when Tone teased him about the admiring looks he was receiving from the ladies of Belfast.[53]

But Russell was not always such a tortured soul: he could also be light-hearted and witty, mocking his own moral failings and bantering as pointedly as Tone. Just as Tone had nicknamed him 'P.P.', he responded by dubbing his friend 'Mr John Hutton', probably after one of Dublin's leading coachbuilders — a gentle swipe at Tone's origins as the son of a coachbuilder. On one occasion when Tone flew into a rage on discovering that his printer had sent him 2,000 prospectuses for the *National Journal* instead of the 2,000 copies of *An Argument on behalf of the Catholics of Ireland* he had requested, Russell gleefully stoked his friend's rage by quoting Seneca, Boethius' *De consolatione* and several other works on the folly of anger.[54]

After they had accomplished their business in Belfast, Tone and Russell set off for Dublin on Thursday 27 October 1791. During the discussions of the past weeks they had acted as spokesmen for Dublin Catholics and radicals, and had been given the task of keeping the capital informed about developments in Belfast. Tone had been in touch with Dublin-based radicals such as James Napper Tandy, Drennan and Hamilton Rowan before his arrival in Belfast, probably through an intermediary, the Dublin printer, John Chambers.[55] Tone and Russell were now given instructions to make official contact with Dublin radicals and to assist them in founding another United Irish club. An embryonic Dublin society composed mainly of Tandy's followers met on 5 November, without Russell or Tone present, though they were balloted and accepted as members *in absentia*. Two days later they attended a meeting with a number of the city's leading radicals, including Tandy, William Todd Jones, Joseph Pollock and William Drennan — Theobald McKenna, William James MacNeven and Richard McCormick represented the Catholic interest. The central purpose of the new society was discussed: Todd Jones was for pressing ahead with Catholic emancipation, without complicating the issue by coupling it with parliamentary reform at this early stage, but Tone and Russell disagreed. Adopting Jones's suggestion would have made the United Irishmen no different from earlier political organisations which had pursued the interest of one sect or interest group. They saw the United Irishmen as being a new kind of political society: one which was dedicated to the interests of the entire nation and they insisted on the adoption of a programme which simultaneously pursued the twin aims of reform and emancipation, and eventually had their way.[56]

They did not, however, have things all their own way. On 9 November the Dublin Society of United Irishmen was formally inaugurated, and Russell and Tone ran into some difficulties by strenuously opposing a test drawn up by Drennan, which read:

> I A. B. in the presence of God, do pledge myself to my country, that I will use all my abilities and influence in the attainment of an impartial and adequate representation of the Irish nation in parliament...I shall do whatever lies in my power to forward a brotherhood of affection, a identity of interests, a communion of rights, and a union of power among Irishmen of all religious persuasions, without which every reform must be partial, not national, inadequate to the wants, delusive to the wishes and insufficient for the freedom and happiness of this country.[57]

According to Drennan they opposed the test because they claimed that it was too vague, too rhetorical and likely to dissuade potential members from joining, but they found little support.[58] Tandy replied to the last of their objections with the observation that 'it was better to have a society knit together and braced by a strong obligation than admit those scrupulous, hesitating, half-way men who would soon damp the zeal and spirit of the meeting'. Drennan was puzzled at the staunch opposition of Tone and Russell to the test, and maintained that most of his fellow members found their stance unreasonable and that as a result they failed to have themselves elected to the society's correspondence committee. In a letter to Belfast he wrote:

> I think Tone and Russell imprudent in rendering themselves unpopular...My chief fault to them is that they are too reserved to some who are entitled to confidence, and that they aim rather at making *instruments* than *partners*. They don't conceal this enough, and therefore, I think, don't know men as well as they will do. They are both sincere and able and zealous. They sometimes speak of being officially representative of the Belfast society, and Tone said if this had not been the case he would not have taken the test.[59]

It may have been that Tone and Russell thought that any oath might prove difficult for some Catholics to take, which would militate against the declared objectives of the society. It could also be that since the Belfast club had initially taken no test, they were wary of adopting anything that might drive a wedge between the northern and southern societies. Significantly, the founders of the United

Irishmen in Belfast had ignored the masonic mumbo-jumbo outlined by Drennan in his circular for the creation of an 'Irish Brotherhood'. Their preference appears to have been for a society that would perform its functions in as businesslike a manner as possible, without the elaborate rules, procedures and bombastic declarations that typified many contemporary clubs. The test was, however, accepted by both the Dublin and Belfast societies, and Robert Simms wrote to Tone from Belfast approving of it and claiming that it would be a useful barrier to the admission of 'lukewarm men'.[60]

But Russell never lost his pronounced distaste for tests and oaths. He was horrified by the way in which the name of God was invoked so lightly and he wholeheartedly agreed with the opinion expressed some years later by a fellow United Irishman, James Hope, that 'good men will not violate their engagement, and you can frame no oath which will bind the villain who would desert the cause of his country and betray his fellow men'.[61] The issue of the test appears to have rankled with Russell — Drennan claimed that he was noticeably cool towards him when they met at a dinner several weeks later.[62]

NOTES

1 Drennan to Sam McTier, 21 May 1791 (Drennan papers, T765/300).
2 Russell's journal, Mar. 1791 (*Journals*, p. 39).
3 Russell's journal, Mar. 1791, 9 Apr. 1791 (*Journals*, pp. 38-9, 47–8).
4 Russell's journal, [2 Mar. 1791], c. Mar. 1791 (*Journals*, pp. 40–41, 42); a new organisation, the Whigs of Belfast, was formed in the early summer of 1791, though it is not known if Russell played any part. It was soon to be absorbed by the United Irishmen; see Haliday to Charlemont, 16 June 1791 (*Charlemont MS*, ii, 140).
5 Madden, *United Irishmen*, 2nd ser. (1843), i, 93, claims Tone as founder, but in 2nd ser., 2nd ed. (1858) he credits him with a lesser role; see also: MacNeven, *Pieces*, p. 17; Frank MacDermot, *Theobald Wolfe Tone: a biographical study* (London, 1939), pp. 59–62; Mac Giolla Easpaig, *Ruiséil*, pp. 40–49; Elliott, *Tone*, pp 124-5; A. T. Q. Stewart, *A deeper silence* (London, 1993), pp. 153–60.
6 Drennan to Sam McTier, 21 May 1791 (Drennan papers, T765/300).
7 Circular on the formation of an 'Irish Brotherhood', June 1791 (Reb. papers, 620/19/24).
8 Sam McTier to Drennan, 2 July 1791 (Drennan papers, T765/302).
9 A. T. Q. Stewart, *A deeper silence* (London, 1993), p. 155; *Journals*, p. 18.
10 Madden, *United Irishmen*, 2nd ser., (2nd ed., Dublin, 1858), p. 11; Edna C. Fitzhenry, *Henry Joy McCracken*, (Dublin, 1936), pp. 51–2.
11 Drennan to Sam McTier, early July 1791 (Drennan papers, T765/307).
12 Bartlett, *Life of Tone*, p. 45.
13 A copy of Tone's resolutions are enclosed in Westmorland to Dundas, 11 July 1791 (P.R.O., HO 100/33/81–2).

14 Tone to Russell, 9 July 1791 (R.I.A., Burrowes MS 23 K 53).

15 Russell's journal, 20 Mar. 1793 (*Journals*, pp. 65–6); Drennan to Sam McTier, c. July 1793 (Drennan papers, T765/435); Elliott, *Tone*, pp. 106–7; Westmorland to Dundas, 11 July 1791 (P.R.O. HO 100/33/81–2).

16 Frank MacDermot, *Theobald Wolfe Tone: a biographical study* (London, 1939), p. 122.

17 Thomas Knox to Lord Abercorn, 17 July 1791 (P.R.O.N.I., Abercorn papers, T2541/1B1/2/27).

18 Bartlett, *Life of Tone*, pp. 46, 119.

19 T. W. Tone, *An argument on behalf of the Catholics of Ireland* (Dublin, 1791), p. 51

20 Hugh MacDermot to Owen O'Conor, 21 Nov. 1791 (Tone, *Writings*, i, 153)

21 Mac Giolla Easpaig, *Ruiséil*, pp. 44–5.

22 Russell's journal, early 1791 (*Journals*, p. 53).

23 Drennan to Sam McTier, c. Nov. 1791 (Drennan papers, T765/309a).

24 P.R.O., HO 100/34/9; according to Drennan, Tone wrote the prospectus: see Tone, *Writings*, i, 129–31.

25 *Northern Star*, 28 Mar. 1792; Drennan to Sam McTier, 5 Nov. 1791, c. Mar. 1792 (Drennan papers, T765/310, 328).

26 Brian Inglis, *The freedom of the press in Ireland, 1784–1841* (London, 1954), p. 97; Rosamond Jacob, *The rise of the United Irishmen, 1791–4* (Dublin, 1937), p. 178; for the *Northern Star*'s circulation figures see [Bernard Dornin], *Sketch of the life of Samuel Neilson of Belfast* (New York, 1804), p. 8.

27 MacNeven, *Pieces*, p. 14.

28 Declaration of the Belfast Volunteers, 14 July 1791 (National Archives, Westmorland correspondence, 1/17).

29 Reply of Belfast Volunteers to the Catholics of Jamestown and Elphin, 4 Oct. 1791 (Reb. papers, 620/19/28).

30 Drennan to Sam McTier, 5 Nov. 1791 (Drennan papers, T765/310); for Russell's contacts with O'Conor see p. 42; for O'Conor's role in Catholic politics see Eamon O'Flaherty, 'The Catholic Convention and Anglo-Irish politics, 1791–3' in *Archivium Hibernicum* xl (1985), p. 17.

31 Russell's journal, July to Sept. 1791 (*Journals*, pp. 57–61).

32 [Sinclair] to [Russell], 4 Oct. 1791 (P.R.O., HO 100/34/10); for the identity of the correspondents see Elliott, *Tone*, pp. 131–2; 427n. The fact that there are copies of so much of this correspondence in the Home Office papers suggests that the mail of the founders of the United Irishmen was already being opened by government officials.

33 [Russell] to [Sinclair?], 8 Oct. 1791 (P.R.O., HO 100/34/13); the 'THJ' referred to was possibly Thomas Harman Jones, Russell's cousin.

34 Bartlett, *Life of Tone*, pp. 47, 119–20.

35 [Russell] to ?, Oct./Nov. 1791 (P.R.O., HO 100/34/41–2); for Russell's authorship of this letter see Curtin, *United Irishmen*, p. 9.

36 Maureen Wall, 'The United Irish movement' in *Historical Studies*, v, ed. J. L. McCracken, (London, 1965), p. 128; Charles Dickson lists the 'co-founders' of the society as Tone, Neilson, Russell and Drennan (*Revolt in the North: Antrim and Down in 1798* (Dublin, 1960), p. 182).

37 Elliott, *Tone*, p. 125.

38 Tone, *Writings*, i, 132.

39 For Russell's contacts with the Catholics, see Hugh MacDermot to Owen O'Conor, 21 Nov. 1791 (Tone, *Writings*, i, 153); The O'Conor Don, *The O'Conors of Connaught* (Dublin,1891), pp. 300–302; Tone, *Writings*, i, 132; Morgan, 'Sketch of Russell', p. 50; Woods, 'Place of Thomas Russell', p. 86; and

Helen Landreth, *The pursuit of Robert Emmet* (Dublin, 1949), p. 21.
40 Tone, *Writings*, i, 144, 148, 209.
41 Russell's journal, 16 Aug. 1793 (*Journals*, p. 101).
42 Westmorland to Hobart, c. 1791–2 . This document is cited in Helen Landreth, *The pursuit of Robert Emmet* (Dublin, 1949), pp. 20–21, but cannot now be traced; on this point see also Woods, 'Place of Thomas Russell', p. 97n.
43 Tone, *Writings*, i, 148, 220.
44 [Russell] to –, Oct./Nov. 1791 (P.R.O., HO 100/34/41–2); for Russell's authorship of this letter see Curtin, *United Irishmen*, p. 9.
45 Bartlett, *Life of Tone*, pp. 17, 481, 578.
46 Tone, *Writings*, i, 148.
47 Tone to Russell, 1 Sept. 1795 (Reb. papers, 620/16/3); Bartlett, *Life of Tone*, pp. 475, 511, 621, 623, 631.
48 Tone, *Writings*, i, 133–49, 152.
49 C. J. Woods points out that this character is to be found in *The works of Alexander Pope, esq.* (London, 1769), iii, 217–26 (*Journals*, p. 31n).
50 Mary Ann McCracken to Madden, n.d. (Madden papers, 873/672v).
51 J. A. Russell to John Gray, 22 Apr. 1843 (Madden papers, 873/669).
52 Madden, *United Irishmen*, 3rd ser., ii, 148.
53 Tone, *Writings*, i, 136.
54 Tone, *Writings*, i, 137.
55 Tone to Chambers, 13 Oct. 1791 (Reb. papers, 620/19/29).
56 Tone, *Writings*, i, 135, 152; Drennan to Sam McTier, Nov. 1791 (Drennan papers, T765/311).
57 Drennan to Sam McTier, Nov. 1791 (Drennan papers, T765/313).
58 Drennan to Sam McTier, Nov. 1791 (Drennan papers, T765/313).
59 Drennan to Sam McTier, [Dec.] 1791 (Drennan papers, T765/315).
60 Tone, *Writings*, i, 159.
61 Russell's journal, 9 July 1793 (*Journals*, p. 83); Morgan, 'Sketch of Russell', p. 56.
62 Drennan to Sam McTier, 24 Dec. 1791 (Drennan papers, T765/318).

CHAPTER FOUR

The Making of a Radical

Since leaving the army in June 1791, Russell had spent his time largely on political work, but once the Belfast and Dublin United Irish societies were in place he found himself at a loose end. By then his lack of a regular income was beginning to make itself felt and he desperately needed to find some means of earning a living, his proposed editorship of the *National Journal* having come to nothing.[1] Through his contacts with the Knox family of Co. Tyrone, on 22 December 1791 he managed to secure appointment to the post of seneschal (a kind of stipendiary magistrate) to the manor court at Dungannon, which carried with it the unpaid position of justice of the peace for Co. Tyrone.[2] There was some irony in the fact that a liberal reformer such as Russell should hold the office of seneschal, which was in effect a vestige of feudalism in the gift of the lords of the manor courts of corporate towns. Many of those appointed to such positions had no legal qualifications and were thoroughly unsuitable to preside over a court. The courts themselves were often held at unsuitable premises such as inns or public houses, and were conducted with little regularity or decorum.[3]

There is little hard information available about Russell's career in Dungannon. By all accounts it seems that he attempted to carry out his duties as diligently and fairly as possible, despite having to contend with deep-rooted sectarian antagonism. Even Samuel McSkimin, an unsympathetic biographer of Russell, concedes that his conduct as a magistrate 'was marked by the strictest justice and impartiality' and that he 'was respected by the people'.[4] Apparently, Russell threw himself into his task so diligently that he managed to have some success in calming religious conflict and produced 'an apparent harmony between...discordant elements in his own immediate neighbourhood'.[5] But when he attempted to co-operate with his fellow magistrates to extend this harmony throughout the county he ran into real difficulties. In dealing with incidents between

Peep o'Day Boys and Defenders he found it hard to accept the anti-Catholic prejudices of his fellow magistrates, who were often reluctant to take action against Protestant wrongdoers but enforced the law strictly against Catholics. Russell believed that, far from seeking to administer justice in an even-handed manner and attempting to keep the peace in the county, they fomented and encouraged local animosities, and he soon found that 'the office of a peacemaker was a thankless one'.[6]

Religious tensions were notably on the increase in Ireland in 1792. Under pressure from London to make concessions to the Catholics, leading members of the Irish government were busily engaged in whipping up sectarian passions.[7] At the heart of these efforts was the 'Castle Cabinet' of John Fitzgibbon, the Lord Chancellor, John Foster, the Speaker of the House of Commons, and John Beresford, Commissioner of the Revenue. For most of the 1790s this cabal dominated the Irish government, adopting a hardline attitude to Catholic relief, parliamentary reform, and law and order. Fitzgibbon, in particular, was staunchly opposed to any broadening of the political nation to include the unpropertied or the Catholics, which he believed, would threaten the connection with Britain he deemed so essential to the maintenance of Protestant ascendancy.[8] Like other conservative Protestants he looked on the elections to the Catholic Convention with great suspicion. This unprecedented level of political activity among Catholics brought forth a storm of staunchly anti-Catholic resolutions from grand juries, contributing to an upsurge in Defender activity and Protestant volunteering, and to a general sharpening of religious animosity in many areas. Throughout the year much of south Ulster and north Leinster was affected to some degree, with Tyrone being a particularly disturbed county. While Russell was attempting to play the role of peacemaker in Tyrone, John Keogh and Tone, who in July 1792 had been appointed assistant secretary of an increasingly radical Catholic Committee, were also trying to damp down sectarian conflict in south Down.[9]

This heightening of sectarian tensions would have made life difficult for an idealistic young magistrate intent on the impartial administration of the law, and Russell's tenure in Dungannon was evidently a frustrating and unhappy period in his life. One of his duties as seneschal entailed administering oaths, for example to those who wished to enlist in the military, and Mary Ann McCracken remembered him expressing regret at the number of men he had helped recruit into the army during his time in Dungannon.[10] One of the very few surviving documents that sheds any light on this period in Russell's life is a letter from a Dungannon liquor-merchant charging him with a bill for spirits bought between June and December 1792 amounting to £5 12s. 9d., which suggests that, to an even greater extent than usual, he was attempting to drown his frustrations in liquor.[11]

Russell's dispiriting experiences in Tyrone probably led to his interest in legal reform. When imprisoned in 1803, in response to a request from the authorities he detailed a series of reforms which he believed would help to alleviate the grievances of the people. Among these was a proposal to curb the powers of local magistrates. Russell claimed 'that the magistrates, from their uncontrolled powers of punishment, were often local tyrants', and their behaviour was so bad that the people were often compelled to 'look to the military officers of England for protection from the oppressions of the gentry'. Anticipating the resident magistrates of the later nineteenth century, he advised the government to appoint suitably qualified and salaried magistrates throughout the country. If they administered justice in an even-handed manner, he believed 'they would be esteemed by the people a blessing, and the expense most cheerfully paid'.[12]

To add to his difficulties with his fellow magistrates, his sympathies for the poor came to the surface and it seems that he managed to antagonise Dungannon's linen merchants by taking the side of local weavers in a trade dispute. According to Madden, his efforts on their behalf 'caused him to be considered a man with dangerous leanings towards the people, in fact, a republican'.[13]

As if taking the side of the Catholic peasantry and the linen weavers was not enough, Russell also found time to write to the newspapers about one of his deepest concerns — the plight of African slaves. The first parliamentary vote on the abolition of the slave trade had been taken at Westminster in April 1791 and had been overwhelmingly defeated. This led to an upsurge of anti-slavery campaigning, particularly by evangelicals and Quakers, and parliament was deluged with petitions in the spring of 1792.[14] In an essay entitled 'Enslavement of the Africans', which he sent to the *Northern Star*, Russell graphically detailed the tortures inflicted on slaves and expressed his outrage at this trade in human beings. He wrote:

> it is a lamentable truth that their oppressors are those who make
> profession of the Christian name, and that the legislature of our

nation encourages this business; as also the consumers of the commodities [of] the West Indies (sugar and rum). It is to be hoped, in charity to the king and his counsellors, as also the public at large, that they cannot be fully sensible of the sufferings of the poor oppressed negroes; for if they were, surely they could not find peace of mind till they put a stop to such iniquitous proceedings, the very relations of which might make the hearts of the peaceful melt with pity, and those of well meaning zealots burn with indignation! While we live under a government, the mildness of which allows us thus with impunity, to speak of its imperfections, and plead without restraint the cause of the oppressed; an act which the religious, in goodwill to mankind, have sometimes found it their duty to perform in opposition to human laws, and through much persecution and sufferings unto death... how much of selfishness and ostentation must we suspect in the boasts of the English, that their laws are thus free, and declarative of the natural rights of mankind, while the same laws hold thousands of our fellow creatures in a bondage worse than that of Pharaoh...

There is perhaps no part of the earth where beasts of burden are so much oppressed as the negroes are in the sugar plantations. They are sixteen hours in the service of their cruel masters; and the shouts of their drivers, and the cracks of the whip on their naked bodies, which cuts out small pieces of flesh at almost every stroke, are heard all day long in the fields... Are they not already sufficiently unhappy in being reduced to a state of slavery... To crown their wretchedness must they be abused, buffeted, murdered and treated worse than brutes. Humanity revolts at the idea of a conduct which nothing but the thirst [for] gold could ever have introduced and of which from that thirst, every day will still, perhaps produce an aggravated repetition, till an enlightened legislative [*sic*] shall put an end to a traffic which disgraces human nature.[15]

This may have been one of a series of letters which Russell had written against the slave trade. Some months earlier a letter which bore some strong similarities to this had appeared in the *Belfast News Letter* signed by 'G'. On the basis of its sentiments and style it is possible that this too was written by Russell. It claimed that Europeans had destroyed the Africans' natural state of 'innocence and peace', and sowed in their communities, even in their very families, 'a spirit of strife and discord', with the result that 'the plantations of the West Indies are saturated with the very blood of Africa'. The writer was hopeful though that 'the arguments of truth and justice' would eventually 'prevail over those of sophistry and interest' and that this vile trade would cease.[16]

Opposition to the slave trade was the great philanthropic cause of the age, drawing adherents from all Christian denominations and from across the political spectrum, but few of its opponents expressed their outrage as passionately as Russell. The essay he sent to the *Star* was not published, though Neilson did print a reply to a 'Dungannon correspondent' in which he maintained that although the *Northern Star*, inspired as it was 'with the principles of general liberty', could not be 'insensible to the sufferings of any part of the human race', nevertheless, because there were 'three million slaves in our native land' the paper's priority was to concentrate on oppression and injustice in Ireland.[17] For Russell, however, recognition of domestic injustice did nothing to diminish his outrage at what he saw as a gross violation of the laws of God. He was a man with a cosmopolitan vision of liberty, outraged by injustice wherever it appeared in the world, and denunciation of the slave trade was one of the recurrent themes of his writings. So strong were his feelings against slavery that, over sixty years later, Mary Ann McCracken remembered his refusal to eat or drink anything containing sugar at the many Belfast dinner parties to which he was invited. Significantly, one of his closest friends in Belfast was Thomas McCabe who in 1786 had strenuously opposed efforts in the town to invest money in fitting out a slave-ship.[18] In his *Letter to the people of Ireland*, published in 1796, the fullest statement of his political views, Russell made sure to include a swingeing attack on the slave trade:

> Are the Irish nation aware that this contest involves the question of the slave trade, the one now of the greatest consequence on the face of the earth? Are they willing to employ their treasure and their blood in support of that system, because England has 70 or 7,000 millions engaged in it, the only argument that can be adduced in its favour, *monstrous* as it may appear? Do they know that this horrid traffic spreads its influence over the globe; that it creates and perpetuates barbarism and misery, and prevents the spreading of civilisation and religion, in which we profess to believe? Do they know that by it thousands and hundreds of thousands of these miserable Africans are dragged from their innocent families like the miserable Defenders, transported to various places, and there treated with such a system of cruelty, torment, wickedness and infamy, that it would be impossible for language adequately to express its horror and guilt, and which would appear rather to be the work of wicked demons than of men.[19]

R. R. Madden, the nineteenth-century biographer of the United Irishmen and a passionate opponent of slavery himself, as well as some later writers, have credited Russell with a series of anti-slavery poems which appeared in the *Star* in 1792.[20] However, although Russell may have been responsible for their inclusion in the paper, these are the work of other authors, for example, the English poet William Cowper.[21] The confusion may have arisen because drafts of anti-slavery verse are to be found in Russell's papers but these are the revision of a previously published work by another writer. In his journal Russell noted 'alter the ballad of the Negro's complaint. Intend to get it publish'd'. However, this was not an original work but a revision from supposed negro dialect to standard English of the poem 'The Negro's Lament', which had appeared in a Belfast songbook published in 1793 and in the *Gentleman's Magazine* of August 1793.[22]

According to McSkimin's account of Russell's career as a magistrate, he was treated by the Knox family 'with the most marked attention'.[23] But Lord Northland and his eldest son Thomas Knox were both conservatives and it is likely that there was considerable tension between them and Russell. Thomas Knox was suspicious of Catholic assertiveness in 1792 and one of the most active figures in advocating the formation of yeomanry corps to resist the United Irishmen in 1796; he and his father also joined the first Orange lodge founded in Dublin in June 1796.[24] Many years later, in a terse reference to this period of his life, Russell remembered that 'he told Mr Knox his sentiments who then left him to himself'.[25] Russell resigned his position in October 1792, according to his nephew, on the grounds that 'he never could reconcile it to his conscience to sit as magistrate on a bench where the practice prevailed of inquiring what a man's religion was before inquiring of what crime he was accused'.[26] This version of events is supported by Drennan, who maintained that Russell should have sought some compensation from the Catholic Committee, since he had sacrificed his position as a magistrate on a matter of principle.[27] Russell's unhappy experiences in Dungannon constitute an important episode in his alienation from the establishment, confirming his hatred of injustice and sectarian prejudice, particularly when supported by biased authority. Having been an army officer and a magistrate he never again served in any official position or sought the patronage of his aristocratic friends.

His resignation from his magistrate's position again left him without employment or income. He decided that since he had 'an enthusiasm for the cause of liberty', he would emigrate to France and join the army of the newly-founded republic. He wrote to Tone seeking advice and letters of recommendation from his contacts in the Dublin United Irishmen and the Catholic Committee. In the paranoid atmosphere that had gripped Paris in the wake of the September massacres this was a dangerous scheme, but Tone approved of Russell's intentions and his spirit.[28]

Before going to Dublin Russell went to Belfast, where a majority had now swung behind Catholic relief. In November several gatherings of Belfast citizens, even the moderate Northern Whig Club, adopted resolutions in favour of complete and immediate Catholic emancipation.[29] At one such meeting, chaired by Samuel McTier, one speaker insisted that the citizens of Belfast should declare for Catholic relief even though 'a rebellion should ensue and the kingdom should be deluged with blood'. An ebullient Neilson wrote to Tone: 'you can form no conception of the rapid progress of union here ... The universal question throughout the country is: when do we begin? Do we refuse hearth money or tythes first?'.[30] On 29 November Russell attended a meeting of the town's leading United Irishmen and was delegated by his colleagues to present a number of resolutions to the Catholic Convention due to meet in Dublin the following week. The resolutions exhorted the Catholics not to accept any half-measures that might retard the 'general freedom of Ireland ... In the present glorious era, we do expect that our Catholic countrymen have too high a value for the rights of man to be satisfied with anything short of them, the more so as their Protestant brethren and fellow citizens are determined to aid in the general recovery of those rights for all Irishmen'.[31] The Catholic Convention delegate for Co. Antrim, Luke Teeling, was appointed to observe and influence events at the convention while Russell, it seems, was given the task of acting as a behind-the-scenes agent and courier.[32]

On his arrival in Dublin on 3 December, Russell was met by a family servant and told that his father's health was failing rapidly. This probably came as no great surprise — his father had stayed with him in Dungannon some weeks earlier and had been in poor health. Russell went immediately to the Royal Hospital and saw that his father was dying. To avoid dwelling on the inevitable they discussed Thomas's affairs. His father approved of his plan to serve with the French and wished him well, telling him that he was going 'among a set of heros, legislators and lawgivers ... [and] that the French would prove the terror and admiration of the world'.[33]

In his journal Russell recorded a lengthy account of his father's last days:

My father's breathing became worse and his life was coming visibly to
a close...He desired me to remember the directions he had given
before when he was ill relative to his funeral...that he should be
buried close to my mother quite privately in the morning without any
military honours.

...He conjectured, I believe (and truly), that I wish'd to have him
enterr'd like a soldier and gave me these directions to prevent such
foppery...Toward morning I read the prayers used to the sick...and
those texts of scripture which so sublim[e]ly set forth the tender mercy
of God to such as trust in him. I was kneeling at the little table and
when praying fervent[t]ly and repeating those exquisite things, the
force of them, the sense of my own unworthiness, and the loss I was
going to sustain, all came on me too powerfully. In spight of all my
efforts the tears ran in torrents from my eyes and my voice fail'd me
so that I was stop'd for a time...The morning of Thurs[d]ay was
fine...I now saw that form I had reverenced from the beginning of
my faculties struggling with death. His eyes became dim, his voice
scarce audible, his hands and arms grew cold...At last, after a long
pause, he shut his mouth, moved in the bed and expired. As soon as
this happen'd I scarce recollect anything for a time but remaining on
my knees in the posture I was in...weeping most violently and talking to my father as if alive, asking his forgiveness for all my faults
which I had most earnestly desired when he was living but had not
from fear of affecting him to[o] much, and not being able to contain
my grief, my brother and the servants urged me to go, but I did not
mind them. My heart required a vent at last...On Saturday the 8
[December] at 8 o'clock Tone and I attended the funeral. He wanted
me not to go. He wept much at it; I was quiet. I look'd into the grave,
heard with pleasure the fine service read and remain'd in the sure hope
of his...blessed resurrection. 'Let me die the death of the righteous
and let my last end be like his!'[34]

For whatever reason — perhaps because his sister, Margaret, had
been entrusted to his care, or possibly because he felt it was better to
remain at home and try to stiffen the resolve of the Catholics —
Russell did not go ahead with his plan to emigrate to France.

During his father's last days Russell had endeavoured to fulfil his
instructions from Belfast and to liaise with the Catholic Convention,
the election of which had so impressed Belfast radicals.[35] Links
between the radicals and the Catholics had been strengthening since
late 1791, when a number of leading members of the Catholic
Committee had joined the Dublin Society of United Irishmen. The
Committee's aristocratic leaders were outraged and these divisions

were exacerbated when a group of radical Dublin Catholics formed a new Catholic Society to agitate openly for the complete abolition of the penal laws. The Castle asked the Catholic Committee to repudiate the forceful language used in their declaration but the majority refused and the conservatives led by Lord Kenmare withdrew, leaving the middle-class radicals in control. In February 1792 a petition from the Catholic Committee was unceremoniously rejected by parliament and its members dismissed as 'a rabble of obscure porter-drinking mechanics, without property, pretensions or influence, who met in holes and corners and fancied themselves the representatives of the Catholic body, who disavowed and despised them'.[36] To demonstrate that they did indeed have the support of the Catholic masses, the Catholic Committee drew up a plan whereby meetings would be held in Catholic parishes throughout the land to choose delegates who would in turn elect the members of a new general committee, which assembled as the Catholic Convention. It was the most genuinely representative body that had ever sat in Ireland, consisting of 233 Catholic delegates from the counties, cities and towns. Nothing could indicate more clearly the new-found assertiveness of Catholics than this bold experiment in democracy.[37]

Russell was no doubt encouraged by the uncompromising spirit shown by the Convention's delegates. The meetings and elections which preceded the convention and the vociferous opposition from hardline Protestants had constituted a profoundly politicising experience for Irish Catholics. One observer noted that for Catholics the year 1792 'had been a continued study of the rights of man and a gradual incitement to assert them'.[38] Imbued with this new militancy, the Catholic Convention readily adopted Luke Teeling's motion that they should seek nothing less than the complete removal of disabilities. They also decided to snub the Castle administration and present their petition directly to the king, proclaiming that 'It is time for us to speak out like men. We will not, like African slaves, petition our task-masters.'[39] Accordingly in mid-December a delegation of prominent Catholics — John Keogh, Edward Byrne, Sir Thomas French, Edward Devereux and Christopher Bellew — accompanied by Tone as secretary, travelled to London. They went via Belfast where, in a gesture of solidarity, some Belfast radicals unharnessed the horses from their carriages and drew them through the town themselves. On 2 January 1793 they were received courteously by George III; a week later at the opening of the Irish parliament the viceroy's speech intimated that further Catholic relief would be granted and throughout January and February negotiations were carried on between the government and Catholic representatives to determine the extent of this relief.[40]

Unlike Tone, Russell had no official position with the Catholic Committee, but he was nevertheless closely involved in a number of shadowy meetings that ran parallel to the official negotiations between the Committee and the Castle. By late January he and Tone had become concerned that Catholic resolve was waning. At a 'council of war' which included Tone, Russell and the leading Catholic activists Sir Thomas French, James Plunkett and Edward Sweetman, they detected a 'sneaking spirit of compromise' creeping into the negotiations between Keogh and Hobart, the Chief Secretary. By this stage the Committee was divided between those who were willing to accept the substantial measure of relief on offer from the government — which included the franchise but stopped short of full emancipation — and those who wished to hold out for the Convention's original demand for the complete abolition of all religious disabilities. Tone and Russell unhesitatingly threw their lot in with the latter group and did their utmost to aggravate the resentment of the Catholic gentry at the possibility that they might be excluded from sitting in parliament. As negotiations progressed the two became increasingly entangled in the internal politics of the Catholic Committee. Early in February, Keogh attempted to monopolise negotiations with the Castle by appropriating all powers into a small informal sub-committee controlled by himself. On hearing the news, Russell mocked Tone as an 'ex-minister' who had lost the confidence of his employers but by rapidly summoning a 'meeting of malcontents' they managed to thwart Keogh's move.[41] Despite this, they feared that the Catholic leadership would reach an accommodation with the government that would fall short of the Catholic Convention's original demands. Their fears were to be realised: the committee accepted a compromise settlement which granted Catholics the franchise for parliamentary elections, the right to sit on grand and petty juries, the right to carry arms subject to a property qualification, and made them eligible for most civil offices and commissions in the army or navy, but crucially it did not concede the right to sit in parliament. Some Catholics felt betrayed: 'The demand of Catholics was total, why is their relief partial?' asked Edward Sweetman. Keogh replied that they had got what they could in the circumstances and that judicious exercise of the franchise would soon achieve what had been denied and most of his colleagues agreed with him. The Catholic Committee then dissolved itself, and although the outgoing members declared themselves in favour of parliamentary reform, they made no provision for any organised agitation to achieve this or the abolition of the remaining penal laws.[42] Russell was deeply disappointed by their decision and in his journal lamented 'the defection of the Catholics'. The events of these weeks made a lasting impression on him, convincing him more than ever that only by maintaining a united front could the Irish people hope to wring real concessions from the government.[43]

This concentration on Catholic matters by Russell and Tone drew the ire of several leading United Irishmen. Neilson was incensed at Tone, and presumably also at Russell, for not being kept informed of the progress of the Convention and Drennan had been critical of the moderate stance taken by Catholic United Irishmen, with the support of Russell and Tone, while the Convention continued to sit. At a United Irish meeting in Dublin in December, Russell led the way in supporting the toning down of a United Irish resolution to resist the prosecution of Archibald Hamilton Rowan and Napper Tandy who had been charged with publishing a seditious address. The society had resolved that the prosecutions should 'be resisted in every stage', but Russell and 'several other papists' were adamant that the word 'legally' be inserted before resisted, and they eventually carried the day. Drennan noted that though 'they would have flamed out a year ago' they were now 'so entwined with Catholic trammels that they cannot act as their heart [sic] leads them'.[44] The rather dismissive attitude of both Russell and Tone to the convention of Ulster Volunteers which met at Dungannon in February 1793 may also have rankled. Delegates from the Volunteer corps of six Ulster counties debated the issues of parliamentary reform and Catholic emancipation for two days and produced resolutions in favour. These, however, were tempered by the convention's strong declaration of loyalty to the existing constitution and its 'abhorrence' of republicanism. Tone was disappointed by the moderation of the Dungannon resolutions and by the convention's failure to condemn the war with France, while Russell appears to have expected little of its deliberations from the start.[45]

The pro-Catholic sympathies of Russell and Tone put them in an awkward position, since many Catholics were wary of identifying their cause too closely with that of radical reform. By late 1792 the tide was already running with them and they were aware that an open alliance with Belfast democrats would have alienated London and moderate Irish Protestants, and allowed Protestant reactionaries to tar them as subversives. A United Irish deputation sent to the Catholic Convention in December 1792 was received courteously but was not allowed to address the assembly. Catholic leaders were coming to see that the threat of an alliance with radical Dissenters was as powerful a weapon as the actual alliance itself.

Thus Russell and Tone were in a quandary. They wanted to lend their full support to Catholic demands for emancipation, but too close an identification with the Catholics could leave them open to charges that they were pursuing a sectional agenda, which was anathema to the spirit of the United Irishmen. However, accusations that Russell had abandoned the cause of the United Irishmen for that of the Catholics alone were misplaced. He remained committed to the society's twin goals of reform and emancipation but, with the Catholics in a strong position to extract concessions from the government in the early months of 1793, he believed it made sense to concentrate on the emancipation issue. Although he had become increasingly involved in Catholic politics during this period, Russell had not neglected the affairs of the United Irishmen. His attendance at several United Irish meetings in the Tailors' Hall in December 1792 and January 1793 and his importance as a courier was noted by the informer, Thomas Collins, as was the fact that he was a member of a committee appointed by the Dublin society on 11 January 1793 to draw up a plan for the reform of parliament.[46]

In March 1793 Russell served as Secretary to the Dublin society, at a time when this was a rather delicate position to hold. Two months earlier the Irish House of Lords had set up a secret committee to enquire into the widespread disturbances in the country. An address from the Dublin Society of United Irishmen was issued on 24 February 1793 under the names of the Chairman, Simon Butler, and the Secretary, Oliver Bond, that challenged the constitutionality of the lords' committee. Butler and Bond were charged with libelling the high court of parliament, fined £500 and sentenced to six months in Newgate.[47] The Wexford United Irishman, Bagenal Harvey, and Russell stepped in to fill their respective positions. On 3 March, two days after the convictions of Bond and Butler, the Dublin society issued another statement, written by Tone, and signed by Harvey and Russell.[48] Addressed 'To the people of Ireland', it criticised the convictions and sentences handed out to Butler and Bond, reaffirmed the commitment of the society to parliamentary reform and Catholic emancipation, denounced the repressive policies of the government and called on the people of Ireland to assemble in a convention and 'pronounce the national will'.[49]

Drennan believed that Russell and Harvey would not be prosecuted; the address was cleverly worded and he felt the government had had its revenge.[50] Nevertheless, on 20 March 1793 Russell received a summons from the lords' secret committee. His attendance, however, was also required at the Omagh assizes, in a case probably connected with his former duties as a magistrate in Co. Tyrone. Since he believed his testimony might help to save the lives of two young men, he decided to postpone his appearance before the lords until after he had attended the Omagh trial.[51] The secret committee was obviously intent on questioning him: some weeks later, while still in the North, he was tracked down in a remote part of Co. Fermanagh by a special messenger and again presented with a summons to appear before the lords. This left him with little choice but to return to Dublin, which he did on 9 May. The advice from all quarters was that he should co-operate with the committee. Another United Irishman, Dr James Reynolds, had been imprisoned for his repeated refusals to testify, and there seemed little point in making another martyr. On 10 May, the morning of his interrogation, Russell had the benefit of a legal briefing from Tone before he was questioned by the committee. Aware that testifying would bring him face to face with the Lord Chancellor, John Fitzgibbon, probably the most implacable enemy of the United Irishmen, Russell's family were genuinely worried about his fate and his young niece Julia begged him to 'take care of that nasty petulant man'.[52] Russell was probably asked about the letter that Tone had sent him in July 1791 in which Tone broached his ideas on separation. Russell was guarded in his testimony and refused to comment on opinions attributed to others and or answer any questions likely to incriminate himself. His replies to questions about the French and volunteering were such 'as could not be pleasing' to the lords' committee, which he dismissed as 'rascals, stupid, unfair and either ill-inform'd or pretending to be so'.[53] Their refusal to reimburse his expenses did nothing to soften his opinion of them.

In the end the secret committee's report proved nothing but it did imply that the Catholic Committee had a hand in Defender disturbances. Fitzgibbon, however, was not prepared to let up in his battle against sedition and publicly denounced Tone in the House of Lords in July, brandishing a version of the letter he had sent to Russell two years earlier.[54] The setting up of the secret committee was a sign of the increasing disquiet in government circles, faced with the growing assertiveness of Catholics and reformers and the prospect of war with France. In February 1793 England declared war on France and the pace of events in Ireland accelerated: the government began to raise a national militia, the Defenders spread throughout much of the country and coercive legislation against potentially subversive activities such as volunteering and extra-parliamentary conventions was passed. Even the government's efforts at conciliation, notably its repeal of most of the remaining penal laws, were made in such a way as to earn little gratitude from Catholics while at the same time aggravating Protestant insecurity. These events had a strongly polarising effect on Irish politics, turning many conservatives into reactionaries and many liberals into radicals. Seventeen ninety-three was the year in which the violent cycle of disaffection and state-sponsored repression, which would erupt into open rebellion in 1798, began in earnest. The attempt to recruit a militia, in particular, resulted in a summer of widespread disorders with over 200 fatalities, five times the number killed in disturbances over the previous thirty years.[55] Three years later Russell remembered the bloodshed it had caused and condemned the raising of the militia as an act by which 'a formidable Irish army was raised, armed and disciplined, to keep Ireland in subjection; the armed peasantry of one county were employed to subdue the peasantry of another'.[56]

During his journey to Omagh in March Russell observed steadily increasing polarisation in the North. He was invited to dine with the Tyrone grand jury and the following night with lawyers of the northern circuit and he noted their staunchly Tory politics and exaggerated fears of insurrection. In contrast, he described the politics of Omagh's linen merchants as 'furious on the other side', and they claimed that most of the people shared their views. In his conversations with local radicals he was informed that the declaration he had signed as secretary to the Dublin society was 'much liked' in the area. He believed that events were still in a state of flux and the outcome would depend on developments in France, the progress of the war and the attitude taken by the Catholic leadership to further political change.[57]

On his return to Dublin in April he found his fellow United Irishmen in subdued mood. The decision of the Catholics to reach a compromise with the government, the setbacks suffered by the French in the Netherlands and the increasingly hardline stance of Dublin Castle had almost extinguished the spirit of the southern reformers. His journals exude a palpable spirit of despair: 'no hopes entertain'd. All despond...reform is out of the question.' His disillusionment was such that he was seriously thinking of emigrating to America. He noted how the government had played a clever waiting-game to undermine the alliance between Catholics and Dissenters. They had promised relief to the Catholics, but immobilised them by delaying the necessary legislation; at the same time they had used the military to intimidate the United Irishmen of Belfast and had taken advantage of the *Northern Star*'s decision to publish an inflammatory address to initiate a prosecution against the paper and cow its proprietors. So frightened and disillusioned were the owners of the *Star* that they were considering selling the paper to the government.[58] Russell believed that since 'now the tyranny of gover[n]men[t] is establish'd by precedent', nobody would be found to resist it. He claimed that he and Tone had warned of this but their advice went unheeded and he lamented a missed opportunity for the United Irishmen: 'we had our day and let it pass. Will it ever return in our time? What can put us up again? I can see nothing but the continuance of the present ruinous war'. In May when attending a meeting of the Dublin Society of the United Irishmen he commented on its decline, counting less than forty members present.[59]

The cause of reform seemed so moribund that some United Irishmen began to contemplate desperate expedients. Russell's journal for May 1793 contained an entry that certainly would have set alarm bells ringing in Dublin Castle. He, Tone and the Catholic activist, Richard McCormick, appear to have been considering the possibility of seeking French assistance. Russell noted that if their plans met with the approval of their colleagues Tone was 'willing, to risk all he has [to] go to an unanointed republic via London'.[60] Just how serious they were is questionable: the frustrations of recent weeks had probably produced a great deal of such loose talk and the plan does not appear to have been followed up with any great intent or vigour. Significantly, when Jackson asked Tone to act as a United Irish agent to France the following year, Tone was reluctant to become involved, pleaded domestic responsibilities and declined.[61] In fact, almost at the precise time that Russell, Tone and McCormick were discussing an appeal to France, a French agent, Eleazer Oswald, was in Dublin sounding out United Irish support for an invasion of Ireland. He met several of the society's leaders but there is no record of any contacts with Tone or Russell. Although some of the United Irishmen expressed interest in the prospect of securing aid from France the general consensus was that the time was not yet ripe.[62]

In May Russell travelled north and met Neilson and McCabe in Belfast. They informed him that 'Derry, Tyrone, Antrim, Down and part of Ardmagh [were] burning with indignation against gover[n]ment', but the northerners were 'disgusted' with the conduct of the Catholics, who they believed had hastily abandoned the cause of reform once the government had bought them off with the franchise. They complained that all their recent exertions to effect a union of Irishmen had been received with apathy or even hostility. They had made up their minds to do no more and claimed that many active northern reformers and Volunteers were equally disillusioned and were emigrating.[63] Neilson believed that for the time being the cause of reform would be best served 'by indulging the present sulky humour of this town and leaving the nation a little to come to its senses'. He not only resented the conduct of the Catholics in Dublin but also that of the United Irishmen closest to them, namely Tone and Russell. He was suspicious that they were keeping him in the dark, telling him nothing of their negotiations with the Catholics and complaining that Russell 'corresponds almost daily with Tone but he never communicates the substance to me'. Neilson noted that Russell's 'ardour induces him to bore us with politics, sometimes, but few pay any attention to him'. On his arrival in Belfast he 'was (as usual) very hot ... but I fancy the present frigid air of Belfast has given him *the cool*'.[64]

Russell sensed the change of mood in Belfast and, though he tried not to despair, he could see little hope of progress. The decline of the reform movement in Ireland combined with the parlous state of his own affairs had a deeply depressing effect on him. His poverty was now so acute that for this latest trip to Belfast he had to raise the money by pawning Tone's watch. A note of self-pity crept into his journal: 'poor Ireland. P.P. has ruined himself in the pursuit of the good of his country'.[65]

By this time poverty had really begun to bite and 1793 was a difficult and unsettled year in Russell's personal life. The loss of his magistrate's position in October 1792 marked a period of over fifteen months during which Russell was without regular paid employment. Aware of Russell's difficulties, in May 1793 Tone contacted their mutual friend, Colonel Henry Barry, in an effort to obtain a commission for him in a newly-formed regiment. Barry promised to do what he could, but nothing came of it.[66] To compound his problems, the death of his father in December entrusted Russell with the care of his elder sister Margaret and deprived them both of a possible place to live. There was also the question of the support of two of his nieces, Mary Ann and Julia, the daughters of John Russell who had moved to England in 1792, apparently after the break-up of his marriage. Margaret, an intelligent woman with radical political views, was to take care of the two girls in his absence. With his father dead and his older brothers abroad, Thomas was effectively head of the family and he took his responsibilities seriously. In October he arranged the details for the marriage of Mary Ann to William Henry Hamilton of Enniskillen, and was deeply upset when the marriage ran into serious difficulties in less than a year. Given his protective attitude to his sister and nieces, he was somewhat horrified when he heard that on a national day of fast for the executed Louis XVI, that all three stood up in public and drank 'the fate of Louis to all crown'd heads', adding a toast to 'George the Last'. With a mixture of exasperation and pride Russell noted that 'P.P.'s women under a bad report. Confidently say'd that they are bloody politicians.'[67]

Possibly because they believed it would be cheaper to live there, Margaret and the girls were to settle in Co. Fermanagh. After a few weeks staying with friends in Enniskillen, they rented a cottage at Drumsluice about six miles north of Enniskillen. From the beginning Margaret did not like her new home, describing it as 'a bitter cold country' with 'firing very dear and scarce'. She hoped that it would be a temporary home until they could live with her beloved brother Thomas. Russell, it seems, had various plans to settle them. First of all, he planned to get a farm near Belfast so that he could be joined by Margaret and the two girls, who teased him that he would make 'but a bad farmer', but it is likely that he could not raise the money for such a venture; then he planned to settle them with a Belfast family where the girls could act as governesses.[68] Neither of these schemes worked out but family problems and the lack of money continued to play on his mind.

Russell's journey to the Omagh assizes in March 1793 marked the beginning of a period in which he travelled more or less continuously between Dublin and Ulster, rarely staying more than a few weeks in any one place. Using the home of Dr James McDonnell in Belfast as his home base, he travelled widely throughout Antrim and Down and made several long journeys to Dublin and to Enniskillen. Coach fares were often beyond his means (the single fare for the twenty-six hour trip from Dublin to Belfast was £1 16*s*. 3*d*.) and so he usually went by foot. On one occasion he hired a chaise horse for six shillings to take him to Hillsborough and almost immediately regretted his extravagance: 'Could have walked it in ½ the time. Drench'd with rain.' His journals show a preoccupation with keeping his travelling expenses to a minimum: chiding himself for his 'extravagance' in paying '6 pence for a stick which the man tells me has broken many a head' or paying 5*d*. for a pot of beer and 2½*d*. for a 'naggin of hardware'.[69]

A typical journey was his walk from Belfast to Enniskillen and back in the autumn of 1793. He set out on 27 September carrying food for three days and walked to Antrim town, where he discussed politics with some locals and was highly pleased by both the fact that one of his publications, the *Lion of old England* was being talked about and was highly thought of, and that he was recognised as the Thomas Russell who had acted as secretary to the United Irishmen. That night he slept at Randlestown and the following morning went to Toome, making notes on the surrounding mountains, and countryside near Lough Neagh and on a beautiful bridge at Toome. At Toome he took a ferry and then made his way to Moneymore, all the time taking notes on the geological features of the countryside he walked through, and then on to Cookstown. Walking through a wild stretch of the mountains he was accompanied by a man who told him tales of ghosts 'walking like coffins in these dreary wilds'. As night was falling this unnerved him slightly and he lost his way for a time before finding a cabin where he was given directions to Pomeroy, where he fortified himself with sixpence worth of whiskey, and the stayed the night. The next morning he set out for Sixmilecross and on to Fintona, with rain and wind in his face for almost the entire thirty-four miles before arriving at his sister's cottage in Drumsluice near Enniskillen that evening. In the three days he walked a distance of just over ninety miles.[70]

These rambles were a significant factor in forming Russell's political outlook. Travelling on foot brought him into direct contact with other pedestrians and the inhabitants of the farms and villages through which he passed. He often engaged them in conversation and found them ready to discuss politics and the great events unfolding in Europe. His journal notes a typical encounter in south Fermanagh with a man who described himself as a 'Methodist'. He told Russell that the great majority of the people throughout north Connacht and south-west Ulster were for the French. The Catholics knew of the abolition of tithes in France and were less and less influenced by the anti-revolutionary propaganda of their clergy. Although 'fond of the king' they were angry at his declaration of war against France. They hated the government and were strong supporters of reform, especially the 'middle orders'. Significantly, he also claimed that sectarian tensions were also on the rise, with Protestants and Catholics each convinced that the other were preparing to massacre them.[71]

It was in the early months of 1793 that Russell's politics began to harden into a radical mould. Following closely on the heels of his disillusionments in Dungannon, he engaged in an intense bout of political agitation during which he had seen the government declare war on republican France, attempt to sabotage the alliance between Catholics and Presbyterians, steadfastly resist reform, disband the Volunteers, raise a militia, attack the liberty of the press and stifle the expression of the popular will by banning extra-parliamentary conventions. In a rapidly polarising political landscape he shed what remained of his Whiggish sympathies and became a fervent democrat. By the spring of 1793 he had become deeply disillusioned with the parliamentary liberals he had once so much admired, having seen 'the opposition, as they call themselves' either support or meekly acquiesce in the government's campaign of coercion.[72] His former 'respect for great names', his deference to authority and the moderation which had characterised some of his earlier political views had by now disappeared. By April 1793 his alienation from both government and reformist Whigs was complete. In response to Grattan's charge that the activities of the United Irishmen had undermined the efforts of the Whigs he declared himself 'heartily glad! If the club has done that, it has served the country by exposing that vile, ped[d]ling, pitiful faction.'[73]

There is little doubt that the behaviour of the Whigs in general and Grattan in particular during 1793 came as a bitter disappointment to Russell and greatly contributed to his disillusionment with constitutional politics. While Grattan continued to snipe at the government on various issues, his opposition to their campaign of domestic coercion had been distinctly half-hearted and he had unreservedly pledged his support for the war against France. As Lecky said of Grattan:

> in times of danger and war there was scarcely any sacrifice he was not prepared to make to support imperial interests. He had nothing of the

French and cosmopolitan sympathies of the English Whigs, and he always made it a vital principle of his Irish policy to discourage all hostility towards England...He looked with undisguised abhorrence on the subversive and levelling theory of government which the French Revolution had introduced into the world; that 'Gallic plant' as he picturesquely described it, 'whose fruit is death'.[74]

Grattan was acutely conscious of the sharp fault lines in Irish society and frequently invoked the spectre of mob rule and a levelling of property. He condemned the United Irishmen's proposal for universal manhood suffrage as one which would give the franchise 'to the scavenger...to every criminal; Whiteboys that break laws and Defenders who steal arms'.[75] Such views fuelled Russell's anger towards a man he had once so admired. At the beginning of the parliamentary session of 1793 Grattan attacked the Irish government 'as one of the most anomalous and most corrupt in Christendom', claiming that it had resisted all reasonable reforms and gone out of its way to insult and alienate the Catholics. Nevertheless, he expressed his steadfast loyalty to the king, the Constitution and the connection with Britain, his complete abhorrence of French principles and his support for the government's plans to put Ireland on a war footing.[76] In August 1793 in a letter to the *Northern Star*, Russell savagely criticised Grattan's behaviour. He maintained that at the beginning of the latest parliamentary session Catholic emancipation and parliamentary reform were there for the taking. And what did Grattan do? He:

peddled and he pranced — he reviled the government, he reviled the French, he reviled sedition and he praised himself. He had all the cant of the Crown and Anchor Association[77] — sedition and mobs — republicans and levellers — and all the long etcetera, propagated by knavery and corruption, and believed by folly and credulity....Mr Reeves himself was not a more effectual *alarmist*...Mr Grattan and his colleagues...were more eager to grant, than the [government] to demand the dispersions of the volunteers, the militia bill, the gunpowder bill, and arbitrary *fines* and *imprisonment*...they deemed a strong government so essential, that for its attainment, both the forms and substance of liberty were to be violated...These circumstances in occurrence with others arising from folly, treachery and want of spirit, at last procured the desired effect: the nation was foiled in its grand pursuit — reform — and, not only so, but liberty, instead of being secured, was shackled with restrictions of a weight and magnitude, which formerly would not have been borne, and from which there at present appears no prospect of emancipation, save through means *too horrid to think of!* ... If this be a true history of the opposition, should it not move indignation to see them endeavour to pass for the friends of Ireland ... surely after such conduct [Grattan] should have the decency to be silent, and not insult [the people's] feelings by obtruding himself on their notice; yet after having assisted at the sacrifice of the happiness of Ireland, we see him once more return to his insignificant opposition, and again declaiming, and grinning and chattering at the abuses of that ministry, which but for him would not now exist ...

One part of his astonishing career remains to be considered ... His conduct relative to the frantic destructive crusade we are engaged in ... he harangued against the French ... and gave the maximum of his assistance to extinguish human liberty and happiness, the pernicious consequences of this war were predicted and are now too plainly to be traced in our starving poor, and our ruined manufactures and commerce ... It was supposed that his political model was the illustrious leader of the English opposition, but on this occasion he disregarded his example and pursued the very contrary. Mr Fox's recent conduct eclipses the lustre of the former part of his life ... he used every effort to prevent so ruinous a measure, but reason and eloquence were insufficient and he became, as he well foresaw, the most unpopular man in England; even his own friends deserted him; in a situation so discouraging he steadfastly remained at his post, and has since maintained it with honour — the time will soon arrive when ample justice will be done to his merits ...

Mr Grattan, whose fortunes were raised by his country, for his exertions on behalf of liberty, eagerly supported this war against liberty, and lavishly granted the treasure and blood of his countrymen, whose guardian he should have been; for a purpose they can never approve — let this be joined to the rest of his conduct, and then let us ask ... whether he would wish that his name should be preserved from oblivion, by infamy?[78]

The very tone of this letter suggests the betrayal of youthful hopes. It is in sharp contrast to the tribute paid by Tone to Grattan in a history of the Catholic Committee, also written in 1793, in which he praised him as 'the early, the steady, and the indefatigable friend of Catholic emancipation'.[79] Two years earlier Tone had cautioned Russell about his excessive respect for Grattan and the Whigs, but by mid-1793 Russell's radicalism had outstripped that of his friend.

NOTES

1 Drennan to Sam McTier, 5 Nov. 1791 (Drennan papers, T765/310).
2 *Commons jn. Ire.*, xvii, dccxvi; Madden, *United Irishmen*, 3rd ser., ii, 150.
3 J. J. Webb, *Municipal government in Ireland* (Dublin, 1918), pp. 196–7.
4 McSkimin, 'Insurrection of 1803', p. 548.
5 Morgan, 'Sketch of Russell', p. 57.
6 Morgan, 'Sketch of Russell', p. 57.
7 Lecky, *Ireland*, iii, 60–1; Thomas Bartlett, *The fall and rise of the Irish nation* (Dublin, 1992), pp. 139–41.
8 For Fitzgibbon see Ann C. Kavanaugh, *John Fitzgibbon, earl of Clare* (Dublin, 1997).
9 See P.R.O., HO 100/34/17 for grand jury resolutions; Lecky, *Ireland*, iii, 212; Bartlett, *Life of Tone*, p. 133.
10 Mary Ann McCracken to Madden, 21 June 1859 (Madden papers, 873/89).
11 John Campbell to Russell, Dungannon, 6 June 1794 (Sirr papers, 868/1, ff 329–30); Mac Giolla Easpaig, *Ruiséil*, p. 57.
12 Russell's statement, Downpatrick, 17 Oct. 1803 (MacDonagh, *Viceroy's post-bag*, pp. 424–6).
13 Madden, *United Irishmen*, 3rd ser., ii, 151; Madden's likely source for this information was Mary Ann McCracken.
14 Roger Anstey, *The Atlantic slave trade and British abolition, 1760–1810* (London, 1975), pp. 267–78.
15 [Russell] to *Northern Star*, 11 Feb. 1792 (Reb. papers, 620/19/56). Although this handwritten draft is unsigned and not in Russell's hand, I am reasonably certain that he is the original author. The views are identifiably those of Russell, and the passionate style studded with biblical allusions is very much his. The article is written from Dungannon where he had taken up residence at the beginning of the year. On the reverse there is a message addressed to the proprietors of the *Star* which reads, 'respected friends, you will much oblige a friend and a subscriber by inserting the within [*sic*] in your paper, if a name is required it shall be made known to you provided it be kept secret'. Given his official position Russell was obviously wary about openly criticising government policy. This desire to maintain a degree of anonymity partly explains why Russell did not pen the article himself in his distinctive scrawl and the very illegibility of his writing provided another reason to employ an amanuensis. Neilson printed a reply to this 'Dungannon correspondent' (*Northern Star*, 10 Mar. 1792), almost certainly intended for Russell (Mac Giolla Easpaig, *Ruiséil*, p. 56).
16 *Belfast News Letter*, 2 Dec. 1791; Mac Giolla Easpaig, *Ruiséil*, p. 52.
17 *Northern Star*, 10 Mar. 1792; Mac Giolla Easpaig, *Ruiséil*, p. 56.
18 For example, the revision of verses in Madden papers, 873/701; Sirr papers, 868/1, ff 77–9; and extracts from *Lion of old Eng.*, pp. 66, 81; 'Chinese journal' in *Northern Star*, 8 Jan. 1795, 26 Feb. 1795; and *Letter to the people*, p. 22; Mary Ann McCracken to Madden, 2 Aug. 1859 (Madden papers, 873/83); Madden, *United Irishmen*, 3rd ser., i, 303.
19 Russell, *Letter to the people*, p. 22.
20 The poems appear in the *Northern Star*, 7 Jan., 18 Jan., 10 Mar., 17 Oct. 1792; Madden, *United Irishmen*, 3rd ser., ii, 159; Brendan Clifford, *Thomas Russell and Belfast*, p. 87; Denis Carroll, *The man from God knows where* (Dublin, 1995), p. 114.
21 Thuente, *Harp re-strung*, p. 91
22 Drafts of an anti-slavery poem by Russell can be found in Madden papers, 873/701 and Sirr papers, 868/1, f. 179; Russell's journal, 5 Nov. 1794 (*Journals,*

p. 174); for Russell's use of this material see Thuente, *Harp re-strung*, pp. 91–2.

23 McSkimin, 'Insurrection of 1803', p. 548.

24 Thomas Knox to Abercorn, 29 Nov. 1791, 17 Jan. 1792 (P.R.O.N.I., Abercorn papers, T/2514/IB1/2/42, T/2514/IB1/3/3); William Richardson, *History of the origin of the Irish yeomanry* (Dublin, 1801), pp. 13–15; R. M. Sibbett, *Orangeism in Ireland* (Belfast, 1914–15), i, 263–4).

25 Russell to McNally, 24 Sept. 1803 (P.R.O., HO 100/113/195–8).

26 J. A. Russell to Madden, n.d. (Madden papers, 873/674, f. 2v).

27 Drennan to Martha McTier, c. Mar. 1794 (Drennan papers, T765/479).

28 16 Aug. 1793 (*Journals*, p. 97); Tone, *Writings*, i, 312; Elliott, *Tone*, p. 194.

29 Henry Joy, *Belfast politics* (Belfast, 1794), pp. 88–9.

30 Westmorland correspondence, 1 Nov. 1792 (PRO 30/8/331, f. 88); Neilson to Tone, 21 Nov. 1792 (Tone, *Writings*, i, 342).

31 Tone, *Writings*, i, 344–5; *Dublin Evening Post*, 6 Dec. 1792.

32 Maureen Wall, 'The United Irish movement' in *Historical Studies*, v, ed. J. L. McCracken, (London, 1965), p. 132; Robert Simms to Tone, 29 Nov. 1792 (Tone, *Writings*, i, 345); Neilson to Tone, 29 Nov., 3 Dec. 1792 (ibid., i, 344, 346); Sam McTier to Drennan, c. 2 Dec. 1792 (Drennan papers, T765/354).

33 Russell's journal, 16 Aug. 1793 (*Journals*, pp. 97–8).

34 Russell's journal, 16, 21 Aug. 1793 (*Journals*, pp. 99–100, 103, 105, 106, 107); the quotation at the end is from the book of Numbers, 23.10.

35 Russell's journal, 16 Aug. 1793 (*Journals*, pp. 98–9).

36 Bartlett, *Life of Tone*, pp. 52, 53.

37 Eamon O'Flaherty, 'The Catholic Convention and Anglo-Irish politics, 1791–3' in *Archivium Hibernicum*, xl (1985), pp. 22–5; Thomas Bartlett, *The fall and rise of the Irish nation* (Dublin, 1992), p. 151.

38 T. A. Emmet, 'Towards the history of Ireland' in McNeven, *Pieces*, p. 31.

39 Bartlett, *Life of Tone*, p. 70.

40 Tone, *Writings*, i, 468–9; Elliott, *Tone*, 197–203.

41 Tone, *Writings*, i, 399, 405–6.

42 Thomas Bartlett, *The fall and rise of the Irish nation* (Dublin, 1992), pp. 165, 168; Sackville Hamilton to Hobart, 25 Apr. 1793 (P.R.O., HO 100/43/238); Eamon O'Flaherty, 'The Catholic Convention and Anglo-Irish politics, 1791–3' in *Archivium Hibernicum*, xl (1985), p. 17.

43 Russell's journal, 4 Apr. 1793 (*Journals*, p. 71); Russell, *Letter to the people*, p. 11.

44 Drennan to Sam McTier, 28 Jan. 1793 (*Drennan letters*, p. 123); Neilson to Tone, c. Dec. 1792 (Tone, *Writings*, i, 346); R. B. McDowell, 'The proceedings of the Dublin society of United Irishmen' in *Analecta Hibernica*, no. 17 (1949), pp. 52–3.

45 *Northern Star*, 20 Feb. 1793; Drennan to Martha McTier, 16 Feb. 1793 (*Drennan letters*, p. 135).

46 R. B. McDowell, 'The proceedings of the Dublin society of United Irishmen' in *Analecta Hibernica*, no. 17 (1949), pp. 47, 50, 52, 59.

47 R. B. McDowell, 'The proceedings of the Dublin society of United Irishmen' in *Analecta Hibernica*, no. 17 (1949), p. 69; P.R.O., HO 100/34/106; Rosamond Jacob, *The rise of the United Irishmen* (London, 1937), p. 141.

48 Drennan to Sam McTier, 4 Mar. 1793 (*Drennan letters*, p. 139).

49 P.R.O., HO 100/34/117.

50 Drennan to Sam McTier, 4 Mar. 1793 (*Drennan letters*, p. 140).

51 Russell's journal, 20 Mar. 1793 (*Journals*, p. 65).

52 Margaret Russell, Enniskillen, to Thomas Russell, 42 Queen St., Dublin, 11 May 1793 (Sirr papers, 868/2, ff 29–30).

53 Russell's journal, 6-10 May 1793 (*Journals*, pp. 74, 76).

54 House of Lords' debates, 10 July 1793 (*Freeman's Journal*, 13 July 1798).

55 Thomas Bartlett, 'An end to the "moral economy": the Irish militia disturbances of 1793' in *Past and Present*, no. 99 (May, 1983), pp. 41–64.

56 Russell, *Letter to the people*, pp. 12–13.

57 Russell's journal, 24 Mar. 1793 (*Journals*, p. 67).

58 Russell's journal, Apr.–May 1793 (*Journals*, pp. 71–2); Drennan to Sam McTier, 1 July 1793 (*Drennan letters*, p. 165); *Northern Star*, 6 Feb. 1793; Russell's journal, mid-Apr. 1793 (*Journals*, p. 72).

59 Russell's journal, 24 Apr., 10 May 1793 (*Journals*, pp. 73–4, 76); see also R. B. McDowell, 'The personnel of the Dublin Society of United Irishmen, 1791–4' in *I. H. S.*, ii, no. 5 (Mar. 1940), p. 15, for attendance figures that correspond with Russell's.

60 Russell's journal, mid-May 1793 (*Journals*, p. 76).

61 Tone, *Writings*, i, 515.

62 Elliott, *Partners*, pp. 60–1; J. J. St Mark, 'The Oswald mission to Ireland from America, 20 Feb.–8 June 1793' in *Éire/Ireland*, xxxiii, no. 2 (summer. 1988), pp. 25–38.

63 Russell's journal, 19 May 1793 (*Journals*, p. 76).

64 Neilson to Drennan, 10 June 1793 (P.R.O.N.I., D516/1).

65 Russell's journal, mid-May 1793, 19 May 1793 (*Journals*, pp. 76, 77).

66 Colonel Henry Barry to Tone, 5 May [1793] (Tone, *Writings*, i, 444).

67 Russell's journal, 24 Apr., 2 Oct. 1793, 3 Nov. 1794 (*Journals*, pp. 74, 130–1, 171).

68 Margaret Russell, Enniskillen, to Thomas Russell, Belfast, 1 Mar. 1793, 29 June 1793, 6 July 1793 (Sirr papers, 868/2, ff 34, 35; 24–5; 33, 36.)

69 Russell's journal, 30 Sept., 1 Oct. 1793 (*Journals*, pp. 125, 130); John J. Monaghan, 'A social and economic history of Belfast, 1790–1800' (M.A. thesis, Queen's University of Belfast, 1936), p. 187.

70 Russell's journal, 29 Sept. to 1 Oct. 1793 (*Journals*, pp. 124–30).

71 Russell's journal, 3 Apr. 1793 (*Journals*, pp. 69–70).

72 Russell's journal, 24 Mar. 1793 (*Journals*, p. 67).

73 Russell's journal, 24 Apr. 1793 (*Journals*, p. 73).

74 Lecky, *Ireland*, iii, 17.

75 R. B. McDowell, *Irish public opinion, 1750–1800* (London, 1944), p. 191.

76 Lecky, *Ireland*, iii, 135–6.

77 A loyalist society founded by John Reeves in London on 20 Nov. 1792. Its official name was the 'Association for the Preservation of Liberty and Property against Republicans and Levellers' (Albert Goodwin, *The friends of liberty* (London, 1979), pp. 264–5).

78 *Northern Star,* 31 Aug. 1793; the letter was signed 'E'. In Russell's journal, 2 Sept. 1793, he speaks of 'E. letter' and on 27 Sept. 1793, he notes, 'Find from Hazlitt that the letter signed E. was known to be mine. They knew the handwriting. It was a good joke to think of disguising my hand!' (*Journals*, pp. 111, 124).

79 Tone, *Writings*, i, 481.

CHAPTER FIVE

Theirs Is the Kingdom of Heaven

Russell is generally accepted as representing the 'radical-populist' strain in United Irish thinking.[1] He sympathised strongly with the poor and believed that more than just political reform was needed to better their lives. These views were intensified on his rambles through the countryside. Given his own poverty he often shared the homes and food of the poor and he developed an enduring respect for them. In a pamphlet written some years later he related his experiences of their generosity:

> It is well known that the traveller will receive in the most wretched cabin in the wildest parts of Ireland all the hospitality that the circumstances of the owner can afford: he will get his share of the milk, if there is any, and of the potatoes; and if he has lost his way he will be guided to the road for miles, and all this without the expectation or the wish for a reward: from such a people the commission of ... crimes are less to be expected, than from those who so falsely and infamously traduce them.[2]

Just as Russell's whiggism hardened into radicalism in 1793 so his general sympathy for the poor hardened into a desire to see a real change in society and an improvement in their position. The comparison between the virtues of the poor and the vices of the rich was a frequent theme in Russell's writings from this time onwards. He points out how the rich, by constantly reiterating the baseness of the lower orders and the dangers of mob government, create a sense of fear that serves only to oppress the poor:

> This mode of reasoning has always appear'd to me a libel on Providence. You say, in effect, God has formed his creatu[r]es so that if left to the facultys he has given them, they would be worse than beasts. We are wiser and will restrain them. And who are their governors — men generally worse than the common run ... Power and

wealth corrupt and harden the heart .... We see that the vices of the rich are so far from being consider'd as shameful that some are honarable — adultery, gaming (that is, robbery), duel[l]ing, luxury. Whence this but from the rich making laws?... He who knew the recesses of the heart loved not the rich.[3]

Going from place to place Russell observed the hardships of the poor at first hand and listened attentively to their political opinions. This frequent exposure to their views meant that he was more in touch with grass-roots opinion than most of his United Irish colleagues and led him to question the accepted belief that the poor were politically ignorant and irresponsible. He noted that this was not just the belief of the 'corrupt and interested. Wise and good men have [been] led into it ... many even in my small circle'. But Russell's contact with working people convinced him of their intelligence and decency. Over a glass of whiskey in the cabin of a mill-worker in Co. Antrim, he was told: 'I think liberty worth risquing life for. In a cause of that sort I think I should have courage enough from reflection to brave death ... it does not much signify now as to myself but it gri[e]ves me to breed up these children to be slaves. I would gladly risk all to prevent that.' Russell reflected: 'When will a man of fortune in Ireland reason thus? Our senators and great think of nothing but their own sordid interests. Here was a peasant interested for the free-dom of mankind. Such I have frequen[t]ly met.'[4] His recognition of the political discernment of ordinary people led Russell to champion their right to participate in the political process. This is a central theme in his main political work — *A letter to the people of Ireland on the present situation of the country* — which stands as the most complete statement of his political philosophy. Although it was not published until September 1796, most of its main ideas are to be found in his journals for 1793–4 and it is representative of his think-ing during this period.

He began by tracing the progress of parliamentary reform from the Volunteer Convention of 1784, claiming that the cause was lost because by excluding the Catholics it was a factional rather than a national effort. This did not stem from any hostility to Catholic rights from rank-and-file Volunteers, but came about because they placed 'too great a confidence in their leaders, who were men of the first lordly and landed interests in Ireland, and who shamefully and meanly deserted the people.' The great mass of the people, the Catholic poor, remained oppressed without relief by landlords,

Church and State. Attempts to redress their grievances met with swift and vicious repression 'while no serious enquiry was instituted into the real or supposed grievances which led these wretched and ignorant beings to transgress laws which they had no share in framing'.[5]

Russell claimed that 'there was no national spirit in Ireland' — in fact, on the anniversary of the battle of the Boyne or the birthday of William III, Irishmen celebrated those very events which had robbed them of their national dignity. An unrepresentative and corrupt parliament had an 'easy, pleasant and lucrative task to govern such a country'. The so-called opposition in this parliament was a mere faction, more concerned with cornering its share of patronage than with the welfare of the country. Once war had broken out they revealed their true colours and co-operated 'heartily in strengthening the hands of that government which they had opposed, and riveting the chains of the people, or to sum up all, plunged this unfortunate country into all the guilt and calamity of the present war'.[6]

A clique of corrupt oligarchs 'governed Ireland with despotic sway'; they could 'plunder and insult the country, and even quarrel among themselves for the division of the spoil with impunity; but whenever a union of the people takes place — when they once consider all Irishmen as their friends and brethren, the power of this aristocracy will vanish'. For this reason the society of United Irishmen was founded. Their efforts, combined with those of the Catholic Convention of December 1792, began to wring concessions from the government and would have produced parliamentary reform and complete Catholic emancipation had they maintained a united front. But once elements of the Catholic leadership began to negotiate with Dublin Castle for their sectional interests, unity was broken and the government was allowed to recover and overawe the people. The Catholic gentry, who should have exerted themselves in protecting their innocent co-religionists from oppression, instead allied themselves with the government. As a result, it came as no surprise that the lower orders, 'conceiving that they were oppressed and without people of knowledge or consequence to advise or protect them, should at times commit unjustifiable actions'. Since the dismissal of the pro-Catholic Viceroy Lord Fitzwilliam in March 1795, 'new laws of an oppressive and sanguinary nature have been enacted and enforced for the purpose of extinguishing any spark of freedom that might yet exist'. Moreover, the government had attempted to foment religious animosities, with some success, but Russell saw this as simply a sign of desperation — 'the last effort of the enemies of Ireland to prevent that union which once effected will terminate their power'.[7]

His survey of recent years complete Russell turned to more general matters. He described how great efforts have been made to exclude the masses from politics. They are told to 'mind your looms, and your spades and ploughs; have you not the means of subsistence;...leave the government to wiser heads and to people who understand it, and interfere no more!'. As a result:

> see what terrible calamities the perfidy, ambition, avarice and cruelty of these rulers have brought on mankind...look at some of that race who inherit great fortunes without the skill or capacity of being useful; those fungus productions, who grow out of a diseased state of society, and destroy as well the vigour as the beauty of that which nourishes them. These are some of the wiser heads; these are the hands in which the people are to repose their lives and their properties; for whose splendid debaucheries they must be taxed; and for whose convenience they must fetter even their thoughts.[8]

Such men derive their fortunes from the toil of the poor. Their vast estates are worthless without the efforts of labour. Therefore:

> let not those then who raise the fruits of it among us be despised. But these are in the language of the great: 'the mob, the rabble, the beggars on the bridge, the grey-coated men whose views are anarchy and plunder, and whose means are bloodshed and murder'. Are such men to be trusted with power? No. Keep them down — do they complain, disregard them — do they resist, dragoon them — send an army to burn their houses, and murder them with the bayonet and the gibbet. The God of heaven and earth endowed these men with the same passions and the same reason as the great, and consequently qualified them for the same liberty, happiness and virtue; but these gentlemen consider themselves wiser than the deity; they find that he was wrong, and set about rectifying his work; they find the moral qualities and political rights of their fellow-creatures commensurate with their fortunes; they punish the poverty which their own insatiable avarice in a great degree creates; and thus, as in every case, when the will of God is departed from, instead of order — confusion, folly, and guilt is produced.[9]

Russell contended that all men have the right, indeed the duty, to concern themselves with government and politics. Only if legislation originates with 'the whole family of mankind' rather than just self-serving minorities, can there be some hope of it reflecting the divine will. No legislative decree can render an unchristian act morally right. If this reasoning is applied to the present war with France and the war is found to be unjust (and 'let every person seriously ask himself what injury did the French do to the Irish') then, 'every man killed in it by the Irish is *murdered*, and every acquisition made by it is *robbery*'. To those who said that Ireland should fight to protect the country's prosperity Russell replied that most of the population derive no benefit from this alleged prosperity. 'If the English, or any other people, think gold a sufficient cause to shed blood — if they are satisfied to fill the world with carnage and misery, that they might acquire cloves and nutmegs, and contracts, and slaves, let it not be so with us — let justice be the rule of our conduct, and let us not, for any human consideration, incur the displeasure of the deity.' Along with his condemnation of the war came a ringing denunciation of slavery, describing it as 'a system of cruelty, torment, wickedness and infamy'.[10]

In order to avoid participation in such inhuman activities the masses should strongly reject the proposition that they 'have no right to meddle in politics, which has been so long and so successfully propagated by these "calm thinking villains" who arrogate to themselves the government of mankind'. Instead, Russell concluded that their efforts should be directed towards the union of all Irishmen, the only way that their grievances could be effectively redressed: 'the means are the most delightful that life can afford, the cultivation of brotherly love to our fellow-creatures and the end the greatest that the imagination of man can conceive, that of being acceptable in the sight of the Almighty, all perfect and adorable author of nature'.[11]

All of Russell's main political ideas appear in *A letter to the people of Ireland*: the corrupt nature of aristocratic government, the right and duty of ordinary people to participate in political life, the need for Christian unity, the primacy of divine law over human contrivance and the iniquity of unjust war and the slave trade. He regarded the work as his political testament. Unlike most radical publications which were anonymous, it was clearly attributed to 'Thomas Russell, an United Irishman'. When taken up on a charge of high treason in September 1796 he presented the arresting officers with a copy and during his imprisonment in Newgate he sent a copy to Edward Cooke, the Castle under-secretary, to counter what he regarded as misrepresentation of his views in the press with a clear and comprehensive statement of his political opinions. Cooke returned the pamphlet with a note saying that he had already read it.[12]

In the work's strident attacks on aristocracy and its championing of the rights of the common man the influence of Paine is evident — but it would be fair to say that most radical tracts of the 1790s owed something to Paine — and Paine himself was as much an effective populariser of contemporary radical ideas as he was an original thinker.[13] Martha McTier's opinion of the work was rather damning. After its publication she wrote to Drennan that 'poor Russell can give no satisfaction. His book is said to want energy, to be ill-written, bad English, to be wicked, to be tame, to be insipid. If you can find any good in it, say so, for pity'.[14] Such criticism was overly harsh. *A letter to the people of Ireland* is no masterpiece of political journalism but it stands as a forthright and passionate statement of the radical position. McTier's use of 'is said' suggests that she may not have read it herself but was reporting opinions she had overheard. The work does have its leaden passages, but the whole cannot be dismissed as 'insipid' — in fact its most striking feature is the genuine rage it exhibits at oppression and injustice. In her eulogy of Russell, Mary Ann McCracken had noted that, 'though his conversational powers were not of the first order, yet when roused to enthusiasm he was sometimes more than eloquent'.[15] This observation could equally be applied to his writings. In *A letter to the people of Ireland*, Russell's survey of recent Irish history is unexceptional but when he deals with topics that he feels particularly strongly about — when he champions the political rights of the common man, or condemns the slave trade — then a real passion is infused into the work that lifts it out of the ordinary.

The identification with the poor shown so clearly by Russell in *A letter to the people of Ireland* strongly characterised his politics from 1793 onwards. He was a member of the United Irish committee which, after much deliberation, produced the society's proposals for parliamentary reform. In the event, it went far beyond the schemes of reform that the Volunteers or the Whigs had proposed, advocating universal male suffrage, annual parliaments, equal electoral districts, payment of MPs and the abolition of property qualifications for those who sat in parliament.[16] Radical though this was, Russell was willing to go beyond purely political reform and intimated that changes in the system of property holding would be necessary to secure social justice for the poor. In a journal entry in which he denounced the laws made by the rich for being more concerned with the preservation of property than human life, he noted that 'property must be alter'd in some measure'.[17] He further maintained that only those who had nothing could be relied on to change the status quo — an observation made more than three years before Tone put his trust in the 'men of no property'. Russell believed that 'the men of property all through Ireland, whether landed or commercial, are decidedly against a struggle which might risque that and will do nothing. The people are begin[n]ing to see this, and in time when they feel their strength and injuries will do it themselves, and then adieu to property. Tant mieux!'.[18]

Russell's cavalier attitude to property would have made many of the lawyers and merchants who formed the leadership of the United Irishmen rather nervous indeed. They were prepared to concede that something should be done to alleviate the plight of the poor, for example, a lowering of taxes or a reform of the tithe system, but any radical tampering with property rights was anathema to them. They sought reform to break the monopoly of the landed establishment on political life, not to indulge in social levelling. While Russell in his days as a magistrate was taking the side of Dungannon weavers in disputes with their employers, the *Northern Star* reported with approval that the Volunteers of Belfast had confronted and put to flight groups of the town's weavers who had demonstrated for higher wages. The Volunteers were praised as 'the steady protec-tor[s] of property'. James Hope, a Presbyterian weaver and leading United Irish activist, and one of the more advanced social thinkers of the movement, later wrote that the defeat of 1798 came as no surprise to him since most of the United leadership had failed to motivate the rank-and-file by engaging with the problems of the poor.[19]

The area of social reform was a problematic one for the United Irishmen. Some historians have seen their failure to produce a detailed plan of social reform as one of the movement's main weak-nesses.[20] As it was, the United Irish proposals for political reform caused considerable dissension and many resignations from the soci-ety, and the leadership recognised that any programme attempting to deal with the society's conflicting views on social and economic issues could have torn the movement apart.[21] In an organisation one of whose earliest rules had been 'to attend to those things in which we agree, to exclude from our thoughts those in which we differ',[22] it was generally judged prudent to steer clear of such a potentially divisive subject. Moreover, the readiness with which the government instigated prosecutions of outspoken radicals, particularly after the outbreak of war in 1793, made advisable a degree of caution in any statements which could be construed as threatening the established social order. An analysis of the debates of the Dublin society in the period 1791–4, reveal that its members, mostly lawyers and merchants, were far more concerned with schemes of constitutional agitation and parliamentary reform than with social issues.[23] Anxious to portray themselves as moderate reformers seeking to restore the 'purity' of the British Constitution, the United Irishmen were sensitive to taunts from supporters of the Protestant ascendancy that they were irresponsible 'levellers', intent on overturning the entire political and social order. They explicitly denied any such intentions, maintaining that they sought reform to break the monopoly of the landed aristocracy on political life, not to eradicate social distinctions. One of its proclamations stated explicitly: 'by liberty we never understood unlimited freedom, nor by equality the levelling of property, or the destruction of subordination'.[24]

On the basis of such evidence most historians have agreed with R. B. McDowell's claim that 'it is doubtful if Irish radicals contemplated making extensive changes in the economic system', that they 'accepted the current orthodoxies of political economy' and gave little thought to changing existing socio-economic relationships.[25] However, as Jim Smyth has noted, the society's stance on social issues was far from monolithic, and an influential group of northern-based United Irishmen — Russell, Henry Joy McCracken, James Hope and James Coigly — strongly sympathised with the plight of the poor. Russell, in particular, was well aware that measures such as parliamentary reform could often seem irrelevant to the poor: the artisan or peasant, burdened by taxes and tithes, paying high rents or receiving low wages and generally struggling for survival, was often either ignorant or sceptical of the blessings that reform might bring, and strenuous efforts would be needed to convince him of the tangible benefits that would accrue from a reformed parliament.[26]

Russell firmly believed that political reform must have a strong social dimension. He shared the characteristic liberal belief that many of the social and economic grievances of the poor were created by the existing political system and could be remedied by a radical reform of that system. The government's neglect of the poor was a result of the dominance of parliament by rich landowners — a parliament that was more representative of the mass of people would obviously be more responsive to their needs. Political reform was therefore an essential first step, to be followed by a series of other reforms that would improve the condition of the people. As the Dublin society proclaimed at its founding: 'with a parliament thus reformed everything is easy; without it, nothing can be done'. United Irish propaganda often linked the issues of political and social reform, implying that a reformed parliament would be a panacea for social ills. The *Northern Star* assured its readers that a reformed legislature would abolish tithes, church rates, the hearth tax and the excise, and reduce county cess. Moreover, it would enquire into agrarian disturbances and attempt to redress the genuine grievances of the poor instead of spending its time passing draconian laws against them. It was significant that the society's published plan of reform was accompanied by an address 'to the poorer classes of the community', telling then that their social and economic grievances could only be redressed by political reform.[27]

From 1793 onwards, Russell's social radicalism could also be seen in his trenchant criticisms of the aristocracy. He denounced them for their part in stalling progress towards reform in the 1780s, for their moral corruption, their unworthiness to govern and their parasitic existence. His attacks on the wealthy were primarily directed at the landed classes; significantly, he excluded those who earned their fortunes in commerce from the accusation that they 'derive their wealth from the labours of the poor'.[28] Given his interest in technology and his friendships with radical Belfast merchants and industrialists, he believed that commercial development could be a force for good. Among his papers are notes that show his approval of the economic liberalism of post-revolutionary France, where the 'Constitution guarantees [the people] the rights of employing their wealth, industry and talents in such channels as each shall deem most productive, without monopolies, exclusive charters or corporations.'[29]

But Russell was far from being an uncritical disciple of *laissez-faire* economics. Unlike some of his politically radical colleagues, he was deeply concerned about the many undesirable social developments that accompanied the early stages of industrialisation. In a draft essay, seeking to explain England's relatively low level of population, he criticised the unwholesome conditions under which people worked in the new cotton mills. He maintained that the health of women employed in factories was so damaged that they have little chance of bearing strong children, that by working long hours and specialising in manufacturing activities they lose all their domestic skills and their ability to manage a household, 'and from such numbers being together they become impudent and depraved in their manners'. In addition, he criticised the inadequate and anomalous provisions of the English poor law and the uncaring attitude of the government in a country where 'poverty is a sort of crime'.[30] Whereas most factory owners, even those of radical political views, took a hostile view of tradesmen's combinations, seeing them as an obstacle to the self-regulating harmony of the market and were often prepared to invoke the law against them, Russell looked upon them with approval and encouraged their formation. He contributed an article to the *Northern Star* in which he praised the rules of an artisan combination formed in Belfast as having 'as much sense and morality as any institution among the great'. He hoped that 'from the obvious utility of such institutions similar ones may be formed elsewhere...and as easily...among labourers and cottagers as among tradesmen'.[31] Given that Belfast had had its fair share of industrial troubles in recent years, with bitter and often violent disputes between journeymen and masters in the textile, shoemaking and baking trades, such an article would have been infuriating to many employers.[32] As one who closely identified with the plight of the poor, Russell had no doubt that they had every right to protect their precarious livelihoods, even though this might contradict the free market nostrums then popular in radical circles. He believed that morality, rather than the market, should determine the common good. In his *Letter to the people of Ireland*, he intimated that since God had bequeathed the earth to all mankind at the beginning of creation, the great landowners simply held their estates in trust and had a moral obligation to provide at least a subsistence for the poor (an idea that Thomas Paine had explored in his *Agrarian justice*).[33] For Russell, a country's prosperity was not to be judged by the fortunes of its great merchants or landowners: only 'if the majority can procure a comfortable subsistence with little labour, and have something to share with those who are in want', could it be said to be truly prosperous.[34]

In terms of temperament Russell had little empathy with the hard-nosed attitudes of free market economics. He had a distaste for many of the practicalities of life and loathed all forms of bargaining and haggling. While on a visit to a Moravian community in Co. Antrim he noted with approval that all articles were sold to the brethren at a fixed price. He complained that in the outside world:

> with what distrust all people regard each other in making a bargain...and this habitual opinion of the dishonesty of mankind

corrupts and debases the mind...Go into a shop and it is shocking to hear the multitude of lies and see the mean artifices employ'd to save or gain a few shillings or pence...If I were to advise a person entering on life, I would tell them to give the prices demanded for any article without hesitation and [to] proportion their expenses accordingly sooner than degrade themselves by the contrary mode. If the maximum price which the French have adopted attains or approximates this principle...I am convinc'd it will have the happ[i]est effects in ameliorating the morals of mankind.[35]

It would, however, be fair to say that like most radicals of the period Russell was generally clearer on what he was opposed to than what he was in favour of. With the exception of Paine's advocacy of an embryonic welfare state in the *Rights of man, part II* and *Agrarian justice,* or Thomas Spence's demands for a sweeping land redistribution, few radicals outlined anything approaching a coherent programme. Russell's views on social reform are characteristically vague; his intimations that the existing system of property 'must be altered in some measure' were never spelled out in detail. In fact, R. B. McDowell points to the entries on social reform in Russell's journals as 'reveal[ing] rather well the unformed attitude of Irish radicalism towards social questions'.[36] Russell seems to have shared the radical assumption that with the end of oligarchic rule and the removal of the power and privileges of kings, lords and prelates, the subsequent abolition of tithes and the reduction in excessive taxes would bring about a state of material comfort for the poor. Most of all he believed that once iniquitous man-made laws were swept away the divine will would manifest itself freely through man's natural benevolence and thus improve the common good. It is not surprising, therefore, that he was far more concerned with the destruction of the existing system than with the creation of blueprints for a new one.

Nevertheless, in the last days of Russell's life, when questioned by government agents anxious to determine the general state of the country and his motivation for rebellion, he did put forward a vague plan of social reform. Asked to list the grievances that led to popular disaffection, he mentioned the system of land holding, the burden of tithes and taxes on the peasantry and the biased and arbitrary administration of the law. He emphasised the tithe as a serious grievance to both Catholics and Presbyterians, and maintained that the Anglican clergy, who should live as simple a life as possible, should be paid out of the state treasury.[37] He also insisted that steps should be taken to establish a more equitable relationship between landlord and tenant. His views on changes in the system of land tenures, though unformed, are the most interesting part of his plan of reform, stemming from a scriptural justification but vaguely anticipating some of the land legislation of the nineteenth century:

> The avarice of the land proprietors keeps the people in a state of beggary and consequent discontent...I suppose it will be vain to expect any remedy for this, as the common objection will be made that land is private property. But land is a property different from all others. All other property is derived from it; all other property has a terminable value; but land will be the same 10,000 years hence as now, should the Creator continue it so long. Monopoly of land is, as everything is derived from it, the greatest evil. The Jews, whose laws were given from above, alone made this distinction. Land could not be sold for longer than seventy years. It then reverted back to the old family, and its accumulation was thus prevented. All other property could be sold forever. The way lands are held makes the people slaves to the landlords. They are too poor to emigrate, and have no way left but to submit or starve. I cannot see why a law should not be made as to the length of leases, as well as for any other purpose; and it might be so managed as the poor should benefit from it, and yet the rich not lose.[38]

Russell's views on social reform had an important influence on some United Irish contemporaries, notably Tone. As one of the key social radicals in the United Irishmen, Russell was to play an important role in convincing Tone that the lower orders could be a force for revolution rather than just a dangerous, ill-organised mob. Unlike Russell, Tone rarely associated with peasants or artisans and had a horror of mob rule. In 1791 he could describe the masses as 'rabble', but by the mid-1790s his view had changed and in letters to Russell from America he expressed a sympathetic interest in the welfare of the Catholic peasantry. A year later, while in France, Tone pinned all his hopes for revolution on 'that numerous and respectable class of the community — the men of no property', and wrote a number of socially-radical manifestos to be distributed to the Irish peasantry.[39] Tone's exile undoubtedly contributed to his growing radicalism but Russell's respect and sympathy for ordinary people also had a considerable effect in curbing his political élitism and encouraging him to rely on the Irish masses.

Russell's radicalism was directly and powerfully influenced by his Christianity and it was the Bible which provided the foundation for his beliefs. Dr James McDonnell, whose friendship with Russell was at its closest in the earlier 1790s, recalled that 'he dwelt much (and this increased upon him) upon religious politics, particularly the obscure parts of scripture ... which he thought he understood and could apply'.[40] Russell saw the hand of God in contemporary events and was convinced that the course of human history was, as he put it, 'written in the records of heaven'. His personal papers reveal attempts to use his knowledge of the classics to examine ambiguities of translation in passages relating to prophetic signs, government by the elect and the coming of a new age, and show a general fascination with millennialist prophecies — the notion of the advent of a divinely ordained era of peace and harmony.[41] There are no explicit millennialist references in Russell's journals, which practically cease at the end of 1794, but there are entries that carry apocalyptic or eschatological intimations. For example in May 1793, as the conflict on the Continent intensified, he noted his long-held belief that 'this war would [be] long, bloody, general and almost the last with which Europe would be infested, and that it would end in republicanism very generally'. Some months later he observed:

> when I see the dreadful catastrophe of the kings, princes, nob[l]es and rich of France, I can't help calling to mind the passage where God says He will visit the sins of the father on the children. I think the same fate attends the great in all the European country[s] at no very remote period. They will persist in their oppressions till veng[e]ance comes.[42]

The turmoil of the 1790s formed an ideal breeding ground for millennialist expectations.[43] The French revolution, following so quickly on the heels of political upheaval in America, created a consciousness of living in an era of unprecedented change and an exhilarating sense that the world could be made anew. For many of those who looked to scripture as their guide, the unfolding of history seemed to furnish evidence of the realisation of biblical prophecies of Isaiah, Daniel and particularly the Book of Revelations. Written in the second century by St John of Patmos during a period of persecution of Christianity, Revelations assured believers that eventually the forces of good would triumph over those of evil and Christ would return to establish a kingdom on earth and reign over it for a thousand years until the Last Judgement. During this time the divine purpose in creation would be fulfilled and the world would again enjoy the happiness of Eden: there would be no more war or oppression, no more poverty or ignorance, no more superstition or religious animosity, and a millennium of peace, justice and plenty would precede the end of the world.

Such ideas had always come to the fore most prominently during periods of war, revolution and international turmoil. Violent events could be readily identified as the blasts of the trumpet, the opening of the seals or the pouring out of the vials which the Book of Revelations had prophesied would herald the advent of the thousand years of Christ's reign on earth. In America one of the driving forces behind the revolution was the notion that Americans were acting in accordance with prophecy and playing a divinely ordained role in bringing about a new age of justice and liberty, not just for themselves but for all the world. Such an interpretation was lent credence when in the aftermath of the upheaval in America revolution erupted in France. Since many Protestants had long identified the Antichrist of the Book of Revelations as the papacy, the overthrow of the French monarchy, which was seen as Rome's main prop, was charged with particular significance and excitement for them. Even the de-Christianisation of France was often interpreted as the clearing away of corrupt Christianity for the pure faith that was to follow.[44]

In the late eighteenth century millennialist views were not simply the preserve of fanatics and cranks (though, as in all ages, they attracted their fair share of these). There were many respected intellectuals who had inhaled the intoxicating utopian atmosphere of the time and believed the world to be on the verge of a new and glorious future.[45] Almost all the writers who influenced Russell, especially Paine, Godwin and Priestley, had a strong millennialist vein running through their work. Even a sceptic such as Wolfe Tone, after an almost uninterrupted series of victories by the French armies and the dethroning and exile of the Pope in 1798, observed 'that there is a special providence guiding the affairs of Europe at this moment, and turning everything to the great end of the emancipation of mankind from the yoke of religious and political superstition'. Many years earlier he had laughed at the millennialist views of Whitley Stokes (a man for whose intellect Tone had the utmost admiration) when he had claimed that the Jews would soon return to Palestine, but by 1798 Tone was prepared to accept that such an event was not altogether unlikely.[46]

At a time when the old certainties appeared to be disintegrating and a new world loomed people cast around for explanations. Secularly-minded thinkers such as Paine and Godwin believed that the golden age would be brought about by human benevolence and the power of reason once oppressive and irrational forms of government had been swept away. But for those who looked to scripture as their guide contemporary events were often interpreted as steps in a divinely ordained plan that would eventually lead to a state of heavenly perfection on earth. They viewed contemporary events in Manichaean terms as a cosmic conflict between the forces of light and darkness — the *Northern Star* for example, commenting on the war in Europe, claimed that Poland was 'fighting the cause of God; Prussia, Russia and Austria fighting the cause of the Devil'.[47] To such minds it seemed in the 1790s that history was at a decisive juncture and the culmination of the war between good and evil was near.

Russell shared these beliefs and was convinced that in accordance with the divine will the end of the current conflict would usher in a millennium of peace and harmony in which humanity would be subject to no law but the law of God. An extract from *The lion of old England* gives some indication of the new world he envisaged:

> And now...methinks I can descry the day
> When all such vanities shall pass away;
> When peace shall dwell on earth, and man shall learn
> The majesty of heaven to discern;
> No more shall tremble at a tyrant's nod
> Nor pay to man the homage due to God.
> Fanatical authority no more
> Forbid the human intellect t'explore
> Its sacred springs — no more the infant voice
> Be taught for slaughtered thousands to rejoice.
> No more shall fiend-like hosts be led along
> To butcher those who never did them wrong;
> And man, forgetful of his nature vie
> With beasts of prey in savage cruelty;
> Rapine and murder shall no more be known
> And rage and jealousy for ever flown;
> But gentleness and love return again
> And dwell amidst the new-born sons of men.[48]

Russell's years in Belfast played an important part in the development of his millennialism. In Ulster there were several well-known Presbyterian ministers such as Samuel Barber, Thomas Ledlie Birch,

William Steel Dickson and William Stavely, who formed an important element in the leadership of the United Irishmen in Ulster and
who fused their advanced politics with apocalyptic beliefs, preaching sermons and published tracts with explicit millennialist themes
throughout the 1790s.[49] Ulster dissent nurtured an intellectual
climate that spawned an intense interest in millennialism, and its
adherents ranged across the spectrum of Presbyterian belief, from
New Lights such as Barber and Dickson to the staunchly orthodox
Birch and to the fervent Covenanter, Stavely.[50] A common theme in
their millennialist writings was that the reign of the Antichrist had
begun when Christianity had been corrupted by the creation of an
unholy alliance between Church and State (usually dated from the
time of Constantine), but that the overthrow of the French monarchy and the weakening of the papacy heralded a return to this
original state of purity.[51] In one of the most influential of these works
William Steel Dickson noted that 'human laws can never justify
measures which those of God condemn', an idea that cropped up in
Russell's writings time and time again. Dickson foretold that with
the coming of the millennium 'then will jealousies cease, discontents
vanish, animosities be extinguished, and the pure spirit of the gospel,
unadulterated by the politics of the world, warm us into mutual
kindness, restore us to confidence, and soothe us into peace'; 'that
blissful period is at hand' since the French republic 'has burst the
chains of prejudice and slavery... [and] sent forth her arms, not to
destroy, but restore the liberty of the world and extend her blessings
to all'.[52]

Millennialism is not a precise ideology and there were many
different interpretations of the prophetic texts of scripture, for
example, between post-millennialists and pre-millennialists. The
former, often associated with Rational Dissent, believed that the
millennium would come about as the result of progressive improvement and stressed the continuity between the existing and future
world, maintaining that the Second Coming would follow the
millennium after humanity had prepared the way by creating a
world worthy of Christ's presence. In contrast pre-millennialism,
which generally had a more populist tone, involved a desire for a
sudden and apocalyptic change through direct divine intervention.
Its adherents believed that the physical coming of Christ would
precede the millennium and that he would act as the primary agent
of change.[53]

To a great extent, Russell shared the post-millennialist views of leading intellectual Dissenters such as Richard Price and Joseph Priestley, who believed that providence, working through human agents, was making society ever more perfect in order to prepare the way for the coming of Christ's kingdom.[54] Progress in science and technology, in economic development, in the spread of literacy and political awareness, and the perceived decline in superstition and religious intolerance, all seemed to offer evidence of a world gradually converging towards a state of perfection.

Priestley, in particular, appears to have been an important influence on Russell. Russell may have corresponded with him and he was certainly familiar with his work, and in his journals makes a reference to procuring 'Priestley's book' — probably Priestley's *Letters to the Rt. Hon. Edmund Burke occasioned by his reflections on the revolution in France* (1791).[55] In one of these letters Priestley discussed the opportunity for the 'general enlargement of liberty, civil and religious' that the revolution had brought about. He claimed that events such as the American and French revolutions were:

> unparalleled in all history, [and] make a totally new, a most wonderful, and important era in the history of mankind...a change from darkness to light, from superstition to sound knowledge, and from a most debasing servitude to a state of the most exalted freedom...
>
> How glorious, then, is the prospect, the reverse of all the past, which is now opening upon the world. Government, we may now expect to see...taking no more upon it than the general good requires; leaving all men the enjoyment of as many of their *natural rights* as possible, and no more interfering with matters of religion, with men's notion concerning God, and a future state, than with philosophy or medicine...we may expect to see...the establishment of universal peace and goodwill among all nations . . . This, Sir, will be the happy state of things, distinctly and repeatedly foretold in many prophecies, delivered more than 2,000 years ago...which good sense, and the prevailing spirit of commerce, aided by Christianity, and true philosophy cannot fail to effect in time.[56]

The intellectual millennialists of Rational Dissent believed that this kind of world could only be created in a liberal society in which all were permitted free inquiry, free association and free expression in order to fulfil their responsibility of creating the required conditions for the millennium. For Price and Priestley the creation of a truly liberal society was inseparable from the establishment of a republic. Only under this rational and broadly-based form of government

would the diffusion of political rights and duties transform the ignorant and oppressed masses into a virtuous citizenry capable of
preparing the way for the coming of Christ's kingdom. Until the realisation of this liberty 'the forces of evil, the Antichrist, and sin would
continue to impede human progress toward the millennium'.[57]

The concept of the establishment of the millennium through the
progressive realisation of liberty offers the key to an understanding of
Russell's career. It explains his fervent opposition to the slave trade, to
Catholic disabilities and to oligarchic government. As well as offending his basic humanitarian instincts, such glaring injustices were
redolent of a world of sin, one which was not yet worthy of Christ's
kingdom. Only with the eradication of these evils could the millennium be realised. This is why Richard Price described slavery as a
'diabolical' institution, just as for Russell it was 'the work of wicked
demons' rather than the work of men.[58] The penal laws — the denial
of liberty to one Christian sect by fellow believers — were particularly
repugnant to him. Likewise he saw the efforts of a privileged minority
to exclude the poor from politics as an attempt to stifle the growth of
that broad-based liberty which alone could bring forth a Christian
utopia. Russell never positively identified his idea of antichrist in his
writings but for him it appears to have been an abstraction: the kind
of political system which benefited only the rich and powerful whose
self-serving rule had undermined the divine law.[59]

This millennialist perspective raised Russell's efforts to establish
his country's independence to a different plane. He was not just
engaging in the struggle of a small nation for self-government but
rather was participating in a broader crusade to establish universal
liberty. Russell fervently believed that 'in promoting the good of my
country, I am certain I was promoting that of mankind', and for this
reason looked upon the founding of the United Irishmen as 'herald-
ing a new age of liberty'. He argued that the only foundation for
liberty was morality and morality could not exist independently of
genuine Christianity.[60] This explains the talismanic quality of words
such as 'virtue' and 'liberty' to Russell (for someone rarely given to
using capital letters they are usually capitalised in his journals). The
exercise of virtue would bring about liberty and as the onward
march of liberty swept away iniquitous man-made laws, the laws of
God would be obeyed on earth and His kingdom would be close at
hand.

He had no doubt that the world was proceeding inexorably to this
point and observed of those governments who set themselves above

the laws of God: 'this assumed power is no wise different from that said to have been claimed by the popes of forgiving sins; for the pretending to authorise the commission of a sin, and the pretending to pardon it after its commission, are equally anti-Christian, and will equally be destroyed'.[61] He believed, however, that the millennium would not come about by purely miraculous means and that rather than passively awaiting its onset it was the duty of all Christians to do their utmost to create the New Jerusalem. As he wrote to a friend: 'I trust that the error of supposing that the affairs of the world can be tranquillised in their present form, does not obtain amongst my friends — this is a most awful crisis — may they be found doing their duty, by exerting themselves to extend virtue and liberty.'[62]

Millennialism provided Russell with a comprehensive and coherent ideology, and formed the essential link between his religious views and his political and social outlook. It was the means whereby his hopes for social justice would be realised — which does much to explain the vagueness of his views on social reform. Because millennialism is an ideology of change, it has often appealed to those who sought radical social transformation. One of the most innovative social thinkers of the period, the English radical, Thomas Spence, who advocated social levelling through a universal redistribution of land, was a convinced millennialist.[63] Millenarian tracts which circulated in the 1790s often prophesied the levelling of rich and poor. *The children's catechism*, a radical handbill which circulated in Belfast in 1794, asked: 'Q. When will *happiness* attend mankind? A. At the extirpation of SLAVERY, Priestcraft, *king*craft, and *Aristocracy* — thence spring fair *Liberty* and *Equality*, that men may enjoy the BLESSINGS OF GOD in an earthly *Paradise*.'[64] The prediction of a return to an egalitarian state of nature and of the Last Judgement as the day reckoning for the rich and powerful had been a staple in millenarian literature since the Middle Ages.[65] The pamphlet *Christ in triumph coming to judgement* seized by two magistrates in Co. Tyrone from an old hawker foretold:

> what happy times will succeed to many people, when the poor will be had in equal (or perhaps superior) estimation with the rich. [On judgement day] all those emperors, kings, princes, and rulers of nations, who have been cruel tyrants and not governed rightly nor cared for the lives of their subjects but made wars for ambition and revenge, then all these will wish that their kingdoms might fall over them and hide them from the terrible face of seeing justice . . . these shall at these

sessions stand shivering dejected and naked...Cobbler and Caesar shall stand at this bar on equal terms.[66]

Referring to a similar outburst of millenarian pamphlets in Britain in the 1790s, J. F. C. Harrison observes that the 'general tone of this literature is critical of the rich and powerful, and sympathetic to the needs and claims of the poor. Always, just below the surface, is the...conviction that social ills can be cured if men would individually follow God's inward revelation.'[67] For those such as Russell, who sympathised with the poor and looked forward to an egalitarian millennium, the language of the apocalypse could equally serve as the language of social revolution.

NOTES

1 Smyth, *Men of no property*, p. 165.
2 Russell, *Letter to the people*, p. 12.
3 Russell's journal, 9 July 1793 (*Journals*, pp. 82–3).
4 Russell's journal, 9 July 1793 (*Journals*, p. 82).
5 Russell, *Letter to the people*, pp. 1–2.
6 Russell, *Letter to the people*, pp. 4, 6.
7 Russell, *Letter to the people*, pp. 6, 8, 11–12, 14–15.
8 Russell, *Letter to the people*, p. 16.
9 Russell, *Letter to the people*, pp. 17–18.
10 Russell, *Letter to the people*, pp. 20–22.
11 Russell, *Letter to the people*, pp. 23–4.
12 –, Belfast, to –, 24 Sept. 1796 (Reb. papers, 620/25/103); Thomas Russell to John Russell, Fort George, 10 Dec. 1800 (copy) (Madden papers, 873/655, f. 6).
13 Smyth, *Men of no property*, p. 92.
14 Martha McTier to Drennan, Sept. 1796 (*Drennan letters*, p. 240).
15 Morgan, 'Sketch of Russell', pp. 44–5.
16 United Irish plan of parliamentary reform, *Northern Star*, 20 Feb. 1794; also P.R.O., HO 100/51/100.
17 Russell's journal, 9 July 1793 (*Journals*, p. 83).
18 Russell's journal, 11 July 1793 (*Journals*, p. 88).
19 *Northern Star*, 23, 30 June 1792; Madden, *Antrim and Down in '98*, p. 108.
20 Oliver McDonagh, *States of mind: a study of Anglo-Irish conflict, 1780–1980* (London, 1983), p. 75; Elliott, *Partners*, p. 369. For a more detailed discussion of this issue, see James Quinn, 'The United Irishmen and social reform' in *I. H. S.*, xxxi, no. 122 (Nov. 1998), pp. 188–201.
21 R. B. McDowell, 'Personnel of the Dublin society of United Irishmen' in *I. H. S.*, ii, no. 5 (Mar. 1940), p. 18.
22 'Resolution of the Society of United Irishmen of Dublin', 30 Dec. 1791 (*Society of United Irishmen* (Dublin, 1794), p. 8).
23 R. B. MacDowell, 'The proceedings of the Dublin Society of United Irishmen' in *Analecta Hibernica*, no. 17 (1949), pp. 3–143.
24 'The Society of United Irishmen of Dublin to the Volunteers of Ireland', 14 Dec. 1792 (*Society of United Irishmen*, p. 45).

25 R. B. McDowell, *Irish public opinion, 1750–1800* (London, 1944), pp. 200, 202. For similar views, see also J. D. Clarkson, *Labour and nationalism in Ireland* (New York, 1925), p. 127; Elliott, *Tone*, p. 418; idem., *Partners*, p. 367; Curtin, *United Irishmen*, p. 283.

26 Draft essay by Russell on parliamentary reform, n.d. (Sirr papers, 868/1, f. 179).

27 'Declaration of the Society of United Irishmen of Dublin', 9 Nov. 1791 (*Society of United Irishmen*, p. 5); *Northern Star*, 17 Mar. 1792; 8 Dec. 1792, see also address 'To the Presbyterians of the province of Ulster', c. Sept. 1792 (Reb. papers, 620/19/101); 'The Society of United Irishmen of Dublin to the people of Ireland', 14 Mar. 1794 (*Society of United Irishmen*, p. 192); 'The society of United Irishmen to the people of Ireland', c. Mar. 1794 (*Society of United Irishmen* (1798), pp. 129–30); according to Drennan, this was written by Thomas Addis Emmet (*Drennan letters*, p. 184).

28 Russell, *Letter to the people*, p. 17.

29 Draft essay by Russell, c. 1797–8 (Sirr papers, 868/1, f. 194v).

30 Notes by Russell on the population of England, c. 1797–8 (Sirr papers, 868/1, ff 323, 188v).

31 *Northern Star,* 14 Nov. 1793; for authorship, see Russell's journal, 14 Nov. 1793 (*Journals*, p. 135).

32 John J. Monaghan, 'A social and economic history of Belfast, 1790–1800' (MA thesis, Queen's University Belfast, 1936), pp. 159–60.

33 Russell, *Letter to the people*, p. 17.

34 Russell, *Letter to the people*, p. 20.

35 Russell's journal, Oct. 1794 (*Journals*, pp. 165–6).

36 R. B. McDowell, *Irish public opinion, 1750–1800* (London, 1944), p. 202.

37 Russell to McNally, 6 Oct. 1803 (P.R.O., HO 100/114/121–2).

38 Russell's statement, Downpatrick, 17 Oct. 1803 (MacDonagh, *Viceroy's post-bag*, pp. 424–6).

39 Elliott, *Tone*, p. 240; Bartlett, *Life of Tone*, pp. 120, 494, see also 'Address to the people of Ireland' and 'An address to the peasantry of Ireland by a traveller, 1796' (ibid. 691–708, 709–14); Tone to Russell, Princeton, 25 Oct. 1795 (Sirr papers, 868/2, ff 13–15).

40 Madden, *United Irishmen*, 3rd ser., ii, 280.

41 Russell's statement recorded by Dr Trevor, 27 Sept. 1803 (P.R.O., HO 100/114/11–12); Russell's notes on scriptural prophecy (Sirr papers, 868/1, ff 3–5).

42 Russell's journal, 7 May 1793, 19 Jan. 1794 (*Journals*, pp. 75, 142).

43 E. P. Thompson, for example, refers to 'a sudden emergence of millenarial fantasies, on a scale unknown since the seventeenth century' in the years 1793–4 (*The making of the English working class*, 2nd edn (London, 1968), p. 127). For works which examine the upsurge of millenarian ideas in western Europe during this period in detail, see J. F. C. Harrison, *The second coming: popular millenarianism 1780–1850* (London, 1979) and Clark Garrett, *Respectable folly: millenarians and the French revolution in France and England* (London, 1975).

44 E. L. Tuveson, *Redeemer nation: the idea of America's millennial role* (Chicago and London, 1968); see also Ruth Bloch, *Visionary republic: millennial themes in American thought 1756–1800* (Cambridge, 1988).

45 Besides the best-known millennialists of the period — Joseph Priestley and Richard Price — J. F. C. Harrison mentions Timothy Dwight (president of Yale) and John H. Livingstone (president of Rutgers) as examples of intellectuals with a strong interest in millennialist scholarship (*The second coming: popular millenarianism 1780–1850* (London, 1979), p. 5).

46 Bartlett, *Life of Tone*, p. 836; for Tone's attitude to Stokes, see ibid. pp. 35, 517, 844.

47 *Northern Star*, 21 Aug. 1794.

48 'The lion of old England', *Northern Star*, 30 Dec. 1793. One cannot be certain about which parts of this work were written by Russell or Sampson, but given Russell's Christian and millennialist views he is a more likely author of this extract rather than the religiously sceptical Sampson. For similar sentiments relating to a future golden age see also Russell's ballad, 'Man is free by nature', *Paddy's resource* (1795), p. 36.

49 Pieter Tesch, 'Presbyterian radicalism' in Dickson, Keogh and Whelan (eds), *United Irishmen*, pp. 46-8; James Donnelly, 'Propagating the cause of the United Irishmen' in *Studies: an Irish quarterly review*, lxix (1981), pp. 16–17.

50 I. R. McBride, *Scripture politics: Ulster Presbyterians and Irish radicalism in the late eighteenth century* (Oxford, 1998), p. 199.

51 William Steel Dickson, *Three sermons on the subject of scripture politics* (Belfast, 1793), pp. 15–16, 55; foreword by William Stavely to Robert Fleming, *A discourse on the rise and fall of the antichrist wherein the revolution in France and the downfall of the monarchy in that kingdom are distinctly pointed out* (Belfast, 1795); Thomas Ledlie Birch, *The obligations upon Christians* (Belfast, 1794), pp. 26–7.

52 William Steel Dickson, *Three sermons on the subject of scripture politics* (Belfast, 1793), pp. 16, 35.

53 W. H. Oliver, *Prophets and millennialists: the uses of biblical prophecy in England from the 1790s to the 1840s* (Auckland, 1978), pp. 20–1.

54 Jack Fruchtman jnr, 'The apocalyptic politics of Richard Price and Joseph Priestley: a study of late eighteenth-century millennialism' in *Transactions of the American Philosophical Society*, lxxiii, pt. 4 (Philadelphia, 1983).

55 Russell's journal, 9 Apr. 1791, 20 Oct. 1793 (*Journals*, pp. 49, 133).

56 Joseph Priestley, *Letters to the Rt. Hon. Edmund Burke occasioned by his reflections on the revolution in France* (Dublin, 1791), pp. 114–16, 119; a copy of this work can be found in Reb. papers, 620/19/41.

57 Fruchtman, 'Apocalyptic politics', pp. 29, 49–50.

58 Russell, *Letter to the people*, p. 14; Richard Price, *Observations on the American revolution* (London, 1784) p. 68; for Price and Priestley's opposition to slavery see also, Fruchtman, 'Apocalyptic politics', pp. 53–4.

59 Russell's journal, 9 July 1793 (*Journals*, pp. 82–3); Russell, *Letter to the people*, pp. 17–18.

60 Thomas Russell to John Russell, 10 Dec. 1800 (copy) (Madden papers, 873/655, f. 1v); [Russell] to –, Oct./Nov. 1791 (P.R.O., HO 100/34/41–2); Russell to Templeton, 5 June 1802 (Madden papers, 873/638).

61 Russell, *Letter to the people*, p. 12.

62 Russell to Templeton, 5 June 1802 (Madden papers, 873/638).

63 Malcolm Chase, '*The people's farm': English radical agrarianism 1775–1840* (Oxford, 1988), pp. 52–3; Iain McCalman, *Radical underworld: prophets, revolutionaries and pornographers in London, 1795–1840* (Cambridge, 1988), p. 70.

64 Joy MSS, Linenhall Library, Belfast.

65 Norman Cohn, *The pursuit of the millennium: revolutionary millenarians and mystical anarchists of the Middle Ages* (revised edn, London, 1970), p. 271.

66 *Christ in triumph, coming to judgement! As recorded in the most holy sacred scriptures by the holy prophets and evangelists* (Strabane, 1796?), enclosed in A. Cole Hamilton to [Dublin Castle], 2 Mar. 1797 (Reb. papers, 620/29/8).

67 J. F. C. Harrison, *The second coming: popular millenarianism 1780–1850* (London, 1979), pp. 83–4.

CHAPTER SIX

Spreading the Word

From their foundation the United Irishmen devoted themselves to agitating and directing popular opinion in favour of parliamentary reform and Catholic emancipation. Imbued with the optimism of the age, they believed that once the people had been persuaded of the righteousness of their cause, then government would have no choice but to concede the demands of a united and enlightened populace. To achieve this they mounted a massive campaign of public education to inform the people of their rights and to encourage them to demand those rights. The movement published and disseminated a wide variety of materials — newspapers, pamphlets, broadsheets and handbills — designed to transform the Irish masses into an informed and virtuous citizenry capable of vigorous participation in the political process.

There also appears to have been the hope, among some of the movement's radicals, that people could be educated into revolution. In July 1793 Russell noted: 'McCabe observes that it's the lower orders alone that will produce a revolution. When the majority *feel* themselves slaves they will resist. Information being diffused will produce this.'[1] Many supporters of the government also believed that the distribution of political propaganda among the people at large could have such an effect. Reports were sent to the Castle that the United Irishmen were merely using parliamentary reform as a pretext 'to promote discord and sedition' by spreading their 'literary mischief...amongst all the lower orders of the people'. Denis Browne, MP for Co. Mayo, claimed that the militia riots in Mayo in the summer of 1793 had been caused by 'the new political doctrines which have perverted the lower orders' particularly by shopkeepers who spread Paine's *Rights of man* and seditious newspapers throughout the countryside, directed by the United Irishmen.[2]

Russell himself soon became one of the United Irishmen's leading propagandists. He had been an occasional contributor to the

Northern Star since its launch and during 1793 he became increasingly involved in its affairs. As part of its offensive against northern
radicalism the government had initiated a prosecution against the
Star for publishing a seditious address. Feeling isolated and disillusioned, the proprietors began negotiations to sell the paper to the
government, with the Whig MP for Co. Antrim, John O'Neill, acting
as an intermediary. Russell and Thomas McCabe senior did their
utmost to persuade them to resist the government's threats. In July
1793 McCabe called a meeting of the town's leading United
Irishmen and the *Star*'s owners to discuss the matter. Those opposed
to negotiating with the government prevailed and publication
continued. In the meantime, the authorities repeatedly delayed the
trial of the proprietors keeping the threat of prosecution hanging
over their heads to intimidate them.[3] To help stiffen their resolve,
Neilson asked Russell to write a defence of the proprietors, which
was published in the *Northern Star* in January 1794. It was of the
utmost importance to the reform movement in Ulster that the paper
should continue to be published. The *Northern Star* played a key
role in informing and shaping opinion in the province: for James
Hope it 'represented the moral force of Ulster, [and] sowed the seeds
of truth over the land'. The paper penetrated into even the remote
areas of the province. In September 1793, while on an excursion to
the Mourne Mountains, Russell noticed 'a little girl with a paper in
her hand in quite a wild part near Ballynahinch. Ask what it is.
Answer'd the N[orthern] Star. Here give them the N[orthern] S[tar]
which they read with avidity'.[4]

Russell often disseminated radical propaganda while on his travels. As well as distributing material on his wanderings throughout
Ulster, there were sightings of him as far south as Portarlington,
where he was reported driving through the streets of the town in a
phaeton handing out seditious leaflets.[5] But it is as one of the *Star*'s
main contributors that Russell's real importance as a United Irish
propagandist lies.[6] In autumn 1793 he began collaborating with
William Sampson, a radical Belfast barrister, on a work entitled *The
lion of old England or democracy confounded*, which was serialised
in the *Northern Star* from September to December. The work is a
review of a supposedly epic poem based on the exploits of 'the lion
of old England' — the lion representing England's martial glory.
Primarily, it sets out to satirise the British government's reactionary
and war-mongering behaviour and contrasts the dignity of peaceful
commerce with the folly and destructiveness of war. It strikes this

keynote in its first canto: 'Scorn the vile traders, who to peace incline/War, raging war, is glorious and divine.'[7]

Why then, ask the reviewers, do nations go to war?

> For as long as people are happy, and can earn a comfortable subsistence by their industry, they will never become soldiers, to fight when they have no quarrel. Nothing but ignorance and misery can make a nation truly warlike...It is by keeping...the nation in a sufficient degree of ignorance, to be good dupes and good soldiers, at the same time sufficiently laborious and industrious to pay taxes, that his Majesty's present ministers have rendered such important services.[8]

The work is unsparing in its criticism of leading government figures, such as Burke and Pitt, who it implies made their reputations as reformers but have now abandoned their principles and become hypocritical place-seekers. For his efforts in defence of privilege and corruption Burke is appointed 'Priest of the Temple of the Constitution', a construction which may 'be justly styled, the envy of all nations, the glory of the earth, the boast of antiquity and the nation's pride: the origin or foundation of it is, according to the best historians, lost in the clouds of antiquity, which proves it divine'.[9] Burke is credited with drawing up a creed for the faithful adherents to this constitution:

> I believe that the law of primogeniture is the law of nature. I believe that kings are the fountain of all honour, justice, wisdom and mercy; and that lords are by birth judges, legislators and counsellors...I believe that the swinish multitude are born only to labour and be governed, and I believe that standing army, national debt, revenue, tax-gathering, pensions, places, ecclesiastical patronage, tithes, bribes, tests, informations, penalties and press-gangs, together with all manner of influence, amicable or hostile, direct or indirect, are the means of governing most consistent with true glory. I believe that the idleness and voluptuousness of absentee bishops is essential to true glory.
>
> I believe that there is such a divine glory in all kings and queens...that whensoever...their dread majesties may be inclined to go to war...that the duty of a liege subject is to despise peace, prosperity, domestic endearments, personal danger, private judgement and public tranquillity; and to fly, if commanded, to the remotest corner of the earth, to carry fire and desolation amongst those who may by any means become obnoxious to his dread sovereign, fellow citizens as well as strangers.[10]

Burke looks back to a golden age when:

> *Kings and nobles stood in true degree,*
> *'Twixt heaven's throne and base-born villainy;*
> *Then slaves were slaves, as 'twas decreed they should*
> *For rights of man were not then understood.*
> *Mongrel philosophers, say if you can,*
> *What mean your wisdoms by the rights of man?*
> *Is it with impious hands to burst the chain,*
> *Which providence in mercy did ordain?*
> *Is it to teach the filthy wallowing swine,*
> *To grunt that kingly power is not divine?*[11]

The war attracts the main criticism of the reviewers and Britain's poor performance against the French during 1793 provides ample scope for mockery: 'Q. Where did the British army triumph last? / A. Where should they triumph last — why — in Belfast.'[12]

In fact, so great are Britain's accumulating military setbacks that even the lion himself becomes disillusioned and, recognising the sins of his past, he confesses:

> *Too much of human carnage have I seen,*
> *Too long the reckless instrument have been*
> *Of vile ambition — too long served the cause*
> *Of those who trample upon nature's laws.*
> *...*
> *The grateful peasant viewed his little hoard*
> *And pleasure crowned his hospitable board;*
> *And dawning science did its beams impart*
> *T'expand his soul and humanise his heart.*
> *Already had he learned himself to scan*
> *And felt the conscious energy of man:*
> *When lo! some cruel monarch's fell command,*
> *Spreads desolation through that smiling land.*
> *How changed the scene! — The harmless rustic now*
> *Forsakes the honest labours of his plough;*
> *And now a soldier stains with human gore*
> *That earth, his guiltless hands had tilled before*
> *From the proud city too, all joy is fled*
> *Where wounded commerce hangs her drooping head.*[13]

The lion is very much a work of 1790s radicalism, with Paine's influence strongly evident. It exploits the well-worn themes of radical protest: the corruption, hypocrisy and obscurantism of monarchy and aristocracy; the unjust persecution of reformers by government and judiciary; the mounting distress of the poor; and, most pointedly, the destructiveness and futility of dynastic wars. It employs ample amounts of ridicule to undermine the respect of ordinary people for their masters, but as with much of the journalism of the *Northern Star* its lampooning of the government stays just on the safe side of the seditious. The authors attempt to establish the respectability of the radical movement by linking those persecuted in the early 1790s — Paine, Muir, Palmer, Reynolds, Bond and Butler — with Whig martyrs of the seventeenth century such as Hampden and Sidney.[14] Their condemnation of unnecessary war as an engine of monarchical tyranny and corruption is also squarely set in the country Whig tradition. Opposition to the war with France was one of the radicals' most powerful weapons in trying to recruit mass support: because it disrupted trade, pushed up prices and caused widespread distress it could be denounced on pragmatic as well as moral and ideological grounds. This was particularly so in places like Belfast where much of the town's commercial middle-class sympathised openly with France, and resented the wartime economic dislocation all the more. As R. B. McDowell notes, for radicals the war 'was a glaring and costly example of the evils consequent upon the British connection'. Moreover, in the face of the repeated setbacks suffered by British forces on land, they could point out that not only was it an unjust war, it was also a disastrous one and that government ministers were not merely immoral but incompetent.[15]

The lion seems to have been a popular work among the farmers and artisans of the north-east. While travelling around County Antrim in September 1793, Russell remarked that many people were talking of it and that it was 'highly praised'. Its popularity was such that it was published in pamphlet form in March 1794.[16]

The adoption by the United Irishmen of conspiratorial rather than constitutional methods from 1794–5 did not mark a relaxation in their propagandist activities. If a mass organisation was to be built up, it remained essential that their message should be spread as widely as possible and inevitably Russell was involved. In January 1795 he and William Sampson began to write the 'Chinese journal' for the *Northern Star*.[17] These journal articles were ostensibly the observations of the secretary of an English peer travelling through China with his master but used the convention of the travel journal to make some thinly-disguised attacks on targets nearer home. In China the two Englishmen find themselves at the court of a great emperor whose:

> armies carry sword and conquest into every land... His alliances are courted by the indigent and artful, for his bounty shines like the genial beams of day upon the unjust as well as the just... Nay, even the Pope, whom he is sworn to abjure and who is styled the Scarlet Whore of Babylon, and the Filthy Beast, is protected by his cavalry.[18]

They are privileged to witness a ceremony in which this great monarch looks towards heaven and prays.

> Oh Thou, to whom the pride of monarchs is but baseness... Make me quick to redress the wrongs of my people... Let none be in authority but those whose souls are pure, for in such only is true nobility. Let none be ennobled but the good and the instructed; for otherwise is nobility a scorn and a reproach. When rumours are spread of treasons and plots, make me wise to those who utter forth such tidings, that they be not themselves plotters: and of him who would shed blood let blood be shed; and let him who would alarm be alarmed.
>
> But if any insurrections shall at any time prevail, let not the poor suffer, nor be put to death by military violence, for their ignorance shall excuse them: but let the mandarins of the district, and those of high degree, be brought to punishment and shame: for in the negligence and corruption of the great originate the vices of the poor... Let the laws of my empire be simple and easy, for where there is mystery there is ignorance and chicane [*sic*]; where there is delay there is bitterness of spirit, and where there is cost, there is oppression. Let all mystery and deceit be far from my children: let them seek truth and find it.[19]

The work also includes a scathing attack by a foreign ambassador on British laws, the character of lawyers, and the bishops and clergy, who are described as:

> at once the most supple slaves and over-bearing tyrants, enjoying large territories, and claiming one tenth of the poor man's industry, to whom he is no otherwise known than by the cruelty of his exactions and the depravity of his example. Their prophet, the Son of God, taught them a religion of meekness and humility: by his example they sanction their intolerance and pride — he taught perfect equality: they are the champions of monopoly and power — he suffered hunger and

thirst: they are bloated with riot and excess — he comforted the poor: they fawn upon the great — he had nowhere to lay his head: they revel in palaces and repose on down — he clothed the poor and naked: they strip the poor naked — he was patient under persecution: they persecute the patient — he returned good for evil: they return evil for good — he filled the hungry and sent the rich away empty; they feed the rich and send the hungry away — he took no care for this world: they take no care for any other... he preached peace: they preach war!... he was the shepherd that guarded his flocks: they are the shepherds that shear them![20]

A year on from the publication of *The lion of old England,* the satire is less restrained, in keeping with the more polarised atmosphere of the times and the increasingly militant attitude of the radicals. While *The lion* had attacked specific ills stemming from the current regime such as the continuation of the war or the government's persecution of radicals, the 'Chinese journal' broadened the attack to the very foundations of the Constitution — Church, State and law. Kings, aristocrats, lawyers and bishops are all lumped together as parasites living off the toil of the masses and, by standing between them and their God, frustrating the divine will and divine justice.

Russell's propaganda efforts were not confined to the *Northern Star.* As James Donnelly has pointed out, when the United Irishmen began to create a popularly-based organisation after 1794, they 'consciously turned to political ballads as a major means of spreading republican ideology and stimulating revolutionary enthusiasm... [and] it was the northerners who took the lead in exploiting this dimension of popular culture'.[21] In 1795 the Belfast United Irishmen published the first edition of *Paddy's resource,* a collection of republican ballads. It proved a popular work and went through a number of editions between 1795 and 1803. *Paddy's resource* was carefully tailored for a lower-class audience. Its songs attacked 'places, pensions, bishops, taxes, tithes, high rents, slavery, monarchy, aristocracy and English influence' and called for 'a union of Irishmen, Catholic emancipation, and emulation of the French'.[22] As with most United Irish propaganda the contributors remained anonymous. The readiness with which the government instigated prosecutions of the *Northern Star* and United Irishmen who had put their names to outspoken addresses made this the most prudent course to take. This, however, provides obvious difficulty in trying to determine the authorship of individual pieces. Evidence suggests that Russell made some contribution to the collection — he probably

wrote the preface and a song entitled 'Man is free by nature'. The
latter appeared in the 1795 and 1803 editions of *Paddy's resource*,
which suggests that the publication of the 1803 version may have
been connected with the attempts at insurrection by Emmet and
Russell in that year.[23] The rather blood-thirsty manuscript version
had to be toned down, but even the published version struck a strident note:

> *Why vainly do we waste our time*
> *Repeating our oppressions*
> *Come haste to arms, for now's the time*
> *To punish past transgressions*
> *They say that kings can do no wrong*
> *Their murderous deeds deny it*
> *And since from us their power has sprung*
> *We have a right to try it.*
>
> *The starving wretch who steals for bread*
> *But seldom meets compassion*
> *Then shall a* crown *preserve the head*
> *Of one that robs a nation.*
> *Such partial laws we all despise*
> *See Gallia's bright example*
> *The glorious scene before our eyes*
> *Let's every tyrant trample.*
>
> *Proud lordlings now we must translate*
> *From senate, see and pensions*
> *Virtue alone must teach the state*
> *In spite of kings' intentions.*
> *These despots long have trod us down*
> *And judges are their engines*
> *Such wretches — minions of the crown*
> *Demand a people's vengeance.*
>
> *The golden age will yet revive*
> *Each man will be a brother*
> *In harmony we all shall live*
> *And share the earth together*
> *In virtue's school enlightened youth*
> *Will love his fellow creature*
> *And further ages prove the truth*
> *THAT MAN IS FREE BY NATURE.*[24]

Set to popular tunes of the day, designed to appeal to as wide an audience as possible and capable of being transmitted even to the illiterate, the political song could prove a particularly effective form of propaganda. Tom Dunne, however, dismisses United Irish songs as crude and cloyingly sentimental, and claims that such 'bland bourgeois propaganda' had little impact on its intended audience.[25] But songs with a genuinely popular appeal *are* very often crude and sentimental, and *Paddy's resource* sold well in its several different editions. Years later, an Ulster contemporary described the impact of United Irish songs in the late 1790s: although they were:

> utterly destitute of the graces of fine writing, yet being adapted to popular airs, being in unison with popular feelings, and containing some times a great deal of simplicity and nature, [they] were alto- gether suited to the taste of the lower orders, and produced in their minds a wonderful degree of political enthusiasm. It had been asserted that the prevalence of those songs did more to increase the numbers of conspirators than all the efforts of French emissaries, or the writ- ings and harangues of all the political philosophers, and age-of-reason men of the times.[26]

Many other reports testified to the effectiveness of propagandist songs. An informer reported that William Putnam McCabe, a lead- ing northern United Irish emissary, had told him 'the songs published by Storey had done wonders among the militia — who were all true fellows'; a loyalist recalled how in the later 1790s 'the country...resounded with blasphemous rhymes, which were called patriotic songs' with the result that 'the most illiterate bumpkin appeared to consider himself a consummate politician'.[27]

Although it is generally accepted that Russell was one of the *Northern Star*'s leading journalists, it is difficult, because almost all the work published in the paper was unsigned or written under pseu- donyms, to be precise about the extent of his contribution. There are many articles and poems denouncing the war, the slave trade, reli- gious bigotry, the injustice done to the poor, the carving up of Poland and the hypocrisy of European monarchs, which may well have been written by Russell but, given that these views were hardly unique to him, they cannot be claimed as his with any real certainty.[28]

It is likely that Russell's propagandist efforts were far more exten- sive than those that can be positively attributed to him. In 1796 a leading government informer noted that Russell was held in high esteem by his United Irish colleagues, having rendered 'very essential service' to the republican cause through his writings.[29] In his journals Russell makes reference to writing a number of political works, for example, in March 1791 'an address to the people of Ireland to be prefixed to the pamphlet', 'a paper' for a radical club in Enniskillen in October 1793 and 'a paper for the county of Down' in November 1793.[30] These may now be lost, cannot be identified as Russell's work or may never have been published.

Russell himself realised that in the area of political writing he achieved less than his potential. On a number of occasions he stated his intention of publishing works on a variety of subjects — a pro-Catholic pamphlet, a philosophical work, a history of Ireland — but sustained effort rarely matched his intentions, and none of these proposed works ever appear to have been completed. Aware of his own shortcomings, he admitted to a friend, 'I have always had an aversion to writing... I am planning two or three things, but am very lazy.'[31] His own opinion of his efforts in verse was that 'I am but a poor poet', and much of the verse he wrote was closely modelled on the works of other authors.[32] Russell even seems to have difficulty in writing letters of any real length and in India was distressed at his inability to write a good letter to his parents. His letter writing abilities improved: Tone for example noted that he 'writes the best stuff of any man in the world. All his letters good', but even Tone felt the need to reprimand him gently 'you have got a trick of beginning your letters by promising me to tell your business in your next. Pray condescend for once to tell it in the letter you are then writing'.[33]

However, political writing formed an important part of Russell's career. He continued to contribute to the Northern Star until his arrest in September 1796 and published a major pamphlet, *A letter to the people of Ireland on the present situation of the country*, days before his arrest. In prison he wrote from time to time and during his exile in France in 1802–03, he may also have written for the *Argus,* a Paris-based English language publication.[34]

NOTES

1 Russell's journal, 11 July 1793 (*Journals*, p. 87).
2 A. Charles Murphy to Dublin Castle, Dublin, 10 Apr. 1794 (P.R.O., HO 100/46/150–1); information of Denis Browne, 6 June 1793 (P.R.O., HO 100/44/118).
3 Russell's journal, 8 July 1793 (*Journals*, pp. 80–1); Drennan to Sam McTier, 1 July 1793 (*Drennan letters*, p. 165); Brian Inglis, *Freedom of the press in Ireland,1784–1841* (London, 1954), pp. 94–5.

4 *Northern Star*, 2 Jan. 1794; Russell's journal, 19–20 Oct. 1793 (*Journals*, 132); Madden, *Antrim and Down in '98*, p. 104; Russell's journal, 2 Sept. 1793 (*Journals*, p. 112).

5 Margaret Russell to Thomas Russell, 7 Sept. 1793, Drumsluice (Sirr papers, 868/2, ff 26–7).

6 Madden, *United Irishmen*, 3rd ser., ii, 159 and idem, *United Irishmen*, 4th ser. (2nd edn, Dublin, 1860), pp. 19–20, and F. J. Bigger, 'The *Northern Star*' in *Ulster Journal of Archaelogy* (1895), p. 33 claim that Russell was one of the main contributors to the *Star*. Letters written by John Russell, William Drennan and Martha McTier suggest that he was closely involved with the paper; see Sirr papers, 868/2, f. 123; *Drennan letters*, p. 239 and Drennan papers T765/540.

7 *Northern Star*, 7 Sept. 1793; *Lion of old Eng.* (rev. edn, 1794), p. 6.

8 *Northern Star*, 14 Sept. 1793; *Lion of old Eng.*, p. 18.

9 *Northern Star*, 31 Oct. 1793; *Lion of old Eng.*, p. 39.

10 *Northern Star*, 31 Oct. 1793; *Lion of old Eng.*, pp. 48–9.

11 *Lion of old Eng.*, p. 84; this extract did not appear in the *Star*.

12 *Northern Star*, 26 Dec. 1793; *Lion of old Eng.*, p. 66.

13 *Northern Star*, 30 Dec. 1793; *Lion of old Eng.*, pp. 85–90.

14 *Northern Star*, 4 Nov. 1793; *Lion of old Eng.*, p. 55.

15 R. B. McDowell, *Irish public opinion, 1750–1800* (London, 1944), pp. 206, 204.

16 Russell's journal, 29 Sept. 1793 (*Journals*, pp. 124–5); *Northern Star*, 3 Mar. 1794.

17 According to the *Northern Star*, 15 Dec. 1794, the author is 'the learned and accomplished commentator upon *Lion of old Eng. of old England*'. This would narrow the field down to Russell or Sampson, but jokes about the illegibility of author's handwriting in the *Star* of 22 Dec. 1794 (Sampson had a clear legible hand) favour Russell as the author. One of the major passages quoted below contains a scathing attack on the law and the character of lawyers, while another extols the virtues of a simple Christianity; since Sampson was a practising barrister and was described as a 'a professed deist' and an 'unbeliever' by Martha McTier (4, 24 Oct. 1794, Drennan papers, T765/527, 531), these extracts are more likely to be the work of Russell. McTier claimed that the work was a co-production of Sampson and Russell, but that Russell had written parts of it alone (25 Jan. 1795, Drennan papers, T765/540). Mary MacNeill cites Russell as the author of the 'Chinese papers' [*sic*], but gives no source in support (*Mary Ann McCracken*, p. 91).

18 *Northern Star*, 8 Jan. 1795.

19 *Northern Star*, 5 Feb. 1795.

20 *Northern Star*, 26 Feb. 1795.

21 James Donnelly, 'Propagating the cause of the United Irishmen' in *Studies: an Irish quarterly review*, lxix (1981), p. 10.

22 Georges Denis Zimmerman, *Irish political street ballads and rebel songs 1780–1900* (Geneva, 1966), p. 38; second and third editions of *Paddy's resource* were published in Belfast in 1796 and 1798. Another was published in Dublin, probably in 1803. Other editions appeared in Philadephia in 1796 and in New York in 1798; Smyth, *Men of no property*, p. 162.

23 *Paddy's resource* (Belfast, 1795) pp. 26–7, 35–7, 50–1. For preface see draft in Russell's hand (Sirr papers, 868/1, f. 61) and for 'Man is free by nature' see draft in Russell's hand (Reb. papers, 620/25/136); Thuente, *Harp re-strung*, p. 163.

24 *Paddy's resource* (1795), pp. 35–6. For the manuscript version see Reb. papers, 620/25/136.

25 Tom Dunne, 'Popular ballads, revolutionary rhetoric and politicisation' in Gough and Dickson (eds), *Ire. and the Fr. Rev.*, pp. 143–5.

26 James McHenry, *O'Halloran; or the insurgent chief, an Irish historical tale of 1798* (Philadelphia, 1824), i, 63.

27 Information of Smith, 28 May 1796 (Frazer MS II/20); Samuel McSkimin, *Annals of Ulster, 1790–1798* (1849, E. J. McCrum ed., Belfast, 1906), p. 31. The 'Storey' referred to is probably John Storey, a United Irishman who worked as a printer on the *Northern Star*; he was hanged in 1798 for taking part in the rising at Antrim.

28 See, for example, *Northern Star*, 14 Jan. 1792, 18 Jan. 1792, 17 Oct. 1792, 8 May 1793, 21 Sept. 1793, 5 Oct. 1793.

29 Smith's information on arrested United Irish leaders, late 1796 (Frazer MS II/40).

30 Martha McTier to Drennan, 25 Jan. 1795 (Drennan papers, T765/540); for the work itself see the *Northern Star*, 31 July to 14 Aug. 1794; *Journals*, pp. 41, 132, 135.

31 Tone, *Writings*, i, 148; Russell's journal, 8 July 1793 (*Journals*, p. 81); 21 Nov. 1797 (Sirr papers, 868/1, f. 2); Russell to Templeton, 14 Feb. 1798 (Madden papers, 873/635).

32 Thomas Russell to John Russell (copy), n.d. (Madden papers, 873/673, f. 2); Russell's journal, 25 Nov. 1794 (*Journals*, p. 179). His 'Mourn lost Hibernia...' published in *The Press*, 4 Nov. 1797, was modelled on Smollett's 'Mourn hapless Caledonia...' (Madden papers, 873/673, f. 2); likewise, a poem attributed to him by Madden, 'The negro's lament', was a revision of the work of another unnamed author (Thuente, *The harp re-strung*, pp. 20, 92).

33 Russell's journal, Nov. 1794 [?] (*Journals*, p. 179); Tone, *Writings*, i, 312; Tone to Russell, 9 July 1791 (R.I.A., Burrowes MS 23 K 53).

34 *Dublin Evening Post*, 22 Dec. 1796; 'The fatal battle of Aughrim', *The Press*, 4 Nov. 1797 and manuscript version in Russell's hand (Reb. papers, 620/53/71); see also R. R. Madden, *Literary remains of the United Irishmen* (Dublin, 1887), pp. 284–5; Lewis Goldsmith, *Secret history of the cabinet of Bonaparte* (4th edn, London, 1810), p. 263.

CHAPTER SEVEN

Reason, Romanticisim and Revelation

In January 1794 Russell's spell without regular employment came to an end when he was appointed librarian to Belfast's Society for Promoting Knowledge, later to be better known as the Linenhall Library. This appointment owed much to his friendship with the Belfast physician, Dr James McDonnell. Russell had met McDonnell soon after his arrival in the town in 1790 and, in between his wanderings, he often used the doctor's house in Donegall Place as his home base. McDonnell was one of the notable figures in Belfast's social and cultural life and played a leading part in founding and running several of the town's most important institutions, including the Belfast Society for Promoting Knowledge.[1]

This institution had originally been founded in 1788 by a number of the town's tradesmen as the Belfast Reading Society. Within a few years it had attracted many of Belfast's professionals and merchants and in 1792, in keeping with the rising social profile of its membership, it assumed its more grandiose title. The influx of new members brought prestige and funds and the society broadened its remit, proclaiming as its purpose 'the collection of an extensive library, philosophical apparatus and such productions of nature and art as tend to improve the mind and excite a spirit of general enquiry... [and] to collect such materials as will illustrate the antiquities, the natural, civil, commercial and ecclesiastical history of this country'.[2] Modelled on Manchester's Literary and Philosophic Society, which had been founded in 1781, such institutions made a valuable contribution to the cultural and intellectual life of many industrial towns. They were in keeping with the progressive ethos of the age and were supported by local industrialists eager to encourage the application of science to commercial uses.

Among the society's members were almost all the leading United Irishmen of Belfast as well as some progressively-minded men of moderate reformist politics such as Henry Joy and Robert Stewart (later Lord Castlereagh). Although the society was ostensibly non-political, politics often intruded into its deliberations. In 1792 it passed a resolution in favour of Catholic emancipation and by November 1793, the chairman of the local Whig club, Dr Alexander Haliday, had become anxious about the direction the society was taking. He complained that there were 'sundry members there whose characters, whose principles, and whose spirits I did not like . . . I was early disgusted by an attempt of some of our profound statesmen to render it a *political* as well as a scientific society, *in which they were with some difficulty baffled*'.[3]

Despite Haliday's misgivings, the radical members of the society were soon able to find an outlet for their political sympathies by electing Russell, well-known for his democratic politics, as the society's new librarian. Russell received the news while in Dublin in January 1794 but at first was unenthusiastic about accepting the position — perhaps because of the small salary it carried. However, Tone and Whitley Stokes persuaded him of the folly of refusing an offer of regular and secure employment, and on arrival in Belfast some weeks later he finalised details of his new post.[4] The salary was a modest £50 a year but the librarian's basic duties were not very onerous: he had to be present in the library from Monday to Saturday between 11a.m. and 2 p.m., write to subscribers who had not returned books on time and attend meetings of the society. The job also involved a number of additional tasks, the first of which was to find a new premises for the society's growing stock of books and specimens, and on 27 February 1794 Russell reported back to the society that he had secured the use of a house in Ann St. He also engaged in research in order to give a series of chemical lectures and in December 1794 began work on creating an up-to-date alphabetical catalogue of the society's books, which was duly published the following April.[5] He appears to have taken his position as librarian seriously and carried out all his duties diligently. While in prison, his correspondence with Templeton and McDonnell indicates that he continued to retain a lively interest in the affairs of the library. After his arrest in September 1796 the library went through a difficult period because of the disturbed state of the country and the society's failure to secure a suitable replacement as librarian. However, it still managed to keep afloat, much to the relief of Russell who prophetically forecast that the library would become 'a fine institution for the province, and, perhaps, the whole country'.[6]

For one with Russell's broad range of interests the position of librarian was a most congenial one, the library's stock of several hundred titles covering a broad range of subjects offering great scope for his enquiring mind. In an age before the establishment of rigid professional standards Russell was typical of those enthusiastic amateurs who had no inhibitions about dabbling in a wide variety of scientific disciplines. Prior to his appointment as librarian, he and the Belfast botanist John Templeton had undertaken a tour of the Mourne Mountains in the autumn of 1793, on behalf of the Belfast society, to collect geological and botanical specimens for a new museum. They spent several days in the area observing its topography and rock-formations and gathering samples, and Russell took detailed notes on their observations and the geological structure of the Mournes. Even when not commissioned to engage in such activities, Russell would take whatever opportunities came his way to make observations and take rock samples, doing so frequently on his travels between Belfast and Enniskillen in the hills to the west of Lough Neagh or the mountains of Co. Fermanagh.[7]

In addition to geology and mineralogy Russell's curiosity was also excited by disciplines as diverse as anthropology, chemistry, physics, biology, botany and medicine. He seems to have had some familiarity with the work of several of the leading scientists of the day, including the French chemists Berthollet, Morveau and Fourcroy.[8] In the late eighteenth century an interest in science often went hand in hand with a desire for political reform and many radicals saw science as an important vehicle for social improvement. There was a widely-held belief that humanity, as well as increasing its command over the natural world, could also discover and master the principles of politics and replace the existing irrational and unnatural system of government with one in harmony with reason and nature. Joseph Priestley, whose work Russell had read and admired, was only one notable example of the many intellectuals who applied their enquiring minds to politics as well as science. In an age in which there was a widespread belief that the human race was advancing on all fronts, many shared the euphoria of the Revd. Samuel Barber, one of the leading 'New Light' ministers of Ulster Presbyterianism, who rejoiced at 'the progress of science, which must ever be favourable to truth and fatal to error. Science enlarges the mind, ascertains the rights of man, and before science, sooner or later, all tyranny will fall.'[9] Like many radicals Russell believed that the diffusion of knowledge would help bring about political enlightenment and enable all to play their rightful role in political life. He was therefore interested in modern notions of education, such as encouraging children to write descriptively rather than them learning verses by rote. He also strongly approved of the establishment of reading societies which he believed could play an important role in the education of the poor and one of his journal entries suggests he believed that women deserved as good an education as men.[10]

Russell read widely and enjoyed the company of intellectuals, numbering among his friends such distinguished Irish intellectuals as Revd. Edward Berwick, chaplain to Lord Moira, and an accomplished author and classicist; Revd. John Stack, a fellow of Trinity College, Dublin, and secretary of the Royal Irish Academy; Whitley Stokes, also a fellow of Trinity College, a physician who published several works on politics, economics and religion — Tone regarded him as the individual best qualified to head a national system of education should Ireland achieve independence.[11] Russell was also acquainted with Richard Kirwan, a close friend of Priestley and one of the most respected chemists and mineralogists of the age, who became president of the Royal Irish Academy in 1799.[12] It is possible that Russell also corresponded with Priestley and Dr Joseph Black, professor of chemistry at Edinburgh University.[13]

Despite his genuine enthusiasm for learning, Russell's intellectual eclecticism, combined with a less than assiduous approach, meant that he spread himself thinly over a number of disciplines without particularly distinguishing himself in any. His friend Dr James McDonnell noted that unlike Tone who was 'perspicuous and discriminating' Russell 'was diffuse, easily taken with novelties, and soon generalised'.[14] Moreover, Russell's scientific experiments could at times be eccentric, not to say foolhardy. On one occasion he allowed himself to be bled and fasted for three days to see the effect that it would have on his pulse.[15] His intellectual impulsiveness was such that before his excursion to the Mourne Mountains McDonnell felt it necessary to give him some advice:

> remember not to observe and reason too rashly, not to jump to conclusions so rapidly, not to move in so straight and direct a line towards the inferences in tracing the position of the strata, the direction of the mountains and the nature of the fossils, in your mineralogical tour, as you seem to have done in your enquiries into the structure of society, for the history of nature is full of turnings and subtleties, which are not seen at one glance as political truths *are* by simple intuition.[16]

As McDonnell's warning suggests Russell's enthusiasm could at times get the better of him. An example of this is a draft essay in which he delved into political economy and sought to explain England's relatively low level of population and its inability to sustain the level of taxes required to fight a long war against France. Russell claimed that the factory system damaged the health and the child-bearing capacity of its female employees, deprived them of domestic skills and generally rendered them ill-equipped to manage households. He also argued that the burden of poor law charges led parishes to forbid the poor to settle within their boundaries, discouraging marriage and encouraging infanticide and abortion among the lower orders. He then went on to claim that one of the main reasons for England's relatively low population was that the country bred an excessive number of horses 'for the purposes of pleasure and trade and especially agriculture' and since a horse required as much food as would sustain four people, 'men may be said to toil for beasts and not beasts for men'. He pointed out the examples of China, Japan and especially India, where horses were rarely used on farms, with ploughing normally being done by cows or bullocks, and that all were very populous countries.[17] Perhaps fortunately for Russell, the essay never seems to have gone beyond the draft stage.

As with his politics, Russell's Christian beliefs were the over-riding influence on his intellectual pursuits. His interest in geology seems to have stemmed mainly from a desire to find evidence in support of scriptural accounts of creation. In a letter to Templeton he recalled that he became interested in the subject when confronted with theories of creation which he believed were 'inconsistent with revelation, and were used as arguments against it'. While observing geological formations on his travels he noted with particular eagerness anything that seemed to support the biblical account of the Great Flood. In response to Templeton's assertion that he was a 'Neptunist' rather than a 'Vulcanist' (i.e. one who held that most geological features had been shaped by the sea rather than by volcanic eruptions) Russell replied that he was 'of no theory except the account contained in the scriptures'.[18] The broad range of Russell's interests can partly be explained by his desire to explore and celebrate the beauty and diversity of God's creation. Templeton was obviously writing to a kindred spirit when he claimed that 'the Almighty Creator... has allowed it to be the purest part of human happiness, to unfold the volume of nature, which gradually exposes to our view the hidden causes of particular effects'.[19] For Russell the appreciation of nature was an emotional and deeply religious experience. While in prison he expressed the hope that he would in the future 'make some pleasant journeys, contemplating the works of nature and adoring its Divine Author'. On his rambles he was enraptured by spectacular natural scenes: those which were 'lonely and wild', by the 'sublime noises of rain and wind' or 'solitude, silence and wildness', by steep mountains, cascading waterfalls and raging torrents.[20]

In his reverential attitude to nature, as in so many other ways, there is much of the stereotypical Romantic about Russell. He was a passionate, introspective man who revelled in his emotions: he held his religious and political beliefs with a fervent intensity and his feelings of love, lust and anguish were invariably taken to extremes; in his tendency to indulge in the private expression of his grief and anguish he seems the very model of the late eighteenth-century 'man of sentiment'.[21] His Romanticism is also evident in his passion for Gothic novels — the works of Ann Radcliffe such as *The romance of the forest* (1791), *The mysteries of Udolpho* (1794) and *The Italian* (1797) were particular favourites.[22] These were novels of pure melodramatic excess, crammed with isolated castles, dingy dungeons, ghostly spectres, fierce thunderstorms, pursued maidens and evil villains.

Another example of his literary tastes which showed a more earthy side to his Romanticism was a small chapbook found among his papers. Besides the anti-slavery poem 'The negro's lament', it contained a lusty drinking song, a love song called 'Answer to the farmer's daughter' about an elopement, and a bawdy ballad entitled 'In praise of the sporting plowman; or Bartly M'Cuskers frolick' which contained lines such as:

> You lasses fair to me repair
> And hear my declaration o
> I'm ready now your lands to plow
> That's fit for cultivation o
> ...
> Should maid's agree I still make free
> Yet never loves to tease them o
> When they are bent or gives consent
> I do my best to please them o

As Mary Helen Thuente notes, a work that contained songs about anti-slavery, a love affair, drinking and philandering seems to be a fair representation of some of Russell's diverse interests.[23]

Some short extracts from Rousseau's *La Nouvelle Héloïse*, one of the seminal works of Romanticism, are to be found copied out in his personal papers.[24] It is not surprising that Russell so admired William Godwin — a writer whose influence was greatest on the Romantic poets — Blake, Wordsworth, Coleridge, Southey and especially Shelley. Hazlitt wrote of the attractiveness of Godwin's ideas to such passionate minds: 'there was nothing better calculated to at once feed and make steady the enthusiasm of youthful patriots than the high speculations in which he taught them to engage on the nature of social evils and the great destiny of his species'.[25] Despite his claim that he found little new in William Godwin's *An enquiry concerning political justice* (1793), Russell considered it a 'masterly' work.[26] Godwin's trenchant criticisms of Britain's political, legal and ecclesiastical institutions struck a chord with Russell. The central idea of *Political justice* was that man should ignore the oppressive apparatus of the state and trust his private judgement. This would allow free scope for the development of his natural benevolence which would enable him to live peaceably and usefully with other men without the restraints imposed by law and government.[27] Similar ideas were espoused by many millennialists such as Russell, who argued that the oppressive nature of government was to blame for most of society's ills and that as government withered away a better world would follow.

Russell firmly believed that the governments of the day were responsible for frustrating the divine plan of liberty and justice for all. It was they who stood between the poor and a decent life. Russell noted with approval Paine's distinction between government and society: Paine argued that 'society is produced by our wants, and government by our wickedness; the former promotes our happiness *positively* by uniting our affections, the latter *negatively* by restraining our vices ... Society in every state is a blessing, but government, even in its best state, is but a necessary evil'.[28] Russell maintained that in future 'gover[n]ments will be almost totally done away [*sic*] and little more than society remain. I think in proportion as gover[n]ments grow more simple, men will be better. His duty to his god and his interest will clash less. As he has less to do with human laws he will have more inclination to respect divine ones.'[29] According to Russell, these human laws:

are to be obeyed so far as they consist with the divine will and no further. No human law can justify a breach of the law of God, and whenever laws are made in contradiction to it, they should be resisted. This respect for and obedience to human laws has been one of the greatest causes of the calamities which fill the annals of mankind. Reason was so corrupted that men conceived themselves justified in killing their fellow creatures and taking their property, and otherwise torturing them, if there was a law commanding it.[30]

Russell's philosophical outlook seems to have owed much to the Romantic commonplaces of the day, such as the 'the noble savage' and the distrust of the omnipotence of reason. The concluding lines of one of his republican songs proclaimed his belief that 'further years will prove the truth / That man is good by nature'.[31] This was a theme that reoccurred frequently in writings which showed his fascination with distant and savage cultures. In his journals and in notes jotted down from travel books he contrasts the ingenuousness and simplicity of uncivilised peoples with the artifice and greed of Europeans. For example, in an anti-slavery essay he quoted the French botanist Michel Adanson's rather fanciful description of the earthly paradise from which the Africans were seized:

> Which way so ever I turned my eyes on this pleasant spot...I beheld a perfect image of human nature...the ease and indolence of the negroes reclined under the shade of their spreading foliage; the simplicity of their dress and manners, the whole revived in my mind the idea of our first parents, and I seemed to contemplate the world in its primitive state; they are generally speaking very good-natured, sociable and obliging, honest in their dealings, friendly to strangers, of a mild disposition, conversible [*sic*], affable, and easy to overcome with reason...The more discerning of them account it the greatest unhappiness that they were ever visited by Europeans, the 'Christians' having introduced the traffic of slaves and banished that peace from amongst them that they formerly lived in.[32]

Because he regarded man as a naturally benevolent creature, Russell, like Godwin, believed that humanity was capable of dramatic improvement, particularly once the oppressive shackles of the state were removed and as human beings grew more virtuous, so society would become more just and equitable.[33] His broad intellectual interests are partly explained by his desire for 'improvement'. Several friends refer to him as an 'improving' companion and his desire to visit places such as the monastic ruins on Devenish island or the Moravian community near Ballymena and take substantial notes of his visits, smack of an earnest desire to turn his talents and his time to the best possible account.[34]

The concept of human perfectibility also found a strong echo in his ideas on the moral reformation of his personal life. Although the chasm between his desire to live piously and the reality of his personal behaviour often left him bewildered and depressed, Russell continued to hope that some day he would mend his ways. One of his main reasons for keeping a journal was that it might in time reveal to him 'a progression in virtue'. During his time in prison he expressed the hope that 'every year I live I shall improve, either in or out of prison'. Time after time he subjected himself to bouts of self-examination, in which he was invariably found wanting. After yet another fall from grace he concluded: 'such I am — so vicious, so imperfect, with wishes and desire for virtue and a firm belief in revelation, and yet lapsing into vice on the slightest temptation. I do not improve'.[35]

Russell's personal problems probably also contributed to his belief in another Romantic tenet — the distrust of the omnipotence of reason. He knew only too well the inadequacy of human reason when it clashed with powerful desires, and he often demonstrated a preoccupation with the irrational, writing of ghosts and the possibility that dreams might foretell the future. For many years he planned to write a work in which he would examine 'the insufficiency of reason' as a philosophical creed.[36] A visit to the Moravian settlement at Ballykennedy, near Ballymena, Co. Antrim, where marriages were arranged by the communities elders set him thinking on the age-old conflict between human passions and reason. Although many of the arranged marriages were successful Russell was relieved to learn that things had not always proceeded in such a rational manner and that some people had quit the community when refused permission to marry those they had fallen in love with. He mused:

> it appears that the power of Love is not dimin[i]sh'd in the regions of Bally Kennedy. It seems indeed to be a passion like all others which may be suppress'd but cannot and perhaps ought not to be extinguish'd. That it will exist independent of reason is evident when an attachment is form'd without an acquaintance with each other's character. Like the other passions it may be regulated and directed to the best purposes. The sensations attending it are far more exquisite than any other.[37]

Perhaps the main reason why Russell was convinced of the inadequacy of pure reason was his belief that reason alone was not enough
to reconcile people to Christianity. Reflecting in his journal on the
philosophy of the ancient Stoics, he noted that 'the light of reason
was sufficient to point out the evil of our present state though not the
remedy, and indeed the necessity of revelation strongly appears from
this'. He believed that the Stoics' disinterested pursuit of virtue for its
own sake could not be emulated by ordinary mortals who needed the
prospect of eternal reward as an incentive to live virtuously.[38]

As a convinced Christian, Russell viewed with deep concern the
progress of deism, a religious creed based purely on reason. He was
the likely author of an article in the *Northern Star* criticising Paine's
Age of reason (1794), by far the most popular statement of deism
written in these years, in which Paine irreverently dismissed most
Christian dogma as nonsense and set out his belief in a Supreme
Being who revealed himself solely through nature. This article maintained that 'revelation is but part of the broad basis on which
religion rests, and that although by taking it away, virtue loses an
able friend she is not entirely without an advocate'.[39] Russell's
nephew claimed that he had a copy of a work written by his uncle
refuting the *Age of reason*.[40] This was probably a work published in
Belfast in 1794 entitled *Paine's Age of reason, with remarks containing a vindication of the doctrines of Christianity from the aspersions
of that author* by 'A citizen of the world'. Russell's papers contain
comments on extracts from the *Age of reason* in which he criticises
Paine's assertions point by point and which appear to be an early
draft for such a work. He takes Paine to task for what he claims was
his repeated misuse of the word 'revelation' and his inaccurate and
selective use of scriptural quotations. Russell himself had an excellent knowledge of scripture. His grasp of the classics was good
enough to allow him to read the Bible in the original Greek and he
even began to learn Hebrew to delve deeper into the texts.[41]

However, the evidence suggests that the more likely author of the
work against the *Age of reason* was not Russell but an acquaintance
of his — the Scottish author and scientist James Tytler, who went by
the name of Donaldson in Belfast.[42] A man of many talents, in 1776
Tytler wrote and edited most of the second edition of *Encyclopaedia
Britannica* and was the first person in Britain to make a balloon
flight — at Edinburgh in 1784. He began to publish a journal in
1791, *The Historical Register,* in which he set out advanced radical
views. In November 1792 he published a hastily written pamphlet in

which he denounced the British House of Commons as 'a vile junto of aristocrats'. After a warrant had been issued for his arrest on a charge of seditious libel he fled to Ireland in January 1793 where he stayed for two and a half years.[43] It seems that the Belfast United Irishmen gave some consideration to using Tytler as an emissary, but in the end decided against it, much to his annoyance. In July 1795 he emigrated to America, where he in 1796 wrote *Paine's second part of the age of reason answered*. Tytler appears to have had a significant influence on Russell, and wrote to him from America.[44] Russell negotiated with Belfast booksellers to improve the terms for the sale of Tytler's work and sent a copy of it to Whitley Stokes. In his *Letter to the people of Ireland,* Russell referred to him as 'the excellent Mr Tytler' and quoted him as an authority on economic matters. Several of Tytler's opinions and discoveries were also cited by Russell in his prison correspondence.[45]

Russell believed that revelation was an essential element in cementing Christian beliefs and that abandoning belief in revelation was the thin end of a wedge that led to atheism. His discussions with Tytler, who was also a keen student of scripture, convinced him of this even more. Mixing in radical circles, however, Russell would have met those who shared Paine's religious views. One account of Russell's life informs us that he 'was frequently obliged to defend Christianity against the sallies of Tone and others of his associates'. Several entries in Russell's journal are written in such a way as to answer objections to traditional religious beliefs, and were probably written up in the wake of arguments with friends.[46] He seems to have crossed swords regularly on this issue with Samuel Neilson, whose Presbyterianism was apparently being gradually supplanted by deism and who admired Paine's *Age of reason*. Russell, while acknowledging that it was more usual for him to receive advice from Neilson than to give it, nonetheless cautioned him to:

> be more circumspect in your conduct...if Christianity should indeed be true, could anything be more dreadful than taking from any living soul the eternal blessing which it offers. No person can be justifiable in acting as though it were false, 'till he has dispassionately weighed the evidences, if it be a revelation from Heaven it is but reasonable to suppose that appropriate evidences will be afforded to such as show due humility...if it is attempted by minds biased by vice and vanity or hardening themselves in incredulity and demanding a sign, it is equally reasonable to suppose that such will be suffered to continue in error.[47]

Although Russell frequently had to play the role of Christian apologist among his close friends, his anti-deist views were widely shared in Irish radical circles. The general reaction of Irish radicals to the *Age of reason* was hostile and a number of them published works criticising it. Most Irish radicals saw no incompatibility between Christianity and democracy and resented that Paine's foray into theology had allowed the authorities to brand them all as atheists.[48]

One of the ways in which Christians countered deist arguments was by claiming that the fulfilling of scriptural prophecies proved the truth of Christianity. Eighteenth-century Christian apologists who sought to reconcile reason and revelation 'encouraged an emphasis upon prophecy as a demonstration of God's power which could be verified by human experience'. Therefore, if biblical prophecies were being fulfilled this would prove the reality of divine power and the truth of the Bible.[49] Thus, the same people were often found propagating millennialist beliefs and attempting to counter the deist assault on Christianity and several of Russell's acquaintances published works in both these areas.[50] Among these was Tytler, who confided his apocalyptic belief to Russell 'that this country and England will be deluged with blood'. Tytler wrote several tracts on revealed religion during his time in Edinburgh, as well as his counter-blasts to Paine in 1794 and 1797, and among his many publications was a millennialist pamphlet in which he applauded the example given by the Americans to Europe in winning their freedom and argued that if the Scots and Irish united against England they could bring 'that proud and tyrannical nation' to its knees. He claimed that the French were 'led and protected by divine power. They have in a great measure overthrown that monstrous system of superstition and spiritual tyranny in scripture called Babylon the Great ... They have denied revelation, and yet they have fought in favour of it. Their cause is that of the whole world.'[51]

Just as millennialism provided a compelling motivation for Russell's political activities, so his interest in scientific matters, in education and in defending Christianity against its detractors can be seen as part of his overall effort to create the conditions for the inauguration of Christ's future kingdom. What has been said of Richard Price and Joseph Priestley, that 'they brought their wide-ranging interests into a synthesis where every aspect of their thought — moral, political, scientific, economic, and theological — was related to and held together by the overall, controlling element of their millennialism', could equally be said of Russell.[52]

Russell's sympathy with contemporary Romantic beliefs was also evident in his interest in folk culture. His position as librarian of the Belfast Society for Promoting Knowledge, one of the aims of which was 'to receive and encourage all communications concerning the antiquities of Ireland', allowed some scope for the development of this interest. The society organised the harpers' festival of July 1792, primarily under the patronage of Russell's friend, Dr James McDonnell.[53] This was followed up by an announcement in March 1793 that the society proposed to publish the tunes collected at the festival, and in October it set up a sub-committee of James McDonnell, William Sampson and George Madden to consult the musician Edward Bunting on the manner of publication. Russell was a friend of Bunting, who was then living with the McCracken family, and he soon became involved in the undertaking. It proved to be a time-consuming and expensive task, and as time dragged on many members of the society, including Bunting himself, began to lose interest. Russell, however, continued to insist that the society should keep up its support of the project, and intervened when it showed signs of flagging. Bunting's *A general collection of the ancient Irish music* was finally published in November 1797, and it would in time provide the foundation text for Thomas Moore's celebrated *Irish melodies*.[54] An entry in Russell's journal suggests that he himself tried his hand at playing these tunes on the harp and throughout his life he maintained a strong interest in Bunting's work. He requested a copy of the published music from Newgate in 1798 and he continued to send tunes to Bunting while in prison in Scotland some years later. On his release from prison in 1802 he wrote to a friend that he was taking his copy of Bunting's work with him to the Continent, where he would do his best to publicise it.[55]

Russell also had an interest in the Irish language. In 1794 he began to take Irish lessons from Patrick Lynch, a Gaelic scholar from Loughinisland, Co. Down; he probably already had some familiarity with Irish from his childhood in counties Cork and Kilkenny. The following year, it is likely that Russell was involved in the publication by the *Northern Star* of an Irish textbook for those who wished to learn the language, entitled *Bolg an tSolair,* which contained a short Irish grammar and vocabulary, and dialogues, verses and songs in Irish with English translations.[56] Some time earlier the *Star*, in an editorial which may well have been written by Russell, had encouraged its readers to learn the Irish language pointing out how this would allow them to 'more easily and effectually communicate our sentiments and instructions to all our countrymen' and thus help forge the union of all Irishmen.[57]

It was probably Russell who introduced his Irish teacher Patrick Lynch to Whitley Stokes, and paved the way for the two to co-operate in the production of an Irish translation of the New Testament. Both Stokes and Lynch discussed the project in their correspondence with Russell in the early months of 1796.[58] Russell may also have introduced Lynch to Edward Bunting, who later employed him to travel through Irish-speaking areas in Connacht collecting the original words for the tunes Bunting had already recorded.[59]

The growing interest in the Belfast of the 1790s in Irish culture drew largely on materials produced by antiquarian scholars during the upsurge of curiosity in the Gaelic past which had begun in the mid-eighteenth century. While some had been interested in this heritage for its own sake, there were also those Irish Protestant nationalists who sought to bolster their demands for greater political autonomy by staking their claim to a separate, distinctive culture. To counteract the traditional English view of Gaelic Ireland as a country sunk in poverty, ignorance and superstition, Anglo-Irish scholars represented it as a land which had nurtured an ancient and heroic civilisation, and which exerted an enlightened influence on European culture in both pagan and Christian times.[60] Similarly, in the 1790s interest in the Gaelic past stemmed from a combination of cultural and political motives. Extolling the glories of Ireland's Gaelic heritage could have obvious political implications, most notably by creating a new pride in being Irish and by implying that if all Irishmen adopted the Gaelic past as their common inheritance, the religious and cultural divisions of previous centuries could be bridged.

Such arguments had an obvious appeal to the United Irishmen and elements within the movement did their best to publicise those aspects of Ireland's past of which all Irishmen could rightly be proud. The *Northern Star* praised 'those admirable specimens of musical composition' collected at the Belfast harpers' festival of 1792 for 'affording a new and very decisive proof of the existence of a very high degree of civilisation among our ancestors, at a period when the greatest part of Europe was buried in the deepest barbarity and ignorance'.[61] The preface to *Bolg an tSolair*, written by Patrick Lynch, extolled the beauties of the Gaelic language since 'many tongues and pens have been employed to cry it down, and to persuade the ignorant that it was a harsh and barbarous jargon, and that their ancestors, from whom they derived it, were an ignorant, uncultivated people'. Lynch maintained that on the contrary the language 'will be found by the unprejudiced ear to excel in the harmony of its cadence...It is also a rich and copious language, abounding with terms of art...never was any language fitter to express the feelings of the heart...[and] no nation ever encouraged poets and musicians more than the ancient Irish'.[62]

In their efforts to strip the United Irishmen of the anachronistic cultural values attributed to them by later nationalists, some modern historians have gone too far in portraying the entire movement as cosmopolitans who were contemptuous of Gaelic culture.[63] Tone's dismissive reaction to the Belfast harpers' festival — *'strum, strum, and be hang'd'* — has been eagerly seized upon as representing the attitude of the entire movement to the Gaelic past. Yet, temptingly quotable as this remark is, it is not even an accurate reflection of Tone's attitude towards Irish music, let alone the verdict of the United Irish movement as a whole towards native culture.[64] The United Irishmen's stated decision to think 'little about our ancestors' did not involve a blanket rejection of the past, but rather of the internecine feuding of previous centuries. Although the United Irishmen were much given to internationalist rhetoric, they also frequently high-lighted the distinctiveness of Ireland's culture and traditions. Much United Irish propaganda, especially songs and verse, extolled the glories of old Ireland and invoked traditional Irish icons and images — St Patrick, Granuaile, Brian Boru, the harp, the shamrock, the colour green — in an effort to stir up national sentiment and stress Ireland's separateness from England. Russell was in the forefront of a group of Irish radicals, which included William Sampson, William James McNeven, Whitley Stokes, and Robert Emmet, that took a real interest in Ireland's Gaelic heritage and sought to create a distinctive national culture in which all Irishmen could share.[65]

It must be conceded, however, that these were tentative moves. The United Irishmen drew only fitfully on Ireland's cultural heritage and never argued that cultural distinctiveness alone justified Irish inde-pendence.[66] As with the United Irishmen in general, it would not do to overstate Russell's interest in Gaelic culture: references to it in his papers are fleeting and it never seems to have exerted anything of the same hold over his imagination as did political or religious matters.

On his rambles through Ulster Russell came into close contact with the culture of ordinary people. He would have almost certainly seen performances of Robert Ashton's *Battle of Aughrim*, which has

been described as the Ulster folk play 'par excellence'.[67] An awareness of this play probably influenced Russell in his writing of a poem
entitled *The fatal battle of Aughrim* — Mary Helen Thuente notes
that 'Russell's poem reads like a poetic gloss' to Ashton's play.[68] In a
letter to his brother Russell wrote that, while brooding 'over the
injuries of my country', he came across a work by Smollett on the
conquest of Scotland beginning 'Mourn hapless Caledonia, mourn',
which inspired him to write a similar work based on the Irish experience. This was published in the *Press* in November 1797:[69]

> *Mourn lost Hibernia, ever mourn,*
> *Thy freedom lost, thy laurels torn,*
> *Thy warriors sunk on Aughrim's plains,*
> *And Britain loading thee with chains,*
> ...
> *Her stern oppression grinds the state,*
> *Its iron hand prescribes thy fate.*
> *Thy nobles, a degenerate race,*
> *Corrupt, rapacious, sordid, base*
> *Anxious their ill-got wealth to save*
> *And slaves themselves — to rule the slave.*
> ...
> *With merciless and ruffian power,*
> *Invade the sacred midnight hour,*
> *Religion, morals, laws effaced,*
> *Devouring flames the cottage waste*
> *And violation stalks around*
> *Murder and lust pollute the ground.*
> *They mock the trembling mother's pain,*
> *The tears of beauty plead in vain!*
> *The rocks resound with widow's cries*
> *The suffering air with orphaned sighs!*
> ...
> *Cowards thy prostrate power deride,*
> *Lost is thy independent pride,*
> *And ceased thy harp's melodious sound*
> *And thy green standard trails the ground.*
> *Thy honour and defence no more,*
> *Defiled with dust, distained with gore,*
> *Thy warriors stretched on Aughrim's plains*
> *And Britain smiling at thy pains,*
> *Thy freedom lost, thy laurels torn*
> *Mourn, lost Hibernia — ever mourn!*[70]

The poem can be read as a lament for the old Gaelic order, but given its condemnation of 'degenerate' nobles, 'vile informers' and the unleashing of the 'ruffian power' of a tyrannical government on a defenceless people, it was intended to say more about the 1790s than the 1690s. The *Press* referred to it as a work 'translated from the Irish', possibly to create a sense of the timelessness of Ireland's struggle. It also had the distinction of being quoted in part in the report of the 1798 parliamentary secret committee as a typical example of the subversive literature that issued from United Irish presses.[71]

The sentiments it contained, however, did not always meet with the approval of Russell's United Irish colleagues. Robert Simms, for one, still clung to the conventional Whig view of the Glorious Revolution and wrote that he had no wish to mourn the outcome of the battle of Aughrim since he believed that:

> it was happy for the world that the English government succeeded. If Lewis [*sic*] had been able to have placed James on the throne of Great Britain and Ireland, despotism would have reigned all over Europe and the human race been thrown back a century, and in place of our seeing a government patronising *Locke on government* we should have seen them patronise passive obedience and nonresistance.[72]

It was just this type of controversy that the United Irishmen hoped to avoid by their decision not to dredge up the events of the past. As Nancy Curtin has pointed out, Irish radicals were generally far more reluctant than their English counterparts to support their demands by reference to precedent. In Ireland to invoke the name of William III and the Glorious Revolution, for example, 'was only to remind Catholics of how their civil and political liberties had been crushed by triumphant Protestantism'.[73] Instead, the more pro-Catholic elements within the United Irishmen often questioned Protestant veneration of such icons. Russell and Sampson's *The lion of old England* mocked the Glorious Revolution as an event which 'preserved us from wooden shoes and left us free to go barefoot'.[74] Russell took particular care to portray a view of the past that offered Catholics some solace. Writing to a Catholic correspondent soon after the founding of the United Irishmen in October 1791, he was anxious to inform him that a new version of Tone's *Argument on behalf of the Catholics* would contain 'a damned hard side blow at King William' and to assure him that 'this is the first strike at his memory, but it will not be the last'.[75] It is possible that Russell's view was influenced by his own family history: with Catholics on both sides of his family he was aware that his own ancestors had been among the victims of the Williamite settlement. In his journal he recalled the dispossession after 1691 of the Catholic O'Clears, the family of his paternal grandmother, with sadness and apparent resentment that they had been sent into life as 'beggars'.[76]

Differing attitudes to the Catholic defeats of the previous century were often a touchstone of the divisions in the United Irishmen between secular republicanism and sectarian Defenderism, and strained United Irish unity and cohesion. Along with several other high-ranking northern leaders, Robert Simms refused to act when rebellion erupted in the south in the summer of 1798 and also rejected Russell's overtures to take the field in 1803. One account of the 1798 rebellion in Ulster tells of a United Irish regiment making its way to battle when a Munster Catholic, who had deserted from the regular army and been given charge of a rebel unit, waved his sword in the air and shouted, much to the consternation of his Presbyterian comrades: 'by J-s, boys, we'll pay the rascals this day for the battle of the Boyne!'.[77]

Significantly, *The fatal battle of Aughrim* never found its way into the *Northern Star*, but was published by the *Press* in 1797, at a time when religious polarisation was rapidly on the increase and some United Irishmen, especially the editors of the *Press*, were prepared to exploit sectarian tensions to enlist support.

NOTES

1 David Kennedy, 'James McDonnell, 1762–1845' in *Capuchin Annual* (1945–6), p. 353; Peter Froggatt, 'Dr James McDonnell' in *The Glynns*, ix (1981), p. 20; Anna McCleery, 'Life of Mary Ann McCracken' in Robert M. Young (ed.), *Historical notices of old Belfast* (Belfast, 1896), p. 189.
2 John Killen, *A history of the Linenhall Library, 1788–1988* (Belfast, 1988), pp. 7–14; Belfast Soc. minute books, 1 Jan. 1794.
3 List of the society's members (Sirr papers, 868/2, f. 196); D. J. Owen, *A history of Belfast* (Belfast, 1921), p. 184; Haliday to Charlemont, Nov. 1793 (*Charlemont MS*, ii, 395).
4 Belfast Soc. minute books, 8 Jan., 20 Feb. 1794; Russell's journal, 18 Jan., 20 Feb. 1794 (*Journals*, pp. 140, 146).
5 Librarian's rules (Reb. papers, 620/20/16); Belfast Soc. minute books, 27 Feb., 4 Dec. 1794; John Anderson, *History of the Linenhall Library* (Belfast, 1888), p. 13; Russell's journal, 9 Mar. 1794 (*Journals*, p. 146); John Killen, *A history of the Linenhall Library, 1788–1988* (Belfast, 1988), p. 19; for the catalogue itself see Reb. papers, 620/20/16.
6 Templeton to Russell, Sept. 1797 (Madden, *United Irishmen*, 3rd ser., ii, 190); Russell to Templeton, 10 Sept. 1797 (Madden papers, 873/634).

7 Russell's journal, 1–4 Sept., 30 Sept. to 8 Oct., 18 Nov. 1793 (*Journals*, pp. 109–21, 125–32, 135).

8 Scientific notes by Russell (Sirr papers, 868/1, f. 88); Russell's journal, 13 Mar. 1795 (*Journals*, p. 185).

9 See, for example, Conrad Russell, *Science and social change 1700–1900* (London, 1983), chapters 6 and 8; *Journals*, pp. 49, 133, 184; W. D. Bailie, 'Revd. Samuel Barber, 1738–1811, national Volunteer and United Irishman' in J. L. M. Haire (ed.), *Challenge and conflict: essays in Presbyterian doctrine* (Antrim, 1981), p. 82.

10 Russell's journal, 11 July 1793 (*Journals*, pp. 84, 86).

11 Bartlett, *Life of Tone*, p. 844; see also the copy of Stokes's *Disputatio inauguralis de respiratione* sent to Russell 'with the affectionate regards of the author' (Reb. papers, 620/20/35) and correspondence between Russell and Stokes (Sirr papers, 868/2, ff 189, 192–201).

12 *D.N.B.* For contacts with Kirwan see Russell's journal, 2 Sept. 1793, 24 Sept. 1794 (*Journals*, pp. 112, 159), Thomas Russell to John Russell, Fort George, 10 Dec. 1800 (copy) (Madden papers, 873/655, f. 7) and Thomas Russell to Margaret Russell, 2 June 1802 (Sirr papers, 868/1, ff 301–2); for Kirwan's friendship with Priestley, see F. W. Gibbs, *Joseph Priestley* (London, 1965), p. 89.

13 Russell's journal, 20 Oct. 1793, 11 July 1793 (*Journals*, pp. 133, 86).

14 Madden, *United Irishmen*, 3rd ser., ii, 280.

15 Russell's journal, 5–8 Nov. 1794 (*Journals*, pp. 174–7).

16 McDonnell to Russell, n.d. (Sirr papers, 868/2, ff 135–6).

17 Notes by Russell, *c.* 1797–8 (Sirr papers, 868/1, ff 187–9, 323).

18 Russell's journal, 4 Sept. 1793 (*Journals*, p. 121); Templeton to Russell, 29 Jan. 1798 (Madden papers, 873/632); Russell to Templeton, 14 Feb. 1798 (Madden papers, 873/635).

19 Templeton to Russell, 19 Mar. 1797 (Sirr papers, 868/2, ff 270–71).

20 Russell to Templeton, 2 Sept. 1800 (Madden papers, 873/636); Russell's journal, 7 May, 3 Sept., 30 Sept. 1793 (*Journals*, pp. 74–5, 118, 129).

21 John Mullan, *Sentiment and sociability: the language of feeling in the eighteenth century* (Oxford, 1988), pp. 15–16.

22 Martha McTier to Drennan, 17 Mar. 1797 (Drennan papers, T765/652).

23 Reb. papers, 620/20/35; Thuente, *Harp re-strung*, pp. 19–20.

24 For extracts from *La Nouvelle Héloïse*, see Sirr papers, 868/1, f. 206.

25 W. C. Hazlitt (ed), *Letters of Charles Lamb* (London, 1886), i, 209; cited in Albert Goodwin, *The friends of liberty* (London, 1979), p. 475.

26 Russell's journal, 20 Oct. 1793 (*Journals*, p. 133).

27 William Godwin, 'Perusal of Dr Parr's Spital Sermon' p. 326, appendix to K. Codell Carter, (ed.), *Enquiry concerning political justice* (Oxford, 1971).

28 Thomas Paine, 'Common sense' (Moncure Daniel Conway (ed.), *The writings of Thomas Paine* (New York, 1967), i, 69).

29 Russell's journal, 9 July 1793 (*Journals*, p. 83).

30 Russell, *Letter to the people*, p. 19.

31 'Death or liberty' ballad, Russell's papers, seized 16 Sept. 1796 (Reb. papers, 620/16/3).

32 'Enslavement of the Africans', [Russell] to *Northern Star*, 11 Feb. 1792 (Reb. papers, 620/19/56) — for Russell's authorship see below p. 80, n. 5 — the work was apparently Adanson's 'account of Goru/Goree and Senegal'; for other notes on this theme see Sirr papers, 868/1, ff 239–40, 251; Russell's journal, 23 June 1793 (*Journals*, p. 79) and Russell, *Letter to the people*, p. 13.

33 Russell's journal, 9 July 1793 (*Journals*, p. 83).

34 W. Irwin to Russell, *c.* 1798 (P.R.O.N.I. T913); Martha McTier to Sarah Drennan, Sept. 1803 (*Drennan letters*, p. 328); Russell's journal, 24 Nov. 1793, 9 Oct. 1794 (*Journals*, pp. 136–7, 163–70).

35 Russell's journal, 3 Nov. 1794 (Sirr papers, 868/1, f. 15); Thomas Russell to Margaret Russell, 22 Nov. 1801 (Sirr papers, 868/1, ff 289–90); Russell's journal, 9 June 1794 (*Journals*, p. 151).

36 Russell's journal, 30 Sept. 1793, June 1792 (*Journals*, pp. 129, 62–3); 21 Nov. 1797 (Sirr papers, 868/1, f. 2).

37 Russell's journal, Oct. 1794 (*Journals*, p. 168).

38 Russell's journal, 14 Aug. 1793 (*Journals*, pp. 91–2).

39 McGiolla Easpaig, *Ruiséil*, p. 88; this claim is based on the reminiscences of Mary Ann McCracken (Madden papers, 873/670); *Northern Star*, 11 Sept. 1794.

40 J. A. Russell to Madden, 27/28 Feb. 1843 (Madden papers, 873/670).

41 Sirr papers, 868/1, ff 209–12; reminiscences of Mary Ann McCracken and memo from J. A. Russell (Madden papers, 873/155; 873/672v; 873/674, f. 3v).

42 Mac Giolla Easpaig, *Ruiséil*, pp. 88–9; Russell's journal, 5 Nov. 1794 (*Journals*, p. 174); Mac Giolla Easpaig's claim that Donaldson was the chief author of the *Vindication* is supported by the evidence of John Smith, the government informer, who refers to a man named 'Titlar' [*sic*] who fled from Scotland to Belfast after the dispersal of the 'Scotch Convention' and took the name Donaldson. 'He was a man of genius but very poor [and] wrote ... an answer to Paine's *Age of reason*' (Reb. papers, 620/27/1).

43 James Fergusson, *Balloon Tytler* (London, 1972), pp. 11, 121–24; *D.N.B.*

44 James Tytler to Russell, Salem, Sept. 1795 (Sirr papers, 868/2, ff 182–3); James Fergusson, *Balloon Tytler* (London, 1972), p. 135.

45 Russell, *Letter to the people*, p. 20; Russell's journal, 5 Nov. 1794 (*Journals*, p. 174); Russell to Templeton, 10 Sept. 1797 (Madden papers, 873/634); compare also Tytler, *The rising of the sun* (1795), p. 22 — 'in the old world, the order of nature instituted by the deity is totally reversed. God hath said that all men are free and equal; but the *gentlemen* say it is not so', with Russell's views in *Letter to the people*, p. 18 — 'these gentlemen conceive themselves wiser than the Deity; they find he was wrong, and set about rectifying his work'.

46 Russell's journal, 6 Nov. 1794 (*Journals*, p. 176); Morgan, 'Sketch of Russell', p. 40; Russell's journal, June 1792, 23 June 1793 (*Journals*, pp. 64, 78–9); for Russell arguing against deism, see his journal, 9 June 1794 (*Journals*, p. 151).

47 Draft letter by Russell to Neilson, n.d. (Sirr papers, 868/1, ff 181, 183).

48 R. B. McDowell, *Irish public opinion, 1750–1800* (London, 1944), p. 176; see, for example, Revd. William Jackson, *Stricture's on Paine's age of reason* (Dublin, 1794); Whitley Stokes, *A reply to Mr Paine's age of reason* (Dublin, 1795); Revd. William Stavely, *An appeal to light, or the tenets of the deists examined and disapproved* (Belfast, 1796).

49 Clark Garrett, 'Joseph Priestley, the millennium and the French revolution' in *Journal of the History of Ideas*, no. 34 (1973), p. 53.

50 Whitley Stokes wrote a pamphlet entitled, *A reply to Mr Paine's age of reason* (Dublin, 1795); the Rev. William Stavely, a Reformed Presbyterian minister from Belfast, wrote the foreword to Robert Fleming's *A discourse on the rise and fall of the Antichrist* (Belfast, 1795), (copy in Reb. papers, 620/22/63) and *War proclaimed, and victory ensured; or, The Lamb's conquests illustrated* (Belfast, 1795), as well as *An appeal to light, or the tenets of the deists examined and disapproved* (Belfast, 1796); James Tytler (Donaldson) in addition to his probable authorship of *A vindication of the doctrines of Christianity* (Belfast, 1794), also composed the tract *The rising of the sun in the west or the origin and progress of liberty* (Salem, 1795), see Reb. papers, 620/22/62.

51 Russell's journal, 10 June 1794 (*Journals*, p. 151); *D.N.B.*; James Tytler, *An answer to the second part of Paine's age of reason* (Edinburgh, 1797); James Tytler, *The rising of the sun* (1795), pp. 11–12 (Reb. papers, 620/22/62); a fore-word informs us that the author had been exiled from Scotland in January 1793 because of 'his writings in the cause of liberty' and has recently arrived in America from Belfast.

52 Fruchtman, 'Apocalyptic politics', pp. 106–7.

53 David Kennedy, 'James McDonnell 1762–1845' in *Capuchin Annual* (1945–6), p. 356; Nancy Curtin claims that Russell was involved in organising this festi-val (Curtin, *United Irishmen*, p. 35n), but Russell was employed as a magistrate in Dungannon in July 1792 and there is no evidence to suggest that he had any direct involvement.

54 Belfast Soc. minute books, 7 Mar., 19 Oct., 27 Dec. 1793; 13 Jan., 23 Oct., 4 Nov. 1794; 3 Sept. 1795; Mary McNeill, *The life and times of Mary Ann McCracken: a Belfast panorama* (Dublin, 1960), pp. 71–2; Russell's journal, 5–6 Nov. 1794 (*Journals*, pp. 174–6); *Belfast News Letter,* 10 Nov. 1797.

55 Russell's journal, 10 June 1794 (*Journals* 152); William Simms to Russell, 22 Jan. 1798 (Sirr papers, 868/2, ff 258–9); Russell to Templeton, Fort George, 2 Sept. 1800, 5 June 1802 (Madden papers, 873/636, 638).

56 Séamas Ó Casaide, *The Irish language in Belfast and Co. Down 1601–1850* (Dublin, 1930), pp. 32–3; *Bolg an tSolair* (Belfast, 1795); Mac Giolla Easpaig made a strong case for Russell's involvement in this work citing his interest in the Irish language, the similarity of some of his personal notes (Sirr papers, 868/1, f. 37) copied from *O'Brien's Irish-English Dictionary* (Paris, 1768) with the published preface of *Bolg* and the fact that, although future numbers of the work were intended, publication stopped in 1795 — at a time when Russell was busily engaged in political activities (*Ruiséil*, pp. 91–2).

57 *Northern Star,* 20 Apr. 1795; Mary Helen Thuente is of the opinion that Russell was 'probably' the author (Thuente, *Harp re-strung*, pp. 10, 95).

58 Mac Giolla Easpaig, *Ruiséil*, p. 92; Sirr papers, 868/2, ff 189–97, 201. Stokes eventually published parts of the New Testament in Irish in 1799 and 1806 (Brian Ó Cuív, 'Irish language and literature, 1691–1845' in T. W. Moody and W. E. Vaughan (eds), *A new history of Ireland, iv, eighteenth-century Ireland 1691–1800* (Oxford, 1986), p. 376).

59 Robert M. Young, 'Edward Bunting's Irish music and the McCracken family' in *U. J. A .* (1898), pp. 175–8; C. M. Fox, *Annals of the Irish Harpers* (London, 1911), pp. 20, 36; Séamas Ó Casaide, *The Irish language in Belfast and Co. Down 1601–1850* (Dublin, 1930), pp. 29–31.

60 John Hutchinson, *The dynamics of cultural nationalism* (London, 1987), pp. 54–6.

61 *Northern Star*, 23 Oct. 1793.

62 *Bolg an tSolair*, pp. iv–vii; for Lynch's authorship see the *Northern Star*, 3 Sept. 1795.

63 R. F. Foster, *Modern Ireland 1600–1972* (London, 1988); Tom Dunne, 'Popular ballads, revolutionary rhetoric and politicisation' in Gough and Dickson (eds), *Ire. and the Fr. Rev.*, p. 143.

64 Tone, *Writings*, i, 213; Thuente, *Harp re-strung*, pp. 5–7; for United Irish inter-est in cultural revivalism see also A. T. Q. Stewart, 'The harp new strung: nationalism, culture and the United Irishmen' in Oliver McDonagh and W. F. Mandle (eds), *Ireland and Irish Australia: studies in cultural history* (London, 1986), pp. 258–69, and Norman Vance, 'Celts, Cartiginians and constitutions: Anglo-Irish literary relations 1780–1820' in *I. H. S.*, xxii, no. 87 (Mar. 1981), pp. 216–36.

65 R. B. McDowell, *Irish public opinion, 1750–1800* (London, 1944), p. 209; Thuente, *Harp re-strung*, p. 143; Curtin, *United Irishmen*, p. 286.
66 On this topic see Kevin Whelan, 'The United Irishmen, the Enlightenment and popular culture' in Dickson, Keogh and Whelan (eds), *United Irishmen*, pp. 269–96; *Northern Star*, 20 Apr. 1795.
67 J. R. R. Adams, *The printed word and the common man: popular culture in Ulster* (Belfast, 1987), p. 70.
68 Thuente, *Harp re-strung*, p. 120.
69 Thomas Russell to John Russell, n.d. (Madden papers, 873/673).
70 Manuscript version in Russell's papers, seized 18 Sept. 1796 (Reb. papers, 620/53/71); published in *The Press*, 4 Nov. 1797.
71 *Rep. comm. sec.*, p. 192.
72 Robert Simms to Russell, Belfast, 10 Aug. 1797 (Sirr papers, 868/2, f. 308).
73 Curtin, *United Irishmen*, pp. 20–1.
74 *Lion of old Eng. of old England* (Belfast, 1794), p. 47.
75 [Russell] to —, Oct. or Nov. 1791 (P.R.O., HO 100/34/41–2); for Russell's authorship of this letter, see Curtin, *United Irishmen*, p. 9.
76 Russell's journal, 30 July 1793 (*Journals*, pp. 89–90).
77 Samuel McSkimin, *Annals of Ulster, 1790–1798* , ed. E. J. McCrum (Belfast, 1906), pp. 74–5.

CHAPTER EIGHT

From Bad to Worse

Much of Russell's time in the late 1793 and early 1794 was spent trying to hold together the fragile alliance between Catholic and Dissenter. Despite occasional moments of euphoric fraternity, suspicions between southern Catholics and the Belfast United Irishmen had never really disappeared. The Catholics for their part had no wish to handicap their cause by too close an identification with the northern 'levellers', while Belfast Presbyterians remained wary of the Catholics reverting to what they saw as their old deferential and sectarian ways. Since the Catholic acceptance of limited emancipation in spring 1793 and their subsequent apathy towards further reform, much of the goodwill that had existed in 1791–2 had evaporated and the alliance had been rent by bitter recriminations.

In August 1793, at a dinner held by former members of the Catholic Committee to honour the pro-emancipation peer, Lord Moira, no toasts were drunk to the northern Dissenters or to the United Irishmen. After such events lists of toasts were often published in the newspapers and were used as a means of giving clear political messages to friends and foes. Whether or not it was deliberate, the decision to omit the United Irishmen was seen as a snub and was the final straw for many northerners. The society had been at a low ebb for some months now and it seemed that leading Catholics had come to view their radical allies as a liability. From Belfast, an angry Samuel Neilson wrote a scathing attack on the conduct of the Catholics to Richard McCormick in Dublin: 'not to speak of their refusal to include us among their friends when they were concluding their business as a convention, they could not when assembled the other day in a festive capacity omit insulting this province... when ransacking the very dregs of royalty, aristocracy and pseudo-patriotism for toasts'.[1] With the trial of the *Northern Star* owners still pending, Neilson no doubt felt particularly aggrieved at the failure of the Catholics to show publicly even the slightest solidarity with the northern radicals.

Russell and Tone suggested that another dinner should be held to effect a *rapprochement*, but this ran into difficulties because of tensions between southern reformers, notably the bitter enmity between John Keogh and Richard McCormick — McCormick having accused Keogh of betraying the Catholic cause by reneging on the convention's original decision to accept nothing less than full emancipation. Considerable difficulties also arose on the question of who should be invited. Keogh was in favour of asking the parliamentary opposition; Tone was doubtful about the wisdom of such an invitation while Russell, given his continued disillusionment with the Whigs, was fervently opposed to it.[2] In such an atmosphere of uncertainty plans for the dinner were soon scrapped.

As a United Irishmen trusted by both northern Presbyterians and southern Catholics, Russell often had to play the role of mediator between the Dublin and Belfast societies. Although he was prepared to make tactical adjustments as circumstances dictated, his commitment to the two original United Irish principles of parliamentary reform and Catholic emancipation remained undimmed, and he still believed that only the complete implementation of these principles could secure true liberty and equality for the Irish people. Most probably he was referring to his and Tone's efforts to mend the bridges between north and south when he noted in his journal: 'while in Belfast frequently hear that only for the confidence placed in Mr H. [Tone] and P. P. things would have gone *to extremity*. Their letters prevented it'.[3]

In these difficult times Russell did his utmost to boost the morale of both Presbyterians and Catholics. On returning to Belfast in October 1793, within the space of two days he wrote a defence of the proprietors of the *Northern Star* and penned strong letters to Richard McCormick and John Sweetman, two leading members of the Catholic Committee. By this stage even Russell — sympathetic though he was to the Catholics — was becoming increasingly concerned at their timidity and he considered publishing an open letter to encourage them to renew their commitment to reform and to press for full emancipation.[4]

For the most part, Belfast radicals were far more militant than their Dublin counterparts in 1793–4. This was partly due to the aggressive military presence in the town: troops had obviously been given tacit licence to intimidate local radicals and tensions between townspeople and the military ran high throughout 1793. In March a party of the 17th Light Dragoons wrecked a tavern displaying republican signs and attacked the houses of leading United Irishmen and the offices of the *Northern Star*, as well as 'cutting and abusing every person they met with in the street in a most unmerciful manner', and only stopped when the town's Volunteers assembled to face them down.[5] Clashes between troops and civilians punctuated the next few months and in April Henry Joy McCracken had to intervene in a brawl between some drunken soldiers and Belfast youths, which almost led to a duel between himself and a young officer.[6] Russell himself was drawn into an ugly confrontation with the military towards the end of the year. On the night of 13 November a dinner was held in honour of Hamilton Rowan and Simon Butler who had returned from Edinburgh after attending the preliminary stages of the radical 'British Convention' as representatives of the United Irishmen.[7] When the celebrations ended and revellers spilled out onto the streets there were several altercations between soldiers and townspeople. On their way home Russell and McCabe were confronted by several officers of the Fermanagh militia. Russell, who had been drinking heavily, approached them; he said nothing, but gave them a look of withering contempt and walked on. They followed him and demanded an explanation for his behaviour, which he refused to give. They were soon surrounded by a crowd and tempers became inflamed. One of the officers was Lord Cole, son of the Earl of Enniskillen, and he angrily challenged Russell to a duel. In doing so he proclaimed that he was Lord Cole so often that an onlooker cried out 'you are very fond of that title; take care, or it may not be long till you lose it!'. However, a fellow officer would not allow the hot-headed young lord to fight and stepped in to take his place. When it was pointed out that both Russell and McCabe were unarmed, the soldiers agreed to postpone the duel to the following day. The next morning, passions had cooled all round and the militia officers called on Russell to apologise to him. While he had been waiting for them to call, McCabe had done his best to persuade him 'that he had been the first offender by a look which, even at moonlight was, it seems, worse than a sentence'. Russell then agreed to write an apology to the officers concerned but before he could deliver it they called and settled the affair amicably.[8]

Russell wrote a brief account of the incident in his journal. He accepted that he was in the wrong in the beginning but felt that the subsequent behaviour of the militia officers aggravated the dispute. Torn between a heightened sense of honour and a desire to live according to genuine Christian principles, he found the decision on whether or not to engage in a duel — an activity which he denounced as a vice of the aristocracy — tormenting:

> Never spent so miserable a time as after I waken'd that morning till I went to town. Remember'd what my friend Knox told me of the night he was to fight McLeod. Sayd if it was his misfortune to be engaged in a second duel he would fight off-hand. What a conflict I had between pride, shame and what I *knew* was my *duty*, and what was my determination to put the duel on them and not fire in return! I had not spirit enough to renounce duel[l]ing, but I will, I trust. Must not drink. With a prostitute that very night when the next day I might be in the presence of God. Terrible![9]

In December 1793, in a move that implied some disillusionment with the United Irishmen, Tone and Russell tried to revive the fortunes of the reform movement in the south by attempting to found a new club that would concentrate on publishing and distributing propaganda in favour of parliamentary reform. They discussed their scheme with leading Dublin radicals but this too foundered on the rock of local animosities. With the alliance between northern Presbyterians and southern Catholics practically dead and deep divisions among Catholic reformers themselves, the public standing of the United Irishmen was at its nadir. Drennan, noting Catholic apathy towards the society, thought that it should hold a meeting to consider dissolving itself.[10] Even the United Irishmen's decision to publish their plan of parliamentary reform in February 1794 was symptomatic of their flagging fortunes and a desperate attempt to inject some momentum into their campaign for reform.[11] Russell's journals for the period exude a palpable note of despair. 'Everything goes on from bad to worse', he noted. The divided and demoralised United Irishmen he described as having, 'no concert. No plan. Every day sinking...Fright, pride and jealousy have laid us asleep.'[12]

Russell spent Christmas and the early new year with Tone in County Kildare, where one of their favourite activities was to go partridge shooting together in the countryside around Tone's cottage in Bodenstown. After spending over a month with the Tones, he received news on 17 January that he had been elected librarian of the Belfast Society for Promoting Knowledge and he decided to return to the North. The following day as he was leaving Dublin both he and

Tone were in low spirits. Tone shared the general disillusionment with the lack of progress of the reform movement and was in a particularly foul mood, venting his spleen on all available targets. He criticised Russell for giving up a secure living in Dungannon and then turned on the United Irishmen of the North whom he dismissed as 'cowards and braggadocios'. The only people from whom anything was to be expected were those Irish *'sans culottes'* who were 'too ignorant for any thinking man to wish to see in power'.[13]

Russell had family business to attend to in the North and before going to Belfast he made his way to Enniskillen to attend the wedding of his niece Mary Ann to William Henry Hamilton, a local army officer of radical political views with whom he was to become closely associated. He declared himself and his family 'much affected' by the wedding in which 'his dear girl was married to that fine young man'. He then travelled on to Belfast on 8 February 1794 to discuss the details of the offer of the librarianship of the Belfast Society for the Promotion of Knowledge. He was less than enthused about accepting the position but he agreed when told that it might lead to a permanent post and the salary was increased.[14] When the decision had originally been taken to appoint him librarian it was decided that 'the expense attending a house for the library, museum, etc. and the librarian's salary should not exceed £30 per annum' but friends of Russell, aware of his poverty, managed to secure an extra £20 a year for his salary in order to give him a living wage.[15]

Securing regular employment, however, did not herald a new period of tranquillity in Russell's personal life. Throughout his life brief bouts of optimism and euphoria appear to have alternated with prolonged periods of deep despair — he may well have suffered from manic depression. Though he was rarely free from such despair for very long, the year 1794 was a particularly difficult time for him, when the coincidence of a number of unfortunate political and personal developments played heavily on his mind. On 10 March 1794 he received a letter from India informing him of the death of his older brother, Captain Ambrose Russell, who had died suddenly in Madras from natural causes on 3 July 1793 at the age of 34. He had served with Ambrose in India and he loved and admired him above all his brothers. Ambrose's obituary praised his 'inoffensive and mild' manners and his 'witty and pleasant' conversation, and noted that he was 'idolised by the soldiers and beloved by the officers with whom he served. In the field he was the intrepid soldier, in private life everything that was admirable'.[16] On 17 January, the very day that he had left Tone in Co. Kildare, a letter for Russell arrived with the news. Tone and his wife, fearing the effect it might have on him given his many other troubles at the time, decided to keep the news from him until a later date.[17] True to their fears, when he received the news of Ambrose's death a couple of weeks later, it had a devastating effect on him. Somewhat strangely, he felt that it was better not to give way to his grief and when he dined that night with William Simms and a group of friends he 'kept up tolerably well'. A week later, however, after an evening when he dined and danced with friends, he was gripped by the notion that he had shown a lack of feeling and he imagined guiltily how upset Ambrose would have been if the situation had been reversed. He described his feelings on returning home:

> this idea seized me so strongly and my affection to him was so excited that I fell into tears most violently so much so that I lay down on the floor to ease myself. How long I continued in this state I know not. I suppose it was something in the way of hystericks. The sound of my own voice in weeping echoing in the room struck me as so like his that it redoubled my anguish and tears. This is all I remember. I was not well for some days, but my mind felt more relieved after it than before.

On many occasions afterwards he had vivid dreams of the times he had spent with Ambrose in his youth and his brother's funeral — the coffin draped with regimental colours, the lines of grenadiers acting as a guard of honour, the solemn music and the final volley of shots at the graveside.[18]

Despite Russell's efforts to put on a brave face among friends, Martha McTier observed his distress and noted: 'now fortune had done its worst, he did not seem to wish it to be known and therefore put on a strange kind of vacant spirits, which made my heart bleed for him'. She also observed that his poverty was such that he could not even afford a black coat in which to mourn his brother. McTier had first expressed concern for Russell after he had become involved in the incident with the militia officers, noting: 'I am very much interested for this seemingly unfortunate young man Russell. He seems very poor, is very agreeable, very handsome and well informed, and possessed of most insinuating graceful manners.[19]

While Martha McTier was no doubt genuinely fond of Russell, she also valued the drama and colour that such a romantic figure brought to the Belfast social scene and she appears to have relished her role as an occasional go-between in the stop-start affair between Russell and Eliza Goddard. Russell also played an active part in the amateur productions of Shakespeare and Sheridan that McTier's set regularly held and she had a high opinion of his dramatic abilities, considering him to be particularly suited to dashing roles such as Hotspur in *Henry IV part 1*. He was also often invited to speak at meetings of radical women at her home and after one particularly powerful address she noted that 'I admire that man much and had I the power, I do believe he would be the first man I would serve'.[20]

While she admired Russell's character and manners, McTier also observed that 'his dress betrays poverty, and he associates with men every way below himself, on some of whom, I fear, he mostly lives'.[21] This was one of the many contradictions in Russell's life: he had the bearing, speech and many of the attitudes of a gentleman — he was, for example, one of the few United Irish leaders given the title of 'esquire' by the government — but he most certainly lacked the means of a gentleman and was well aware of his penury. During a discussion with some Belfast friends who argued that money was a matter of no importance in determining happiness he repeated the phrase 'a man must *dine*' to every such argument, and said it in such a tone that it 'almost thrilled' Martha McTier.[22] His personal circumstances were made even more difficult by the need to support his sister Margaret, who like most single women from poor middle-class families was dependent on her male relatives. Since the death of Ambrose, apparently the most responsible and level-headed of all the Russell brothers, Margaret relied completely on Thomas. She was his most regular correspondent — sending a constant stream of letters complaining of her loneliness and debts and asking him to visit her or send money. Thomas was well aware of his responsibilities towards Margaret and often was often guilty about the manner in which he discharged them. He noted: 'She was left me in charge by my venerable father. I owe to, and feel for, her the tenderest love and affection, and she is [in] solitude and want, cut off from any friend whose conversation could sooth or amuse her. I am here in pleasing society which however at times only aggravates the recollection of her situation.'[23]

Margaret's loneliness was aggravated when her two nieces left her care: Mary Ann to marry William Henry Hamilton in January 1794 and Julia to be with her father in September 1794. Her other brothers seem to have made little or no contribution to her support.

Relations between Margaret and John were strained. John, who shared Thomas's carelessness about money, did little or nothing for her support and Margaret was impatient with his interfering and his impractical schemes, wishing that 'he would keep his romantic schemes to himself and let us be as happy as our situation will admit'.[24] Thomas later disapproved when John formed a relationship with Biddy, a family servant, but they still remained close and in their letters John teased him about his proclivity for women. 'Does your cheek ever come into contact with a woman's? I am glad to see that you are so reform'd. I'm told you never meddle with the sex — you have that great model Pitt in your eyes. I seldom meddle — not above once a week...Thank God poor Biddy is very moderate in her passions.'[25]

John was a good friend of Theobald Wolfe Tone, who advised him after the breakup of his marriage in September 1792 to go to London to try his hand as a writer. Even Tone, though deeply fond of him, thought that he lacked 'resolution and energy — too much of the milk of human kindness. Poor fellow!' John took Tone's advice and left Ireland in November 1792 after bidding farewell to Tone at Sallins.[26] He travelled to London where he tried to make a living by writing but with little success. Although he eventually secured a commission in the West London militia, he lived one step ahead of the bailiffs for most of the time.[27]

The remaining brother, Will, was by all accounts the most irresponsible of all and very much the black sheep of the family. References to his unreliability, selfishness and ingratitude crop up frequently in family correspondence. He was staunchly anti-French and his brothers were wary of discussing politics with him. While in Dublin he lived off John's wife: he 'makes her get whiskey for him and drinks a great deal — he then begins to talk of the French till she is tired of him'. He neglected his own wife — a 'big, ugly woman...that slapped the wet stockings in Mrs Tone's face for asking her if she was a whore to both brothers...Next morning she broke Tone's flutes on his father's head.' He borrowed repeatedly from John when living in London and, much to John's annoyance, left the aforementioned wife for him to support. It seems however that John was more forgiving of William than was Thomas, who avoided all contact with him. While William was staying in Dublin John asked Thomas: 'why don't you write to him — he is a good-natured creature and takes much to heart your never writing him a line'.[28] It was probably Will that Martha McTier had foremost in mind when she spoke of the 'unfortunate' character of some of the Russell family.[29]

Martha McTier was one of the many people acquainted with Russell who developed an affectionate and protective attitude towards him, looking upon him as 'a younger, rasher brother'. His 'very wild words and actions' and his moods of despondency worried her and she wondered: 'God knows how his little pittance is paid, but this I know, that he does not eat when left in his melancholy lodging, without a living being but himself, and situated in a dark and gloomy entry'.[30] She was so concerned that she sought her brother's advice on ways to help him. Drennan thought that it would be best to apply to John Keogh for some payment to Russell for his efforts on behalf of the Catholics. Before winding up its operations the Catholic Committee had voted considerable sums of money to those who had helped it achieve the concessions granted in April 1793: £1,500 was voted to Tone, as secretary to the committee; £1,000 to William Todd Jones, who had been an advocate of Catholic relief since the 1780s and had published several pro-emancipation pamphlets; £500 to Simon Butler, who had compiled a digest of the penal laws in 1792; and £100 to Samuel Neilson.[31] Russell himself received nothing and, though he himself made no comment on his omission, Drennan certainly was puzzled by it and thought that the Catholics had treated Russell shabbily since he had been 'so active an agent in their cause'.[32] But Russell's efforts on behalf of the Catholics had been carried out largely behind the scenes while those of Tone, Todd Jones, Butler and Neilson had a much higher public profile. It probably would have been difficult to persuade the committee to vote money for services most of its members knew little about. In the event, once the euphoria of the moment had died down, subscriptions to the fund were disappointing: Tone and Butler were the only two to receive even partial payment and even then it was paid over in dribs and drabs.[33] But Drennan believed that Russell had a genuine claim on the Catholics and advised McTier to:

> give Keogh a simple statement of Russell's situation, say you have heard he was an active instrument in the Catholic cause and for his principles lost a livelihood at Dungannon ... say that if Tone received £1,500 ... his friend who was equally zealous, though perhaps not equally able in literary capacity, should certainly receive some gratification, hint that the Catholics are suspected in the North of not

having long memories with respect to their friends, and that anything done in the present instance would have the best consequence, from the very great esteem in which Russell is held in Belfast.[34]

She did write to Keogh but by this stage he had lost much of his influence among the Catholics and her efforts were unsuccessful.[35]

Martha McTier's schemes to help Russell did not end there. She discussed with William Sampson the possibility of encouraging Russell to give chemistry lectures 'which would be both agreeable and lucrative' to him. Though Russell liked the idea and began to do some preparatory reading, he eventually decided against lecturing because he believed that 'the political state of the country would prevent [it] being beneficial at present'.[36] McTier also suggested that he should set up a periodical, though Russell was not very enthusiastic about the idea. He mentioned that he had already attempted this with a group of colleagues in Dublin (perhaps the *National Journal*), and that after its failure he was wary of engaging in a similar venture again.[37]

Russell also made some efforts on his own behalf. In September he tried to seek financial help for Margaret from his brother's widow, Nancy, who had returned from India with a sum of £10,000 bestowed on her by the East India Company, but he seems to have had no success.[38] It appears that with his £50 a year failing to cover his expenses he considered moving to England and enquired to his brother John about employment prospects in London. John believed that it would be the ideal place for the employment of his brother's literary talents; by co-operating together they 'might make something by play-writing' or he could become a House of Commons reporter, although he realised that a typesetter would have difficulty in reading his near illegible hand. If all else failed he might even find himself a wife, although John advised him that 'a wife is easier had with a red coat on your back — if you could begin with that it might be better'.[39]

Russell's worries about money and family matters were compounded by his continued anguish and confusion over Eliza Goddard. She still exerted a strong hold over his imagination although their relationship had all but finished. Since their first meeting in April 1791, it seems that they had only seen each other infrequently, though Russell singled out a day in June of that year when he accompanied Eliza on an excursion to Cave Hill as the happiest of his life. There is no other mention of any meetings between them until Russell refers to a dinner, probably held at the end of November 1792, just before he travelled to Dublin to liaise with the Catholic Convention. He recalled how 'she was pensive at supper and looked more beautiful than ever I saw her. A lock of hair hung across her bosom'. That night, Eliza complained of her father's overly protective attitude towards her, which meant she was rarely allowed to venture out in public. She told Russell that even if there were no other barriers to their relationship — and Russell's poverty represented a formidable barrier — his politics alone 'would be an insuperable one, for she was sure if I was the first duke in the land her father would refuse me, such was his abhorrence of Democracy'.[40]

But in the months and years that followed Eliza was never far from his thoughts. He remembered a visit to the Mourne Mountains with his brother John in the spring of 1792, when they had enjoyed the beauties of nature and talked about 'the rapturous, the to me fatal, sensations of love'. He recalled that 'though I have had great anguish yet when our passion first commenced my pleasures were exquisite. It gri[e]ves me to think that so cunning a pattern of excelling nature should fall off. A flower that smelt so exquisitely sweet that the sense ach'd at it. I am now near her no more!'[41]

Some time later he spoke to Martha McTier about her: he was told that Eliza considered the affair to be finished and she believed Russell was of the same opinion. Nevertheless, she still looked fondly upon him as a friend. He was not entirely convinced that these were her true feelings and claimed that he would not marry before she did or until he was sure that his marriage would not hurt her. He even wrote to Martha McTier asking her to find out once and for all if Eliza cared for him or not, in order to set his mind at rest. Mrs McTier, however, refused to put such a direct question to her, but she did mention some days later that she had met Eliza and told her of Russell's illness following Ambrose's death. Eliza was very concerned and hoped that he was receiving proper medical care. She knew that her father would not allow her to go to Belfast to visit him but she added: 'he might very safely, for my mind *is made up* as to him, *never* to marry him'. She added, however, that although she would love to visit Mrs McTier in Belfast, she could not bear to do so if she would find Russell there looking unwell or unhappy. Such contradictory signals left Russell more confused than ever and still he agonised: 'Does she love me or not?'[42]

Months later he was still puzzled and pained about the relationship and, to add to his distress, money and family problems weighed heavily upon him. It was during the low points of his life that his feelings for Eliza seemed to take on an even greater intensity. He noted in his journal: 'thus circumstanced, what folly, what madness to think of love, and yet in defiance of reason and common sense and pride, I love! It occupys my thoughts and biasses my actions'.[43]

As a way out of his difficulties he was considering marriage with 'a certain lady of competent fortune', though he claimed he sought financial security on his sister's behalf rather than his own. He committed his tangled thoughts to his journal:

> I am as certain as I can be...that were I married I should be kind and indulgent to my wife and endeavour to make her happy; and I think it probable that I could conceal and in time overcome my present attachment. What then is to prevent my trying? I should beside lead a virtuous life, which from my propensity to women I hitherto have not done. E[liza] has from prudential reasons relinquished all thoughts of me. Neither of us have any fortune. She even told me that I was indifferent to her, and another lady that she had made up her mind never to marry me. Am I not then at liberty in every point of view to pay my addresses to any other? Beside have I not been told that her understanding is not good, that she never could be qualified to be a companion to me. Still, after the vows I made to her I am not certain but she may think I will not marry. I am not certain but that it might make her uneasy and, as I was wrong in the outset in endeavouring to gain her affections, am I not bound in honor to take care that whatever I might suffer she shall not be unhappy, or does this proceed rather from vanity in thinking that I am yet dear to her...The emotion I feel when I see her or even when I hear her name mentioned is so great that I doubt at times whether I would be just[i]fy'd in attempting to marry any other, as it might make them unhappy...I fear with all this there is some nonsencical choemera floating in my brain of the possibility of our future alliance, though I dare not avow it to myself. Thus I fluctuate and balance and dream, and the prime of my life passes away. What shall or what can I do?[44]

Eliza stayed in Belfast for some months towards the end of 1794 but Russell went out of his way to avoid meeting her. Martha McTier reflected on him sitting alone in his 'melancholy lodging...while the lovely girl he adores, and who I believe to be sensible of his accomplishments, shines in circles he once was courted to'.[45] In December he saw Eliza unexpectedly during an evening at a friend's house in Belfast. He became extremely nervous and could not bring himself to approach her: he 'wish'd to quit the room and to stay to see her and not to see her'. He was unable to concentrate on conversation and his hosts noticed his bad spirits; Russell excused himself by saying he had a headache. Eventually, he worked up the courage to speak to Eliza and she appeared equally agitated, which convinced him that she could not be completely indifferent to him. At supper he could not eat and could not stop himself from gazing at her, noting that:

> her attention was as much employ'd in observing me when I look'd away, as I did when I met her eyes. She look'd beautiful and innocent and I loved her if possible more than ever. Latterly as I got, as it were, more courage, when I met her eyes I look'd at her without turning away, and she look'd at me so mild, so placid, so gentle, that it penetrated my very soul.

When the gathering broke up, Eliza left immediately and Russell followed her home. He walked up and down outside her house for an hour in the hope of seeing her again. Although he could make out a figure standing at a window he could not be certain if it was Eliza. He waved his handkerchief and the figure remained at the window for about five minutes and then withdrew.[46]

That evening may well have been the last time that they spoke. Soon afterwards, at her father's insistence, Eliza was engaged to an army officer named Kingston, 'a sensible well-behaved young lad of twenty-two and said to have a fortune of £6,000 independent of his father'. Within a few months they were married and living in Dublin and by September 1795 Eliza was expecting her first child.[47] But Russell never forgot her. On his journey north in July 1803 he spoke of her as he passed by her former home and while awaiting execution at Downpatrick in October 1803, some of his last dreams were of Eliza Goddard.[48]

Russell never married. Mary Ann McCracken admired him and appears to have been strongly attracted to him; she was to prove one of his most faithful and loyal friends, but the attraction does not seem to have been mutual.[49] Drennan suspected that he would marry a Miss Clark of Belfast, a sister of Eliza, wife of James McDonnell, and Grace, wife of William Sampson, but it came to nothing.[50] There was also a Miss Hamilton in Belfast to whom he paid some attention. He thought her 'very handsome...very like E[liza] in the expression and manner of her face', but he noted that she 'opens her mouth too much'.[51] Some years later he may have formed an attachment to a daughter of Hampden Evans, a wealthy United Irishman with whom he was imprisoned, and there was some talk of their getting married.[52] The 'lady of competent fortune' he had in mind as a prospective wife in November 1794 was probably Mary Simms, sister of the Belfast radicals, William and Robert. Russell shared an interest in music with her; she had 'a fine voice and sang exquisitely' and he thought her 'very agreeable'. It appears that Mary Simms harboured strong feelings for Russell and she fainted on hearing of his death.[53] He wrote of his proposed match to his sister who replied that 'nothing would make me happier than to hear of its taking place. I am not much surprised at the lady's not having B[eauty?] or fortune, I never did suppose either would have any effect on you, but I am certain she has accomplishments of a kind to make you happy'. Although he believed he would be accepted, he was uncertain how to proceed and thought it best to postpone his offer until his political duties were less onerous. In 1796 he wrote to Matilda Tone seeking advice, which she gave 'like an honest republican':

> I entirely disapprove of it. Friendship, honour and principle all forbid it, unless you have the approbation of her family and prospects, which I confess I cannot foresee. Though a young man, you are not a boy, and you have much experience — for my part I cannot conceive your being led away by passion (particularly at this time) to involve a lovely girl in inevitable ruin, for I will not one moment suppose your intentions are not serious... Nothing could induce me to wound your feelings, but to save you from involving yourself and the woman you love in lasting misery and ruin. I shall say no more on this, as I trust you believe me that what I have said was dictated by the most affectionate regard.[54]

If Matilda Tone's brutal common sense was not enough to kill off Russell's marriage plans then his arrest on a charge of high treason a few days later certainly was.

To compound Russell's depression, the prospects for political progress during 1794 were also bleak. The frustration and disillusionment evident in his journal at the beginning of the year was aggravated by events in spring and early summer. Since the militia riots of the previous summer Defenderism was on the decline and the countryside was quieter that it had been for years. The government had stepped up its offensive against the United Irishmen —

Hamilton Rowan, William Drennan and the proprietors of the *Northern Star* had all been charged with seditious practices — and the radical reform movement was now largely cowed.[55] Average weekly attendance at United Irish meetings in the capital had dwindled to less than thirty-five. On a visit to the Dublin society in January, Samuel Neilson had denounced it as being infested with informers and called for the setting up of a secret committee to transact all business. This had caused further dissension within United Irish ranks between those who favoured an open approach, claiming that the society had nothing to hide, and those who believed their deliberations should be held in secret. As for the northern United Irish societies, very little had been heard from them for some time, and Drennan, for one, was baffled by what they hoped to achieve through their 'system of eternal silence'.[56]

By 1794 the United Irishmen were more isolated and demoralised than ever. Far from resolving their differences with the parliamentary Whigs to present a common front against the government, the gap between the two groups had grown wider. In March the Whig leader George Ponsonby introduced a reform bill, which advocated the enlargement of some boroughs and the return of an additional member from county constituencies, but his proposals fell far short of United Irish demands for universal male suffrage and annual parliaments. By this stage the continuing war with France and the increasingly radicalisation of the French revolution under the Jacobins had made any reform, however moderate, seem potentially subversive and, despite its moderation, Ponsonby's bill went down by 142 votes to 44 in the Commons.[57]

Whereas in Britain radicals could at least console themselves with Fox's opposition to the war, there was no such comfort for Irish radicals. At the opening of the 1794 Irish parliament Grattan had gone out of his way to declare that Ireland should grant Britain 'a decided and unequivocal support' in her contest with revolutionary France. With the United Irishmen in disarray and the parliamentary opposition quiescent, the government were well pleased with their efforts to curb radicalism and the Chancellor of the Exchequer, Sir John Parnell, could speak with satisfaction of 'the great tranquillity of Irish politics'.[58]

According to Thomas Addis Emmet this was a time when the 'expectations of reformers had been blasted, their plans defeated and decisive means had been taken by the government to prevent their being resumed'. It was this feeling of despair that led prominent

United Irishmen such as Rowan and Reynolds to give a sympathetic reception to the mission of the French agent, Revd. William Jackson. Tone also became embroiled in the affair and was severely compromised when a memorial he had drawn up at the behest of Rowan, which claimed that Ireland was ripe for revolution, fell into the hands of the authorities. This dabbling in treason gave the government the opportunity it needed to strike against the ailing Dublin Society of United Irishmen. On 25 May 1794 a United Irish meeting at the Tailors' Hall was raided by the police, papers were seized and those present ordered to disperse, an event that has traditionally been seen as marking the end of the constitutional phase of the United Irishmen.[59]

NOTES

1 Neilson to McCormick, 26 Aug. 1793 (Tone, *Writings*, i, 499).
2 Russell's journal, Jan. 1794 (*Journals*, pp. 139–40).
3 Russell's journal, 9 Sept. 1793 (*Journals*, p. 123).
4 Russell's journal, 19/20 Oct. 1793 (*Journals*, p. 133).
5 *Northern Star,* 13 Mar. 1793; Neilson to [Tone], 11 March 1793, Robert Simms to [Tone] (Tone, *Writings*, i, 415–17).
6 Sam McTier to [Martha McTier], 22 Apr. 1793 (Drennan papers, T765/410)
7 Albert Goodwin, *The friends of liberty* (London, 1979), pp. 295–304. An assembly of British radicals styling themselves the British Convention met in Edinburgh from 6 Nov. 1793 until their dispersal on 6 Dec. 1793.
8 Martha McTier to Drennan, 16 Nov. 1793 (*Drennan letters*, pp. 174–5).
9 Russell's journal, 14 Nov. 1793 (*Journals*, pp. 134–5).
10 Drennan to Sam McTier, 16 Aug. 1793 (*Drennan letters*, p. 169).
11 Curtin, *United Irishmen*, p. 27.
12 Russell's journal, Dec. (?) 1793, 22 Jan. 1794 (*Journals*, pp. 140, 143).
13 Russell's journal, 18 Jan. 1794 (*Journals*, p. 141).
14 Russell's journal, 29 Jan. to 20 Feb. 1794 (*Journals*, pp. 144–6).
15 Morgan, 'Sketch of Russell', pp. 57–8.
16 *Freeman's Journal*, 6 May 1794.
17 Tone to Russell, 12 Mar. 1794 (Sirr papers, 868/2, ff 299–300).
18 Russell's journal, 10–20 Mar. 1794 (*Journals*, pp. 147–9).
19 Martha McTier to Drennan, 17 Mar. 1794 (Drennan papers, T765/478); Martha McTier to Drennan, 16 Nov. 1793 (*Drennan letters*, p. 175).
20 Russell's journal, 30 June 1793 (*Journals*, pp. 155–6); Martha McTier to Drennan, 4 Sept., 24 Oct., Nov. 1794 (Drennan papers, T765/527, 528, 533).
21 Martha McTier to Drennan, 16 Nov. 1793 (*Drennan letters*, p. 175).
22 Martha McTier to Drennan, c. Oct.–Dec. 1794 (Drennan papers, T765/533); for the government styling Russell 'esquire', see 8 Geo. III c. 78 (*The statutes at large passed in the parliaments held in Ireland*, xviii, 1130).
23 Russell's journal, 3 Nov. 1794 (*Journals*, p. 171); most of the letters sent to Russell in the Sirr papers, 868/1–2, are from his sister Margaret.
24 Margaret Russell to Thomas Russell, 13 Sept. 1793 (Sirr papers, 868/2, ff

20–1), 30 Dec. 1793 (Sirr papers, 868/2, ff 32, 37).

25 John Russell to Thomas Russell, 3 May 1795, 16–18 Aug. 1796 (Sirr papers, 868/2, ff 121, 125–6).

26 Tone, *Writings*, i, 284, 295–6, 323.

27 Sirr papers, 868/2/114–15, 122–3, 127–8.

28 Margaret Russell to Thomas Russell, 30 Dec. 1793 (Sirr papers, 868/2 f. 32, 37); John Russell to Thomas Russell, 29 Mar., 11 April , 1 June, 16/18 Aug. 1796, 18 Oct. 1798 (Sirr papers, 868/2, ff 122–3, 114–15, 127–8, 125–6, 107–8).

29 Martha McTier to Drennan, 16 Nov. 1793 (Drennan papers, T765/449).

30 Martha McTier to Drennan, Sept. 1796 (*Drennan letters*, p. 241); Martha McTier to Drennan, c. Oct. to Dec. 1794 (Drennan papers, T765/533).

31 Mac Giolla Easpaig, *Ruiséil*, p. 67; Russell's journal, mid–Apr. 1793 (*Journals*, p. 72).

32 Drennan to Martha McTier, 13 Mar. 1794 (*Drennan letters,* pp. 193–4).

33 Frank MacDermot, *Theobald Wolfe Tone: a biographical study* (London, 1939), p. 120.

34 Drennan to Martha McTier, Mar. 1794 (Drennan papers, T765/479); for more correspondence on this issue see Drennan papers, Mar. to Dec 1794, T765/477, 478, 483, 533, 534.

35 Martha McTier to Drennan, c. Oct. to Dec. 1794 (Drennan papers, T765/533).

36 Russell's journal, 9 Mar. 1794, 3 Nov. 1794 (*Journals*, pp. 146, 173).

37 Martha McTier to Drennan, 22 Mar. 1794 (Drennan papers, T765/482).

38 Martha McTier to Drennan, 3 Sept. 1794 (Drennan papers, T765/526); see also John Russell to Thomas Russell, 19 Mar. 1794 (Sirr papers, 868/2, ff 131–2).

39 John Russell to Thomas Russell, 4 Aug. 1795, n.d. (Sirr papers, 868/2, ff 116–17, 145).

40 Russell's journal, 9 June, 30 June 1794 (*Journals*, pp. 150, 155).

41 Russell's journal, 3 Sept. 1793 (*Journals*, p. 118).

42 Russell's journal, 30 June 1794 (*Journals*, p. 157).

43 Russell's journal, 3 Nov. 1794 (*Journals*, pp. 171–2).

44 Russell's journal, 3 Nov. 1794 (*Journals*, pp. 172–3).

45 Martha McTier to Drennan, *c.* Oct. to Dec. 1794 (Drennan papers, T765/533).

46 Russell's journal, 9 Dec. 1794 (*Journals*, pp. 180–3).

47 Martha McTier to Drennan, 25 Jan., 24 June, 21 Sept. 1795 (Drennan papers, T765/540, 562, 563); see also Mary Ann McCracken to Madden, 13 Nov. 1857 (Madden papers, 873/70).

48 Madden, *United Irishmen*, 3rd ser., ii, 214; Martha McTier to Drennan, 4 Nov. 1803 (*Drennan letters,* p. 332).

49 In his 'Mary Anne [*sic*] McCracken: Belfast revolutionary and pioneer of femi-nism' in Dáire Keogh and Nicholas Furlong (eds), *The women of 1798* (Dublin, 1998), pp. 47–63, John Gray discusses the relationship between Russell and Mary Ann McCracken, and dismisses the claims in works such as Helena Concannon, *Women of 'ninety-eight* (Dublin, 1919) and Mary McNeill, *The life and times of Mary Ann McCracken: a Belfast panorama* (Dublin, 1960) that Mary Ann McCracken's political activities can be largely explained by the fact that she was in love with Russell, and notes that the evidence for this 'presumed love' is non-existent (p. 58). However, the description of Russell given below on pp. 27–8 is McCracken's and at the very least it indicates a strong physical attraction. My own opinion is that McCracken was indeed attracted to Russell but that this did not greatly influence her politics, which arose out of her own principles and convictions.

50 Drennan to Martha McTier, Feb. '95; Martha McTier to Drennan, 21 Sept.

    1795 (Drennan papers, T765/544b, 583); *Journals*, 172n.
51 Russell's journal, 4 Nov. 1794 (*Journals*, p. 174).
52 Statement of James Farrell, 24 Oct. 1803 (P.R.O., HO 100/114/23).
53 Mary Ann McCracken to Madden, 13 Nov. 1857 (Madden papers, 873/70); see
    also an affectionate letter from Mary Simms to Russell, 27 Aug. 1797 [?] (Sirr
    papers, 868/2, ff 309–10).
54 Matilda Tone to Russell, 11 Sept. 1796 (Reb. papers, 620/25/136).
55 *Drennan letters,* pp. 187, 202, 204.
56 R. B. McDowell, 'The proceedings of the Dublin Society of United Irishmen' in
    Analecta Hibernica, xvii (1949), pp. 98, 107; Drennan to Sam McTier, 16 Feb.
    1794 (*Drennan letters*, p. 188).
57 Lecky, *Ireland*, iii, 21.
58 Lecky, *Ireland*, iii, 225–6, 231.
59 MacNeven, *Pieces*, p. 70; Tone, *Writings*, i, 504–8; Cooke to Nepean, 26 May
    1794 (P.R.O., HO 100/52/72–3).

CHAPTER NINE

Violent Democrat

The events of 1793–4 led to a disillusionment with constitutional politics, and transformed many United Irishmen from reformers to revolutionaries. Russell, who had harboured near revolutionary sentiments for some time, had begun to feel that the Irish masses were ripe for armed rebellion by the early part of 1794. On his travels in south Ulster Russell met a boy on the road who told him that the Defenders in Monaghan were armed and in contact with France. Throughout Cavan and Monaghan he found the common people staunchly pro-French. They rejoiced to see the republic's armies being led by ordinary tradesmen and they hatred aristocracy every bit as fervently as did the French *sans culottes*. Russell believed that the common people offered the only real hope for change and prophetically noted that 'nothing can hinder a revolution in this country...It must be in four or five years'. He observed that 'the people are in that state of expectation of some great event taking place in their country, which will of itself produce it'.[1]

Meanwhile in Dublin there were also stirrings. The dispersal of the United Irish meeting in May 1794 had not in fact killed off the society. During the summer it continued to meet under the direction of the Sheares brothers, John and Henry, two militantly republican lawyers, although it maintained a lower public profile than previously. Gradually it began to revive, with the Sheareses and Thomas Addis Emmet, the latter a close friend of Russell and Tone, playing the leading roles in its resurgence. Russell made several visits to Dublin in the summer of 1794 in June and July, and in August he and Tone were admitted as members into the restructured club.[2] By October membership had grown to about 250 and to avoid the lax security which had plagued the earlier society the Sheares proposed that it adopt a cellular structure. The club was to be divided into local sections of no more than fifteen members that were each to return a delegate to a central committee every week. Drennan, who

157

had been tried for sedition in June 1794 and acquitted, met Russell and Tone in August and believed that they were closely involved in the reorganised society. He resented that they did not include him in their confidence, complaining to his brother-in-law in Belfast that he was being kept in the dark as he thought were most of the northerners except Russell, Neilson and possibly Simms. Drennan had been badly shaken by his trial and disapproved of the revolutionary potential of the new cellular structure; he was adamant that he would not be a party to 'these private plotting meetings'.[3]

As Nancy Curtin has noted, there was a considerable level of continuity between the 'constitutional' and 'militant' phases of the United Irishmen, and there was a hard core of members willing to contemplate insurrection well before they were forced underground.[4] The existing organisation of the United Irishmen in Belfast in 1794 already lent itself to restructuring on more conspiratorial lines. Samuel Neilson, when questioned by the secret committee in 1798, claimed that the 'affiliated system' had begun early in 1792 and had gradually increased since then.[5] These societies kept a lower profile than that in the capital, issuing none of the bombastic addresses and declarations of their Dublin counterpart, and as a result attracted far less attention. Despite the concern of some Dublin-based United Irishmen at their apparent inactivity, the Belfast societies had played an important behind-the-scenes role between 1791 and 1794, disseminating radical propaganda and attempting to influence larger organisations such as Volunteer corps, masonic lodges and the Catholic Committee.[6]

In his evidence before a parliamentary secret committee in 1798 Thomas Addis Emmet maintained that the initiative for a more secretive style of movement came from a Belfast United Irish society in the latter half of 1794. According to Emmet this Belfast society had continued to meet throughout the year and had avoided the attention of the authorities because of 'the obscurity of its members'. These men were 'mechanics, petty shopkeepers and farmers' and were assisted by another club composed of men with similar occupations. With opportunities for public meetings and debate curtailed they decided to institute a system of secret societies, but they continued to use the name of United Irishmen and an oath based on the society's original test.[7] The oath of the new society was, however, amended to allow a more radical interpretation of the society's aims. In the original wording members had sworn to seek 'an impartial and adequate representation of the Irish nation in parliament' while, in the new version, the reference to parliament was dropped and members pledged themselves to work for 'an equal, full and adequate representation of all the people in Ireland'.[8] According to Emmet the goal of the new societies was 'a republican government, founded on the broadest principles of religious liberty and equal rights', while their means was to harness the efforts of the Irish masses — in effect to 'make every man a politician'.[9]

Emmet claimed that even in Belfast the existence of the new United Irish clubs was for a long time unknown to most of the town's leading radicals, who only became involved with the new societies when they saw how popular they were among the lower orders. In March 1795, noting the increasing involvement of the working classes in politics, Martha McTier observed that in the town 'the democratic party are now established in strength and numbers... Persons and ranks long kept down now come forward, and with a degree of information which might shame their betters'.[10] However, it is unlikely that Belfast's leading democrats such as Neilson, Russell and McCracken remained unconnected with these developments for very long. In particular, it is probable that Russell, a well-known figure in the town, renowned for his radical politics, was closely involved in the rise of popular republicanism in Belfast from an early stage. Martha McTier often commented on his friendships with 'men every way below himself' and he was singled out in the report of a Belfast loyalist as someone who had been engaged in 'corrupting the minds of the lower orders of the people'.[11] In his journal for November 1794 Russell indicated that he was no stranger to the town's working-class militancy by noting that 'the young men are far more violent than the others'. They were suspicious of prominent middle-class radicals, such as the proprietors of the *Northern Star*, who they believed were 'not ready enough for the field'. But they thought better of Russell: 'P.P. stands well with them. They think to[o] he would be ready to act. This [is] a great compliment as few are so counted'.[12]

Some of Russell's more respectable friends were deeply concerned about his close association with plebeian militants. He was held in such high regard in the town 'for his literary taste, general deportment, and unbounded love of liberty', that when they feared 'he might entangle himself beyond recovery in dangerous schemes, every effort was made to detach him from the United Irishmen'.[13] One of those who attempted to dissuade him from the path of republican militancy was Dr James McDonnell, but his efforts were unsuccessful. He gave up, claiming that although he had done his best to reason with Russell, 'no power on earth can make any impression on him. It is part and parcel of his existence'.[14] As a former army officer who could provide radical leadership for Belfast's working classes, Russell was seen as a real threat by the authorities and it seems that efforts were made to divert him from democratic politics. In August 1794 he was offered an ensigncy in a militia regiment through an officer named Fortescue, with a promise of rapid promotion to lieutenant, but he turned it down.[15]

Russell's ability to move with ease in different social settings was one of his key attributes as a revolutionary organiser. He was respected by both the radical professionals and merchants who had been present at the society's founding and the artisans and labourers who formed its the rank and file in its later phase. Just as he often acted as a mediator between north and south, so he also served to bridge the gap between different social strata within radical circles. Through his frequent contact with working people in Ulster and north Leinster he became aware of their increased levels of politicisation and of their revolution-ary potential. This was to be a crucial factor in his commitment to the transformation of the United Irishmen from a small number of exclu-sive clubs into a mass movement.

It seems to have been towards the end of 1794 that the Belfast United Irishmen began to abandon the idea of reform in favour of revolution. According to Russell's own notes, the republican variant of the test was drawn up and adopted by existing societies during the winter of 1794–5. This period also saw a steady growth in the number of United Irish clubs in Belfast and its hinterland.[16] The resurgence of United Irish activity in and around Belfast began to alarm loyalists. An inhabitant of Hillsborough complained that these new United Irish societies are attempting 'to excite nothing less than rebellion in these parts ... Hand bills are dispensing throughout the country and the shop boys of Belfast and Lisburn are traversing the country on various pretences to diffuse their poison. Jacobin clubs under the specious names of book clubs and literary societies in every town and village kept all private as if masonic'.[17] From Carrickfergus came reports that the disaffected were 'well supplied with arms and ammunition' and that 'wicked and designing men in Belfast' were spreading dangerous doctrines and attempting to convince the people that they would 'bring all people on a level, no one to exceed another in the property of lands'.[18] Russell played a prominent part in the establishment of these new societies: it was reported that a United Irish club had been founded at Lisburn — 'a man of the name of Russell most forward in it', and he was denounced by a government informant from Belfast as 'one of the most violent democrats on the face of the earth'.[19]

In the early months of 1795 the growth of United Irish societies in Ulster was steady rather than spectacular but the dismissal of the pro-Catholic Lord Lieutenant, Earl Fitzwilliam, accelerated their spread. Fitzwilliam had been appointed viceroy on 13 December 1794 as one of the conditions of the Portlandite Whigs for joining Pitt's government. But after he arrived in Ireland on 4 January 1795 his actions sent nervous tremors through Whitehall. He dismissed some leading conservatives from the Irish administration, notably John Beresford from the revenue, and made clear his support for further Catholic relief. Pitt was not prepared for such far-reaching measures and Fitzwilliam was recalled in March and replaced by the conservative Earl Camden. The government's action was a slap in the face to Catholics and Protestant liberals: Tone's friend George Knox noted that Fitzwilliam's dismissal had alienated 'all the middling people ... driving them back into a tendency to French principles which they had lately completely relinquished'.[20] Lecky maintained that this was the defining moment in the history of the 1790s and that afterwards disaffection spread throughout the land creeping, as Grattan claimed, 'like the mist at the heels of the countryman'.[21]

The important point is, however, that Fitzwilliam's recall and the publicity given to seditious activity by the trial of Revd. William Jackson in April 1795 gave impetus to a movement already in motion. As increasing numbers joined the United Irishmen the movement soon began to outgrow its rudimentary organisation and consequently, delegates from seventy-two societies met in Belfast on 10 May 1795 to adopt formally a new constitution and structure.[22] Individual societies were to consist of no more than thirty-six members and were to be co-ordinated by a hierarchical series of committees rising from baronial, through county and up to provincial level. In mid-June a committee for Co. Antrim was established, followed by the Down committee towards the end of the month and later in the summer the Ulster provincial committee came into being.[23] Early in June a government official from Belfast noted that there were sixteen different societies of United Irishmen in the town and that 'the generality of the people here ... are very ripe for a revolution'.[24]

There were also several shadowy radical clubs established in Belfast closely linked to the United Irishmen, such as the Irish Jacobins. There is no record that Russell was a member, but friends such as William Sinclair, Henry Haslett, William Tennent and William Sampson were, and the staunchly Paineite stance of the Irish Jacobins would have been in keeping with his political views from 1793 onwards.[25] He was certainly a leading member of an influential body known as 'the Mudler's club', which met in a tavern and was ostensibly a drinking club, but its real purpose was as a front for the United Irishmen; McCracken and Neilson were also important members. The club was a common port of call for trusted radicals from Belfast's hinterland who came to town on business. Apparently, it acted as a confidential forum for discussion and for planning strategy.[26] The trio of Russell, Neilson and McCracken were those most closely involved in the restructuring of the United Irish system. The notes made by Russell on this matter suggest a close involvement with the reconstituting of the society, as does the fact that, when negotiating with the government in 1798, it was to Russell that William James MacNeven wrote looking for details on the adoption of the new test and constitution.[27]

There are intimations of revolutionary intentions and expectations throughout Russell's journals of 1793 and 1794, but it is not until April or May 1795 that we first find him making an explicit commitment to rebellion.[28] This occurred during one of his intermittent visits to Dublin to see Tone who, having been seriously compromised by his entanglement with the French agent, William Jackson, was obliged to reach an agreement with the authorities to accept exile in America in return for immunity from prosecution. The two friends walked out to Thomas Addis Emmet's villa in Rathfarnham. Emmet was building a new study in his garden which he intended to use for meetings and Tone 'begged of him, if he intended Russell should be of the party, in addition to the books and maps it would naturally contain, to fit up a small cellaret, which should contain a few dozens of his best old claret...[Emmet] acknowledged [this] to be essential, and we both rallied Russell with considerable success'. When they got down to more serious business Tone proposed that on arrival in Philadelphia he would visit the French ambassador, inform him of the state of Ireland and seek a recommendation to the government in Paris. He would then travel to France to solicit assistance in overthrowing British rule. Russell and Emmet strongly approved of the plan and the next day Russell returned to Belfast.[29]

Towards the end of May Tone and his family arrived in Belfast, which was to be their port of embarkation for America. They stayed for three weeks, during which there was 'no lack of whiskey, claret and burgundy'. Tone was grateful for the generous hospitality shown to him by his friends and remembered the period with great fondness, particularly a number of memorable excursions to local beauty spots. The first of these was to Cave Hill, where Tone, Russell, Neilson, Simms, McCracken and a few others climbed to the top of McArt's fort and made a solemn promise — 'never to desist in our efforts until we had subverted the authority of England over our country, and asserted our independence'. Before he left for America, Tone informed the town's leading United Irishmen — Simms, Neilson and Charles Teeling — of his intentions to seek French aid, and they also approved. On his last night in Belfast he was at Neilson's when the prospect of seeking help from France was discussed: Frank McCracken, brother of Henry Joy, announced that 'the Irish could free themselves without any assistance from France'. Tone replied that 'If you act on that principle...you may pursue your ropeworks and sail manufacture long and prosperously enough; for there will never be an effectual struggle in Ireland without invasion'.[30]

A government official in Belfast had taken careful note of the movements of Tone and Russell during these weeks and divined Tone's intentions, even if his account was inaccurate on some points. He informed the Castle that although Tone was pretending to go to America, his real destination was France and that he was to be accompanied by Russell. He alleged that their excursions from Belfast were far from innocent, but that Tone and his colleagues had been charting the coast, and 'if his and Russell's papers were examined I would forfeit my existence if some useful discoveries were not made'.[31] The authorities, however, were anxious to be rid of Tone and took no action against him. On 14 June Tone bid his friends farewell and he and his family sailed on the *Cincinnatus* for America. Tone and Russell never saw each other again.

The evidence for Russell's involvement in the transformation of the United Irishmen to a mass organisation is, not surprisingly, fragmentary. Recording such activities in writing would have been very foolhardy and Russell's journals peter out after 1794. He was, however, a central figure in building up the revolutionary movement. As C. J. Woods notes, Russell's position as librarian with the Belfast Society for Promoting Knowledge was the ideal 'cover' for a United Irish organiser, allowing him time for his political activities and regular access to Belfast radicals.[32] Russell was regularly cited as a leading United Irish organiser in the reports of informers but, for the most part, he seems to have operated with considerable caution, often working through intermediaries.[33] John Smith (alias John Bird), a government agent well-informed about the activities of the Belfast societies, could only say of Russell — 'of him I know nothing but by report — he was always spoken of as a man of the strictest republican principles on whose integrity the committee reposed the greatest confidence'.[34]

By the mid-1790s Russell's radical democratic views had taken on an even harder edge and he had become one of the most fervently anti-aristocratic of the United Irish leaders. Tone, writing from America in September 1795, anticipated Russell's delight when he informed him that:

> We are splitting here fast into two great parties, the rich and the poor... and I know you will rejoice to hear that against all the might of property and government influence, democracy is daily gaining ground... I see now what aristocracy is however modified! I suppose as much has been done as could well be done to neutralise it in the constitution of America but in vain, it still retains its noxious activity... Liberty must destroy aristocracy under every possible modification or surrender her existence... She must, to borrow Grattan's expression, when he was surprised by his passion into a fit of honesty, 'extinguish aristocracy or aristocracy will extinguish her'.[35]

In a letter to a newspaper he wrote in December 1976 Russell described the Irish aristocracy as 'bigoted, corrupt, rapacious, cruel and ignorant'.[36] A draft ballad, written by him about 1795, left no doubt as to the kind of treatment the nobility might expect should revolution break out:

> *Proud bishops then may well translate*
> *Around priestcrafted martyrs*
> *The guillotine on peers shall wait*
> *And knights shall hang on garters*

Now one for all the work's begun
We'll clear the Augean stable
A moment lost is [word unclear]
Let's strike while we are able.[37]

Perhaps intended for the 1795 edition of *Paddy's resource*, this verse had to be toned down for the published version.[38]

One of the intermediaries through whom Russell worked was James Hope, a Presbyterian weaver from Templepatrick in Co. Antrim. Hope was an intelligent, self-educated man and, like Russell, founded his dedication to the radical cause on strict Christian principles and was convinced that sweeping social change was needed to improve the lot of the poor. The two struck up a firm friendship. They first met in Belfast in about 1795 when Hope, who had become a member of the United Irishmen but objected to the society's preoccupation with oath-taking, was explaining his reasons to colleagues, and Russell, who was passing by, was called on to adjudicate. Hope claimed that good men would always keep their word and 'you can frame no oath which will bind the villain who would desert the cause of his country and betray his fellow men'. Russell carefully weighed up Hope's words and then as 'he stretched out his left hand to tender the grasp of union, he looked like one who has found a man after his own heart'.[39] Hope fought bravely at the battle of Antrim in 1798 and was one of the few northerners willing to resort to arms again in 1803, but it was as an indefatigable emissary that he did greatest service to the United Irish cause. As a working man himself, Hope was adept at winning the confidence of his own class. Among his more important assignments was a mission to Dublin in the spring of 1796 to establish the United system among the artisans of the capital. According to Hope, his instructions came mostly from Russell and Henry Joy McCracken.[40]

McCracken and Russell had been close friends since soon after the latter's arrival in Belfast in 1790. Russell's political principles made a strong impression on McCracken, who shared Russell's republican and socially-radical views, and he formed strong links with Belfast's working classes. Strangely enough, there is no mention of McCracken in Russell's journals, which largely cover the years 1791–4, though it seems that he was in the confidence of leading United Irishmen from the society's foundation.[41] As a United Irish organiser, however, he seems to have come into his own when the society began to expand its popular base, particularly when the United Irishmen began to make overtures towards the Defenders.[42]

The Defenders were a shadowy organisation that had emerged out of sectarian feuding in Armagh in the early 1780s. In this populous and prosperous county competition for land had been intensified by the repeal of penal laws which enabled Catholics to buy land and Protestants found their position threatened. They became all the more anxious when some Catholics exhibited their rising status by openly carrying arms. Protestant vigilantes took it upon themselves to enforce the prohibition on Catholic ownership of arms and their custom of raiding Catholic homes at dawn led them to be termed Peep o' Day Boys. Catholics then banded together in groups known as Defenders, which soon developed a lodge structure and oaths which owed something to freemasonry. Clashes continued throughout the 1780s and by the early 1790s had become more frequent and widespread. As tensions grew the Defender movement spread from Armagh into neighbouring counties in south Ulster and north Leinster. By this stage Defenderism was much more than a response to intimidation but had taken on a more aggressive character and often involved raiding Protestant homes for arms. Its aims had also broadened beyond the purely sectarian and, although varying from place to place, they usually involved regulating tithes, rents and food prices. The Defenders also turned their attention to politics. By the early 1790s social and sectarian oppression was widely associated with the state apparatus and the Defenders' resentment was focused on the entire social and political structure rather than on specific local grievances, making them potential allies of the United Irishmen.

Some United Irishmen, for example Samuel Neilson, had reservations about recruiting the Catholic masses into the republican movement, but he realised that 'their number makes them formidable, their wrongs make them desperate, [and] with proper leaders they might be made of very great service to the cause'.[43] The large numbers of Defenders in militia regiments was a further incentive to their recruitment. Therefore from 1795 onwards, once the United Irishmen had decided to create a mass movement, they attempted to tap the great well of Catholic disaffection and began to incorporate Defender lodges into their organisation.[44]

By the mid-1790s Defenderism had spread through most of the northern half of the country but its real heartland was in south-east Ulster and north Leinster, especially the southern parts of counties Armagh and Down. In this region a small number of key individuals and families provided the core of the movement's leaders. Several of these already had links with the United Irishmen before any formal decision was taken to ally the two bodies. Among the most important Defender leaders were the Teelings, John Maginnis, Bernard Coile, Alexander Lowry, Valentine Derry and Fr. James Coigly. Coile and Coigly were key organisers in Armagh, Maginnis and Lowry were the leading figures in Down, Charles Teeling moved between Antrim and Down, while Derry and Bartholomew Teeling operated out of Dundalk, where they were later joined by Coigly.[45] They were a close-knit group, linked together by family and business ties: Maginnis had married into the Teeling family and Coigly and Derry were related; the Teelings, Maginnis, Lowry and Coile were all prominent in the linen trade, which greatly facilitated contact with the radical merchants and manufacturers of Belfast. These networks helped to provide the infrastructure for the expansion of a radical popular organisation through much of Ulster and north Leinster.[46]

By May 1795 government informants were reporting increased contacts between Defenders and United Irishmen. From Carrickfergus, one claimed that 'three emissaries are to be sent from Belfast. The societies wish to co-operate with the deluded people in Louth, Meath etc.'. Another, from Strokestown, Co. Roscommon, wrote that 'by considering the different movements and progress of the Defenders, a person would be led to think that their daily instructions came from Belfast, or some other northern direction'.[47] Before departing for America in June, Tone related his intention of seeking French assistance to Charles Teeling, one of the leading figures in the Defenders. Tone then considered himself qualified 'to speak fully and with confidence for the Catholics, for the Dissenters and for the Defenders of Ireland'. In a memorial on the state of Ireland he prepared for the French government in February 1796, probably trying to convince the French of the existence of a popular non-sectarian republican movement in Ireland, he maintained that the Defenders in Ulster were directed more by the Dissenters of Belfast than by their co-religionists in Dublin.[48]

Even before the beginnings of their merger with the United Irishmen, Russell had some contact with Defenders, conversing with them and their sympathisers in his rambles through south Ulster and north Leinster early in 1794. Such contacts probably facilitated the more formal overtures to absorb the Catholic peasantry into the republican movement made throughout 1795–6. His attitude towards the Defenders was always strongly sympathetic. He lamented a massacre of Defenders in north Meath in 1793 and claimed that they had been the victims of an unprovoked attack. His *Letter to the people of Ireland* empathised with the grievances of the Catholic peasantry and claimed that since they had been deserted by the Catholic gentry it was hardly surprising that they 'should at times commit unjustifiable actions'. Russell compared the fate of alleged Defenders in Connacht, arbitrarily arrested and transported or sent to the fleet in 1795, with the plight of African slaves torn from their homes.[49] He was also probably the author of a *Northern Star* article on clashes between Defenders and the militia in Co. Leitrim which strongly sympathised with the Defenders. After the killing of eleven revenue officers by Defenders at Drumcollop, Co. Leitrim, on 23 April 1795, a party of the Derry militia sent to recover the bodies was harassed by Defenders and responded by killing as many as 100 of them in a battle at Drumsna. The militia then mounted a series of punitive raids and attacked and routed Defenders throughout Leitrim, giving them no quarter. It was reported that 'from the great quantity of blood on the roads and through the county it is impossible to form any idea of the vast numbers that are killed or wounded'.[50] The *Northern Star* article lamented this bloodshed:

> When I read those daily accounts in the papers which . . . advertise the cruelties committed by and upon this wretched race of people I feel all that is Irish within me melt with compassion. When will this social war cease? When will the heart whisper — these are my *country-men* . . . How my heart beats when I think that all this bloodshed may be owing to the want of mutual explanation . . . Jesus wept — O! were He to revisit this earth, where would He be found? Would it be at a visitation of the clergy? Would it be at the episcopal tables or with stall-fed theologians? . . . He would be found in the cottier's cabin . . . His hand would pour balm on the mangled body of the expiring husband; and His eyes would spread the consolation of heaven upon the wretchedness of an Irish peasantry.[51]

Russell and McCracken were the Belfast United Irish leaders most closely involved in liaising with the Defenders.[52] Both men, free from anti-Catholic prejudice and sympathetic to the plight of the poor, were more inclined than many of their colleagues to feel solidarity with the Catholic masses. In the summer of 1795 McCracken moved to Holywood, Co. Down, where he was frequently joined by Russell, and from here the two were busily engaged in promoting 'the business of the union'. McCracken spent much of his time in the years 1794–6 helping those Catholics who had been the victims of sectarian outrages to seek legal redress. As well as winning the confidence of persecuted Catholics this no doubt also provided a convenient entry into local Defender networks and McCracken's influence became such that he was appointed to command a large body of Defenders.[53]

Forging links between the United Irishmen and the Defenders was not always smooth going and the alliance took anything up to a year to formalise. In outlook and organisation there were considerable differences between the two organisations: the visceral Catholicism of the Defenders often conflicted with the pluralistic republicanism of the United Irishmen and decentralised Defender lodges were not always easily incorporated into United Irish hierarchical structures. It took considerable amounts of negotiation, the dissemination of much propaganda and repeated journeys through Defender strongholds by United Irish emissaries to create the alliance.

Russell's precise role in the expansion of the United Irishmen is vague (as he would have wished it to be) but available evidence suggests that he ranged far and wide recruiting new members, founding new clubs and preaching his political ideals with religious fervour. Madden credits him with 'a very active part in propagating the system in the counties of Antrim, Down, Tyrone and Donegal' while a report from a government informer has Russell 'at or near Sligo, no doubt promoting union among Irishmen'. In Sligo he may have been renewing the contacts he had with Catholics in north Connacht in 1791.[54] Another informer noted his contacts in Enniskillen with William Henry Hamilton and claimed that there was 'a chain of societies' extending from Belfast to Derry and 'the connexion between Enniskillen and Belfast is strong, young Hamilton ... visits the latter place occasionally and is an intimate confidential friend of Russell's ... This connexion runs also to Ballyshannon, to Keenan, formerly a delegate to the Catholic Committee.'[55]

Russell's recruiting efforts were directed at Presbyterians as well as Catholics. His knowledge of scripture and sincere religious convictions made him a respected figure among Ulster Presbyterians and, according to Madden, 'his efforts to gain over persons of the Presbyterian persuasion, notorious for their hostility to those of the Roman Catholic religion, met with more success than those of any other northern leader'.[56] The roving mission of United Irish emissary was well suited to Russell and we can only guess at the immense distance he must have covered on his travels during 1795–6. During these years he was too busy even to find time to visit his sister Margaret: she complained that she had not seen him in over a year and that 'you tell me you are very busy but not a word of in what manner'.[57]

Nancy Curtin has correctly cited Russell as one of the key figures in demonstrating the continuity between the United Irishmen in the constitutional and militant phases, but her claim that he 'travelled about the north in 1793 enrolling lower-class members in a manner strikingly similar to United Irish recruiters in the second half of the decade' is an exaggeration.[58] We know that in 1793 he often took the political temperature of the areas through which he travelled, that he occasionally distributed United Irish propaganda and that in all he probably established contacts which he later used when the United Irishmen were expanding their popular base. He did, for example, help to 'lay the foundation of a club' in Enniskillen in October 1793,[59] but because the United Irishmen did not at first aim at mass membership, his efforts to recruit new members on a major scale were confined to the years 1795–6.

These years saw Russell make his most significant and distinctive contribution to the United Irish movement — travelling throughout Ulster spreading his gospel of republicanism, Christian unity and social revolution. At times it is likely that he used contacts previously established but he also appears to have travelled to areas where he knew nobody in order to make new converts. His activities in this regard found their way into Ulster folklore: *The man from God-knows-where*, the popular ballad written about Russell, begins with him riding into an Ulster townland on a snowy night in the winter of 1795–6, being friendly but guarded with the local people, and then riding off into the night on United Irish business.[60]

Most reports of his activities in the mid-1790s are vague, such as the account of Russell and Charles Telling borrowing the horses of James Dickey of Crumlin, Co. Antrim, and going on noctural expeditions 'organising the country and rapidly inspecting the progress of and preparations for their projected enterprise'. But there is at least one more substantial account of his recruiting efforts, which gives us some idea of how Russell went about enlisting United Irishmen. This occurred on Rathlin Island, off the north Antrim coast: Russell told Robert Gage, the owner of Rathlin, that he had come to the island to explore geological formations and he was invited to stay as a guest at Gage's house. Given Russell's genuine interest in geology he may well have spent some time observing rock formations, but in addition he also had considerable success as a United Irish emissary:

> He held frequent conversations with the people, in which he endeavoured to instil his principles into their minds, but in order to avoid suspicion he was obliged to assemble them in some secluded spot where he might harangue them without fear of observation. For this purpose he fixed on a large cave on the eastern coast called Brackens Cave ... It would easily contain a hundred men; there the secret meetings took place and there they were persuaded to take the United Irishman's oath, before doing which they insisted on an additional clause declaring that they would not injure Mr Gage or any of his family.[62]

Russell's millennialist leanings lent themselves well to his revolutionary proselytising. In addition to the intellectually respectable millennialism of scholarly Dissenters there was a folk tradition of prophecy and apocalyptic expectation, which in Ireland, as elsewhere, came to the fore strongly during the troubled years of the 1790s.[63] In the face of accelerating economic change, growing political and sectarian polarisation, and increasing levels of violence in the Irish countryside, slumbering hopes and fears took on a new immediacy. The dawning of a new era seemed imminent and people were increasingly susceptible to prophecies that land would be redistributed, that poverty and injustice would be swept away and 'heretics' would be converted or exterminated. Predictions such as the one found posted up on a house in Glenarm, Co. Antrim, in May 1795 etched themselves into people's minds:

> *We have had a frosty winter and a cold spring*
> *We will have a bloody summer and a headless king.*[64]

The oaths and catechisms of the Defenders were steeped in millenarian imagery: 'The gates are open. — How many? Twelve. — For whom? The children of Abraham. — Where? In paradise'.[65] As Thomas Bartlett has pointed out, in these formulae 'the theme of deliverance, the central feature of Gaelic literature for more than 200 years, was fused with the very real prospect of French help to form a revolutionary dynamic, and it was this fusion that, in the final analysis, made Defenderism an altogether new force in Ireland'.[66]

Apocalyptic prophecies that strongly focused the inchoate resentments of the poor against the rich and powerful and prepared their
minds for revolution were a powerful propaganda weapon for the
United Irishmen. Millenarian tracts such as those by Richard
Brothers, Robert Fleming or James Bicheno were frequently adver-
tised in the *Northern Star.*[67] Fleming's work in particular seemed
infused with prophetic insight. He was a Scottish Presbyterian
follower of William of Orange who in 1701 had forecast that the
French monarchy would be toppled in 1794 at the latest. Some
United Irishmen such as Samuel Neilson showed some embarrassment about using such propaganda: on receiving 'a foolish old
prophecy' Neilson said he included it only 'to please his country
readers',[68] but many of Neilson's colleagues, among them Russell,
had no such reservations about disseminating prophecies for political purposes. Russell's interest appears to have straddled both
scholarly millennialism and the more popular forms of millenarianism. At least two folk prophecies held in the Rebellion papers at the
National Archives in Dublin have what appears to be Russell's signature on the reverse and seem likely to have been in his possession at
some stage. One of these, written in Irish with an accompanying
English translation, claimed to be an 'ancient prophecy' foretelling
the 'eight remarkable eras of Ireland': 'The first era the learned
bereft of right. The next era the Geralds will pose their might. The
third era my race is at a stand, the fourth the Britains [*sic*] overcome
the land. The fifth era, in wily plots they pride. The next they're
plucked and vanquished every side. The next, dismay by land,
despair by sea. But last of all, the Erins win the day'. It was accompanied by a prophecy of 'Mother Shiptons' which foretold of crop
failures and great defeats for England in battle, and warned that
'dams shall swell, and mills be turned with blood'.[69] The other, which
may have been copied out by Russell, is labelled 'Part of Collon Kills
prophescy [*sic*] in the year 1412' and chronicled the events of the
1790s as follows:

> 1790/There will be a rebellion against the French king. 1791/A war
> amongst many powers...1794/No religion observed in France.
> 1795/Destruction [and] divisions amongst the powers of
> Europe...1797/Will appear Gog and Magog who will make war
> against the inhabitants of the earth...1799/Will come a descendant
> of David who will perform great acts of grace from the power of
> heaven and destroy Gog and Magog and cause the remnants of all

nations to be one religion and banish war from the earth and man shall live in friendship and love...[70]

The authorities viewed the increasing number of 'pretended prophets' spreading their doctrine of sedition with deep concern.[71] A leading Castle politician complained that:

> the utmost pains have been taken by those devils, the United Irishmen, to prepare the minds of the different classes of the people for mischief...They have a vast number of emissaries constantly going through the country to seduce every person they can and swear them; they have songs and prophecies, just written, stating all late events and what is to happen, as if made several years ago, in order to persuade the people that, as a great part of them has already come to pass, so the remainder will certainly happen. These and every other species of contrivance to mislead a silly and superstitious people they practise.[72]

Russell may well have made use of such prophecies as a United Irish emissary; utilising a range of prophetical material provided an effective means of commanding attention from different traditions. Just as his revolutionary gospel when couched in the language of Daniel or Revelations was more likely to appeal to a Presbyterian audience for whom scripture was the ultimate sanction, so folk prophecies that carried the stamp of the Gaelic tradition would have enabled him to tap in to the apocalyptic expectations of the Defenders. Millenarianism provided a means to awaken in an unevenly politicised population the prospect of far-reaching political and social change, and to convince them that they had a part to play in bringing it about. As John Gray has noted, far from representing evidence of detachment or lack of realism, Russell's combination 'of a populist political agenda with religious millenarianism rendered him particularly in tune with the Ulster of the 1790s'.[73]

As the popular organisation advanced throughout 1795, Irish republicans began to think more and more of seeking the assistance of their revolutionary mentors in Paris. Late in the year, when a proposal from the Antrim county committee to open communications with France appeared before the Ulster directory, it was informed (possibly by Russell) of the progress of Tone's mission.[74]

On his arrival in America in August, Tone travelled to Philadelphia and composed a memorial on the state of Ireland for Pierre Adet, the

French ambassador. Adet received him politely but without enthusiasm. He informed Tone that he would convey his memorial to the French government with a recommendation that they should act on it, but he strongly discouraged him from travelling to France to try and persuade the government in person. Tone, considering himself to have fulfilled his mission, set about buying some land in New Jersey and prepared to settle down and become a farmer.[75] But he did not like America, and he greatly missed the company of his Irish friends, particularly Russell; he wrote to him of his

> most unqualified dislike of the people...Those of Philadelphia seem a selfish, churlish, unsocial race totally absorbed in making money — a mongrel breed, half English, half Dutch, with the worst qualities of both countries. The spirit of commerce hath eaten up all other feeling...Send me by the first safe conveyance...a full state of everything in Ireland since my departure together with all manner of papers, pamphlets etc. relating to Irish affairs; let me also know how my old masters the Catholics got on or whether they got on at all. You know me better than any man knows me and suit your letter accordingly...
>
> Believe me, dear Tom, the greatest of the numberless heavy losses I sustained in leaving Ireland, and especially in leaving Belfast, my adopted mother, was the loss of your society; and I speak for us all. There does not a day lapse that we do not speak of you nor a ridiculous or absurd idea or circumstance arise that we do not regret that you are not with us to share and enjoy it with us. You know how exactly our humours concurred, and that particular style of conversation which we had framed for ourselves and which was to us exquisitely pleasant; those strained quotations, absurd phrases and extravagant sallies, which people in the unreserve of affectionate intercourse intimately indulge themselves in — all these we yet enjoy, but woefully curtailed by your absence — if anything brighter than ordinary occurs the first idea is 'Ah, poor Tom! I wish he was here with us now!'
>
> It is a selfish wish — never come here, unless you are driven. Stick to your country to the last plank...much as I regret your absence, I cannot in conscience wish you were with us...Writing thus to you, and recalling so many of those I most regard...is making me almost too melancholy to proceed. I will therefore stop here, wishing you and them health, happiness and liberty. You have a country worth struggling for, whose value I never knew until I had lost it.[76]

Tone's plans for a quiet life were interrupted by the arrival of letters from Russell, Keogh and the two Simmses. These were sent on the advice of the Belfast executive directory and acquainted Tone with the rapid growth of disaffection throughout Ireland.[77] Defenderism was spreading into counties which had previously been undisturbed and pro-French sentiments were gaining ground. The letters urged Tone 'in the strongest manner, to fulfil the engagement I had made with them at my departure, and to move heaven and earth to force my way to the French Government in order to supplicate their assistance'.[78] These entreaties encouraged Tone to approach Adet again in November. On this occasion he received a far warmer reception. The ambassador, possibly reassured about Tone's bona fides, displayed much more interest in his plan and encouraged him to sail for France to press the government to mount an expedition to Ireland. Tone then wrote to his younger brother, Arthur, who was living in New Jersey, to make his way immediately to Philadelphia. There, Tone acquainted him with his plans and entrusted him with the task of returning to Ireland to inform Neilson, the Simmses and Russell in Belfast, and Keogh and McCormick in Dublin, of the mission he was undertaking. Arthur sailed on 10 December and had made contact with Russell by early January.[79]

Tone himself arrived in France on 1 February 1796. He was to spend many lonely and trying months negotiating with the French government and throughout the period he continually lamented Russell's absence. To keep his mission as secret as possible he mostly kept to himself and often after a night at the theatre or a bottle of wine he noted in his diary how much more enjoyment he would have derived from it had he shared it with Russell. He complained that:

> The French have an abominable custom of adulterating their Burgundy with water... I cannot but respect the generous indignation which P.P. would feel at such a vile deterioration of that noble liquor, and the glorious example he would hold out for their imitation. He would teach them how and in what quantities generous Burgundy ought to be drank[sic]. I would gladly pay his reckoning today en numeraire, which would be no small sum, for the pleasure of his company.

But it was more than just Russell's sociability he missed: he valued his friend's help every bit as much in political matters. Soon after his arrival in Paris Tone lamented: 'I never wanted the society, assistance, advice, comfort, and direction of the said P.P. half so much as at this moment. I have a pretty serious business on my hands, with a grand responsibility, and here I am alone... without a single soul to consult with.' On being asked by the French government to compose a manifesto that would be issued by French invasion forces on their arrival in Ireland and finding himself unable to write, he 'wish[ed] to God that P.P. was here' to advise and assist him. Often he thought about how he would spend his future with his family and with Russell, and the desire to impress him was a constant motivation during his difficult early months in Paris:

> I frame no system of happiness for my future life in which the enjoyment of his society does not constitute a most distinguishing feature...When I think I have acted well, and that I am likely to succeed in the important business wherein I am engaged, I say often to myself, my dearest love and my friend Russell will be glad of this.[80]

Tone was also anxious to promote Russell's political career in whatever way he could. When the French foreign ministry suggested sending an agent to Ireland to test the waters for invasion, Tone decided that it would be safer if he was to make contact with only one member of the United Irish leadership and recommended that that man should be Russell. He realised that in doing this he would 'put him in the post of danger and honour, though I love him like a brother. I wish Ireland to come under obligations to the said P.P.'. Some months later, on 29 October 1796, while waiting to sail with Hoche, Tone learned that Russell, Neilson and several other Belfast United Irishmen had been arrested six weeks earlier on charges of high treason. He fully expected that the government would stop at nothing to hang them and, though anxious for them all, he was particularly concerned for Russell. He winced at the manner in which he had made fun of him in the past and grimly noted 'that levity exists no more'. From this time onwards, a new note of deadly earnestness entered Tone's journal: he discarded the nickname of 'P.P.' when referring to Russell and swore solemnly that, if he landed in Ireland with a French army after his friend had been harmed, he would not rest until he had avenged him.[81]

In his letter to Tone, Russell had informed him that the United Irishmen were 'gaining ground, and our opponents rapidly losing', but he believed that talk of an immediate rising was folly. It might prove to be a useful diversion for the French but it would only dissipate the society's momentum at a time when the tide was flowing in its favour. Likewise, he believed that the issuing of a declaration of assistance from the French, a move favoured by some United

1. Betsborough, Kilshannig, Co. Cork, photo by J.G. White, 1909

2. Royal Hospital, Kilmainham, Dublin, by Christopher Machell
(Courtesy National Gallery of Ireland)

3. Lt John Russell (R.R. Madden, *United Irishmen*)

4. Theobald Wolfe Tone (R.R. Madden, *United Irishmen*)

5. High Street, Belfast, in 1786

6. Interior of the Belfast Assembly Rooms in the 1790s

7. Samuel Neilson (1761–1803)

8. Dr James MacDonnell (1764–1845)
by Christopher Moore (1844)
(Courtesy the Trustees of the National Museums
and Galleries of Northern Ireland)

9. Martha McTier (Courtesy the Trustees of the National Museums and Galleries of Northern Ireland)

10. Henry Grattan by Gilbert Stuart (Courtesy National Gallery of Ireland)

11. John Keogh (Denis Gwynn, *John Keogh*)

12. Thomas Addis Emmet (R.R. Madden, *United Irishmen*)

13. Henry Joy McCracken (1767–98), by Sarah Cecilia Harrison (1926)

14. James Hope (R.R. Madden, *United Irishmen*)

15. Thomas Russell (R.R. Madden, *United Irishmen*)

16. Caricature of Russell, 'The Librarian at Belfast'
(Courtesy Linenhall Library, Belfast)

17. McArt's Fort, Cave Hill, Belfast, c.1828, by Andrew Nicholl

18. Newgate Prison, Dublin (MacGiolla Easpaig, *Tomás Ruiséil*)

19. Fort George (Courtesy Historic Scotland)

20. Robert Emmet (Courtesy National Gallery of Ireland)

21. Execution of Thomas Russell at Downpatrick Jail, October 1803
(*Ulster Jn. Of Arch*. XIII, 1907)

22. Russell's grave, Downpatrick Church of Ireland graveyard
(Courtesy Down County Museum)

23. Downpatrick Church of Ireland graveyard
(Courtesy Down County Museum)

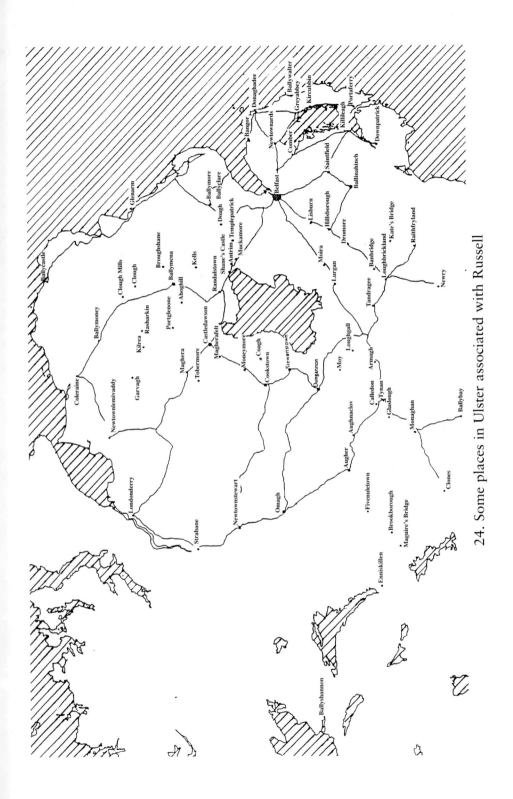

24. Some places in Ulster associated with Russell

Irishmen, could only serve to alert the government and intensify repression, resulting in the imprisonment, exile or death of all the society's leaders and the frustration of any insurrection. He continued: 'believe me, Tone, I am for no unnecessary procrastination. I think the hour is rapidly approaching, and our business at present is preparation. Not the fixing a time, or saying "when the crops are in, or the corn secured" or any other definite time; but when we are prepared let us embrace the first favourable moment that offers.'[82] It was to this preparation for insurrection that he devoted himself until his arrest in September 1796.

These measures included the stock-piling of arms and attempts to suborn members of the militia and regular army. The militia, containing large numbers of Catholics, was a particularly tempting target, into which Defenderism had already made inroads, and the unreliability of certain militia regiments was a recurrent theme in the letters of anxious loyalists. Russell's involvement in this activity is unclear, though as an ex-soldier he would have been well-suited to recruiting among the military. He certainly had contact with the militia as early as September 1793: his journal records a meeting with two militia sergeants at the home of a Belfast radical. He was impressed by their levels of politicisation and noted that the raising of a nationwide militia 'will serve further to make people know each other in this kingdom, which is all that is wanted'. Russell may also have had contact with the militia and Defenders in Dublin. In a letter to Tone, William Simms remarked that someone referred to as 'R' had just returned from the capital with a report that five or six thousand militiamen had taken the Defender oath.[83]

In addition to its attempts to enlist military allies, by 1796 the United Irish organisation was itself beginning to take on an increasingly military character. When examined after the '98 rebellion most leaders placed this development as late as possible in the year, implying it was a response to the enforcement of the draconian insurrection act or the sweeping arrests made in the autumn. It would seem, however, that the United Irishmen were in possession of significant quantities of arms by the autumn of 1795 and by May 1796 were well on the way to constructing a military organisation.[84]

Under the rules of the militarised United Irishmen, the colonels of each county returned the names of three persons to the executive, who appointed one of them to serve as adjutant-general, in effect commander-in-chief, of that county. Russell was appointed adjutant-general of Down in the summer of 1796.[85] He was a popular choice.

According to Charles Teeling, the 'chief command in Down had been early assigned to Russell and the military organisation of this county was considered complete when talent and virtue were combined in the person of its chief'.[86] Admittedly, Teeling rarely stinted when praising his United Irish colleagues, but there is strong evidence to confirm that Russell held a special place in the esteem of both the movement's leaders and its rank-and-file. Though he had never progressed beyond the rank of ensign in his army days, he was generally given the more respectful title of 'Captain Russell' by his friends, and this became the title by which he was normally referred to by friend and foe alike. While he was imprisoned in Newgate, a letter from Thomas Potts, an active republican from Belfast, assured him that 'although you have been so long immured within the walls of a loathsome dungeon, suffering for the cause of the people, your name, even among those who never had the pleasure of your acquaintance, is alive and much revered'. Before he was hanged in 1798, Henry Joy McCracken was anxious that his sister should write to Russell to inform him of his death and to assure him that he had done his duty. While awaiting execution in July 1798 William Michael Byrne, a member of the Leinster United Irish directory, wrote one of his last letters to Russell, addressing him as 'my virtuous countryman, whose censure or approbation, next to my God's, I alone regard.'[87] Besides the respect he evinced, his local knowledge and many contacts in east Ulster, as well as his experience of soldiering, made him an obvious choice as a military commander. His seniority in the movement was soon brought to the attention of the government. In September 1795 a Carrickfergus weaver had alleged that 'Capt. Russell of Belfast has been appointed to the command of all the societies in the province of Ulster'.[88] Some time later, one of the government's most reliable agents informed the Castle, 'the United Irishmen...are now ready at a call, they are hourly expecting arms and ammunition...Russell who was an officer in the 64th [is] at the head of those deluded people. He and Mr Tone were the original founders of United Irishmen here, and he now conducts all their plans'. Reviewing the leadership of the movement, the Lord Lieutenant, Camden, was of the opinion that Neilson, Haslett and Russell had been the 'leading characters in Belfast'.[89]

It seems that the controlling body behind the expansion of the United Irishmen was an executive committee which sat in Belfast. According to a Co. Down informer all important business was planned by an 'executive directory', which then communicated with

the Ulster provincial committee, and Camden, considered this directory to be 'the centre of motion of the whole machine'.[90] John
Mitchell of Ballynaslee, Co. Antrim, reported that he had been
present at meetings where money was collected to be forwarded to
the 'general committee of Belfast' which controlled all the societies
of United Irishmen in the province and planned 'to overthrow the
government'. This directory supervised the creation and direction of
new societies, received subscriptions from the local clubs and
dispatched and financed the emissaries required to spread the system
throughout the country. It took all the main policy decisions affecting the movement and sought to co-ordinate the activities of local
clubs by issuing instructions through the provincial and county
committees. The precise membership of this directory is not known
for certain but the informer John Mitchell maintained that it was
composed of Neilson, McCabe, Haslett, Sinclair and Russell.[91]

By the summer of 1796 reports from loyalists were flooding in
detailing the great numbers of United Irishmen who had been sworn
in, the widespread disaffection in the militia, the landing of large
quantities of arms in Ulster and warning of the imminence of rebellion. 'It is to be hoped that a civil war might be averted', wrote a
Belfast loyalist, 'but be assured if something be not speedily done, it
is impossible to say what might take place'. Another, an insider in
the northern United Irish organisation, wrote that preparations were
well advanced, insurrection would erupt after the harvest and that
'the present government stood on the precipice and before three
months were past 'twould be no more'.[92]

The county of Down, Russell's main sphere of operations, was a
particularly troubled one. The tenants of Lord Moira were
reported to have been corrupted by 'the infernal *Northern Star* and
the politics of Belfast' and others intended to refuse to pay tithes,
cess or rent. The town of Ballynahinch was reported to be
completely organised by the United Irishmen, who were 'increasing
by thousands' especially in the areas around Dromore, Rathfriland
and Saintfield. Lord Downshire's agent reported 'that a flame may
and will burst forth is surely to be apprehended. The emissaries of
the United Irishmen are astir in every quarter'; and Major Robert
Ross of Rostrevor informed his lordship that 'if even a privateer
and crew were to land, an insurrection would be the consequence,
and before winter is over I really believe you'll have some very
unpleasant work'.[93]

John Goddard, father of Eliza, whose 'abhorrence of democracy' Russell was already acquainted with, took care to point out Russell's activities to Lord Downshire. He had learned that Russell had been out of circulation for a month and was publishing a pamphlet 'to inform the people how they have been imposed on by their governors since 1782, to exhort them to unite, and if the measures of their rulers do not meet with their perfect approbation, to refuse payment of taxes. To this he intends putting his name'. Reports of intended insurrection were now so frequent that Goddard claimed that 'those who used to laugh at the alarmists are completely frightened now'.[94]

The intensification of sectarian warfare in Armagh contributed significantly to the inflamed state of Ulster. After the foundation of the Orange Order in September 1795, following a Protestant victory over a large body of Defenders at Loughgall, attacks on Catholics were carried out in an increasingly violent and systematic manner. Many hundreds were forced to flee, spreading resentment and panic wherever they went, and rumours of an Orange oath to exterminate all Catholics circulated widely. Sectarian warfare had always horrified Russell: writing to Tone of the strife in Armagh in September 1795, he lamented how 'that county has always been a plague to us'.[95] But as the months passed these disturbances began to work to the advantage of the United Irishmen. Frightened Catholics flocked to the United Irish standard and the alliance between the society and the Defenders began to solidify.[96] The United Irish leadership were not above playing on sectarian fears and their publications often included a version of the alleged Orange extermination oath. In 1798 the movement's leaders admitted that the United Irishmen were 'most exceedingly indebted' to the persecution of Catholics in Armagh. Dublin Castle became deeply concerned at how Belfast republicans had taken advantage of events in Armagh to forge links with the Defenders in the west and midlands, and noted that emissaries had been sent among the Catholics to convince them that their persecution had been sponsored by the government 'to excite them to join the United Irishmen, and to fill them with hopes of a French invasion'.[97]

By the autumn of 1796 such reports were producing genuine anxiety in government circles. A draconian insurrection act passed in March, which gave magistrates wide powers of search and arrest and made administering illegal oaths a capital offence, had done nothing to calm the province.[98] Harvest time was always a period of heightened expectations and in August the lord lieutenant was warning London that the United Irishmen planned to rise once the crops were in and to establish an independent republic with the aid of the French. The state of the north-east provided most cause for concern. A meeting of Dublin Castle's 'inner cabinet' — Fitzgibbon (now Earl of Clare), Foster, John Beresford, Sir John Parnell and Arthur Wolfe, the attorney general — concluded that the conspiracy organised in Belfast was becoming increasingly dangerous. They believed the province to be in a state of 'smothered rebellion' and discussed the possibility of arresting the main agitators, but were aware that they had little hard evidence that could be used to secure convictions against them in court. Therefore, they thought that it might be necessary to recall parliament to pass legislation suspending habeas corpus, which would enable the suspects to be held indefinitely without trial, and decided to request royal consent for a bill should it be required at any point in the near future.[99]

Towards the end of August 1796, Lord Castlereagh, by now a strong supporter of the government and soon to be entrusted with the duties of chief secretary, undertook a tour of east Ulster to see things for himself. He found Antrim and Down to be extremely disaffected, with United Irish societies proliferating, and all the evidence he unearthed confirmed that Belfast was pulling the strings.[100] Some weeks later the authorities decided to act. On 7 September two troops of the 22nd Light Dragoons were sent to Belfast and six days later Castlereagh and General George Nugent, the British military commander in Belfast, met the Marquis of Downshire at Hillsborough Castle in Co. Down to make arrangements for an immediate move against the northern United Irishmen. They decided on a mass arrest of the United Irish leadership, and drew up warrants for the purpose. It emerged during their discussions that one important document was missing, namely the warrant for the arrest of Russell. The Marquis was 'extremely desirous to have a warrant against Russell of Belfast', and he requested that it be sent immediately. On the list of the arrest warrants, alongside Russell's name alone were written the words 'take great care of this man'.[101] Russell's popularity in the North, his political writings, his contacts with the Defenders and with the radical artisans of Belfast, coupled with his military experience and personal charisma, singled him out to the authorities as a particularly dangerous character.

The morning of Friday 16 September was a fair day in Belfast and a large crowd of people from the neighbouring countryside had gathered. They looked on as a sizeable body of troops entered the town, accompanied by Lords Castlereagh, Downshire and Westmeath, colonel of the locally stationed Westmeath militia, and John Pollock, Crown solicitor and Downshire's attorney. The town was placed under military government, guards were set up at all its approaches and soldiers patrolled the streets. The offices of the *Northern Star*, the library of the Belfast Society for Promoting Knowledge and the houses of leading radicals were searched. Henry Haslett was the first to be arrested, and then other United Irishmen — Rowley Osborne, Samuel Kennedy, Daniel Shanaghan and John Young — who had been cited as leading conspirators by the informant John Smith. Three United Irishmen were also arrested in Lisburn on the same day, among them Charles Teeling.[102]

Russell and Samuel Neilson were not among those initially taken up, but later they surrendered themselves to the authorities when they learned that warrants had been issued for their arrest. An observer recalled seeing William Sampson stopping Samuel Neilson in the street and telling him: 'Sam, they are looking for you'. Neilson did not appear overly concerned and replied: 'I have some little private business to attend to and then I will give myself up'. The morning also had its lighter moments. The private life of one of the most active arresting officers, the Earl of Westmeath, had become public knowledge in the previous months after he had divorced his wife for adultery. A well publicised court case had laid bare such embarrassing details as her lover hiding in her bedroom. When Westmeath searched Sampson's home, he insisted on searching his wife's bedroom, where Mrs Sampson was in labour. Sampson assured him that there was no need for this, since his wife 'was not, as some other ladies are, in the habit of privately harbouring gentlemen'.[103]

According to Russell's own account of the arrests, he walked through streets crowded with soldiers on several occasions during the day and since no attempt was made to apprehend him, he believed that the authorities wanted him to escape so that they might be rid of him without the necessity of bringing him to trial. The readiness of both Russell and Neilson to surrender themselves suggests that they may have expected to be arrested and had decided to call the government's bluff by giving themselves up and standing trial. Russell maintained that he had behaved with extreme nonchalance throughout, informing the arresting officers that he had taken his time before surrendering in order to read the newspapers and that he was completely unconcerned by any charges against him. However, an account from a sympathetic observer noted that although Russell tried to affect an attitude of unconcern by presenting the arresting magistrates with a copy of his *Letter to the people of Ireland*, he nonetheless 'seemed much agitated'.[104] The authorities had decided to imprison those arrested in Dublin, away from the northern strongholds of the United Irishmen, and accordingly prisoners were placed in separate carriages, with an armed guard in each, and at three o'clock in the afternoon the convoy set off for Dublin accompanied by a strong escort of dragoons. They made a halt at Lisburn to pick up the prisoners arrested there and arrived in Dublin at 11 o'clock on Saturday night.[105]

The following morning the prisoners were brought before a magistrate to be served formally with their committals. During their committals an incident occurred which showed clearly the rather earnest side of Russell's character. When addressed by the magistrate, Judge Boyd, Neilson interrupted him and made some humorous remarks questioning his sobriety. Teeling recalled that these remarks:

> excited a feeling of merriment impossible to repress. The gravity of poor Russell, however, seemed to have been offended. No man regarded etiquette and the punctilios of politeness more. He looked solemn, stroked up his fine black hair, and with a sweetness of countenance peculiarly his own, and in a gently modulated but sufficiently audible tone of voice he begged of his friend Neilson to respect the dignity of the bench and the personal virtues of the learned judge. Russell's admonition had the desired effect; Neilson bowed respectfully and with a half-suppressed smile assured his friend that he esteemed the learned judge the most chaste and temperate of mankind.[106]

Most of the prisoners were sent to Kilmainham jail but Russell, Rowley Osborne, John Young and Samuel Musgrave of Lisburn were imprisoned in Newgate.[107]

NOTES

1   Russell's journal, 18 Jan., 22 Jan., 1 Feb. 1794 (*Journals*, pp. 141–3, 145).
2   Hamilton to Nepean, 14 July 1794 (P.R.O., HO 100/52/159); Drennan papers, T765/511, 514, 520, 522; Drennan to Sam McTier, 20 Aug. 1794 (*Drennan letters*, p. 213).
3   Drennan to Sam McTier, 2 Aug., Oct. 1794 (Drennan papers, T765/519, 523;

Drennan letters, pp. 214–5).
4   Nancy J. Curtin, 'The transformation of the Society of United Irishmen into a mass-based revolutionary organisation, 1794–6' in *I. H. S.,* xxiv, no. 96 (Nov. 1985), pp. 463–92.
5   *Report comm. sec.,* p. 232.
6   Nancy J. Curtin, 'The United Irish organisation in Ulster: 1795–8' in Dickson, Keogh and Whelan (eds), *United Irishmen,* p. 211; for concern at northern inactivity see, Drennan to Sam McTier, 16 Feb. 1794 (*Drennan letters,* p. 188).
7   MacNeven, *Pieces,* pp. 76–7.
8   *Report comm. sec.,* pp. 5, 77–8, 237, 307.
9   MacNeven, *Pieces,* p. 77.
10 MacNeven, *Pieces,* pp. 77–8; Martha McTier to Drennan, Mar. 1795 (Drennan papers, T765/548).
11 *Drennan letters,* p. 175; — to Dublin Castle, Belfast, *c.* 1796 (Reb. papers, 620/54/29).
12 Russell's journal, 3 Nov. 1794 (*Journals,* p. 173).
13 George Benn, *History of the town of Belfast* (London, 1877), i, 644.
14 Madden, *United Irishmen,* 3rd ser., ii, 280.
15 J.A. Russell to Madden, 1836? (Madden papers, 873/654); Madden, *United Irishmen,* 3rd ser., ii, 181.
16 Note by Russell on the United Irish constitution, n.d. (Sirr papers, 868/1, f. 1v); Morgan, 'Sketch of Russell', p. 59 — based on evidence given by Mary Ann McCracken; for McCracken's evidence see Madden, *United Irishmen,* 3rd ser., ii, 137; MacNeven, *Pieces,* p. 77.
17 Michael Thompson to Dublin Castle, 12 April 1795 (Camden papers, U840/0144/8).
18 John Ford to John Lees (postmaster of Belfast), Carrickfergus, 27 April 1795 (Camden papers, U840/0144/20/1).
19 Robert Johnston to John Lees, 8 May 1795 (Camden papers, U840/0146/3); Rowland J. O'Connor, Belfast, to Sackville Hamilton, Dublin Castle, 7 June 1795 (Camden papers, U840/0147/4/1).
20 Charles H. Teeling, *Personal narrative of the Irish rebellion of 1798* (London, 1928), p. 8; George Knox to Abercorn, 12 March 1795 (P.R.O.N.I., Abercorn papers, T/2541/1132/6/12).
21 Lecky, *Ireland,* iii, 321–2.
22 For this meeting see: A[ndrew] M[cNevin] to John Pollock, 9 May 1795 (Camden papers, U840/0146/7); Dean [Richard] Dobbs to Francis Dobbs, 27 June 1795 (Camden papers, U840/0147/13/2); and Russell's notes (Sirr papers, 868/1, f. 1v).
23 Note by Russell on the United Irish constitution (Sirr papers, 868/1, f. 1v); MacNeven, *Pieces,* pp. 101, 109.
24 Rowland J. O'Connor, Belfast to Sackville Hamilton, Dublin Castle, 7 June 1795 (Camden papers, U840/0147/4/1).
25 For a list of the members of the Irish Jacobins (which does not include Russell), see Camden papers, U840/0147/4/2.
26 Madden, *Antrim and Down in '98,* p. 10.
27 Curtin, 'Transformation of U.I.', p. 471; note by Russell on the United Irish constitution (Sirr papers, 868/1, f. 1v); W. J. MacNeven to Russell, *c.* Sept. 1798 (Reb. papers, 620/16/3).
28 Curtin, 'Transformation of U.I.', pp. 463–92; Smyth, *Men of no property,* p. 98; see Russell's journal, 11 July 1793, 18 Jan. 1794 (*Journals,* pp. 87, 141).
29 Bartlett, *Life of Tone,* pp. 105–6.
30 Bartlett, *Life of Tone,* pp. 107–8; Thomas Russell to John Russell, 13 June

1795 (Madden papers, 873/330/II); Madden, *United Irishman*, 3rd ser., i, 132 — the conversation at Neilson's on the French invasion was reported by Dr James McDonnell.

31 Rowland J. O'Connor, Belfast, to Sackville Hamilton, Dublin Castle, 7 June 1795 (Camden papers, U840/0147/4/1).

32 Woods, 'Place of Thomas Russell', p. 89.

33 For references by informers to Russell, see Reb. papers 620/2241, 620/23/197, 620/54/29 and Frazer MS II/16.

34 Smith's information on arrested United Irish leaders, late 1796 (Frazer MS II/40); see also Smith's statement to the parliamentary secret committee in 1797 in which he mentions Russell as one of the 'active men' among the United Irish leadership (J. T. Gilbert (ed.), *Documents relating to Ireland, 1795–1804* (Dublin, 1893), p. 113.

35 Tone to Russell, 1 Sept. 1795 (Reb. papers, 620/16/3).

36 Written in Newgate, 19 Dec. 1796; the letter appeared in the *Dublin Evening Post*, 22 Dec. 1796 and *Northern Star*, 26 Dec. 1796.

37 Russell's papers, seized 18 Sept. 1796 (Reb. papers, 620/25/136).

38 *Paddy's resource* (1795), pp. 35–6, and below, p. 112.

39 Madden, *Antrim and Down in '98*, p. 143; Morgan, 'Sketch of Russell', p. 56.

40 Madden, *United Irishmen*, 3rd ser., i, 243; Madden, *Antrim and Down in '98*, p. 97.

41 Mary Ann McCracken to Russell, 18 July 1798 (Reb. papers, 620/16/3); Madden, *Antrim and Down in '98*, p. 9.

42 For McCracken's activities, see information of J. W., 1795 (Reb. papers, 620/10/121/26); examination of Michael Phillips, Nov. 1795 (Frazer MS, II/13); Browne notebook, mid–1796 (Reb. papers, 620/54/7).

43 Information of John Bird (alias Smith), *c*. 1796 (Reb. papers, 620/27/1).

44 Marianne Elliott, 'The Defenders in Ulster' in Dickson, Keogh and Whelan (eds), *United Irishmen*, p. 231.

45 L. M. Cullen, 'Political structures of the Defenders' in Gough and Dickson (eds), *Ire. and the Fr. Rev.*, p. 131; Marianne Elliott, 'The Defenders in Ulster' in Dickson, Keogh and Whelan (eds), *United Irishmen*, pp. 222, 228, 232; Madden, *Antrim and Down in '98*, p. 13; for the Teelings see *Northern Star* journey account book (Reb. papers, 620/15/8/6); for Maginnis, see examination of Michael Phillips, 5 Dec. 1795 (Frazer MS II/2, and II/13); for Coile, see Reb. papers, 620/15/8/6, and information from J. W. (ie. Leonard McNally), 1795 and Bryan Egan, 29 Nov. 1796 (Reb. papers, 620/10/121/26, 620/26/109); for Lowry, see Browne notebook, *c*. mid–1796 (Reb. papers, 620/54/7) and information of Smith, July 1796 (P.R.O., HO 100/62/141); for Coigly and Derry, see information of Boyle, *c*. 1796 (Reb. papers, 620/18/3/2 and 620/54/7), Dáire Keogh (ed.), *A patriot priest: The life of Father James Coigly 1761–1798* (Cork, 1998) and Brendan McEvoy, 'Father James Quigley' in *Seanchas Ardmhacha*, v (1970), pp. 247–59.

46 Smyth, *Men of no property*, p. 119; L. M. Cullen, 'Internal politics of the United Irishmen' in Dickson, Keogh and Whelan (eds), *United Irishmen*, p. 179.

47 Digest of information on the Defenders, Camden to Portland, 27 July 1795 (P.R.O., HO 100/58/186).

48 Bartlett, *Life of Tone*, pp. 108, 610; Smyth, *Men of no property*, p. 118.

49 Russell's journal, 18, 19 Jan. 1794 (*Journals*, pp. 141–2); Russell, *Letter to the people*, pp. 12, 22.

50 *Faulkner's Dublin Journal*, 5 May 1795; Liam Kelly, '*A flame now quenched*': *rebels and Frenchmen in Leitrim 1793–1798* (Dublin, 1998), pp. 38–41.

51　*Northern Star,* 18 May 1795. As with most of the content of the *Star,* it is difficult to prove conclusively the authorship of the piece. The article is signed 'A Native', a pen-name that also accompanies a review of a travel book on China in the *Star* (4 June 1795) which contains a number of religious views which are very similar to Russell's. Russell, as author of the 'Chinese journal', was strongly interested in foreign cultures and would have been a likely reviewer of such a work. In the article quoted the extremely emotional style and references to Christ's return and his compassion for the poor, which are recurrent themes in Russell's writings, strongly suggest his authorship. Compare it, for example, with the following lines taken from Russell's *A letter to the people of Ireland,* p. 18, 'How different was the conduct of Him in whom we profess to believe? What did He who knew the hearts of men say of the great and powerful? He did not revile the poor — He comforted, he instructed, he blessed them'.

52　L. M. Cullen, 'Political structures of the Defenders' in Gough and Dickson (eds), *Ire. and the Fr. Rev.,* p. 131; idem, 'Internal politics of the United Irishmen' in Dickson, Keogh and Whelan (eds), *United Irishmen,* p. 179.

53　Madden, *Antrim and Down in '98,* pp. 8, 13–14; see also evidence given in Frazer MS II/13, Nov. 1795, and Browne notebook (Reb. papers, 620/54/7) for McCracken's activities among the Defenders.

54　— to Dublin Castle, Belfast, c. 1796 (Reb. papers, 620/54/29); Madden, *United Irishmen,* 3rd ser., ii, 180. For Russell's contacts in north Connacht see below, pp. 47, 49.

55　Information of J.W. (ie. Leonard McNally), c. 1795 (Reb. papers, 620/10/121/26); the 'Keenan' referred to may have one of the Kiernan family, associates of Hamilton. See Russell journal, 2 Oct. 1793 (*Journals,* p. 131) and C. J. Woods, 'More on the Kernans of Enniskillen: Randal Kernan (1774–c. 1844) and others' in *Clogher Record,* x, no. 1 (1979), pp. 23–5).

56　Madden, *United Irishmen,* 3rd ser., ii, 180.

57　Margaret Russell to Thomas Russell, 2, 9 Jan. 1796 (Sirr papers, 868/2, ff 72–3, 76).

58　Curtin, 'Transformation of U.I.', p. 469; Woods, 'Place of Thomas Russell', p. 92; on this point see also Smyth, *Men of no property,* p. 210n; review of Smyth by C. J. Woods in *I. H. S.,* xxx, no. 117 (May 1996), p. 136.

59　Russell's journal, 2, 12 Oct. 1793 (*Journals,* pp. 131–2).

60　Florence Mary Wilson, *The coming of the earls* (Dublin, 1918), pp. 9–12.

61　W. J. Fitzpatrick, *The sham squire* (new edn, Dublin, 1895), p. 340.

62　[Catharine] Gage, *A history of the island of Rathlin, 1851* (Coleraine?, 1995), p. 78.

63　On the use of the words 'millennialist' and 'millenarian' I generally follow the distinction originally made by E. L. Tuveson. 'To the earlier opinion — which expects the physical return of Christ – I have given the name "millenarian" To the belief that history, under divine guidance, will bring about the triumph of Christian principles, and that a holy utopia will come into being, I have assigned the name millennialist' (E. L. Tuveson, *Redeemer nation: the idea of America's millennialist role* (Chicago, 1968), p. 34.

64　Camden papers, U840/0146/7.

65　Camden to Portland, 29 July 1795, digest of information on the Defenders (P.R.O., HO 100/58/193–210).

66　Thomas Bartlett, 'Select documents XXXVIII: Defenders and Defenderism in 1795' in *I. H. S.,* xxiv, no. 95 (May 1985), p. 377.

67　*Northern Star,* 28 May, 15 June, 6 Aug. 1795.

68　Information of Smith, c. 1796 (Reb. papers, 620/27/1).

69 Reb. papers, 620/54/126.
70 Reb. papers, 620/48/46. For the link with Russell see David W. Miller, 'Presbyterianism and "modernisation" in Ulster' in C.H.E. Philpin (ed.), *Nationalism and popular protest in pre-Famine Ireland* (Cambridge, 1987), p. 100n — 'Russell's name is written several times on the back of the document, but it is struck out in all but one case — as if someone were perhaps practising to forge Russell's signature. Christopher Woods...believes that the document may be in Russell's hand, but that it is more deliberate in style than his usual hand.' Like Dr Woods I would be cautious about claiming that the chronicle was written by Russell, but the signatures on the reverse certainly seem to me to be in Russell's hand. It seems to have been a habit of his to write his name on old correspondence and then cross it out, as if practising his own signature. See for example, Reb. papers 620/16/3 or ibid. 620/15/6/3, p. 101.
71 Lord Altamont to Cooke, 27 July 1796 (Reb. papers, 620/24/62).
72 John Beresford to Lord Auckland, 4 Sept. 1796 (*Beresford corr.*, ii, 128); for similar observations see also Samuel McSkimin, *Annals of Ulster, 1790–1798*, ed. E. J. Crum (Belfast, 1906), pp. 31–2.
73 John Gray, 'Millennial vision...Thomas Russell re-assessed' in *Linen Hall Review*, vi, no. 1 (spring, 1989), p. 9; see also David W. Miller, *Queen's rebels, Ulster loyalism in historical perspective* (Dublin, 1978), p. 55 and idem, 'Presbyterianism and "modernisation" in Ulster' in C. H. E. Philpin (ed.), *Nationalism and popular protest in pre-Famine Ireland* (Cambridge, 1987), p. 101.
74 MacNeven, *Pieces*, p. 110.
75 Bartlett, *Life of Tone*, pp. 111–12.
76 Tone to Russell, 1 Sept. 1795 (Reb. papers, 620/16/3).
77 Robert and William Simms, Russell and Keogh to Tone, Sept. 1795 (Bartlett, *Life of Tone*, pp. 239–42); for the identity of the authors to the letters to Tone see, C. J. Woods, 'The authorship of a letter received by Tone in America in 1795' in *Eighteenth-Century Ireland*, v (1990), pp. 192–4; MacNeven, *Pieces*, p. 110.
78 Bartlett, *Life of Tone*, p. 113.
79 Arthur Tone to Russell, 2 Jan. 1796, Margaret Tone to Russell, 26 Jan. 1796 (Sirr papers, 868/2, ff 18–19, 18v).
80 Bartlett, *Life of Tone*, pp. 468, 487, 736; ibid. p. 475; ibid. p. 510 and pp. 478, 500, 574, 578, 621, 736; ibid. p. 32.
81 Bartlett, *Life of Tone*, pp. 501, 635.
82 [Russell] to Tone, 21 Sept. 1795 (Bartlett, *Life of Tone*, pp. 239–40); the letter is simply attributed to 'one of the leaders of the United Irishmen in Belfast'. C. J. Woods has examined the authorship of this letter and comes to the conclusion that 'it is very probable that Thomas Russell was the author' (C. J. Woods, 'The authorship of a letter received by Tone in America in 1795' in *Eighteenth-Century Ireland*, v [1990], pp. 192–4).
83 A[ndrew] M[cNevin] to John Pollock, 9 May 1795 (Camden papers, U840/0146/7); Russell's journal, 9 Sept. 1793 (*Journals*, pp. 122–3); see also journal for 24 Nov. 1793, in which he appears to record contact with the militia in Enniskillen (*Journals*, p. 137); [William Simms] to Tone, [21] Sept. 1795 (Bartlett, *Life of Tone*, p. 240).
84 *Rep. comm. sec.* (1798), pp. 5, 225, 231–3; information of Smith, Sept. 1795 (Frazer MS, II/17), May 1796 (Frazer MS, II/18); examination of John Mitchal [*sic*], Billeston, Co. Antrim, 13 June 1796 (Reb. papers, 620/23/172).
85 Madden, *Antrim and Down in '98*, pp. 33, 122; see also Hope papers, 7253/2, f. 4.

86 Charles H. Teeling, *Personal narrative of the Irish rebellion of 1798* (London, 1928), p. 224.
87 Potts to Russell, 23 June 1797 (Reb. papers, 620/31/140); Mary Ann McCracken to Russell, July 1798 (Reb. papers, 620/16/3); Byrne to Russell, 24 July 1798 (Reb. papers, 620/39/109); for similar sentiments see also W. Irwin to Russell, *c.* 1798 (P.R.O.N.I., T913).
88 Examination of William Hart, 22 Sept. 1795 (Reb. papers, 620/22/41).
89 Captain Andrew McNevin to Edward Cooke, 27 June 1796 (Reb. papers, 620/23/197); Camden to Portland, 17 June 1797 (P.R.O., HO 100/69/397–9).
90 John Macarra to Gen. Nugent, 8 Aug. 1797 (B.L., Pelham papers, Add. MS 33105/204); see also: Camden to Portland, 27 July 1795 (P.R.O., HO 100/58/182); Andrew McNevin to Pelham, 6 July 1795 (Camden papers, U840/0148/2/1).
91 Examination of John Mitchell, Ballynaslee, Co. Antrim, *c.* 1796 (Frazer MS II/16); Nancy J. Curtin, 'The United Irish organisation in Ulster' in Dickson, Keogh and Whelan (eds), *United Irishmen,* p. 217.
92 — to Dublin Castle, Belfast, *c.* 1796 (Reb.papers, 620/54/29); information of Smith, 15 July 1796, July 1796 (Frazer MS, II/22–3); see also Cooke to Pelham, 30 July 1796 (P.R.O., HO 100/62/154) for predictions of rebellion; for the unreliability of the armed forces, especially the militia, see information of Smith, May 1796 (Frazer MS II/18), July 1796 (P.R.O., HO 100/61/141–4); William Bristow to Dublin Castle, Belfast, 24 May 1796 (Reb. papers, 620/23/122) and anonymous informant, *c.* 1796 (Reb. papers, 620/54/29); for the arrival of large arms shipments in Ulster, see Charles McNeill to John Beresford, Ballynahinch, 2 Aug. 1796 (Reb. papers, 620/24/76).
93 Thomas Lane, Hillsborough, to Lord Downshire, 4 Feb., 24 Mar., 24 May, 19 June, 16 July 1796 (P.R.O.N.I., Downshire papers, D/607/D/27, 43, 62, 73, 102); Joseph Pollock to Downshire, 2 Aug. 1796 (P.R.O.N.I., Downshire papers, D/607/D/109); Ross to Downshire, 2 Sept. 1796 (P.R.O.N.I., Downshire papers, D/607/D/146).
94 John Goddard to Lord Downshire, 2 Sept. 1796 (P.R.O.N.I., Downshire papers, D/607/D/149); Russell's journal, 30 June 1794 (*Journals,* p. 155).
95 Lecky, *Ireland,* iii, 429–30; [Russell] to Tone, 21 Sept. 1795 (Bartlett, *Life of Tone,* p. 240).
96 Camden to Portland, 22 Jan. 1796 (P.R.O., HO 100/62/18); information of Smith, *c.* May 1796 (Frazer MS II/18); Browne notebook, *c.* mid–1796 (Reb. papers, 620/54/7).
97 *The Press,* 12 Oct. 1797; MacNeven, *Pieces,* p. 178; Cooke to Pelham, 6 Aug. 1796 (P.R.O., HO 100/62/153–62).
98 Roger Wells, *Insurrection: the British experience 1795–1803* (Gloucester, 1983), p. 55.
99 Camden to Portland, 6 Aug. 1796 (P.R.O., HO 100/62/154, 160–63).
100 Castlereagh to Pelham, 23 Aug. 1796 (Lecky, *Ireland,* iii, 465).
101 *Belfast News Letter,* 9 Sept. 1796; John Pollock to Cooke, 13 Sept. 1796 (Reb. papers, 620/25/56a); list of warrants delivered by Cooke, 17 Sept. 1796 (Reb. papers, 620/18a/3).
102 *Northern Star,* 16 Sept. 1796; Pelham to duke of York, 22 Sept. 1796 (B.L., Pelham papers, Add. MS 33113, f. 51); Smith's information, Reb. papers, 620/27/1–2.
103 William Grimshaw, *Incidents recalled or sketches from memory* (Philadelphia, 1848), p. 13; Martha McTier to Drennan, 16 Sept. 1796 (*Drennan letters,* p. 240); *Northern Star,* 16 Sept. 1796.

104 Thomas Russell to John Russell, Fort George, 10 Dec. 1800 (copy) (Madden papers, 873/655, ff 4v–5); anonymous letter from Belfast, 24 Sept. 1796 (Reb. papers, 620/25/103).
105 *Belfast News Letter*, 19, 23 Sept. 1796.
106 Charles H. Teeling, *Personal narrative of the Irish rebellion of 1798* (London, 1928), pp. 35–6.
107 *Northern Star,* 23 Sept. 1796.

CHAPTER TEN

Newgate

Newgate jail was located in a run-down quarter of Dublin off North King Street, surrounded by 'filth[y] horrible streets', with a 'heavy and gloomy' appearance. It had been built in the 1770s but by 1796 was already in very poor repair. A report from an inspector of prisons described it as 'dirty beyond description', its cells as 'stinking, shocking places'. The prison administration was inept and corrupt, with the jailer deeply involved in a variety of dubious practices, including selling spirits to the inmates. Drunkenness was endemic and minor riots common, while hardened criminals terrorised the other prisoners. In June 1782 the famous prison reformer, John Howard, reported to a Commons committee that Newgate was 'in every respect the very reverse . . . of a perfect and well-regulated jail'. Prison conditions improved somewhat in the early 1790s, largely due to the efforts of Sir Jeremiah Fitzpatrick, the energetic inspector general of prisons, and political prisoners were spared the jail's worst excesses by being held in individual cells rather than the common hall that housed most of the criminal inmates, but Newgate was still a particularly grim and unpleasant prison.[1] Russell was to be held there for two and a half years. At first he and his United Irish comrades were placed in solitary confinement and denied the use of writing materials but the prison regime did relax after a few weeks.[2]

Russell's arrest even attracted attention in Whitehall. Lord Grenville, the foreign secretary, wrote to Dublin enquiring whether anyone by the name of Russell had been arrested on charges of sedition or treason in Ireland and requested further details on the matter. Grenville's interest probably stemmed from the fact that Russell had recently been cited in an English newspaper as a leading United Irish conspirator. The article in question appeared in the *Sun* (described by the *Northern Star* as 'one of the venal prints of the English administration') two months after Russell's arrest.[3] It stated that:

among the persons who have been arrested for seditious, perhaps we may say treasonable, practices in Ireland is a man of the name of Russell, who has been particularly favoured by government upon many occasions and who had no motive of pique or disappointment to justify his conduct. It appears that this man is strongly tainted with Jacobinical notions and had assumed the office of secretary in the communications which the insurgents had with France. It is said that this man has offered to turn evidence, as he is better informed of the intended proceedings than all his associates, it is probable he will be admitted as a witness against the rest — though it is much to be regretted that such a monster of ingratitude, as well as disloyalty, is likely to escape the punishment he so well deserves.[4]

Russell did not allow such charges to go unanswered, publishing a reply in December:

I am...charged with being 'strongly tainted with Jacobinical principles'. My political principles I have published and have affixed my name and designation to as a United Irishman; from those principles I shall, I trust, never swerve; and that I have no fear arising from them or any political act of mine, was, I apprehend, sufficiently evinced by my *voluntary* surrender to the chief magistrate of Belfast as soon as I knew that there was a warrant issued to apprehend me for high treason...I never assumed, or had conferred on me, the office of secretary to any body of insurgents and that I never as secretary, or in any other manner, held communication with the French. I utterly deny the existence of any species of insurrection or insubordination in that part of the North in which I lived...The contrary is represented only by such dependants of the government as wish to magnify their zeal at court and who have a natural antipathy to those who wish for a reform of parliament or else by those...who, in their distempered imagination see no security but in a government of *force* and not *affection*. I deny also the existence of any species of insurrection in Ireland, except in parts of the county of Armagh and its vicinage, by those fanatics styling themselves 'Orange Boys' whose principles and actions are equally detestable and who are, I am convinced, tools in the hands of wicked and designing men.

[As for accusations that he intended to inform]...I here affirm that if I was so utterly lost to every sense of shame, of honour, of virtue and religion, as for a moment to have the most distant idea of becoming...one of those profligate, nefarious and execrable pests of society — *an informer* — I could not, if I adhered to the truth injure any person — I could inform of nothing but what I glory in, having felt it in common with the most virtuous, and I hope the *most numerous*

part of the people, a conviction of the fatal effects of religious prejudice on the liberty, morals and happiness of our country, and of having
strenuously, and not unsuccessfully, laboured to create a spirit of
union and brotherly affection among the people.

I hope that it is not yet a crime to avow that we think no man shall
be deprived of his civil rights on account of his religious opinions; that
we saw with regret and indignation the commerce of Ireland restricted
in such a manner as accorded neither with good policy nor national
prosperity and honour; enormous sums levied off the people and
prodigally squandered; no efforts made to ameliorate the situation of
the poor by any general plan of instruction and education; the country plunged by ministers into this unnecessary, unjust and disastrous
war; and for these and many other evils, we are persuaded that the
ONLY remedy is a reform in the Commons House of Parliament,
which has been repeatedly demanded by the people . . . a reform which
would place the representation where, conformably to the theory of
the British Constitution and to common sense, it should be placed, in
THE HANDS OF THE PEOPLE, and not in the hands of a bigoted,
corrupt, rapacious, cruel and ignorant aristocracy — and I trust we
are not to be deterred, for a moment, by the dread of imprisonment,
exile or death from endeavouring as far as in us lies, to obtain by
constitutional means, that great object so essential to the liberty and
happiness of Ireland.[5]

It was an effective if somewhat disingenuous reply. Martha McTier,
for example, who had been critical of his *Letter to the people of
Ireland,* praised it highly.[6] On the basis of this letter one of Russell's
biographers plays down the revolutionary side of Russell's activities
in the years 1795–6.[7] But the letter contains no explicit denial of
such activities. What Russell said was strictly true — there was no
evidence to suggest that he was in direct communication with France
or that he had acted as 'secretary' to any body of rebels. His efforts
to promote the United Irishmen and establish an alliance with the
Defenders are implicitly included in the admission of having
'laboured to create a spirit of union and brotherly affection among
the people'. Russell was undoubtedly equivocating, but he was
hardly likely to make a full confession of his revolutionary activism
only three months after his arrest on a poorly substantiated charge
of high treason.

While in Newgate Russell's habitual state of financial hardship
was eased to some extent. As political prisoners the United Irishmen
were paid a state prisoner's allowance by the government which,

added to subscriptions raised in Belfast for their support, probably gave him a better income than ever. He even had enough to send money to his sister and his niece Mary Ann who continued to rely on him, and to help out some of the poorer prisoners in the jail.[8] But this modest degree of financial security was little consolation to Russell, who found imprisonment very difficult to cope with. Besides the appalling conditions that had to be endured in Newgate, his restless spirit pined for the freedom to wander at will and enjoy the beauties of nature. Moreover, he was largely powerless to contribute to what he saw as his mission in life — spreading the message of the United Irishmen, and this at a time when sectarian tensions and political polarisation were on the increase. On the whole he seems to have found his confinement so dispiriting that, besides some desultory reading, he made little constructive use of his time, despite the frequent advice from friends on how he should spend his days. James McDonnell, for example, who regarded Russell's radicalism as rather naïve and simplistic, noting that 'as you have the most wanton and . . . illiberal contempt for all precedent and work all upon fundamental principles, it is a pity to waste instruction upon you', nonetheless advised him to improve his knowledge 'by incessant reading, writing and application . . . in every branch of useful literature'. By this means he could become 'not only clear, but deep, and strong, not in passion and emotion, but in reasoning and solid facts of observation'. Martha McTier, in her characteristically didactic manner, advised him to 'every day write a copy in order to improve your hand' and to 'pursue some good and honest purpose either for yourself or others'.[9] Russell does not seem to have heeded their advice. Since the state prisoners often succeeded in passing written material to visitors it would have been possible for him to continue his political journalism. However, he admitted to Templeton that confinement had aggravated his normal disinclination to writing, and though we cannot be certain about his literary output from prison, it appears to have been slight.[10]

Though chided by friends about the infrequency of his letters, he did manage to write from time to time and had some interesting correspondence with his friend John Templeton, the Belfast botanist. They generally discussed their intellectual and scientific interests — political matters are only mentioned obliquely, as this subject was obviously forbidden by the authorities. Russell's prison correspondence offers further testimony to the wide range of his interests: the subjects discussed include geology, mineralogy, Dublin's new botanical gardens, the construction of scientific apparatus, Bunting's music, some of the travel books that Russell had read, experiments to determine the nature of infections and James McDonnell's efforts to found a new fever hospital in Belfast.[11]

Russell's lassitude during his term in Newgate can be partly explained by the fact that his health suffered in the prison's unwholesome environment. He had a number of serious bouts of illness — one during the winter of 1797–8 of such severity that he thought it would be his last. During this time he was tended by his friend Whitley Stokes and at one stage he asked Templeton to seek McDonnell's advice, since 'of late, I am apt to spit blood in a morning, just before I rise, which is of a very vivid crimson... Between ourselves, I look on it as a very bad symptom'.[12] To add to physical debilitation, Russell also had to contend with his habitual mental anguish. Incarceration did not bring any respite from the temptations which had plagued him on the outside: alcohol and prostitutes were easily available in Newgate to those with ready money. Russell also claimed an allowance of a bottle of wine a day on the basis of his ill-health and he appears to have been frequently drunk. Once when Robert Simms visited Russell he found him so intoxicated that he felt it necessary to reprimand him some days later: 'I regret... that whiskey had taken the lead when I called on you... I would strongly recommend you to be more on your guard with respect to drink for I really think you give way to it too often'.[13]

Such chiding was nothing compared to Russell's own disgust at his moral lapses. He continued to subject himself to self-examination, and to accuse himself of many failings. He acknowledged that he was 'too much given to drink... thinking too much on women... not sufficiently appr[eciative] and grateful to my friends, too careless about my domestic affairs, with not turning my talent to account by endeavouring to benefit my fellow creatures, and *many many* other vices'.[14] On 21 November 1797, his thirtieth birthday, he indulged in a particularly severe bout of self-excoriation:

'I will commence with my heart in my chamber and be still' — Psalms. I am this day thirty years of age, I have been confined fourteen months, and to my sorrow I think I am not so good as I was a year since. I have relapsed into fornication and lust and my temper is become more irritable, my respect for veracity [is] not so great, and [my] swearing has increas'd... This is a melancholy picture, may the grace of God enable me to mend, 'for the good which I would, I do not; but the evil which I would not, that I do. Oh wreched man that I am, who shall deliver me from the body of this death!'

I have perceived that in proportion as I have daily read the Bible I have lived more virtuously, and when I have acted vihously I am asham'd and afraid to open that book. May my next self-examination be more comfortable. I will endeavour in future to avoid intoxication on any account, which I am now less liable to fall into than before, this will prevent my swearing which I have avoided except when in that state, and this will enable me likewise to guard more against women, and I hope when releas'd from this prison to abstain from them till marriage. I will endeavour to gain a compleat mastery over my passionate temper... and ... to obtain all useful information that may enable me ... [to] engage in some work of utility. I hope if this year of my life is spar'd to begin my long planned book on the insufficiency of reason, above all to ... pray for humility and charity. Let me not forget that in the past year the worst accthion of my life was committed, to which the allurements of woman or rather my own lust and wickedness betray'd me — oh Lord God Almighty... thou knowest the secrets and sorrows of my heart, that I humble myself before thee. Thou knows that it is not from thy justice before which I stand condemned that I expect salvation, but from thy tender mercy that I hope for pardon and forgiveness, through my Lord and Saviour, Jesus Christ.[15]

During his time in Newgate the millennialist strain in Russell's thinking became increasingly pronounced.[16] Prison gave him ample time to study, reflect and brood on the troubled state of the world around him, and more and more he found sense and solace in biblical prophecies. Included in his prison reading was Isaac Newton's *Observations upon the prophecies of Daniel and the apocalypse of St John* (1733). In a series of notes and tables, some of which are copied from Newton's work, Russell appears to be making his own attempt to fit world history into a millennialist framework. From the Book of Daniel he drew the conclusion that 'at first Europe, and afterwards the world at large, will be govern'd and inhabited by men of pure morality and uncorrupted Christianity'.[17] During his imprisonment, much of his correspondence was concerned with millennialist matters. A letter to Templeton written after Russell had spent a year in Newgate reveals the direction that his thought was taking:

The weather here is cold, rainy and tempestuous to a great degree, and I apprehend will injure the harvest much; perhaps it is influenced by the comet which is now observed; of old, people expected great

events, not in the natural, but in the moral and political world, from
such phenomena; whether this one portends any such, is to be seen. I
hope that if it does, that it is of a benign aspect; if what I read of it be
true it has something of a revolutionary appearance, as it has a very
short tail, or, in other words, is a croppy. I think General Lake and his
satellites would do well to have an eye on it...[18]

Perhaps his most important correspondent on millennialist matters
was Francis Dobbs, a member of the Irish parliament from 1798 to
1800, who lent him a copy of Newton's *Observations upon the
prophecies*. Dobbs, who had been an active Volunteer and Patriot
polemicist in the early 1780s, published in 1787 a *Universal history*
which sought to prove how messianic prophecies were being
fulfilled. He believed Ireland to be a divinely favoured nation in
which the Second Coming of Christ would take place. In a speech
delivered to the Irish parliament on 7 June 1800 he opposed the
government's plans for union on the grounds that, by obliterating a
country whose independence 'is written in the immutable records of
heaven', they contravened scriptural prophecy. He reasoned that
because Revelations had described the army of the messiah as 'harp-
ing on their harps' and 'clothed in fine linen' it was clear they would
be Irish; it was foretold that they would gather at a place called
Armageddon, which he construed as the Hebrew for Armagh;
finally, he maintained that since all snakes had been expelled from
Ireland, 'Satan, the great serpent, is here to receive his first deadly
blow'.[19] It is not known to what extent Russell shared these particular views but he read some of Dobbs's work while in Newgate and
in their correspondence Dobbs advised him on Biblical texts relating
to 'the personal Antichrist' and 'the happy state of the earth and the
restoration of the Jews'. Russell took his ideas seriously enough to
devote himself, in the days before his death, to writing a commentary on one of Dobbs's millennialist tracts, 'tending to enforce that
writer's interpretation of certain prophecies'.[20]

Millennialist ideas held an obvious attraction to one of Russell's
temperament. In his periods of despair he often comforted himself
and others with the observation that personal or political setbacks
were all part of God's plan and that 'providence orders all for the
best'.[21] His conviction that he was playing his part in hastening the
day of the millennium was probably a source of great consolation
and strength to him. He was, clearly, deeply troubled by his moral
failings but it is significant that he often contrasted his shame at his

personal behaviour with pride in his political activism: in the last weeks of his life he wrote to a friend: 'politically I have done nothing but what I glory in, morally I acknowledge myself a grievous sinner'.[22] In his speech from the dock in October 1803 he admitted that, while he had 'many faults to answer for', he looked back on the thirteen years of his political career 'with entire satisfaction'.[23] Given his deep concern about the fate of his soul, his efforts in pursuit of universal liberty and justice, which he believed to be in accordance with God's will, were in many ways a form of atonement for his moral lapses. He firmly believed that 'our Lord and Saviour will, in eternal life, reward those who laboured for the welfare and happiness of mankind'.[24] Given that he accepted that he was a 'grievous sinner', his commitment to bringing about Christ's kingdom on earth was the only real avenue of spiritual redemption open to him.

Throughout Russell's imprisonment, Dublin Castle was well aware that it had little hard evidence to substantiate the charge of high treason against him. Their main informer against the northern United Irishmen had only the vaguest notion of Russell's activities and was in any case unwilling to appear in court. The immediate difficulty was solved by pushing a bill suspending habeas corpus through the Irish parliament a month after the arrest of the northern radicals. But the government frequently showed a nervousness in its dealings with Russell. Days after his arrest, the attorney general wrote to the Castle to insist that for the time being he should be denied access to legal counsel. According to Russell, in the early weeks of his imprisonment he was approached by an agent, who he believed was acting on behalf of the government, and told that he could secure his release by agreeing to go into exile in England, but he refused to accept these terms.[25]

Throughout 1797 several of his fellow prisoners were released on bail: Henry Joy McCracken for example, arrested a month after Russell, was released in November 1797. On several occasions Russell wrote to the Castle requesting similar treatment. When it was put to him that he could be freed if he would offer security for his good behaviour, he again refused, on the grounds that this would imply 'of having done something wrong, which he never would admit'.[26] In all his dealings with the authorities he tended to demonstrate an extreme high-mindedness, so much so that his friend John Templeton, under the impression that Russell had refused to make any application to the government until he had received an apology, reprimanded him for 'sacrificing his life to *punctilio*'. Russell denied this, pointing out the numerous applications he had made to be brought to trial or released, which had all been ignored. He added:

> neither my religion nor my reason would suffer me to sacrifice my health and my talents (such as they are) to *punctilio*; and for a man to look for personal atonement to his pride or his feelings, from a government by which such dreadful tragedies have been, and still continue to be, acted in this unhappy country, it would afford no great proof of his judgement or his patriotism.[27]

Russell may not have been quite as other-worldly as some of his friends suspected but it is worth noting that they felt the need to warn him against excessive rectitude. It is also significant that in the aftermath of the 1798 rebellion, when government and state prisoners tried to reach an agreement on halting executions, Russell proved to be far more reluctant than most of his colleagues to engage in negotiations.

Throughout his time in prison he did, however, keep up a constant barrage of letters to the government, notably to the Chief Secretary, Henry Pelham, his successor Lord Castlereagh, and anyone else in authority who he felt might have some influence, asking to be released on bail or brought to trial. He reminded them that he had surrendered himself to the authorities and that those arrested with him had been freed, while 'my life and my health are wasting in a prison...It is now near eighteen months (an alarming reduction from the life of man) since I surrendered myself...Of the justice of my cause...I am as much convinced now as I was then'.[28] On the rare occasions when his letters were answered he was invariably given the response that current circumstances did not permit his release.

Several attempts were made on his behalf to secure his release. According to Russell, a friend persuaded a 'nobleman high in military command and in the full confidence of the government', to apply to the government on his behalf. Apparently, Pelham spoke 'handsomely' of Russell's character to this anonymous intermediary (possibly Lord Moira) and admitted that the authorities had no specific charge against him, but they believed that he was one of the most important figures in the United Irishmen and they were determined to keep him imprisoned for the duration of the war. Similar applications were made by other friends of Russell, including the respected scientist, Richard Kirwan, but to no effect.[29] Perhaps the most curious intervention made on Russell's behalf was by the informer, John Bird (alias Smith). In a letter written to the lord lieutenant, and later published in the *Press*, he deplored the fact that although there was no charge against Neilson and Russell they were still detained. The penitent informer claimed he was so determined to free them that he would risk imprisonment himself and threatened that if they were not released he would 'place in Lord Moira's hands such documents as shall strike your boldest orators dumb and raise through the *three kingdoms* such a tornado of execration as shall penetrate the *inmost recesses* of the *cabinets* of London and Dublin!'[30] By this stage the government was well used to the hyperbole of informers and Bird's threats probably did little to impress them.

Neilson was freed in February 1798 because of his poor health. This left Russell as the only leading United Irishman of those arrested in September 1796 who was still detained. He took considerable satisfaction from the fact that although the government was extremely anxious to obtain information against him, and he was in a position where he could have been compromised by many 'whom it is the fashion to revile under the epithets of common people and mob', yet no one could be found to inform against him. In this he does not appear to have been completely correct, for it seems that in March 1797 a former United Irishman from Co. Tyrone was released from prison after 'lodging a strong information against that unfortunate man Mr Russell'.[31]

As the political situation deteriorated throughout 1797 and early 1798, Russell was not a man that Dublin Castle wanted to see at liberty, particularly as they believed that he was still making mischief from prison. Although his contributions to United Irish publications were few during these years, the authorities firmly believed him to be the author of at least one notorious article: an attack on the Earl of Clare, the Lord Chancellor, published in the *Press* in March 1798 and addressed to 'The author of coercion'. It accused Clare of carrying out a campaign of oppression against the Irish people and warned him:

> The hand of fate seems upon you, and you still go on foolishly confident, and as madly gay as the insect that flutters round the torch, or the bird that cannot resist the fascinations of the serpent's jaws that are extended to devour him . . . Ireland can afford the clearest evidence of your crimes; the unanimous voice of its inhabitants will pronounce you guilty. On such an occasion, our disgust against the duty of the

executioner, will be suspended, and men will contend for the honour of terminating so destructive an existence.[32]

The piece was written under the pseudonym 'Dion', but Camden forwarded a copy to Portland the day after its publication with a note stating: 'there is reason to believe from the manuscripts seized [that it] was composed by Captain Russell who has been confined in Newgate under a charge of high treason'. However, the style of the article does not appear to be Russell's and Madden later credited it to John Sheares.[33] Russell would probably have agreed with many of the sentiments expressed in the article and it is possible that he may have disguised his style, but Sheares was the more likely author. The authorities, however, believed that it was Russell who had called for Clare's assassination, confirming their suspicions that he was one of the most dangerous of the United Irishmen and destroying any slim chance he had of being released.

NOTES

1 Diary of [Capt.] Thos Law Hodges of the West Kent militia, 20 Sept 1798 (B.L., Add. MS 40166N); *Commons jn. Ire.*, x, dxxxiii; Bernadette Doorly, 'Newgate prison' in David Dickson (ed.), *The gorgeous mask: Dublin 1700–1850* (Dublin, 1987), pp. 121–31.
2 Charles H. Teeling, *Personal narrative of the Irish rebellion of 1798* (London, 1928), p. 36.
3 Grenville to Pelham, 23 Dec. 1796 (Reb. papers, 620/26/148); *Northern Star,* 2 Dec. 1796.
4 *The Sun,* 18 Nov. 1796; the letter was reprinted in the *Dublin Evening Post,* 22 Dec. 1796 and the *Northern Star,* 26 Dec. 1796.
5 Thomas Russell, Newgate, 19 Dec. 1796; it appeared in the *Dublin Evening Post,* 22 Dec. 1796 and *Northern Star,* 26 Dec. 1796.
6 [Martha McTier] to Russell, n.d. (Sirr papers, 868/2, ff 268–9).
7 Mac Giolla Easpaig, *Ruiséil,* pp. 105–8.
8 Mary Ann Hamilton, Enniskillen, to Russell, 29 Nov. 1797 (Sirr papers, 868/2, ff 40–3); Thomas Russell to Margaret Russell, 23 Oct. 1798 (Sirr papers, 868/1, ff 266–7); Mary Dalton to Russell, n.d. (Sirr papers, 868/2, ff 288–9).
9 McDonnell to Russell, Belfast, [Apr. 1797], 30 June 1797 (Reb. papers 620/16/3; Sirr papers, 868/2, ff 213–14); Robert Simms to Russell, 30 June 1797, [Martha McTier] to Russell, n.d. (Sirr papers, 868/2, ff 215–17, 268–9).
10 Russell to Templeton, 14 Feb. 1798 (Madden papers, 873/635).
11 For a published version of Russell's prison correspondence see Madden, *United Irishmen,* 3rd ser., ii, 187–97.
12 Questioning of Stokes, 19 April 1798 (TCD MS 3363); Russell to Templeton, 14 Feb. 1798 (Madden papers, 873/635); see also: Templeton to Russell, 19 Mar. 1797, 29 Jan. 1798 (*United Irishmen,* ii, 187, 194); Robert Simms to Russell, 1 Jan. 1798 (Sirr papers, 868/2, ff 277–8).

13 Russell to Castlereagh (draft), n.d., to Edward Cooke (draft) 17 September 1798 (Sirr papers, 868/1, ff 25v, 168); Robert Simms to Russell, Belfast, 10 Aug. 1797 (Sirr papers, 868/2, f. 307).

14 Russell's journal, 5 June [1797/8?] (Sirr papers, 868/1, f. 6).

15 Russell's journal, 21 Nov. 1797 (Sirr papers, 868/1, f. 2); the lines quoted at the end of the first parargraph are from Romans 7. 19, 24. I have found no further information on what constituted 'the worst accthion of my life'.

16 Almost all the surviving correspondence relating to this theme is dated from the years 1797–1802.

17 Russell's notes in Sirr papers, 868/1, f. 3; see also Thomas Mercer to Russell, 8 Aug. 1798; Francis Dobbs to Russell, 15 Sept., 5 Dec. 1798 (Sirr papers, 868/1, ff 13–14, 26, 29). For the influence of Newton, compare some of Russell's notes in Sirr papers, 868/1, ff 3–5, with Isaac Newton, *Observations upon the prophecies of Daniel and the apocalypse of St John* (Dublin, 1733), pp. 18–19, 47, 77–8.

18 Russell to Templeton, 10 Sept. 1797 (Madden papers, 873/634).

19 *Memoirs of Francis Dobbs esq. Also genuine reports of his speeches in parliament on the subject of a union and his prediction of the second coming of the Messiah with extracts from his poem on the millennium* (Dublin, 1800), pp. 44–6.

20 Alexander Marsden's account of the insurrection of 1803 (*Emmet memoir*, ii, 98); for correspondence on millennialist matters, see Dobbs to Russell, 15 Sept. 1998 (Sirr papers, 868/1, f. 26); for Russell receiving books written by Dobbs, see Thomas Mercer to Russell, 8 Aug. 1798 (Sirr papers, 868/1, ff 13–14).

21 Russell to Templeton, 5 June 1802 (Madden papers, 873/638).

22 Russell to Frank McCracken, Oct. 1803 (copy) (Madden papers, 873/642); for similar sentiments see also Russell to Templeton, 10 Sept. 1797 (Madden papers, 873/634); Revd. Forster Archer to —, 3 Oct. 1803 (Reb. papers, 620/50/21).

23 Russell's trial speech (Madden papers, 873/700, ff 3, 1).

24 Russell to —, 5 June 1802 (Madden papers, 873/673).

25 Smith's information on arrested United Irish leaders, late 1796 (Frazer MS II/40); Lecky, *Ireland*, iii, 459; Arthur Wolfe to Cooke, Sept. 1796 (Reb. papers, 620/25/130); Thomas Russell to John Russell, Fort George, 10 Dec. 1800 (copy) (Madden papers, 873/655, f. 5v).

26 Thomas Russell to John Russell, Fort George, 10 Dec. 1800 (copy) (Madden papers, 873/655, f. 6v).

27 Templeton to Russell, 29 Jan. 1798 (Sirr papers, 868/2, ff 274–5); Russell to Templeton, 14 Feb. 1798 (Madden papers, 873/635).

28 Russell to Pelham, 9 Mar. 1798 (Reb. papers, 620/16/3); see also Russell to Pelham, 9 Sept. 1797 (Reb. papers, 620/15/6/2) and draft letters (Sirr papers, 868/1, ff 168–174).

29 Thomas Russell to John Russell, Fort George, 10 Dec. 1800 (copy) (Madden papers, 873/655, ff 6v –7).

30 John Bird to Camden, *c.* Feb. 1798 (*Memoirs of William Sampson* (New York, 1807), pp. 394–5); published in *The Press*, 20 Feb. 1798.

31 Thomas Russell to John Russell, Fort George, 10 Dec. 1800 (copy) (Madden papers, 873/655, ff 7 –7v); Revd. Armstrong to Mr Knox, Dungannon, 4 Mar. [1797] (Reb. papers, 620/29/51).

32 'To the author of coercion', *The Press*, 6 Mar. 1798.

33 Camden to Portland, 7 Mar. 1798 (P.R.O., HO 100/75/183–4); R. R. Madden, *United Irishmen*, 4th ser., (2nd edn, Dublin, 1860), p. 221.

CHAPTER ELEVEN

A Bloody Summer

The arrests of September 1796 marked the beginning of an intensified government campaign against the United Irishmen. In the following year about 400 people were taken up on political charges. The seizure of the society's most experienced and dedicated leaders served a serious blow to the northern United Irish organisation but it recovered quickly. Reviewing the state of the country in June 1797, the Lord Lieutenant believed that although the arrest of 'leading characters' such as Neilson, Haslett and Russell had stalled the advance of the United Irishmen for a time, they soon began to organise 'with as much system and more vigour than before'.[1] In fact some Ulster republicans later claimed that the September arrests were a critical turning point in the history of the organisation, decisively setting it on the road to armed rebellion. At a meeting in Randalstown in October 1796 a member of the Ulster directory was reported to have announced that the time had come to abandon constitutional methods since the 'government were laying hands on some of our friends and that we must prepare for the worst by arming ourselves'.[2]

Meanwhile Tone's exertions in Paris had borne fruit and he sailed from Brest for Ireland on 15 December 1796 with an invasion force of almost 14,000 men led by General Lazare Hoche. The expedition was scattered by storms and Hoche's ship was detached from the main fleet, but a substantial French force still managed to reach Bantry Bay. Contrary winds prevented them from landing on shore and after a few days they returned to France, much to Tone's bitter disappointment.

Although the United Irishmen too were obviously disappointed, the publicity gained for them by this near invasion was invaluable. For many people the fact that such a large French force under one of the republic's most famous generals had been destined for Ireland transformed the society into serious players in international politics and growing numbers flocked to their colours. By the spring of 1797 the United movement in Ulster was thriving. Writing to her imprisoned brother of the movement's progress Mary Ann McCracken claimed: 'there cannot be more extraordinary revolutions in politics than what have taken place of late in the minds of many people here...It is very evident that since the people have appeared to be the strongest party their cause has gained many friends...It is generally thought that ere long we will be out of the king's peace'. She mentioned that Russell would be surprised and pleased to hear that even the apolitical John Templeton had 'at last turned his attention from the vegetable to the human species' and after much deliberation had decided to become a United Irishman.[3]

The government, badly shaken by the invasion scare, had no intention of allowing disaffection to grow unchecked and General Lake was given a free hand to break the northern United movement. Ulster was placed under strict martial law in May and Lake's troops set about disarming suspected rebels, employing a variety of brutal methods, including floggings and house-burnings, to ensure that hidden arms were handed up. In the face of Lake's exertions the optimism of the spring began to give way to demoralisation and fear, and some local United Irish committees clamoured for a rising before the spirit of the republican movement was finally broken. Russell's old command of Co. Down led the way in calling for immediate action. At a meeting held in Dublin in June northern delegates pressed the national executive to commit itself to a rising without waiting for a French invasion, but cautious elements in the leadership prevailed and no firm decision was taken.[4]

Russell was kept fully informed of the deteriorating state of the province by several northern correspondents who graphically related to him details of the military campaign to crush the Ulster United Irishmen. 'Sullen silence is observed everywhere', wrote Samuel Musgrave, while William Sampson assured him that 'croppies lie down is now the word'.[5] Many of those at the sharp end of government coercion were probably known to Russell from the days when he had operated as a United Irish emissary. He appears to have been acquainted with William Orr — the young Antrim farmer who became the first United Irish martyr. Orr was convicted of administering an illegal oath to two Fifeshire Fencibles in April 1796, which was a capital offence under the provisions of the insurrection act. The evidence against him was rather dubious and the verdict of guilty was delivered by a packed jury that had allegedly been plied with drink. Despite many pleas for clemency Orr was hanged in Carrickfergus in October 1797.[6]

Russell was also most likely in receipt of information from friends active in the United movement who visited him in Newgate. Henry Joy McCracken and Robert Simms, both of whom were released from prison in 1797, and Lord Edward Fitzgerald, the key figure in planning a rising in Leinster, were among his prison visitors.[7] Although Lake's campaign had considerable success in weakening the United Irishmen in Ulster, by early 1798 the centre of gravity of the United movement and the threat of insurrection, had shifted from Ulster to Leinster. The army was unleashed on Leinster in the spring of 1798 and on 30 March the privy council declared the country to be in a state of rebellion and imposed martial law. In some places the military terror managed to cow the United Irishmen, but in others the excesses of the troops, or the expectation of their arrival, greatly inflamed tensions. On 12 March the government arrested most of the United Irish leadership still at large by surprising a meeting of the Leinster directory at Oliver Bond's house in Bridge Street. The only prominent leader who was not taken up in this sweep was Lord Edward Fitzgerald, who went into hiding.

Russell could do little as these events unfolded. As Ireland moved ever closer towards open conflict his imprisonment must have weighed all the more heavily upon him. His experiences of that bloody summer proved to be vicarious ones, related by those friends and colleagues arrested and brought to Newgate before or during the insurrection. Among these was Lord Edward Fitzgerald, who was betrayed by an informer and arrested on 19 May after a violent struggle in which he was badly wounded. He was taken to Newgate and Russell managed to spend some time with him on his first night in the jail. Russell had not known Fitzgerald before his imprisonment but during his visits to Newgate they became friends. He came to admire the young nobleman greatly and maintained that 'so much information, modesty, disinterestedness and virtue I never saw combined . . . His death was like his life. He died a hero and a saint'. Though separated from Fitzgerald by order of the government, Russell managed to see him before he died on 4 June; on this last visit Fitzgerald gave him a lock of his hair to send to his cousin, Charles James Fox. Russell also spoke to the United Irish leaders John and Henry Sheares and received the valedictory address of William Michael Byrne before all three were hanged at Newgate.[8]

The rising in Leinster finally erupted on 23 May. The plan was for a series of co-ordinated county risings to defeat local Crown forces and for the insurgents then to converge on Dublin, which was to be secured by United Irishmen within the city. Risings broke out in late May in Kildare, Meath and Carlow; although large numbers turned out they were poorly armed and badly led, and were routed with great slaughter by the army and militia. Only in Wexford and Wicklow did the insurrection enjoy some success: a detachment of North Cork militia and local yeomanry was almost wiped out by the insurgents at Oulart Hill. They went on to seize and occupy Wexford town and Enniscorthy but, after heavy fighting, failed to take the strategic towns of New Ross (5 June) and Arklow (9 June). Forced back onto the defensive they regrouped at Vinegar Hill, near Enniscorthy. It was here that the rebel army was finally broken by Lake in a bloody battle on 21 June.

Had the plans of Samuel Neilson succeeded, Russell might have been directly involved in the insurrection. After his release in February 1798 Neilson became active in preparations for the rising in Dublin. He had intended to begin the insurrection in the city with an attack on Newgate to liberate the state prisoners held there. Remembering how the seizure of the Bastille had ignited revolution in France, he hoped that the seizure of Newgate might have a similar effect in Ireland. He was particularly anxious to rescue Fitzgerald, the most popular of all the United Irish leaders, but according to an informer he was also desperate 'to get out Russell, a commander and chief person'.[9] However, Neilson's efforts came to nothing — he was arrested on the night of 23 May while reconnoitring the jail, and the force he had assembled nearby dispersed when he did not return.[10]

In the event, the absence of effective leadership was one of the main reasons why the rebellion fizzled out so rapidly in Dublin. Large groups of United Irishmen did assemble inside and outside of the city's boundaries but they waited in vain for orders to strike. According to the account of one loyalist, 'the columns of the rebels which surrounded the town waited for the other to begin, and had any daring officer been found to lead his men under fire, the others from Ringsend, Eccles St, Clontarf, and Harold's Cross, in all which places were large bodies of them, would have probably followed the example, which might have been of the worst consequences as the garrison was so weak'.[11] Had Russell been free, his military experience and physical courage might have gone some way in supplying the decisive leadership that was so obviously lacking in the capital.

Likewise in Co. Down, where Russell had been appointed military commander in 1796, the absence of capable leaders was a crucial factor in the poor showing of the United Irishmen. In Co. Antrim Henry Joy McCracken eventually brought the United Irishmen into the field but Down lagged behind. Eventually the relatively unknown Henry Monro, a United Irish colonel from Lisburn, Co. Antrim, took command of the Down forces but their delayed and uncoordinated efforts were quickly crushed.[12] We can only guess at Russell's deepening anguish in the summer of '98 as he learned day after day of the defeat of the rebels, the bloody reprisals and the executions of friends and colleagues.

In the aftermath of the rebellion, which at times had owed more to sectarian fury than republican ideals, some United Irish leaders attempted to distance themselves from it. Russell, however, refused to dissociate himself from the efforts of the rebels. Even though the rebellion was thoroughly defeated, far from dismissing it as a hopeless *jacquerie*, he regarded it with genuine admiration. In a letter written some years later he maintained proudly that Britain's 'colossal power was shaken from its summit to its base by the gallant peasantry of a few counties, ill-armed and ill-led'. Questioned about these events in prison in 1803, he denied accusations that the rebellion had been motivated solely by religious animosities. When confronted with specific atrocities such as the murder of more than a hundred mostly Protestant loyalists in a barn at Scullabogue in Co. Wexford, he regretted them, but claimed that the people were 'goaded to those excesses' because of 'the ravishings, house-burnings and torture' carried out by the military.[13]

In July 1798 the government began to try United Irish leaders for complicity in the planning of the insurrection. The testimony of Captain John Warneford Armstrong, a militia officer John Sheares had attempted to suborn, was sufficient to convict both Sheares brothers. Evidence supplied by Thomas Reynolds, a member of the Leinster United Irish directory who had turned king's evidence, would do likewise for his colleagues on the directory — John McCann and William Michael Byrne. The Sheareses were hanged at Newgate on 14 July and McCann five days later.[14] With Byrne and Oliver Bond condemned to suffer the same fate and several others unsure of their own, many of the remaining prisoners were anxious to come to terms with the government.

It seems that the first move came from Samuel Neilson, whose attorney, James Crawford, advised him in mid-July that since the rebellion had been defeated any further resistance was pointless and it was now time to conclude a treaty to end unnecessary bloodshed. Neilson broached the matter with his fellow prisoners, most of whom agreed with Crawford.[15] The prisoners then applied to the Whig magnate Lord Charlemont to act as guarantor of any agreement. Charlemont approved of the measure but pleaded infirmity and appointed his friend Francis Dobbs, MP for the borough of Charlemont, as a mediator; Dobbs was assisted by Henry Alexander, MP for the city of Derry, a relation of Oliver Bond. Neilson informed Alexander that if the terms of the prisoners were met he would reveal to them 'every muscle, sinew, nay, fibre of the internal organisation' and Alexander urged him to put his proposal in writing.[16] On 24 July, the day before Byrne was due to be executed, Dobbs called on the Chief Secretary, Castlereagh, with a written proposal signed by most of the prisoners. In exchange for the lives of Byrne and Bond and an assurance that other prisoners would not be prosecuted, they agreed to give full details of the organisation and aims of the United Irishmen and to submit to banishment for life in a neutral country, although they would not implicate any named individuals.[17]

On the same day Neilson discussed the proposal with Russell, who expressed 'great repugnance' at the idea of treating with the government, but was eventually convinced by Neilson's arguments that a general amnesty would put an end to the bloodshed still occurring in parts of the country. Russell declared that he 'would make any sacrifice consistent with [his] conscience and honour to save the blood of any individual' but was adamant that he would not advise those 'who had engaged in the contest to withdraw even for a moment from it, because [he] had...the most perfect confidence of the easiness of accomplishing the object wished for by the people'. He only agreed to add his signature to the agreement with great reluctance and after much anguished reflection. He insisted on declaring that his only motive was to save the lives of others and, had he been among the condemned, he would not have negotiated with the government to save himself. There is no reason to doubt Russell's claim in this regard: his career would show that he held his honour and his principles more dearly than his life. He maintained that all the state prisoners signed in the same spirit and all believed that they had made 'a great personal sacrifice'. Several other United Irishmen shared his reservations: Arthur O'Connor and William Sampson did not sign the initial drafts and William Dowdall and Roger O'Connor never signed.[18]

The recently appointed Lord Lieutenant, Cornwallis, was immediately attracted to the offer, which fitted in well with his aim of restoring peace through a policy of firmness tempered by leniency. In early July he had issued a proclamation offering a general pardon to rank-and-file rebels who surrendered their weapons and took the oath of allegiance, and he had already formed the opinion that banishment was the most suitable punishment for the leaders. But his law officers cautioned against accepting an agreement that not all the prisoners had signed and he knew that such an apparently lenient step would infuriate loyalists, who were in such a mood that 'nothing but blood will satisfy them'. He therefore allowed the execution of Byrne to go ahead on 25 July.[19]

Byrne's execution concentrated the minds of the prisoners and most of those who had refused to sign the agreement were persuaded by their colleagues to do so. On 26 July Dobbs called on Castlereagh and informed him that the dissidents, including O'Connor, were now willing to sign and that they agreed to leave the time and place of their liberation to the discretion of the government, so long as they were not to be transported as felons. Cornwallis again summoned his law officers, who on the basis of this new offer agreed to postpone Bond's execution to 30 July.[20]

Although loyalists continued to grumble at the government's moderation, for Cornwallis 'the Kilmainham Treaty', as it came to be known, had more to do with expediency than leniency. He claimed that if he had had any real evidence that could have convicted the rebel leaders, he would have gone ahead and hanged them but he realised that with the possible exceptions of Neilson and MacNeven almost all the prisoners were likely to escape punishment.[21] Much of the evidence they had against them was vague and came from informers who were anxious to retain their anonymity. A typical report came from General Nugent, commander of the Crown forces in Ulster, who claimed that he had a witness who could convict Russell and several other northern United Irishmen of high treason, but that he refused to testify in open court.[22] The Castle had seen in the past how skilful defence counsel could tear reluctant or vague witnesses to pieces and believed that it was unlikely they could even establish the guilt of Neilson, who had been caught red-handed planning an attack on Newgate jail, and that every acquittal would be a victory for the rebels. The agreement, therefore, offered the Castle a convenient means of getting rid of a large number of troublesome agitators who otherwise would have to be detained indefinitely without charge.[23]

Cornwallis regarded comprehensive confessions from the United Irish leaders as 'more important than the lives of twenty such men as Oliver Bond', and his most important advisors — Castlereagh, Cooke and even Clare — all agreed with him.[24] By establishing the existence of a widespread conspiracy the government would justify the draconian security policy it had adopted in recent years; the confessions might also damage relations between the United Irish leadership and rank-and-file, and drive a wedge between the United Irishmen and France, destroying the prospects of any future invasion. Crucially, all of this would be accomplished without the Castle having to reveal its informants. Moreover, the signature of Arthur O'Connor on the agreement was a particular prize, since the government hoped that his testimony would discredit opposition politicians in both Dublin and Westminster, such as Grattan, Fox and Sheridan, who had endorsed his political principles and stood as his character witnesses during his trial for high treason at Maidstone. All in all, Cornwallis thought the agreement 'the most complete triumph both in England and Ireland'.[25]

However, negotiations between the prisoners and the government were plagued by suspicion and bad faith. As part of the pact the prisoners agreed to give a written memoir of the United Irish movement to the government and also agreed to be questioned by parliamentary secret committees. In both cases they portrayed themselves as moderate reformers forced into revolution by a repressive government. Their evidence was characterised by a tone of defiance and made clear that although they wished to end unnecessary bloodshed their principles remained unchanged.[26] The prisoners' memoir was suppressed and edited versions of their testimony to the secret committees were published, with most of their attempts at self-justification removed. Misleading extracts of their testimony which included the names of colleagues were also published in Dublin newspapers. In reponse the prisoners published a notice in the press which claimed that the published versions of their testimony were a 'gross and . . . astonishing misrepresentation', bearing no real relation to the evidence they had given, and they specifically denied that they had implicated any of their colleagues.[27] The fact that the notice had been published immediately after the landing of the French in Co. Mayo was not seen as a coincidence. Loyalists were outraged and claimed that prisoners had broken their agreement and should now be tried by martial law.[28]

Relations between the two sides deteriorated further when a draft of the proposed banishment bill appeared in the English newspaper, the *Courier*, on 6 September, alleging that the state prisoners 'had acknowledged their crimes, retracted their opinions and implored pardon'. Now it was the prisoners' turn to be outraged. Neilson informed Castlereagh that he intended to write to the *Courier* to make clear that the state prisoners had neither changed their principles nor begged pardon, but had entered into an agreement with the government as an equal party to bring about an end to unnecessary bloodshed. He was immediately visited by Cooke and Alexander Marsden, the Castle under-secretaries, who threatened that such a step would annul the agreement and bring about a resumption of executions.[29] The prisoners were not prepared for such a drastic step and a vague compromise was reached whereby Neilson would forgo writing to the *Courier* and Cooke would attempt to have the wording of the bill softened. However, this came to nothing and the bill was passed stating that the prisoners 'being conscious of their flagrant and enormous guilt, have expressed their contrition for the same, and have most humbly implored his majesty's mercy'.[30]

The government also negotiated with individual prisoners. In September Francis Dobbs acted as an intermediary between the government and Russell. He expressed his concern to Russell that his imprisonment had continued for so long and intimated that the government might be prepared to release him in the near future. He asked Russell to write a letter to the authorities stating the manner in which he was willing to agree to go into exile.[31] In this letter Russell again firmly reiterated that 'I never retracted any political opinion or confessed any political guilt, for politically I acted to the best of my judgements and in conformity to my conscience; when I signed the paper on which the bill is founded I had no motive but to save the lives of others'. Because of his long imprisonment, he asked for four months to settle his personal affairs and offered security to surrender himself to the authorities on twenty-four hours notice. He would then agree to emigrate to any country that he and the government could agree on. Dobbs forwarded this letter to the government with an endorsement stating that, since Russell was a man of his word, they could 'safely comply with this request', but his intervention achieved nothing.[32]

The government, however, wanted to be rid of the United Irish prisoners, aware that even from prison they could still cause trouble. Of the ninety prisoners who eventually signed the Kilmainham Treaty, Cornwallis believed that only fifteen of them were sufficiently important for their place of exile to be a matter of any real concern.[33] In December most of those who had signed the banishment act were given permission to emigrate to neutral countries and many of those not included in the act who had already been convicted by court martial were later transported to Prussia to serve in her armies.[34] But the problem remained — where to send the leaders? Their preference was to emigrate to a neutral German state, but since this would give them easy access to France, they were told they must go to America.[35]

Most of the active United Irish leaders were opposed to this, regarding the American government as no better than the British and the federalist president John Adams as an American version of Pitt. The distaste was reciprocated and Cornwallis was uncertain about how the Americans, who had recently passed swingeing Alien and Sedition Acts, would react to receiving this 'cargo of sedition'.[36] His doubts proved well-founded: the American ambassador in London, Rufus King, assured the British authorities that their plan to off-load the prisoners to the United States was entirely unacceptable since the principles of the United Irishmen were 'so dangerous, so false, and so utterly inconsistent with any practicable or stable form of government'. On 16 September Alexander Marsden informed the prisoners that the American government would not allow them enter the country: pressed for a reason, he answered that 'perhaps Mr King does not desire to have republicans in America'. With the option of sending them to America blocked, Portland decided that there was no viable place of banishment for them and advised Cornwallis to keep the leading prisoners in custody 'as long as the war lasts, or it is thought necessary'.[37]

Russell, who was one of those the government decided to detain indefinitely, was strongly opposed to accepting banishment to America, preferring instead to remain on the Continent.[38] Tone's unflattering description of the country three years earlier may have influenced him but his main reason for opposing exile in America was probably the practical difficulties involved in renewing the struggle at such a distance.

By November 1798 Tone was foremost in Russell's thoughts. After the failure of the Bantry Bay expedition, he had spent another twenty more months on the Continent attempting to organise another invasion. Russell's fate was often on his mind. 'I am more distressed than I can express about poor Russell. Poor fellow. But what good does my compassion do him, and if we were to lose him, what degree of vengeance would recompense his life? You know I am no threatener beforehand: it leads to nothing; let us therefore say no more on this subject.'[39] On the receipt of news that rebellion had broken out in Ireland, the French decided to send a number of small expeditions. Waiting at Brest to embark for Ireland, Tone wrote to his wife and inquired of Russell's fate with the usual mixture of affection and mockery: 'is poor Russell at last out of the scrape? I hope he may not bully Pelham again. Would he were in Holstein, with all my soul. I am afraid he would break parole and come to Paris, if it were only to see you and Maria. If that should happen take care of him, and let him imbibe...poor Tom, bless his five wits.'[40] Tone finally sailed in September and was captured after a fierce fight when the French fleet was intercepted off the north-west coast of Ireland. He was taken to Dublin, where on 10 November he was convicted before a court martial at the Royal Barracks and sentenced to be hanged. Russell did his best to save his friend's life. He wrote to the Kilmainham prisoners demanding that they should take some action on Tone's behalf. On their behalf a distraught Thomas Addis Emmet replied that they would do anything they could to save Tone's life but he was deeply pessimistic about the prospects of preventing his execution. He pointed out that when they had negotiated for Oliver Bond's life they had something to offer the government — information and exile — now they had nothing left to give. It was inconceivable to think that the government would do them the slightest favour 'when we have been in vain soliciting the very small favour of good faith being kept with us'. Emmet had already been informed by Clare that Tone had signed a confession prior to his exile, which meant that he would certainly be hanged if he should ever attempt to set foot on Irish soil again. The only possibility he could see of saving his life was that the government might be dissuaded from executing him if the French authorities threatened to take reprisals against a captured British officer and interference by the prisoners could only damage this slim hope. Russell also wrote to Tone's old friend, Peter Burrowes, then a leading Dublin barrister who, despite political differences, remembered Tone with affection and promised to do all he could to assist him. Burrowes believed, however, that the case was almost hopeless and that the best that could be hoped for was a postponement of any sentence of death, to be followed by a trial by jury. Such speculations were cut short by Tone's own actions. After the court martial had passed sentence on him, he asked to be shot by firing squad rather than hanged, but this was refused and he was sentenced to be hanged the following day. He was informed that because of the 'peculiar circumstances of his case', his execution 'should be in the most public manner, for the sake of a striking example' and that he was to be executed publicly in front of Newgate gail. A public hanging in such close proximity to Russell could only have compounded the anguish felt by the two men. Tone spared them both this ordeal by cutting his throat on the night of 11 November in his cell in the Provost prison in the Royal Barracks; he inflicted a near fatal wound on himself and died eight days later.[41]

During this time negotiations on the banishment bill had continued. By December both sides were in deadlock, with the prisoners angry at the government's interpretation of the agreement. They had believed that they would be released soon after the conclusion of the agreement and offered some say in their place of exile, but they received neither of these concessions. Emmet complained that the government began by promising prisoners 'the utmost liberality and good faith', that it continued the same language until the prisoners had fulfilled their undertaking, and then it acted with pettiness and vindictiveness.[42] As the months in custody dragged on with no sign of their release, the prisoners grew increasingly bitter about their treatment and their resentment soon found a tangible outlet. One informer claimed that the state prisoners had never been sincere in their dealings with the government and that 'every mischief possible is now and has been doing by the state prisoners since they made the agreement with the government'. He claimed that the prisoners were encouraging their colleagues still at large and telling them that 'it is now that the real business is beginning'.[43]

In the aftermath of the rising much of the Irish countryside had remained disturbed, the counties in the neighbourhood of Dublin particularly so. The severe reprisals of Crown forces had left behind a legacy of sullen resentment among the Catholic peasantry, several rebel bands continued to hold out in isolated regions and the expectation of a French invasion was widely held. Early in 1799 an army officer noted that although 'the kingdom at large appears to wear a face of tranquillity, it more resembles the pause of expectation and the silence of fear'. Parts of Antrim and Down were reported to be preparing for a new insurrection, the counties of Wicklow and Wexford remained disturbed and the government saw the hand of the United Irishmen in recurrent agrarian violence in the south and west.[44]

By the turn of the year some of the state prisoners in Dublin, believing that the pact made with the government was void, were attempting to capitalise on this widespread disaffection. Leaders such as Russell and Arthur O'Connor, who had been reluctant adherents to the agreement in the first place, saw their misgivings confirmed and were to the fore in attempts to revive the movement.[45] The new organisation was based on an acceptance that the United Irishmen were not in a position to mount an effective insurrection themselves, but that they should await the arrival of the French. They adopted a simplified structure, no longer based on a hierarchy of committees; instead the Dublin-based directory would appoint a number of colonels throughout the countryside, who would in turn form local regiments which they would call out once the French had landed.[46] This new streamlined movement was designed to be difficult for informers to penetrate and to be activated rapidly when required.

With the adoption of this pared-down revolutionary organisation, the United Irishmen became completely dependent on a French invasion, which the movement's leaders seem to have expected was imminent. According to James McGucken, a Belfast attorney and United Irishman who had turned informer but who still continued to act for the state prisoners, Russell had received a letter from a United Irish agent in London (probably William Putnam McCabe or George Palmer) who was in contact with the French. On the basis of this information Russell claimed he was 'confident' that an invasion fleet would be ready to sail from Brest by the end of January, and Arthur O'Connor, MacNeven, Sweetman and Emmet were also reported as sharing his hopes. McGucken's information was confirmed to the Castle by reports received in London that preparations were in train at Brest for an expedition destined for Ireland and that the United Irishmen in Dublin had received assurances from France that it would arrive in March or early April. The Irish government certainly expected their arrival and reacted with alarm to signs of naval preparations in France's western ports.[47]

The reports of informers suggest that Newgate was the militant centre of this conspiracy and that Russell was a driving force behind United Irish plans for another attempt at insurrection.[48] Probably to compensate for his enforced inactivity during the previous summer, Russell threw himself into the task with great energy. Given his belief that the Irish people had come within a whisker of victory in the late rebellion, he was convinced that a renewed effort would certainly succeed. For a time he regained the pivotal role he had in the United Irish transformation of 1795–6, and he appears to have been the focus of efforts to enlist support from the French and from some more unlikely allies closer to home.[49]

A novel feature of United Irish planning at this time was that they hoped to make use of Orange discontent at the proposed act of union to enlist their former enemies in the struggle against British rule. Plans for a legislative union had been broached in the autumn of 1798 and a lively pamphlet debate followed. Once the pacification of the country had been achieved, Cornwallis's brief was to force through a union which, coupled with Catholic emancipation, Pitt hoped would remove the causes of Irish disaffection once and for all and allow him to concentrate on the war against France. However, the proposed abolition of the Irish parliament was greeted with hostility by many loyalists. The United Irishmen were generally divided on the issue: some were opposed to Ireland being riveted closer than ever to Britain, while others, including Russell, were largely indifferent to the abolition of Ireland's 'mock parliament'.[50] McGucken reported that whereas the Kilmainham state prisoners had instructed their lawyer friends to oppose the union at a meeting of the bar, those in Newgate had encouraged them to support the measure 'in order to inflame the Orangemen'.[51] This was not quite as far-fetched as it sounds, since the Orangemen were among the most vehement opponents of the proposed union. There were complaints to the Orange Grand Lodge that some members had sought to make common cause with the United Irishmen, and in January 1799 the informer Leonard McNally warned the government that 'the orange and green are making rapid approaches towards each other'.[52] Many loyalists saw the proposed abolition of the Irish parliament as a betrayal by the British government — particularly as many expected union to be accompanied by Catholic emancipation; the yeomanry in particular regarding it as a poor reward for their vigorous efforts in quashing rebellion the previous summer. Members of the Dublin yeomanry proposed that they should stage a mass resignation in protest, while some rural corps threatened open revolt. By 1799 the terms Orangeman and yeoman were virtually synonymous and the growth of disaffection in this large and volatile armed body was viewed with deep concern by the government. In the end, despite the misgivings of many of its members, the order as a whole adopted a position of neutrality in relation to the union and the yeomanry remained loyal.[53]

Of all the movement's leaders Russell seems to have been most hopeful that the Orange society would support the United Irish cause. He was reported to have confided in McGucken that 'the Orangemen of Dublin have offered arms to the United Irishmen and are going about in order to destroy all parties [and] factions and have a common cause'. He allegedly claimed that if the Dublin yeomanry turned against the government they would be supported by other corps throughout the country.[54] Such a view was not altogether incompatible with opinions that Russell had expressed in the past. Although he had been a fierce critic of the Orangemen, describing some as 'execrable villains and plunderers', he had always believed that many of them were 'very ignorant' and had 'no real interest' in religious persecution, but had been set in motion by the 'instigation of artful and wicked men'.[55] Once they showed the merest signs of disaffection towards the government, as some yeomanry corps undoubtedly did when the prospect of union was mooted, Russell, with his boundless capacity for wishful thinking, was willing to believe that they had finally come to their senses and would now make common cause with the United Irishmen against British coercion. A 'letter to the people', written in prison, which the United Irish executive intended to have published and circulated throughout the country, contains several ideas and phrases on the issue of sectarian strife that appear in works written previously by Russell, suggesting his authorship or at least his influence.[56] The letter denounced Pitt's plans for union and encouraged an alliance with the Orangemen, while admitting:

> they have been base and barbarous; but they are still your country-men, and many of them have been more deluded than criminal. With weak understandings and strong passions, they have been instruments in the hands of cool, designing, mercenary villains . . . No Irish arm is unworthy of being employed in its country's cause, and even a last repentance should obtain forgiveness from every generous mind. The English yoke once broken, such parricide will never be renewed, for the prime source of civil and religious dissension will be forever dried up . . . Embrace as a friend and a brother every man of any sect or party (whatever his past errors) who shall take arms in his country's cause, and make her interest his religion.[57]

The government was kept well informed of the conspiratorial activities of the state prisoners and on the morning of 16 January an armed guard searched their cells and seized their papers. Among these papers were found notes of a conversation held by Russell, Neilson and a number of their colleagues at Newgate repudiating their pact with the government and discussing the 'probable success' of an insurrection given the disturbed state of the country. With the agreement of his colleagues Russell was alleged to have drawn up a request to the French to dispatch to Ireland a contingent of experienced officers in plain clothes. These would take charge of the people who would then 'emancipate the leaders and renew the struggle with redoubled energy'.[58]

The seizure of their papers seems to have done little to disrupt their organisational efforts and disturbing reports continued to arrive at the Castle. From Ulster came accounts of deserters from the Kerry militia drilling large bodies of men in Co. Down, and reports of James Hope organising in Co. Antrim. Information was received that in Dublin a United Irish executive, with great influence among the clerks and shopkeepers of the capital, continued to make mischief. Its leading spirit was Thomas Addis Emmet's younger brother, Robert.[59] Reports of preparations in surrounding counties were even more alarming. The Castle was informed that the United Irishmen had established communications with Joseph Holt's rebel band, still holding out in the Wicklow Mountains. Operations had been orchestrated by:

> an executive that met in Kilmainham and Newgate... The entire province of Leinster are under orders to hold themselves at a moment's warning; they don't hold any committee meetings, or any other...; they want no organisation, being sufficiently prepared...; they declare that when they next rise they will not submit but with their lives, they are very desperate... The organisation is going on rapidly, meetings will be held through the province of Leinster in the course of the week... to settle plans. They are encouraged by the prisoners, formerly their leaders.[60]

By this stage the government was genuinely worried. Cornwallis observed that the 'United Irishmen look on with pleasure' at the growing disturbances in the country 'and are whetting their knives to cut the throats of all the nobility and gentry of the island'. McGucken had earlier warned that, regardless of what steps were taken to guard the prisoners, they would still find ways to communicate with the outside world and he advised that they should be sent away. Reports of the prisoners communicating with disaffected groups in London spurred Whitehall to insist early in March that the removal of the state prisoners was 'a measure which is indisputably and immediately necessary'.[61] Cornwallis therefore decided to implement a recommendation he had made months earlier and pack the prisoners off to a fort on the edge of the Scottish Highlands to keep them from doing mischief. To prevent the possibility that they might leave behind instructions they were given only a few hours notice of their impending departure and were not told of their destination. On 19 March the leading state prisoners, including Russell, were taken on board the *Ashton Smith* in Dublin Bay and dispatched to Scotland.[62]

NOTES

1 Camden to Portland, 17 June 1797 (P.R.O., HO 100/69/397–9); R. B. McDowell, *Ireland in the age of imperialism and revolution* (Oxford, 1979), p. 573.
2 Evidence of Robert McCormick, 1798 (P.R.O.N.I., McCance collection, D272/6).
3 Mary Ann McCracken to Henry Joy McCracken, 16 Mar. 1797 (Madden papers, 873/151).
4 Pelham to Lake, 3 Mar. 1797 (N.L.I., Lake correspondence MS 56/31–2); Elliott, *Partners*, p. 133; Charles Dickson, *Revolt in the North: Antrim and Down in 1798* (Dublin, 1960), p. 117.
5 Musgrave, Lisburn, to Russell, 4 Jan. 1798 (Sirr papers, 868/2, ff 311–12) and Sampson to Russell , n. d., (Sirr papers, 868/2, ff 230–1); see also letters to Russell from: James McDonnell, Belfast, 30 June 1797 (Sirr papers, 868/2, ff 213–14); William Sampson, Belfast, Mar. 1797 (Reb. papers, 620/53/12); Rowley Osborne, Belfast, 4 Jan. 1798, 22 Feb. 1798 (Sirr papers, 868/2, f. 245, ff 266–7); James Smith, 15 Aug. 1797 (Sirr papers, 868/2, ff 241–2); Robert Simms, Belfast, 13 Aug. 1797, 26 Nov. 1797 (Sirr papers, 868/2, ff 232–3, 247).
6 F. W. Smith, Carrickfergus, to Russell, 19 Sept. 1797 (Sirr papers, 868/2, ff 234–5) and Robert Simms to Russell, 10 Aug. 1997 (Sirr papers, 868/2, ff 307–8).
7 Thomas Russell to John Russell, Fort George, 10 Dec. 1800 (copy) (Madden papers, 873/655, f. 3v).
8 Thomas Russell to John Russell, Fort George, 10 Dec. 1800 (copy) (Madden papers, 873/655, f. 3); Russell to –, 23 Oct. 1797 (Reb. papers, 620/16/3); William M. Byrne to Russell, 24 July 1798 (Reb. papers, 620/39/109).
9 Samuel Sproule to John Lees, 21 May 1798 (Reb. papers, 620/51/23).
10 Richard Musgrave, *Memoirs of the different rebellions in Ireland*, (3rd edn, Dublin, 1802), i, 262–3; P.R.O., P.C. 1/3118, f. 51; Madden, *United Irishmen*, 4th ser., (2nd edn, Dublin, 1860), pp. 58–9; J. E. Walsh, *Ireland ninety years ago* (Dublin, 1876), p. 154.
11 Revd. William Bennet, notes on Musgrave's Irish rebellions (N.L.I. MS 637, p. 435).
12 L. M. Cullen, 'Political structures of the Defenders' in Gough and Dickson (eds), *Ire. and the Fr. Rev.*, p. 131; Nancy J. Curtin, 'United Irish organisation in Ulster' in Dickson, Keogh and Whelan (eds), *United Irishmen*, pp. 219–20.
13 Russell to —, 5 June 1802 (Madden papers, 873/673); Russell to McNally, 5 Oct. 1803 (P.R.O., HO 100/114/119).

14 Thomas Pakenham, *The year of liberty* (London, 1969), pp. 286–7; Lecky, *Ireland*, v, 25, 28.

15 Thomas Russell to John Russell, 10 Dec. 1800 (copy) (TCD, Madden papers, 873/655, ff 11–12); Charles H. Teeling, *Sequel to personal narrative of the 'Irish rebellion' of 1798* (Belfast, 1832), pp. 294, 307; William Sampson, *Memoirs* (New York, 1807), p. 25.

16 Madden, *United Irishmen*, 4th ser. (2nd ed., Dublin, 1860), pp. 62–3; Henry Alexander to Thomas Pelham, 26 July 1798 (Lecky, *Ireland*, v, 32n).

17 Memorial from state prisoners, [24] July 1798 (Reb. papers, 620/39/231).

18 Thomas Russell to John Russell, Fort George, 10 Dec. 1800 (copy) (Madden papers, 873/655, ff 7v–9v). For Russell's reluctance to deal with the government and his scepticism of their good faith, see also Russell to Hugh Wilson, 10 Dec. 1798 (Reb. papers, 620/41/112); W. J. MacNeven, *Pieces of Irish history* (New York, 1807), p. 191.

19 *Castlereagh corr.*, i, 149; Cornwallis to Portland, 8, 26 July 1798 (*Cornwallis corr.*, ii, 359, 372–4).

20 Arthur O'Connor to Castlereagh, 4 Jan. 1799 (Charles H. Teeling, *Sequel to personal narrative of the 'Irish rebellion' of 1798* (Belfast, 1832), p. 297; 28 July 1798 (Reb. papers, 620/4/29/15); *Castlereagh corr.*, i, 347–8; Cornwallis to Portland, 26 July 1798 (*Cornwallis corr.*, ii, 374).

21 Cornwallis to Pitt, 25 Oct.1798, Cornwallis to Portland, 26 July 1798 (*Cornwallis corr.*, ii, 425, 372–4).

22 General Nugent, Belfast to Cooke, 14 Aug. 1798 (Reb. papers, 620/39/172); the informer in question was the Co. Down farmer, Nicholas Magin. For a brief account of Magin's life as an informer see Charles Dickson, *Revolt in the North: Antrim and Down in 1798* (Dublin, 1960), pp. 164–6.

23 Cooke to Pelham, 9 Aug. 1798 (B.L., Pelham papers, Add. MS 33106, f. 48); Cooke to Wickham, 28 July 1798 (*Cornwallis corr.*, ii, 378).

24 Cornwallis to Portland, 26 July 1798 (*Cornwallis corr.*, ii, 374); Ann C. Kavanaugh, *John Fitzgibbon, earl of Clare* (Dublin, 1997), p. 347; Cooke to Pelham, 9 Aug. 1798 (B.L., Pelham papers, Add. MS 33106, ff 49–50); Clare to Auckland, 1 Aug. 1798 (*Auckland corr.*, iv, 38–9); Cooke to Wickham, 28 July 1798 (*Cornwallis corr.*, ii, 378).

25 Cornwallis to Ross, 30 July 1798 (*Cornwallis corr.*, ii, 381); Clare to Auckland, 1 Aug 1798 (*Auckland corr.*, iv, 38–9); Wickham to Castlereagh, 13 Aug 1798 (P.R.O. HO 100/66/359); 15 Aug. 1798 (N.L.I., Melville papers, MS 54A/145).

26 *Memoir of the Irish union* (London, 1802?).

27 *Reports of the committees of secrecy*, pp. 225–36; *Dublin Evening Post*, 25 Aug. 1798; *Freeman's Journal*, 23 Aug. 1798; *Faulkner's Dublin Journal*, 23 Aug. 1798. For the prisoners' replies see *Saunders' Newsletter*, 27 Aug. 1798 and *Hibernian Journal*, 31 Aug. 1798.

28 *Faulkner's Dublin Journal*, 28 Aug. 1798; Lecky, *Ireland*, v, 52.

29 Madden, *United Irishmen*, 4th ser. (2nd ed., Dublin, 1860), pp. 73–4.

30 T. A. Emmet to Russell, [*c.* Sept. 1798] (Reb. papers, 620/15/2/14); 38 Geo. III c. 78 (*Stat. Ire.*, xviii, 1129).

31 Thomas Russell to John Russell, Fort George, 10 Dec. 1800 (copy) (Madden papers, 873/655, ff 11–12).

32 Russell to Francis Dobbs, 14 Sept. 1798 (Reb. papers, 620/16/3).

33 Cornwallis to Portland, 29 Oct. 1798 (*Cornwallis corr.*, ii, 427–8); for a list of prisoners included in the terms of the agreement see 38 Geo. III c. 78 (*Stat. Ire.*, xviii, 1129–30).

34 Castlereagh to Wickham, 2 Jan. 1799 (P.R.O., HO 100/85/7); Samuel Neilson to Thomas Russell, 5 Dec. 1998 (Reb. papers, 620/16/3); *Cornwallis corr.*, ii, 427.

35 Cornwallis to Portland, 29 Oct. 1798 (*Cornwallis corr.*, ii, 427–8).
36 T.A. Emmet to Cornwallis, 11 Oct. 1798 (Reb. papers, 620/15/2/13); Castlereagh to Wickham, 29 Oct. 1798 (*Castlereagh corr.*, i, 414); 13 Sept. 1798 (*Cornwallis corr.*, ii, 403).
37 Rufus King to Portland, 13 Sept., 17 Oct. 1798 (P.R.O. HO 100/66/369, 373–4); T. A. Emmet to Rufus King, 9 Apr. 1807 (MacNeven, *Pieces*, p. 291); 12 Nov. 1798 (*Cornwallis corr.*, ii, 435–6).
38 Russell to Francis Dobbs, 14 Sept. 1798 (Sirr papers, 868/1, ff 24–5); Francis Dobbs to Russell, 5 Dec. 1798 (Sirr papers, 868/1, f. 29).
39 J. S. [i. e. Tone], Rouen, to Matilda Tone, 22 April 1798 (Tone (Dickason) MS).
40 Tone to Matilda Tone, 22, 23 Aug. 1798 (Tone (Dickason) MS).
41 T. A. Emmet to Russell, [early Nov. 1798] (Reb. papers, 620/15/2/15); Peter Burrowes to Russell, 9 Nov. 1798 (Sirr papers, 868/2, ff 279–80).
42 Neilson to Russell, 5 Dec. 1798 (Reb. papers, 620/16/3); Charles H. Teeling, *Sequel to personal narrative of the 'Irish rebellion' of 1798* (Belfast, 1832), pp. 308–9; T. A. Emmet to Cornwallis, 11 Oct. 1798 (Reb. papers, 620/15/2/13); Bridewell prisoners to Cornwallis, 17 Sept. 1798 (Reb. papers, 620/40/65).
43 Boyle, [Sept. 1798] (Reb. papers, 620/18/3), see also information of McGucken, 5 Jan. 1799 (Reb. papers, 620/7/74/3).
44 John Brown to — , 29 Aug. 1798 (Reb. papers, 620/39/227); Boyle, 8 Sept., 22 Dec. 1798] (Reb.papers, 620/18/3); John Sidwell to Cooke, 3 Jan. 1799 (Reb. papers, 620/46/3); Cornwallis to Portland, 16 Jan., Mar. 1799 (P.R.O., HO 100/85/87–8, 195–6); Buckingham to Grenville, 11 Mar. 1799 (H.M.C., *Dropmore MS* (London, 1892–4), iv, 496–8); diary of Captain Hodges, Feb. 1799 (B.L., Add. MS 40166); Cornwallis to Portland, 14 Feb. 1798 (*Castlereagh corr.*, ii, 174).
45 Elliott, *Partners,* p. 247.
46 Elliott, *Partners*, p. 248; McGucken, 29 Dec. 1798 (Reb. papers, 620/3/32/19), 3 Jan., 29 Jan., 2 Feb., 7 Feb., 15 Feb. 1799 (Reb. papers, 620/7/74/2, 5, 7, 8, 11); Boyle, 13, 17 Mar. 1799 (Reb. papers, 620/18/3).
47 Information of McGucken, 3 Jan., 7 Feb. 1799 (Reb. papers, 620/7/74/2, 8); see also Elliott, 'Despard conspiracy' p. 49; idem., *Partners*, p. 243. For signs of alarm in the Irish government see Wickham to Castlereagh, 28 Feb. 1799 (P.R.O., HO 100/85/281–3) and John Beresford to Lord Auckland, 31 Jan. 1799 (*Beresford corr.*, ii, 205).
48 Information of McGucken, 3 Jan. 1799 (Reb. papers, 620/7/74/2); information of John Pollock, 29 Dec. 1798 (Reb. papers, 620/3/32/19); Madden, *United Irishmen*, 3rd ser., ii, 184; Elliott, *Partners*, p. 247.
49 Thomas Russell to John Russell, Fort George, 10 Dec. 1800 (copy) (Madden papers, 873/655, f. 8). For Russell's contacts abroad see information of McGucken, 10 Feb. 1799 (Reb. papers, 620/7/74/10).
50 Russell to —, 5 June 1802 (Madden papers, 873/673). Neilson actually welcomed the measure, see Neilson to his wife, 21 July 1799 (Madden, *United Irishmen*, 4th ser. (2nd edn, Dublin, 1860), pp. 105–6). For the views of some United Irishmen on the union see Denis Taaffe, *The probability, causes and consequences of an union between Great Britain and Ireland* (Dublin, 1798); William James MacNeven, *An argument for independence in opposition to a union* (Dublin, 1798); William Drennan, *A protest from one of the people of Ireland against an union with Great Britain* (Dublin, 1800).
51 Information of John Pollock (via McGucken), 3 Jan. 1799 (Reb. papers, 620/7/74/2).
52 'J. W.' [Mc Nally] to —, 20 Jan. 1799 (Reb. papers, 620/10/121/124). Hereward Senior, *Orangeism in Ireland and Britain, 1795–1836* (London, 1966),

pp. 122–4. For the United Irishmen hoping to capitalise on Orange discontent see also Lecky, *Ireland*, v, 198.

53 Allan Blackstock, *An ascendancy army: the Irish yeomenry 1796–1834* (Dublin, 1998), pp. 181–6; Hereward Senior, *Orangeism in Ireland and Britain, 1795–1836* (London, 1966), pp. 126–7; Castlereagh to Portland, 2 Jan. 1799 (*Castlereagh corr.*, ii, 81); Cornwallis to Portland, 16 Jan. 1799 (P.R.O., HO 100/85/87).

54 Information of John Pollock (via McGucken), 29 Jan. 1799 (Reb. papers, 620/7/74/5).

55 Russell, *Letter to the people*, p. 14.

56 Compare the extract quoted on p. 216 with Russell's comments on the Orangemen in *Letter to the people of Ireland* (1796) pp. 14–15 and Russell's letter in *Dublin Evening Post*, 22 Dec. 1796 (below, pp. 191–2).

57 Copied by McGucken, 19 Feb. 1799 (Reb. papers, 620/7/74/12).

58 Madden, *United Irishmen*, 2nd ser., (2nd ed., Dublin, 1858), i, 178; Thomas Russell to John Russell, Fort George, 10 Dec. 1800 (copy) (Madden papers, 873/655, f. 12); Madden, *United Irishmen*, 3rd ser., ii, 184–5.

59 Statement of Robert Henry, Antrim jail, 27 July 1799 (Reb. papers, 620/47/100); McGucken, 29 Jan. 1799 (Reb. papers, 620/7/74/5); examination of Thomas Wright, (P.R.O., HO 100/86/301–2).

60 Information of Boyle, *c.* Mar. 1799, 13, 17 Mar. 1799 (Reb. papers, 620/18/13/3).

61 Cornwallis to Major-General Ross, 13 Feb. 1799 (*Cornwallis corr.*, iii, 60); information of McGucken, 5 Jan. 1799 (Reb. papers, 620/7/74/3); Portland to Cornwallis, 5 Mar. 1799 (P.R.O., HO 100/86/9); Wickham to Castlereagh, 26 Mar. 1799 (*Castlereagh corr.*, ii, 169).

62 Cornwallis to Portland, 13 Sept. 1798 (*Cornwallis corr.*, ii, 403); Castlereagh to Wickham, 19 Mar. 1799 (P.R.O., HO 100/86/163–4).

CHAPTER TWELVE

Exile

After a detour to Belfast to collect five northern prisoners, the *Ashton Smith* landed at Gourock at the mouth of the Clyde on 30 March 1799. The convoy then made the long overland journey via Greenock and the Gorbals of Glasgow to the military base of Fort George on the Moray Firth in north-eastern Scotland. Throughout the journey the prisoners' coaches were guarded by a strong escort and were observed by curious crowds along the way. Some were heard to remark that they must be '*very great men*, or they would not be escorted by such a large retinue'. The prisoners behaved with a certain amount of bravado, letting down the coach windows so that they could be seen. They made a strong impression on the watching crowds, with Arthur O'Connor resplendent in his green uniform and the others 'completely cropped with moustachios *aprés la mode française*'.[1]

They arrived at Fort George on 9 April. The fort, located about nine miles east of Inverness, had been built after the Jacobite rising in 1745, and was one of the largest and most secure fortresses in Britain, capable of holding almost 2,000 men. As it was not completed until the 1760s, when the Jacobite threat had receded, it served no strategic function but was used as a mustering station for Highland regiments and was garrisoned by an invalid company.

On the journey to Fort George the prisoners had been well cared for and treated with civility by their guards. This heralded a marked change for the better in their prison conditions. The regime at Fort George was to prove far more benevolent than those which they had experienced previously. The prisoners were lodged in separate, reasonably well-furnished rooms and even had servants to wait on them. Their food gave little cause for complaint. According to one prisoner:

> we have very fine salmon twice or thrice a week ... Our beef, mutton, pork, lamb, etc. are remarkably good. Latterly we have had plenty of

garden stuffs or sallading — and some young ducks and peas . . . Our wine and porter all have been uniformly good. And at supper we occasionally had very fine crabs and lobsters'.[2]

The fort's position on a spit of land jutting out into the firth and its isolation enabled the prisoners to be kept in safe custody but given reasonable freedom of movement and initial restrictions on their freedom to associate together were gradually relaxed. Eventually they were allowed out of their cells for most of the day, and were given ample opportunities for exercise — walking the ramparts, playing football and handball and even swimming in the sea. They were also permitted to buy books and newspapers in nearby Inverness, and these circulated freely among them. The benign regime at Fort George was mostly down to the fort commander, Colonel James Stuart. Russell developed a deep respect for Stuart, whose humanity and selfless dedication to duty reminded him of his late father.[3]

The sea air and improved conditions made for a wholesome environment and Russell fully recovered his health. After a time, the families of some inmates were allowed live in the fort and the imprisoned United Irishmen formed a small community, with the presence of women and children helping to normalise prison life. Prisoners acted as tutors to the sons of Neilson and Emmet, with Russell taking on the role of mathematics teacher. Some sought to improve their own education by studying sciences or languages, or learning to play musical instruments. By the middle of their term of confinement, one prisoner admitted that 'we have enjoyed every accommodation, and every means of health and comfort which [our] situation could admit; nor have we laboured under a single restraint which safe custody did not require'. All could not help comparing the abysmal conditions and petty tyrannies experienced in prisons in Dublin and Belfast with their liberal and dignified treatment at Fort George, and they believed that any new attempts to impose restrictions or privations on them originated with Dublin Castle.[4]

Though Russell wanted for little in Fort George — in fact, he probably enjoyed greater material comfort than had he been free — the welfare of his poverty-stricken sister, Margaret, continued to play on his mind. Towards the end of 1800 she moved from Co. Fermanagh to Dublin in the hope of improving her circumstances, but with little success. Russell was reluctant to apply to friends in Dublin on her behalf, probably having sought their help on several occasions in the past. He himself sent whatever little money he could manage, though it was rarely enough to cover her needs. Her situation became so desperate that she considered travelling to Fort George to ask her brother's help in person, but was dissuaded by friends. Money troubles again reared their head with Russell's release, when he and his sister were forced to apply to friends again. The ever generous Mary Ann McCracken made an effort to alleviate Margaret's poverty by raising a subscription among Russell's acquaintances, but the general response was very lukewarm.[5] By this stage some of those applied to had had enough. An exasperated Drennan complained that Russell 'writes to his friends here in the true spirit of a martyr and demands a supply of £50 in the spirit of the poor Grecian philosophers who used to leave the support of their widows and daughters to some of their rich neighbours'. Drennan's annoyance can be accounted for by more than Russell's supplications: by this stage he was anxious to distance himself from his former United Irish colleagues. Alienated by the transformation of the society into a conspiratorial organisation and horrified by the events of 1798, he now favoured a gradualist approach to reform and, in what may have been a swipe at Russell, he dismissed the 'leavened democrats' of the movement as 'aristocracy in a shabby coat, aristocratic self-sufficiency, aristocratic vengeance, aristocratic intolerance, under a Maratism of language and manners'.[6]

In Fort George too there was dissension, aggravated by prolonged imprisonment. Preferential treatment for certain prisoners, especially Arthur and Roger O'Connor, led to resentment and suspicions among some of their colleagues. Since one of the prisoners, Robert Hunter of Belfast, was passing information on their discussions to the authorities, it soon became apparent that there was an informer in their midst and accusations and counter-accusations of treachery were traded. A long-standing breach between Arthur O'Connor and Thomas Addis Emmet gradually developed into a bitter enmity. The two intended to fight a duel after their release but were dissuaded by the pleading of their colleagues.[7] Their antipathy, however, continued to fester and proved deeply divisive and damaging to United Irish efforts to revive their movement on the Continent. The dispute was partly a clash of personalities and partly due to a difference of opinion on the question of soliciting aid from France. In the months leading up to the insurrection of 1798 O'Connor had favoured a rising of the Irish people even without a French invasion, whereas Emmet thought they should take the field only after the arrival of the

French. This caution led O'Connor to accuse him of cowardice.[8] Ironically, by the early 1800s their positions had reversed with Emmet having become far more suspicious of French intentions towards Ireland than O'Connor.

Russell took the side of Emmet. As well as being a close friend, he shared Emmet's reservations about Bonaparte. Moreover, he had little sympathy with the aristocratic O'Connor's élitist political leanings. James Hope related an account of a heated dispute which occurred at Fort George when O'Connor and Robert Simms stated that the 'present constitution of France was too good for Ireland'. The Belfast tailor, Joseph Cuthbert, angrily disagreed with them, maintaining 'that no constitution could be too good for Ireland'. Russell did not speak his mind on this occasion, possibly anxious to avoid divisive political arguments while in custody but Hope assures us that he did not share O'Connor's opinion.[9] After their release Russell and O'Connor found themselves at odds as they attempted to renew their political activities on the Continent: looking back on the divisions of the exiled United Irishmen in 1802–3, O'Connor singled out Russell as the leading member of the rival United Irish faction in Paris.[10]

Some prisoners at Fort George steered clear of either faction. Indeed, there were those such as Samuel Neilson who, heartily sick of imprisonment and uneasy at the form the rebellion of 1798 had taken, seem to have grown entirely disillusioned with politics.[11] But Russell, who had spent longer in jail than any of his colleagues, suffered no dilution of his revolutionary zeal and was determined to renew the fight at the first available opportunity. His millennialist outlook had only been stoked by the bloodshed of previous years. He believed that the deaths of friends such as Tone and McCracken had imposed 'a greater obligation on the survivors to persevere in the great cause'. The combined effect of the continuation of the war in Europe, its spread to the Middle East and the bloody summer of 1798 in Ireland, seem only to have intensified Russell's belief that the world was presently experiencing the time of troubles which Revelations had foretold would precede the coming of Christ's kingdom. In a letter written to his brother in 1800 he described the war as a conflict:

> which embraces every quarter of the globe... [and] the fate of the human race. [It] is not a contest for relative power or riches, whatever momentary hues it may assume, but is a contest between the two

principles of despotism and liberty and can only terminate in the extinction of one or other. Reason and religion leave one no doubt which will triumph...The sacred volume...evidently points out the impending vengeance of Almighty God on those individuals and those nations who obstinately persist in supporting injustice and tyranny, by fraud, cruelty and superstition.[12]

However, imprisoned in Fort George there was little that Russell could do. The government had hoped that by detaining the United Irish prisoners in such a remote location they would have little influence on political events and that they could press ahead with passing a legislative union without any disruption from the United Irishmen. So it proved, and the union faced little effective opposition from Irish radicals, most of whom shed few tears at the demise of a parliament they regarded as corrupt and unrepresentative.

Nevertheless, a hard core of the prisoners shared Russell's determination to continue the struggle and sought to enlist whatever allies they could. In the autumn of 1801 they planned to disseminate republican propaganda throughout Scotland and attempted to open communications with elements of the Scottish militia. Apparently, however, this attempt was thwarted by Hunter, who notified the authorities.[13] The extent of Russell's involvement in this effort is unclear, but he was rarely found lagging behind in these matters. Significantly, an Irish soldier named Arthur Devlin, with whom he may have become acquainted during his time at Fort George, later acted as a link between Russell and the Wicklow rebel leader, Michael Dwyer, during preparations for the 1803 insurrection.[14] Some verse written by Russell in Fort George may well have been related to this episode. This plea for pan-Celtic solidarity, a favourite theme of one of Russell's mentors, the Scottish intellectual James Tytler, was entitled *Erin's address to Caledonia.*

> *Alike our fate, no foreign force*
> *Could e'er our valiant race subdue;*
> *The Roman eagles stopped their course*
> *When near our rugged coast they drew.*
> *While union was our children's boast,*
> *The gallant conquering Romans failed;*
> *When discord hovered o'er our coast,*
> *A cruel sordid foe prevailed.*
>
> ...

And can your sons for war renowned
Endure that hostile feet should thread-
Should spurn the consecrated ground
Where Fletcher spoke and Wallace bled?
Like us, unite, and in the field
Full soon shall haughty England feel
That fraud to valour still must yield
And India's gold to Carron's steel.[15]

By the autumn of 1801, however, opportunities for militant agitation were on the wane as the war between Britain and France finally appeared to be coming to a close. In August the two countries signed the Leoben peace preliminaries and within a few months the government began to release some of the state prisoners. Dickson, Robert Simms, Dowdall, Tennent, Dowling and Hunter, who had not signed the 'Kilmainham Treaty' and were therefore not included in the banishment act, were allowed to give security for their good behaviour and to return to Ireland. But those the authorities believed could still act as a focus for disaffection, among them Russell, Neilson, Thomas Addis Emmet and Arthur O'Connor, were not released.[16] The government was particularly worried that, although the banishment act forbade the state prisoners to return to Ireland, they were not prohibited from basing themselves in Britain and emergency legislation was quickly passed to cover this eventuality.[17] They were eventually released after the conclusion of the peace of Amiens in June 1802. At that stage, it seems that most of the prisoners would have settled for exile in America but, as in 1798, Russell could not bear the thought, aware that it would be almost impossible to renew the struggle from across the Atlantic.[18] Letters written before his departure from Fort George make it abundantly clear that there had been no weakening in his commitment to take up the fight again or in his confidence of ultimate success. In a letter smuggled out to an unnamed Dublin friend he wrote:

I am sure the people of Ireland, that are determined to be free, are capable of becoming so. I look on the cause of liberty, on the eve of breaking out, with fresh vigour... Ireland stands on *better* ground than ever; by our union, the people were taught to love each other, to know their strength and valour in the field — by their defeat they had been taught to know their *enemies*, and are now ready to resume the contest, and that successfully, when there comes a favourable opportunity of doing so. To accelerate that, by exerting every faculty of my mind and body, is my determination. How I can do that best, I can only know when I am at large ... So far from being tired of the pursuit of liberty, or esteeming it a phantom, my attachments strengthen every day — I have no more doubt of the success than I have of the justice of the cause. Who indeed, that entertained our opinions ... could live to insult the memory of the heroes who fell for Ireland, by trampling on their unhonoured graves? Who that knew that colossal power was shaken from its summit to its base, by the gallant peasantry of a few counties, ill-armed, and ill-led, could ever cease to promote a general and effectual movement? Who could walk the streets of your city and see the great houses where *free* legislators of a great and good people should now be sitting, abandoned by its mock parliament, and converted into a temple of mammon, and not wish the earth to gape and swallow him up, to save him from witnessing such unparalleled infamy and disgrace? ... We will continue to promote the cause of virtue and liberty, with every prospect of success, and with the certainty that should we fall, as many of our gallant friends have, our Lord and Saviour will, in eternal life, reward those who laboured for the welfare and happiness of mankind.[18]

Imprisonment and exile had cocooned Russell from the widespread demoralisation that had come in the wake of the events of 1798. Once the aftershocks of disaffection had subsided, fear and disillusionment had spread a torpor over Ireland and, vested interests aside, even the debate on the act of union was largely greeted with apathy among the wider population. Russell, however, failed to recognise how things had changed. In a letter to John Templeton written days before his release, he dismissed the defeat of the late rebellion as a 'temporary miscarriage of the cause'. He maintained that 'so far from conceiving the cause of Ireland lost, or being weary of its pursuit, I am more than ever, if possible, inflexibly bent on it ... All the faculties I possess shall be exercised for its advancement.' He had wanted to return to Ireland to ascertain the state of the country and see how he might be of use in promoting another insurrection but, denied that opportunity, he would do his utmost to accomplish his object from the Continent. He concluded: 'every motive exists to stimulate the generous mind — the widows and orphans of my friends, the memory of the heroes who fell, and the sufferings of the heroes who survive. My very soul is on fire; I can say no more'.[20]

In his reply Templeton did his best to damp down the fire in Russell's soul:

From what I can see or hear, there is little danger to apprehend another rebellion in Ireland until the past is completely forgotten. A mutual jealousy subsists between all descriptions. The poor will not readily trust the rich, nor the rich the poor; each thinking the other acting under the immediate influence of self-interest ... Every friend to liberty has before his eyes a multitude, who, with enthusiasm, worshipped the goddess and hailed her as the rising sun that was to enable them to enjoy every happiness; yet, dazzled by the blaze of victory, and the pomp and pageantry of regal shows, they forget the blood that flowed from their friends and countrymen and, with exultation, submit to a fortunate usurper.[21]

It was a reply, however, that fell on deaf ears.

After the conclusion of the peace of Amiens between Britain and France, the government decided to release the remaining United Irish prisoners. On 30 June 1802 they were put on board a ship for the Continent. They landed at the neutral port of Cuxhaven, part of the free city of Hamburg, on 4 July and then scattered in various directions. After a few days Russell, Thomas Addis Emmet and his family, and five of their colleagues sailed for Amsterdam. They reached their destination on 1 August after a long voyage of twenty days caused by unfavourable winds.[22] While in Amsterdam Russell almost certainly met up with Robert Emmet. Emmet had been expelled from Trinity College in 1798 because of his radical political views; thereafter he operated as a United Irish organiser in Dublin until forced to flee in May 1799. In 1800 he visited his elder brother at Fort George and afterwards went to the Continent, where he acted as an agent for the United Irishmen.[23] We know little of how the friendship between the two men developed but it certainly seems that Russell developed a deep affection and respect for Emmet, whom he later described as having 'all the fascinating charms of youth and innocence'.[24] Nothing is known of their activities in Amsterdam, but the likelihood is that two such dedicated revolutionaries at least discussed the prospect of another attempt at insurrection.

After a couple of weeks in Holland Russell made his way to Paris. He reached the city on 22 August and put up at the Hotel d'Angleterre in the Faubourg St Germain. Paris was still a centre of United Irish activity with a sizeable community of Irish exiles, many of whom had been in the city since the 1790s. Russell was able to renew his acquaintance with old colleagues such as Richard McCormick and William Henry Hamilton from Enniskillen, who had married his niece Mary Ann. Hamilton had taken part in Hardy's expedition to Lough Swilly in 1798 — the same expedition on which Tone was captured — but he had managed to escape detection by passing himself off as a Frenchman. It is almost certain that Russell took the opportunity to visit Tone's widow Matilda who was at this time living in straitened circumstances near the Sorbonne with her three children, only one of whom survived into adulthood.[25]

Russell was visited in Paris by his brother John in September 1802, who claimed that he found him 'living in a very retired manner'. It was almost ten years since they had seen each other but despite their long separation they remained close. John spent about six weeks in Paris and was introduced to his brother's Irish friends. However, his visit was interrupted when he became extremely ill. He was treated by Thomas's friend Dr William James MacNeven and had to leave France on 30 October in great distress, the brothers parting with much 'anxiety and sorrow'.[26]

Concern for his brother's health was only one of the worries that played on Russell's mind during these months. As ever, he was still dogged by poverty, along with many of his exiled colleagues who eked out a precarious existence on meagre allowances from the French government. With funds so short, Russell pleaded with members of his family to send him some money. He also seems to have lapsed into the depths of depression during his exile in France: Arthur O'Connor painted a picture of Russell in a state of the deepest misery at this time, and claimed that it was the desperation engendered by this misery that drove him into a hopeless rebellion.[27]

Little is known of how Russell spent his time in Paris. We know that at Christmas 1802 he took communion with a Jansenist congregation — a sect, incidentally, with a strong leaning towards millenarian theology.[28] He may also have made attempts to renew his interest in literary and scientific matters. On his release from Fort George he had stated his intention 'to see something of the present state of science after so long a seclusion from the world' and asked his Irish friends to help him secure letters of introduction into literary and scientific circles on the Continent.[29] In the event, his relatively short stay in France — only about seven months — was devoted more to conspiratorial than literary activities. However, one of Russell's closest friends in Paris was John Delaney, a native of Kerry who had been educated at the Irish College and 'was considered a young man of talent and an accomplished scholar', who may well have introduced him into Parisian literary circles. Russell did at least make some effort to continue with his political journalism, contributing to the English language newspaper, the *Argus*, and made enough of an impression on his French hosts to be included in a poetic tribute written by Pierre François Tissot in 1804, entitled *Les trois conjurés irlandais*.[30]

Russell, though, was less than impressed with France under the Consulate. He had adopted several different attitudes towards the French revolution as it changed direction over the years. In his whiggish phase he had expressed concern that a powerful National Assembly, unhindered by checks or balances, might act as an instrument of tyranny. By October 1792, he had shed these reservations and intended to join the army of the newly-founded republic. Subsequently, he seems to have identified with the revolution's more radical elements — for example, taking the part of Georges Danton in an argument with the Fermanagh parson, John Stack. He also appears to have accepted the harsh measures invoked in defence of the revolution: writing to Tone in America, he noted how, at first, the relatively peaceful progress of the revolution had won widespread support for the French, but it was only their 'firm friends' who 'were able to withstand the repeated shocks which a different conduct afterwards produced'.[31] But he regarded Bonaparte, who had reimposed authoritarian government on France and re-introduced slavery in France's overseas colonies, as a traitor to the revolution, and his government as a tyranny which 'tramples on liberty in France, suspends its progress in the world, and madly attempts its total destruction'. While his coup had been 'justified by men espousing the cause of freedom,...the republicans of the nation were driven out by the bayonet'. Had Bonaparte been the sponsor of an Irish invasion, the result would have simply been 'a change of masters' — the substitution of a French tyranny for an English one. Russell also saw Bonaparte's government as morally bankrupt: he believed that France had for several years now been governed by 'professed atheists and deists' who had introduced 'boundless profligacy by their marriage laws', wielded power without mercy and imposed a crushing despotism on the French people. He regarded their 'detestable hypocrisy' as a dire warning to those who made the mistake of linking 'the cause of irreligion with that of liberty'.[32] While many of his United Irish colleagues in exile joined the French army, Russell deliberately held aloof from a course of action he had been intent on a decade previously. Moreover, the French government's neglect of Matilda Tone and her family —

despite the fact that Tone had died wearing the uniform of a French officer, it was not until May 1804 that they began to pay her a pension — can only have added to Russell's contempt for the Bonapartist regime.[33]

During these months the Irish exiles became caught up in the petty squabbling typical of impotent *émigré* groups, as the different factions sought to represent themselves as the true voice of the United Irishmen and to get the ear of influential figures in the French government. The most bitter rivalry was between the Emmet-Russell faction and that of Arthur O'Connor.[34] Compared to Tone some years earlier, Russell and his colleagues were in a completely different position in their dealings with the French government. Tone, though not completely blind to the shortcomings of the Directory, saw it as attempting to consolidate the Revolution and was loath to criticise French government policy. He was negotiating at a time when the United Irishmen were a respected organisation in France and seen as important allies in the war against England. In contrast by the early 1800s, because of their squabbling among themselves, their constant complaints of neglect and the overly optimistic information they had supplied as an enticement to invasion, the United Irishmen had largely been discredited in the eyes of the French authorities.[35] While Tone and most of his counterparts in the French government had largely shared the same ideology, there were marked ideological differences between the exiled republicans of 1802–3 and the increasingly authoritarian Bonapartist regime. More than ever their relationship was driven by expediency rather than fraternity. Both sides now viewed each other warily, while still prepared to use the other to advance their aims.

While in Paris John Russell heard his brother and his fellow United Irishmen 'always expressing the greatest dislike of the French government (both as to their politics and their morals) and the chief consul'. In a conversation with a fellow United Irishman in March 1803, Russell forthrightly condemned the 'tyranny and corruption' of the French government which he 'cordially detested'. He had seen how they hoodwinked Polish exiles by diverting them into an invasion force for the West Indies and he believed that given half a chance they would do the same thing to the Irish. He particularly singled out Talleyrand, Bonaparte's foreign minister, for his corruption and treachery. Jean Joseph Humbert, who had led the French force that landed at Killala in 1798 and who befriended Russell in Paris, told him that Talleyrand had done all he could to frustrate expeditions intended for Ireland. He alleged that he had betrayed plans to the British and blocked finances for Humbert's attempts at another invasion. In his opposition to the establishment of an independent Irish republic he was backed up to the hilt by Bonaparte, who, Russell claimed, 'hated Ireland, and would rather see it sunk in the sea than yield the disaffected in it any assistance'.[36]

By this stage Bonaparte made little effort to disguise his contempt for republicans and Jacobins, particularly foreign ones, and at best regarded the United Irishmen as a useful bargaining chip in his dealings with Britain. During the negotiations which led to the peace of Amiens he had offered to expel the United Irishmen from France if London would agree to take similar action against its community of French *émigrés*, and the United Irishmen believed that given a chance he would 'deliver up the United Irishmen, tied neck and heels to England'.[37] In discussions with Arthur O'Connor (who had little difficulty reconciling himself to Bonaparte's burgeoning authoritarianism) on the preparations being made for insurrection in Ireland in 1803, Bonaparte had 'expressed himself unfavourably of the attempt and of those engaged in it'. Not surprisingly, Bonaparte leaned strongly towards O'Connor's faction which favoured an 'intimate political connexion' between Ireland and France, perhaps even a union of the two countries, once separation from Britain had been achieved.[38] But despite their well-founded suspicions, most Irish republicans were convinced that some form of French assistance was necessary to accomplish the overthrow of British rule in Ireland. Even Russell, though he would undoubtedly have preferred to see the Irish people free themselves by their own efforts, believed that France had a role to play. In one of his flights of millennialist rhetoric he spoke of the French army as 'the instruments God would use ... [to] subdue the whole earth' in his efforts to establish the reign of justice and liberty. Russell believed that the French would attempt an invasion of England, which would be defeated — and were he an Englishman, he was adamant that 'he would lose a hundred lives in resisting them'. After this failure, he concluded that Bonaparte would have no choice but to strike at England through Ireland and thus help free the Irish people in spite of himself. In fact, he was so convinced that a French army would invade England in the near future and that the renewed war would be one of unprecedented ferocity, that he wrote to his brother John advising him to resign his commission in the English militia.[39]

Despite the contempt he held for the Bonapartist regime, the Irish government later believed that Russell had been 'the man who had the most direct communication with the French government' during the spring of 1803. From the correspondence of other United Irishmen it would also appear that Russell was the main focus of communications among the exiles based on the Continent in 1802–3, with contacts as far afield as Rotterdam and Lyons. Arthur O'Connor singled out Russell as the most influential individual in the United Irish faction which opposed him in Paris. O'Connor also claimed that Russell 'pushed the faction to excite Robert Emmet to the mad and utterly desperate attempt he made and which gave the finishing blow to the United Irish confederacy'.[40]

Russell regarded the peace of Amiens as 'a hollow truce', likely to prove short-lived, and believed that on the renewal of war between France and Britain the time would be right to strike a blow in Ireland.[41] While in Paris he associated with disgruntled republican generals, especially Humbert. He was probably introduced to him by James Joseph MacDonnell, a barrister from Co. Mayo who had joined the French when they landed and had escaped to Paris after 1798. MacDonnell had been a prominent member of the Catholic Convention for Co. Mayo and one of the most active United Irishmen in Connacht. It is possible therefore that Russell already knew him.[42] Jacobin generals like Humbert had been pushed aside by the Bonapartist regime and were anxious to involve themselves in projects that might help to re-establish their reputations. Moreover, according to Russell, they 'were warmly attached to the Irish'. Humbert in particular was intent on mounting another expedition to Ireland. He maintained that he loved the Irish nation and would like nothing better than to settle in an independent Ireland.[43] Perhaps time had softened his view since his capture in 1798 or perhaps he was simply misrepresented, when he reportedly spoke to a British officer of 'his contempt and disgust at the Irish he had come to assist'. He claimed that they had stolen his watch and his money and his aide-de-camp's horses; they were 'the most beggarly, rascally, cowardly scoundrels he ever knew…he was forced to shoot several and flog others to preserve any discipline whatever', and he added that 'he should take care he never came again'.[44]

Although he claimed that 'the freedom of Ireland occupied all his attention', it appears that Humbert's main efforts towards the end of 1802 were devoted to planning an invasion of the West Indies. The object of this expedition was to create a federal republic of the Caribbean islands on the model of the United States. This would weaken Britain by depriving her of the valuable sugar islands and her position of maritime pre-eminence in the West Indies. Russell maintained that he had been informed by an official in high authority that negotiations had been held with some of the leading men in Jamaica and the other islands, and that most had declared themselves in favour. Humbert thought that given the disposition of the inhabitants the project could be accomplished easily and apparently the French expected that Irishmen in France and America would assist in this project. But Russell, though perhaps initially attracted to the project as a means of striking a blow against the international slave trade, suffered from no illusions as to how the Irish might be used as cannon fodder in the West Indies, and when a French force sailed for the Caribbean in November 1802, it contained no significant Irish participation.[45]

By this stage the settlement reached at Amiens was looking increasingly shaky and the United Irishmen were again coming into favour with the French government. During the latter months of the uneasy peace an abundance of rumours about possible expeditions circulated throughout Paris. One Irishman staying in Paris, Robert Carty, reported that he had been called on by Russell and Humbert, who were trying to recruit exiles for an invasion of Ireland. The force was to consist of four or five thousand men and to be led by Humbert. Another Irishman, Michael Quigley, reported that Humbert's associate, MacDonnell, 'who was very intimate with Russell and Hamilton', was attempting to enlist Irishmen into a large French force destined for Louisiana. According to an account later drawn up by Dublin Castle, this expedition was to act as a cover for the invasion of Ireland. To allay suspicions Humbert was to resign from the French army in feigned exasperation and, accompanied by a number of troops posing as settlers, pretend to embark for America. Instead they would land in Connacht, where MacDonnell and Michael Gannon, a Mayo priest who had assisted the French in 1798, were to have preceded them and prepared the way for a successful invasion. Russell, Hamilton and the indefatigable United Irish emissary William Putnam McCabe were all reported as participating closely in the organisation of the project. Russell was given the responsibility for dispensing funds and had engaged in negotiations to buy arms.[46]

While it would appear that genuine preparations were made for this particular expedition, many of the projects that were spoken of in these months seem to have existed more in the imagination of their planners than in reality — partly a result of the French

government's desire to create as much uncertainty about their intentions as possible. John Russell related some of the plans that he had
heard being discussed among the Irish in Paris to James Farrell, a
United Irishman living in London. The exiles had claimed that the
American ambassador in Paris, Robert R. Livingston, was strongly
sympathetic to the cause of Irish independence and that he would do
all he could to help the United Irishmen effect a revolution. This
included promising them a large loan to buy a 30,000 stand of arms.
Moreover, the famous French general, Jean-Baptiste Bernadotte,
would be appointed to command this Irish invasion force. Farrell
claimed that he laughed at John Russell's reports, dismissing them as
'the bombast and gasconade of a few desperate fanatics'.[47]

Whatever the truth of many of these claims there would seem to
be little doubt that Russell, Humbert and MacDonnell were busily
engaged in trying to mount an expedition to strike at British interests somewhere on the globe with the ultimate aim of securing Irish
independence. But Russell, wary as he was of any excessive reliance
on French aid, would have looked more favourably on any project
initiated and controlled by Irishmen. In October 1802 Robert
Emmet spent a short time in Paris, and with a renewal of the war
between Britain and France looming, it is likely that he and Russell
discussed plans for another insurrection in Ireland. During this time
Emmet had an interview with Bonaparte which convinced him that
France and Britain would be at war again within a year and that an
invasion of England would take place in August 1803. Though he
was aware that Bonaparte saw Ireland as 'a mere side-show' to help
weaken England, Emmet was still mindful that an invasion of Britain
would denude Ireland of troops and provide an excellent opportunity to mount a successful insurrection. The likelihood is that he
shared this information with Russell. Soon after, apparently having
received news that things were stirring in Ireland, Emmet decided to
return. He assured Russell that he would keep him informed of
developments and summon him over at the appropriate time.[48]

As part of this effort, towards the end of 1802 William Henry
Hamilton returned to Ireland to test the waters for insurrection and
help raise the funds required. The response he met with was sufficiently generous, and the state of the country sufficiently disturbed,
to convince him that another rising stood a real chance of success,
even without the intervention of French troops. On his return to
Paris in February he conveyed his impressions to his United Irish
colleagues and preparations began to gather momentum. Hamilton

travelled to Brussels where he persuaded Thomas Addis Emmet and MacNeven to come to Paris to act as United Irish ambassadors. On 5 March he returned to Ireland with the Kildaremen, Michael Quigley and Brian McDermott. If Dublin was to be seized then the response of Kildare would be crucial and Quigley and McDermott were sent immediately by Robert Emmet to their native county to gauge its willingness to rise. They found enough simmering disaffection in the county to report back optimistically.[49]

Most probably, it was Hamilton who passed the word to Russell that his presence was now required in Ireland. After a few weeks, Russell managed to secure a passport from the British embassy under an assumed name and set out for Ireland. Travelling via Calais and Dover, he arrived in London at the end of March and spent three days there with his brother John.[50] He may have intended to remain longer but his stay was cut short by his near discovery. While walking across Westminster bridge, Russell noticed a passenger in a carriage looking intently at him. The man drew back when he returned his gaze, but not before Russell recognised him as John Claudius Beresford, son of the commissioner of revenue. Beresford, now MP for Dublin city in the Westminster parliament, was a leading Orangeman and had gained notoriety in Dublin in 1798 as captain of 'Beresford's Bloodhounds', a yeomanry corps that had ruthlessly hunted down suspected rebels. Aware that he could be apprehended at any moment, Russell hurried on to his brother's home, had his hair cut to help alter his appearance and left that night for Liverpool.[51]

NOTES

1 Dickson, *Narrative*, pp. 188–200; *Edinburgh Advertiser*, 2–5 April 1799.
2 Dickson, *Narrative*, p. 139.
3 *Cornwallis corr.*, ii, 377; Dickson, *Narrative*, pp. 113–26, 128; Neilson to Anne Neilson, 20 Apr. 1800 (Madden, *United Irishmen*, 4th ser. (2nd edn, Dublin, 1860), p. 115); Thomas Russell to John Russell, Fort George, 10 Dec. 1800 (copy) (Madden papers, 873/655, f. 3).
4 Thomas Russell to Margaret Russell, 18 Jan. 1801 (Sirr papers, 868/1, ff 279–80); William Neilson to Anne Neilson, 20 Feb. 1802 (Madden, *United Irishmen*, 4th ser. (2nd edn, Dublin, 1860), p. 133); Dickson, *Narrative*, pp. 147, 149.
5 Thomas Russell to Margaret Russell, 26 Oct. 1800, 31 May 1802 (Sirr papers, 868/1, ff 275–6, 299–300); Anna McCleery, 'Life of Mary Ann McCracken' in Robert M. Young, *Historical notices of old Belfast* (Belfast, 1896), pp. 189–90.
6 Drennan to Martha McTier, 16 June, 27 Oct. 1802 (*Drennan letters*, pp. 294, 321).
7 *Emmet memoir*, i, 336–8.
8 Lecky, *Ireland*, iv, 257; L. M. Cullen, 'The internal politics of the United Irishmen' in Dickson, Keogh and Whelan (eds), *United Irishmen*, p. 195.

9 'Memoir of James Hope' in Madden, *Antrim and Down in '98*, p. 117.
10 Madden, *United Irishmen*, 3rd ser., iii, 66.
11 Neilson to Anne Neilson, 20 Apr. 1799 (Madden, *United Irishmen*, 4th ser. (2nd edn, Dublin, 1860), p. 104).
12 Thomas Russell to John Russell, Fort George, 10 Dec. 1800 (copy) (Madden papers, 873/655).
13 MacDonagh, *Viceroy's postbag*, p. 258; Madden, *Antrim and Down in '98*, p. 117; Hunter to Skinner, Nov. 1801; Hunter to Pelham, 5 Nov. 1801 (MacDonagh, *Viceroy's postbag*, pp. 258–60).
14 Charles Dickson, *The life of Michael Dwyer* (Dublin, 1944), pp. 253, 338n.
15 R. R. Madden, *Literary remains of the United Irishmen* (Dublin, 1887), pp. 285–6.
16 Hardwicke to Pelham, 31 Oct. 1801 (P.R.O., HO 100/104/216); Thomas Russell to Margaret Russell, 20 Dec. 1801 (Sirr papers, 868/1, ff 291–2).
17 Castlereagh to Marsden, 28 Nov. 1801 (Reb. papers, 620/10/116/16); — to Hardwicke, 9 Nov. 1801 (P.R.O., HO 100/104/209).
18 Martha McTier to Drennan, *c.* Jan. 1802 (*Drennan letters*, p. 315).
19 Russell to —, 5 June 1802 (Madden papers, 873/673).
20 Russell to Templeton, 5 June 1802 (Madden papers, 873/638).
21 Templeton to Russell, 9 June 1802 (copy) (Madden papers, 873/631).
22 Neilson to Anne Neilson, 4 July 1802 (Madden, *United Irishmen*, 4th ser. (2nd edn, Dublin, 1860), p. 137); Thomas Russell to Margaret Russell, Amsterdam, 2 Aug. 1802 (Sirr papers, 868/1, ff 305–6).
23 Robert Emmet to John Patton, 7 Aug. 1802 (Reb. papers, 620/12/146); Lecky, *Ireland*, v, 255–6; R. R. Madden, *The life and times of Robert Emmet* (New York, 1856), p. 9; for Emmet's activities as a United Irish agent in 1799, see the information of James McGucken, 2 Feb. 1799 (Reb. papers, 620/7/74/7) and Thomas Wright P.R.O., HO 100/86/301–2).
24 Russell's trial speech, Oct. 1803 (Madden papers, 873/700, f. 2).
25 Thomas Russell to Margaret Russell, Paris, 5 Sept. 1802 (Sirr papers, 868/1, ff 307–8); Madden, *United Irishmen*, 3rd ser., ii, 211; Bartlett, *Life of Tone*, pp. 892, 904; Elliott, *Tone*, p. 404; Wickham to King, 25 Sept. 1803 (P.R.O., HO 100/113/191–4).
26 Madden, *United Irishmen*, 3rd ser., ii, 210; see also Thomas Russell to John Russell, Paris, 15, 17 Sept. 1802 (Reb. papers, 620/12/145); examination of John Russell, *c.* Oct. 1803 (copy) (P.R.O., HO 100/113/143–6); John Russell to Margaret Russell, 27 Nov. 1802 (copy) (P.R.O., HO 100/113/91–4); see also Thomas Russell's statement, 2 Oct. 1803 (P.R.O., HO 100/114/9–10).
27 Thomas Russell to Margaret Russell, 5 Sept. 1802 (Sirr papers, 868/1, ff 307–8); Thomas Russell to John Russell, 15 Sept. 1802 (Reb. papers, 620/12/145); Arthur O'Connor to Madden, n.d. (Madden papers, 873/744, f. 3v).
28 Revd. Forster Archer to —, Kilmainham, 3 Oct 1803 (Reb. papers, 620/50/21). For the millenarian strain in jansenism see Clark Garrett, *Respectable folly* (London, 1975), pp. 21–4, 29–30.
29 Russell to Templeton, 3 June 1802 (Madden papers, 873/637); for attempts to gain letters of introduction see also Thomas Russell to Margaret Russell, 2 June 1802 (Sirr papers, 868/1, ff 301–2) and Thomas Russell to John Russell, 17 Sept. 1802 (Reb. papers, 620/12/145).
30 Byrne, *Memoirs*, iii, 169; Russell considered Delaney 'one of the first scholars and poets of the age', 2 Oct. 1803 (P.R.O., HO 100/114/9–10); Lewis Goldsmith, *Secret history of the cabinet of Bonaparte*, 4th edn (London, 1810), p. 263; P. F. Tissot, *Les trois conjurés irlandais; ou l'ombre d'Emmet* (Paris,

1804), cited in Woods, 'Place of Thomas Russell', p. 99n. Dr Woods also notes that Russell also merited an inclusion in the *Biographie nouvelle des contemporains*, xviii (1825), pp. 313–14.

31 Russell's journal, *c.* Mar. 1791 (*Journals,* pp. 42–3); Margaret Russell to Thomas Russell, 10 May 1794 (Sirr papers, 868/2, f. 45); [Russell] to Tone, 21 Sept. 1795 (Bartlett, *Life of Tone*, pp. 239–40).

32 Russell to —, 5 June 1802 (Madden papers, 873/673); Russell to Templeton, 5 June 1802 (Madden papers, 873/638).

33 Bartlett, *Life of Tone,* p. 903; Elliott, *Tone*, p. 404.

34 Arthur O'Connor to Madden, n.d. (Madden papers, 873/744).

35 Elliott, *Partners*, pp. 323, 279.

36 Examination of John Russell, 1 Oct. 1803 (P.R.O., P.C. 1/3582, f. 50); enclosures in P.R.O., HO 100/114/113–23 and ibid. 100/122/220–3; examination of James Farrell, 24 Oct. 1803 (P.R.O., HO 100/114/123).

37 Cornwallis to Hawkesbury, 3 Dec. 1801 (*Cornwallis corr.*, iii, 403); T. A. Emmet to MacNeven, Brussels, n.d. (*Emmet memoir*, i, 333).

38 Madden, *United Irishmen*, 3rd ser., iii, 66, 68; Frank McDermott, 'Arthur O'Connor' in *I. H. S.*, xv, no. 57, (Mar. 1966), p. 62.

39 Revd. Forster Archer to —, Kilmainham, 3 Oct. 1803 (Reb. papers, 620/50/21); examination of James Farrell, 24 Oct. 1803 (P.R.O., HO 100/114/123); Thomas Russell to John Russell, 25 Mar. 1803 (copy) (P.R.O., HO 100/114/117).

40 Wickham to King, 25 Sept. 1803 (P.R.O., HO 100/113/191–4); T. A. Emmet to MacNeven, Brussels, Oct., 8 Nov. 1802 (Madden, *United Irishmen*, 3rd ser., iii, 23–6); ibid., iii, 66; Arthur O'Connor to Madden, n.d. (Madden papers, 873/744, f. 3v).

41 Russell to –, 5 June 1802 (Madden papers, 873/673); Madden, *United Irishmen*, 3rd ser., iii, 27.

42 Sheila Mulloy, 'James Joseph MacDonnell, 'the best known of the United Irish chiefs of the west' in *Cathair na Mart: Journal of the Westport Historical Society* (1985), v, 67–9; for Russell and Humbert, see examination of James Farrell, 24 Oct. 1803 (P.R.O., HO 100/114/123) and also report from Michael Quigley, 15 May 1804 (P.R.O., HO 100/122/220).

43 Examination of James Farrell, 24 Oct. 1803 (P.R.O., HO 100/114/123); C. W. Flood to Dublin Castle, 27 Oct. 1803 (P.R.O., HO 100/114/127).

44 Diary of [Capt.] Thomas Hodges, 20 Sept. 1798 (B.L., Add. MS 40166N); see also Castlereagh to Portland, 10 Sept. 1798 (P.R.O., HO 100/78/324–6); Cooke to Wickham, 11 Sept. 1798 (ibid. 100/78/330).

45 Michael Quigley's report, 15 May 1804 (P.R.O., HO 100/122/220); Elliott, *Partners,* p. 300.

46 Information of McNally, 10 Nov. 1802 (Reb. papers, 620/10/121/19); examination of Robert Carty, Aug. 1803 (P.R.O., HO 100/112/363–4); *Emmet memoir*, i, 308n; Wickham's account of the insurrection of 23 July 1803 (*Colchester corr.*, i, 445–6); examination of Michael Quigley, 15 Nov. 1803 (*Emmet memoir*, i, 306–8).

47 Examination of James Farrell, 24 Oct. 1803 (P.R.O., HO 100/114/123).

48 Madden, *United Irishmen,* 3rd ser., iii, 62–3; ibid. ii, 212.

49 Elliott, *Partners*, pp. 302–3.

50 Statement of James Farrell, 24 Oct. 1803 (P.R.O., HO 100/114/123); Wickham to King, 24 Oct. 1803 (P.R.O., HO 100/114/113); Wickham's account of the insurrection in Dublin , 5 Dec. 1803 (B.L., Hardwicke papers, Add. MS 35740, f. 202).

51 J. A. Russell to Madden, n.d. (Madden papers, 873/674, f. 3).

CHAPTER THIRTEEN

In the Vortex

After his arrival in Dublin in October 1802, Emmet re-established contact with United Irish veterans of '98 such as James Hope. Though preparations were not begun immediately, he sounded these men out on their attitude to a future action and found them well-disposed. But according to Hope, Emmet was not the originator of the plan of insurrection. Instead he claimed that it was the work of a number of influential figures in Dublin and had existed before Emmet's return to Ireland. It seems that Emmet was notified of a plan of insurrection while in Paris, encouraged to return to Ireland to assume leadership on the ground, and promised financial and moral support. Soon after his arrival in Dublin he informed Hope that he had come at the invitation of 'some of the first men of the land'. Hope later identified two of these influential figures as Gerald Fitzgerald, the brother of the knight of Glyn, and Lord Wycombe, the eldest son of the first marquis of Lansdowne. Fitzgerald was probably a United Irishman and it seems that Emmet and Russell encouraged him to command an uprising in Limerick and north Kerry. Nothing is known of Wycombe's involvement, although he was a disaffected aristocrat who had associated with United Irishmen in 1798.[1] Even in his trial speech, in which he went out of his way to avoid implicating others, Emmet was anxious to assure Lord Norbury that 'I am not the head and life's blood of this rebellion. When I came to Ireland, I found the business ripe for execution . . . You have given to the subaltern all the credit of the superior'; there were men involved in the conspiracy 'before the splendour of whose genius and virtues I should bow with respectful deference, and . . . who would not disgrace themselves by shaking your bloodstained hand.'[2] Similarly, when Russell was attempting to raise the North, he 'particularly dwelt on the number and respectability of their friends', and after his own conviction noted that there were several individuals more implicated than he was.[3] In his account of the events of 1803, Madden alluded to certain 'very influential persons' who were aware of the preparations for a rising and actively promoted it from behind the scenes. He implied that among these were John Keogh and John Philpot Curran. There is certainly evidence to show that Emmet met figures such as Keogh and Curran while he was preparing for a rising. In October 1802 the Castle received a report that Keogh was having meetings with a number of suspicious characters, one of whom had recently set out for Paris. The following March, Keogh wrote to James Ryan, a Dublin merchant who was active in Catholic politics, that he had 'prevail[ed] on our friend R. E. to meet you at dinner today...Mr Curran...said he would come also'.[4]

The conspiracy may well have been encouraged by some influential figures but they appear to have shied away as the day set for the rising approached. Most of the financial support Emmet had been promised was not forthcoming and the lack of money proved to be one of the main obstacles to completing the required preparations. In the end the money used for manufacturing arms was Emmet's own — a bequest of £2,000 left to him by his father who had died in December 1802 — and that of Philip Long, a wealthy Dublin merchant, who delivered on his financial promises. Long was to play a central role in the conspiracy and with Emmet, Russell and Hamilton, was considered by Wickham as 'the very life and soul of the treason'.[5]

Emmet's insurrection, therefore, was not intended to be an isolated or desperate effort: a number of influential Irishmen had indicated that they would lend their support, it met with the approval of several leading United men in Paris, it was planned to coincide with an expected French invasion of England in August 1803 and it was to be accompanied by a similar rising in England.[6] The leadership of the English conspiracy has generally been attributed to Colonel Edward Marcus Despard. Despard, born in Queen's County, was a soldier who had served for many years with courage and distinction in the West Indies, earning the friendship and admiration of his comrades, including Horatio Nelson. For his services he was appointed superintendent of Honduras in 1784, but he became entangled in disputes with local settlers who accused him of autocratic behaviour and he was recalled to London on half-pay early in 1790. Although he was found to have done no wrong, he was told that he could not be re-instated as the government had decided to abolish his former office. Angry at his treatment, he turned to political radicalism and joined the London Corresponding Society, becoming a committee member, and later joining the United Englishmen and helping to found the Society of United Britons in 1797. In April 1798 he was arrested and imprisoned in severe conditions at Coldbath Fields prison until March 1801. After his release he helped to revive the United Britons, regularly holding meetings in working-class taverns, and was particularly successful in recruiting disaffected soldiers.[7]

The main link between the conspiracies in Dublin and London was William Dowdall, one of the state prisoners granted early release from Fort George. Dowdall, a former secretary of the Whig club, had been arrested in England in 1798 for seditious activities. Taken back to Ireland he was held with Russell in Newgate and was one of his main co-conspirators in plans to reactivate the United Irishmen after the rebellion. Soon after his release in January 1802 he travelled to Dublin where he helped to revive the local United Irish organisation. Not having been included in the banishment bill, Dowdall operated as liaison officer between Britain and Ireland. In February it seems that he met Despard, who had settled temporarily in Ireland after his release from prison. By now Despard's resentment towards authority was more inflamed than ever and Dowdall enlisted him into the conspiracy and he returned to London. By March regular communications between Irish and English republicans had been reopened. In July 1802 Dowdall travelled to London, intending to join up with his co-conspirators in France. As cover for his mission he acted as an agent in a business deal between Philip Long and William Putnam McCabe, who had set up a textile business in Rouen. However, his journey was cut short by the receipt of a letter from Long, who had joined McCabe in France, which advised him to return to Ireland to forward preparations for a rising. Long and McCabe, it seems, had been encouraged by indications of support from the French government and the determination of the exiled United Irish leaders, especially Russell, to assist an insurrection in Ireland.[8]

Dowdall travelled to Dublin in autumn 1802 to notify interested parties of developments in England. While in Dublin he behaved indiscreetly, boasting of his mission while drunk and received a stern warning from James Hope, who had now become involved in the preparations.[9] Besides Dowdall's loose tongue, information from its own sources alerted the British government that something was stirring among the disaffected in London. They continued to receive reports, in which Despard's name figured prominently, that attempts were being made to persuade London-based guardsmen to stage a coup. When they learnt that Despard and a group of soldiers were to meet at a tavern the following evening to discuss what appeared to be a plan to assassinate the king on his way to open parliament, they decided to act. On 16 November 1802 the Oakley Arms in Lambeth was raided and Despard and a number of his alleged co-conspirators, many of them Irish, were arrested. By this stage, however, the London conspiracy was still at an early stage and by nipping it in the bud the government failed to discover its full ramifications. Significantly, they did not discover that Despard had any real connection with Irish-based republicans until information came to light after the collapse of Emmet's insurrection in July 1803. It may well have been that, far from inciting disaffected soldiers to action, Despard had been trying to restrain the enthusiasm of those who wanted to strike immediately, a move which would have wrecked the co-ordinated plans of the wider conspiracy.[10]

The authorities came up with very little hard evidence against those arrested and it took some dubious testimony to convict Despard and six others of high treason the following February — a verdict that was widely seen as another example of the government's vindictiveness towards an innocent man.[11] Nor does it appear that the execution of Despard and his accomplices put an end to insurrectionary planning in England. In March and April 1803 United Irish emissaries were reported to be active in Lancashire and days before the outbreak in Dublin, Leonard McNally notified the government that 'the disaffected in Dublin look forward to a serious rising in London, in case England should be attacked'.[12] In the event, Emmet's insurrection collapsed so quickly that it allowed little scope for sympathetic actions, but Marianne Elliott makes a convincing case for the Despard and Emmet episodes primarily as 'premature manifestations' of a larger conspiracy which was to involve co-ordinated actions by Irish and British republicans and a French invasion.[13]

Russell's knowledge of the wider dimensions of the plot is uncertain. As was the case with Despard and Emmet, after his arrest he was anxious not to implicate others and he took his knowledge of the conspiracy to the grave. There is evidence, however, which suggests that he had some connection with events in England. An important link in this respect is his brother, John, who, after Thomas's arrest, came under the scrutiny of the authorities. Though John claimed that his politics differed markedly from his brother's,[14] much of his correspondence gives a contrary impression. His views may have lacked something of Thomas's militancy but he appears to have been largely in agreement with his brother. In some letters John makes veiled references to seditious conversations with radical friends and on one occasion he attempted to persuade Thomas to travel to London to assist the radical cause. Likewise, in Thomas's letters, there is a clear assumption that his brother shares his political views. Writing to John just before his visit to France, Thomas implied that he had important information to convey to him and concluded by 'wishing and expecting to see you in free Ireland'. Many of John's contacts offer further evidence of a radical disposition. He mingled freely in London radical circles, associating with members of the London Corresponding Society and with United Irishmen such as the O'Connor brothers and William Sampson. In February 1798, at a time when the London Corresponding Society was at its most militant, a 'John Russell' acted as secretary at one of its meetings.[15]

John Russell's visit to Paris in September 1802 is also rather suspicious. When questioned by the authorities he claimed that it was undertaken for personal and professional reasons, but it seems strange that it occurred at this particular time given that he had probably not seen his brother since 1794 and had never visited him during his six years in prison. While in Paris it is also clear that he was party to discussions on proposed French invasions of Ireland. A government report later alleged that John Russell had kept 'the very worst company both in London and Paris'. Besides mingling with his brother's republican friends in France, he was acquainted with Despard, Sir Francis Burdett and London-based United Irishmen such as James Farrell; perhaps most significantly, the report maintained that he had associated with Philip Long, one of the key organisers of the 1803 insurrection.[16]

After his arrest in September 1803, Thomas, when questioned about his brother John's contacts, tried to explain away his acquaintance with so many suspicious characters. He maintained that John's relationship with Despard was an entirely innocent one: the two men had at one stage served together in the army and both had family connections with Queen's County. John, he claimed, had been in Paris on the instructions of the Duke of York, researching French military education for a new manual he had planned to write. Naturally enough, Thomas did introduce his brother to his friends, many of whom were republicans and because they dined in public they met many people of various political persuasions, but they always discussed 'common topics' rather than politics. He completely denied that John had any involvement in the conspiracy.[17]

In the end, little hard evidence of John Russell's complicity in the insurrection was discovered besides the fact that he had known that his brother, and his son-in-law William Henry Hamilton, had passed through London earlier in the year. The authorities were also probably mollified by the fact that he did not appear to be the stuff of which hardened conspirators are made: Tone, who liked him, noted that he lacked Thomas's 'strength of character' and James Farrell assured the government that John Russell was 'the most harmless and credulous man on earth'.[18] But the evidence still points to him as acting as a conduit of information between Thomas Russell and London republicans. It strains credibility to believe that his friendships with Despard and Farrell, his close involvement in London radical circles, his dealings with Emmet's paymaster, Long, and his visit to Paris at a time when plans for revolt were taking shape, were all entirely innocent. At least one authority sees John Russell as being 'deeply implicated in the Emmet affair'.[19]

Thomas Russell spent some days with his brother when travelling through London and also met James Farrell. Farrell had played an important role in the reorganisation of the United Irishmen in Dublin after the 1798 rebellion. Apparently, in this activity he worked closely with both Russell and Dowdall, both of whom were reported as being very concerned at his arrest in 1798 lest he might reveal information that could harm them.[20] Farrell was released after spending eighteen months in prison on condition that he exile himself from Ireland. He eventually travelled to London, part of an influx of United Irishmen who took refuge in the metropolis in the aftermath of the 1798 rebellion and who brought a new militancy to the local republican movement. In London he feigned loyalty by joining a local volunteer corps but he remained an active United Irishman and he became a focus for the communications of associates based in England and France. He was known to have links with several of the main United Irish conspirators, including Dowdall and Long, and introduced Dowdall to John Russell in London in the autumn of 1802.[21] As well as assisting Thomas Russell's journey to Ireland from France in March 1803, he also helped William Henry Hamilton in his travels through London in late 1802 and early 1803.[22] Hamilton provides yet another link with the republican movement in London. After his marriage in January 1794 to

Russell's niece, Mary Ann, he had gone to London to study law. Here he had associated with radicals and become a member of a secret committee of the United Britons set up in London in 1798 to co-ordinate the activities of Irish, Scottish and English republicans. Significantly, the membership of this committee also included Colonel Despard.[23]

In the summer of 1802 several leading figures in Emmet's insurrection, including McCabe, Dowdall and Long, converged on London and contacted leading English radicals. Dowdall met up with Burdett and McCabe with Despard. It may also be that John Russell had dealings with Despard at this time. After his visit to London, Long then travelled in the autumn to Paris, where he met United Irish exiles.[24] All in all, a picture emerges of a complex conspiracy taking shape, with a network of leading republicans, with whom the Russell brothers were closely connected, travelling between Dublin, London and Paris during 1802–3, seeking to co-ordinate activities in all three cities.

By the early months of 1803 relations between France and Britain were deteriorating rapidly and in March Emmet began his preparations for insurrection in earnest. His original intention seems to have been to rise in August, to coincide with the expected invasion of England.[25] His plan of action was based on the pared-down United Irish organisation of 1799: rather than transmit orders through a series of hierarchical committees, influential local leaders would call out the people, who would be armed at the last moment. In personnel, too, the plan owed much to the preparations for revolt in 1799 — names such as McCabe, Dowdall, Farrell, Quigley and Russell feature prominently in both episodes. It is almost as if conditions at last allowed for the activation of the plan thwarted by the removal of the state prisoners to Fort George.

Russell arrived in Dublin at the beginning of April 1803 to find preparations for a rising already in motion.[26] It was more than six and a half years since he had set foot in Ireland as a free man. During his imprisonment and exile he had spent much of his time brooding on events in Ireland while many friends and colleagues had sacrificed their lives. Emmet's planned insurrection now gave him his long-awaited opportunity to make up for lost time.

The key to Emmet's plan was the capture of Dublin. This was to be accomplished by seizing the Castle and a small number of other important buildings. Columns of insurgents from Kildare and

Wicklow would then march on the city and complete the job. Emmet had set up a number of arsenals throughout the city to manufacture arms — mostly pikes and a variety of explosive devices to compensate for his lack of artillery — which were to be distributed immediately before the rising.[27] To stretch Crown forces to the limit Emmet also hoped for a co-ordinated uprising in Ulster.

The plan would require careful timing and depended on the maintenance of absolute secrecy. For this reason not all of Emmet's lieutenants approved of Russell's return. When funds for arms were so scarce, they were sceptical about the wisdom of spending money to bring home well-known leaders whose presence could only alert the authorities and who were liable to be arrested at any moment. But, as far as Emmet was concerned, Russell's participation was crucial. As a United Irish veteran, present at the founding of the society, well known and respected among Irish republicans and a link with the martyrs of '98 such as Tone and McCracken, Russell was seen by Emmet as bringing much needed prestige and experience to the venture. In particular, Emmet regarded Russell's reputation in the North as invaluable in giving the proposed insurrection a truly national character.[28] All in all, Russell's influence on Emmet seems to have been significant — one of Emmet's biographers notes that it was 'very great indeed'. His determination to carry on the struggle for independence and his optimism at the expected outcome seem to have been important factors in encouraging Emmet to return to Ireland and begin his preparations. It also appears that Russell's brand of revolutionary Christianity was shared to some extent by Emmet. Commenting on Emmet's religious views Thomas Gamble, chaplain to Newgate, who attended him at his execution, regarded him as 'a visionary enthusiast', and in his speech from the dock Emmet spoke of his intention to destroy that 'government which upholds its dominion against the Most High, which displays its power over man as over beasts of the field, which sets man upon his brother and lifts his hands, in religion's name, against the throat of his fellow who believes a little more or less than the government standard'.[29]

On his arrival in Dublin Russell became a member of an executive committee headed by Emmet and including Hamilton, Dowdall, Quigley and Nicholas Stafford, a Dublin baker, which directed operations from a house in Butterfield Lane in Rathfarnham, just to the south of Dublin.[30] Some days later a group of about thirty United Irishmen arrived there, anxious to hear Russell's news from France.

His report on the prospects of French assistance was not very encouraging: as had been the case so often in the past, the French government had made no firm commitments. This did nothing to dishearten Russell who 'expressed his own decided opinion that the Irish people should begin at once and free themselves'. He was adamant that once a beginning was made 'the North would rise to a man'. Most of his colleagues, more aware than Russell of how feelings had changed in Ulster since the mid-1790s, did not share his optimism but decided to send a mission north to gauge the level of support for a rising. James Hope spent two weeks in Ulster sounding out opinion and returned with a report that was more promising than had been expected. News of the outbreak of war seems to have brought a revival of United Irish activity in the North, with William Tennent, Frank McCracken, brother of Henry Joy, and the Revd. William Steel Dickson allegedly involved. The Ulstermen spoken to by Hope had expressed the 'greatest veneration and admiration' for Russell and claimed that they would be 'proud to have him once more at their head to lead them to victory' and they promised that they would take the field once they had learned that Emmet had taken Dublin.[31]

Russell remained in Butterfield Lane for some weeks, assisting Emmet and helping to test some new explosive weapons they had devised. Generally he and his co-conspirators kept themselves hidden from view, venturing out of doors only after dark. However, at least one government spy discovered that Russell had returned from France and was residing in Dublin. The report of his return attracted some attention in Dublin Castle but the government later claimed that the information was too vague for it to take any action.[32] The authorities also received a report from Leonard McNally that a French emissary was in Dublin and the Dublin United Irishmen expected a rising in London. Ironically, it was two friends of Russell's, Peter Burrowes and George Knox, who gave the most accurate reports to the government. Burrowes had received information that a rebellion was being prepared in Dublin and notified Knox, then MP for Trinity College. His source, obviously close to the rebels, was well-informed about their preparations, organisation and aims. Knox claimed that he passed this information on to Wickham but that Wickham disregarded it.[33]

During this period Russell engaged in discussions with his colleagues about the objectives of the planned rising. James Hope, who represented United Irish social teaching at its most advanced, was in favour of issuing a proclamation allowing for sweeping changes in the system of land-holding, but Emmet was strongly opposed, claiming he 'would rather die than live to witness the distress which that would bring on many families', and that such a measure would have to be decided by the people themselves. William Henry Hamilton also broached this issue with Michael Dwyer and his men, instructing them 'not to think of recovering the forfeited estates — it would create a civil war among ourselves'.[34] According to Hope, Russell agreed with the stance taken by Emmet and Hamilton on the land issue. It is likely that this did not signify a dilution in Russell's social radicalism but rather he had adopted this position to avoid the panic and bloodshed such a proclamation might produce. One of Russell's main concerns was that the rising should be as bloodless as possible. 'We are now in the vortex', he said, 'if we can swim ashore let it not be through innocent blood'. He was convinced that he was engaged in a sacred mission and noted that 'if the people are true to themselves we have an over-whelming force, if otherwise, we fall to save their lives ... Following our redeemer's example we hope for his mercy, and then the work devolves on other hands and we will have done our duty.'[35]

In the weeks following the collapse of the insurrection, the author-ities sought to denigrate it by pointing to the low social standing of its participants. They asserted that it was little more than the rising of an unruly mob, intent on plunder and bloodshed. At Emmet's trial his accomplices were dismissed as 'ostlers, bakers, carpenters and old clothes men'.[36] It was true that most of those enlisted by Emmet were working men, but in the circumstances, the social composition of the rebels had its strengths. One of the legacies of the 1798 rebel-lion had been an increase in suspicion and polarisation between the social classes. Many rank-and-file rebels, particularly in Ulster, believed that they had been betrayed by their middle-class leaders, who had put their property ahead of their cause.[37] This was one of the reasons why most of the second-rank leadership in the 1803 insurrection was composed of ordinary working men, such as Hope, a weaver, Felix Rourke, a clerk, Nicholas Stafford, a baker, and Henry Howley, a carpenter, who had the confidence of their social peers and who brought a hard-edged realism to proceedings. The important part played in the conspiracy by working men later led James Connolly to praise the 'proletarian character' of Emmet's revolt and to single it out as the first real effort of the Irish working class to secure 'political and social emancipation'.[38] In the event, however, the social content of Emmet's proclamation was slim: tithes were to be abolished and church lands nationalised. The provisional government assumed the protection of Irish property and claimed that it would 'punish with the utmost rigour any person who shall violate that property and thereby injure the resources and future prosperity of Ireland'.[39]

During these discussions a phrase used by Russell was seized upon by some historians in their efforts to construct a variety of conspiracy theories around the insurrection of 1803. He was reported to have claimed that 'this conspiracy originated with the enemy'.[40] Madden alleged that this was an acknowledgement that they had been duped into revolt. He claimed that the conspiracy was orchestrated by an Orange faction intent on using the event to show how indispensable they were to the government. Helen Landreth's slant was that Emmet and Russell were ensnared into a Castle plot, known to Wickham, the Chief-Secretary, and orchestrated by Marsden, the under-secretary. She intimated that the uprising was largely the work of Pitt (then out of office) and his sympathisers in the Irish government to discredit Addington's administration.[41] Both alleged that elements within the authorities were well-informed of the conspiracy all along and could have stifled it had they wished, but allowed it to develop to forward their ambitions. More recent scholarship lends little credence to the theories of either Madden or Landreth.[42] Emmet and Russell were not dupes and the most likely explanation of Russell's remark is simply that they had been forced into conspiracy by the repressive policies of the government.

While in Dublin Russell managed to contact Arthur Devlin, who may have been a soldier at Fort George during his imprisonment and was a relative of the Wicklow rebel leader, Michael Dwyer, who had been holding out in the Wicklow mountains with a band of rebels since 1798. Devlin was asked to use his connection to arrange a meeting. He agreed and some time later Dwyer arrived at Butterfield Lane, where he stayed for three days discussing the plan of insurrection. Russell was impressed with Dwyer, considering him 'a man of vast capacity'.[43] He told him of his plans to raise the north and although both he and Emmet expressed their admiration for Humbert, it seemed to Dwyer that neither was anxious for a French invasion. The wily Dwyer was cautious about committing himself but promised that his forces would join the insurgents if they managed to seize Dublin and hold it for two days. After these discussions he maintained that he never saw Russell or Emmet again. When captured some months later he claimed that, since he was convinced that their insurrection would fail, he felt free to promise anything, knowing that he would never be called upon to deliver. Though he seems to have had some admiration for Russell, he mentioned that he had little confidence in Emmet, expressing the opinion that 'if Emmet had brain to his education he'd be a fine man'.[44]

Taking Dwyer at his word, Emmet was pleased with the progress of his preparations and in May he dispatched an envoy, Patrick Gallagher, to Paris to inform the United Irish exiles of developments. Gallagher was instructed to notify them that communications had been opened between north and south and, contrary to expectations, 'very proper and respectable men' had offered their services in Ulster; that contact had also been established with Scottish republicans who had agreed to co-operate; and that preparations in Dublin and in counties Kildare and Wicklow were well advanced. Secrecy had been preserved so far but, as this could not be maintained indefinitely, Thomas Addis Emmet was instructed to apply to the French Government for 'money, arms, ammunition and officers' — the arrival of which would be the signal for the rising to begin.[45] Over the next few months, Emmet spent a frustrating time attempting to see Bonaparte, but was generally fobbed off with meetings with subordinate figures and vague promises of an invasion. He eventually became utterly disillusioned with the French and emigrated to America in 1804, later condemning France as the headquarters of 'fraud, deceit and despotism, and under its present rulers, no nation or people that love liberty need look for its honest co-operation'.[46]

In the meantime preparations continued in Dublin. Russell was to lead the rebellion in Ulster and was given the rank of general and a 'splendid green uniform'. Early in the summer he attempted to establish channels of communication between Dublin and the north. He summoned a number of emissaries from Ulster to Dublin, probably William Metcalfe and William Farrell, who returned home with instructions from the executive committee.[47] Russell himself made a visit north at the end of May to sound out support and reconnoitre the province. He met several of his old friends but found them reluctant to commit themselves to an insurrection.[48] Though disappointed, he returned to Dublin still convinced that he could effect a major rising in the province. An emissary was also dispatched from Ulster to Scotland. The man sent was James Witherspoone, of Castlereagh, Co. Down, a dedicated republican known to Russell since his days as a United Irish organiser in the mid-1790s. His reports from Scottish republicans, who said they would assist the Irish if they mounted an insurrection, were delivered to Dublin by Metcalfe who reported back to James Hope in the Liberties. After his visit to Dublin Metcalfe was active in Co. Down, especially around Loughinisland and Saintfield, encouraging the locals to commit themselves to a rising and spreading the word that Russell would take command.[49] Russell may have had contact with an old comrade from the North and fellow prisoner in Fort George, the Revd. William Steel Dickson. Early in July Dickson was reported to be in Dublin trying to raise money from Catholics, while some weeks later it was claimed that he was hiding out in the Mourne Mountains awaiting the arrival of a French shipment of arms.[50]

William Henry Hamilton and James Hope were assigned to Russell to assist him in raising the North. The loss of Hope, a figure greatly respected by his fellow working-men, was a deep disappointment to rebel forces in Dublin. Looking back on the failure of the rising in the capital, Miles Byrne lamented Hope's absence. He believed that his courage, energy and leadership qualities would have been invaluable in bringing out the people, particularly the weavers of the Liberties whom he had already organised. When it had been suggested in Dublin that James Hope might be better employed organising the working-men of the capital Russell had responded dramatically — 'you may keep him, you certainly take off my right arm, but I will march myself with an imposing force from the north on Dublin'. This speech even produced an indulgent smile from the sanguine Robert Emmet. Hope himself later came to the opinion that Emmet had placed too much stock in the optimistic reports that he had received from the North and agreed with Byrne that his efforts would have been more effectual in Dublin.[51]

NOTES

1 Madden, *United Irishmen*, 3rd ser. iii, 99–100, 102n, 106–7; James Hope on the 1803 conspiracy (Hope papers, 7253/1, f. 3); J. A. Gaughan, *The knights of Glin* (Dublin, 1978), pp. 89–92; G.E.C., *The complete peerage*, ed. H.A. Doubleday and Howard de Walden (London, 1929), vii, 429.
2 Emmet's speech from the dock, 19 Sept. 1803 (Madden, *United Irishmen*, 3rd ser., iii, 239, 244).
3 McSkimin, 'Insurrection of 1803', p. 551; B.L., Add. MS 33112, f. 75.
4 Madden, *United Irishmen*, 3rd ser., iii, 85–6; George Shee to Marsden, 23 Oct. 1802 (Reb. papers, 620/63/47); John Keogh to James Ryan, Mar. 1803 (National Archives, Official papers, [OP] 153/24).

5 Madden, *United Irishmen*, 3rd ser., iii, 100–1; diary of T. A. Emmet, c. 31 May 1803 (*Emmet memoir*, i, 342); digest of information on the insurrection of 1803 (P.R.O., HO 100/114/183); Madden, *United Irishmen*, 3rd ser., iii, 89–90; Wickham to Carew, 25 Sept. 1803 (P.R.O., HO 100/113/181–3).

6 Madden, *United Irishmen*, 3rd ser., iii, 66–7.

7 [James Bannantine], *Memoirs of the life of Colonel E. M. Despard* (London, 1799); Madden, *United Irishmen*, 3rd ser., iii, 33–9; ibid., 4th ser. (2nd edn, Dublin, 1860), pp. 293–303; Charles Oman, *The unfortunate Colonel Despard and other studies* (London, 1922), pp. 1–21.

8 Information of John Pollock (via McGucken), 29 Dec. 1798 (Reb. papers, 620/3/32/19); see Reb. papers 620/65/196 for those pardoned or not included in the banishment bill; Elliott, 'Despard conspiracy', pp. 56, 58–9; Elliott, *Partners*, pp. 290, 293; anonymous information, Jan. 1802 (Reb. papers, 620/10/121/2); information on James Tandy, 1804 (Reb. papers, 620/13/169/3).

9 Madden, *United Irishmen*, 3rd ser., iii, 29–30.

10 J. A. Hone, *For the cause of truth: radicalism in London 1796–1821* (Oxford, 1982), pp. 104, 107; Elliott, 'Despard conspiracy', p. 60; Albert Goodwin, *The friends of liberty* (London, 1979), p. 467n; Elliott, *Partners*, pp. 293–5; McSkimin, 'Insurrection of 1803', p. 550.

11 Elliott, *Partners*, p. 296.

12 McNally to Marsden, 19 July 1803 (MacDonagh, *Viceroy's postbag*, p. 278); R. Fletcher to J. King, 8 Apr. 1803 (Reb. papers, 620/67/33).

13 Elliott, 'Despard conspiracy', p. 61.

14 Examination of John Russell, Sept. 1803 (P.R.O., HO 100/113/143–6); J. A. Russell to Madden, 8 Mar., 1 Apr. 1843 (Madden papers, 873/659, 666).

15 John Russell to Thomas Russell, 4 Aug. 1795, 29 Mar., 11 Apr., 1 June 1796 (Sirr papers, 868/2, ff 116–17, 122–3, 114–15, ff 127–8); Thomas Russell to John Russell, 15, 19 Sept. 1802 (Reb. papers, 620/12/154); Mary Thale (ed.), *Selections from the papers of the London Corresponding Society, 1792–1799* (Cambridge, 1983), p. 420; this John Russell cannot be positively identified as Thomas Russell's brother.

16 Examination of James Farrell, 24 Oct. 1803 (P.R.O., HO 100/114/123); Wickham to King, 25 Sept. 1803 (P.R.O., HO 100/113/191–4) and information of McNally 24 Sept. 1803 (P.R.O. HO 100/113/195).

17 McNally's report of a conversation with Russell, 24 Sept. 1803 (P.R.O., HO 100/113/195–8); statement of Thomas Russell, 2 Oct. 1803 (P.R.O., HO 100/114/9–10).

18 Bartlett, *Life of Tone*, p. 33; examination of John Russell, (P.R.O., HO 100/113/143–6); Wickham to Carew, 2 Oct. 1803 (ibid. 100/114/5–7); Wickham to King, 24 Oct. 1803 (ibid. 100/114/113); examination of James Farrell, 24 Oct. 1803 (ibid. 100/114/23).

19 Roger Wells, *Insurrection: the British experience 1795–1803* (Gloucester, 1983), p. 242.

20 Wickham to Carew, 14 Sept. 1803 (P.R.O., HO 100/113/121–3); information of John Pollock, 29 Dec. 1798 (Reb. papers, 620/3/32/19); for Farrell's career, see J. E. Walsh, *Ireland ninety years ago* (Dublin, 1876), pp. 158–65.

21 See James Farrell's papers, (Reb. papers, 620/12/145); Wickham to Carew, 15 Sept. 1803 (P.R.O., HO 100/113/131–2); examination of James Farrell, 17 Sept. 1803 (P.R.O., HO 100/113/143–8), ibid. 100/113/103; examination of Philip Long, 18 Aug. 1803 (Reb. papers, 620/11/138/4).

22 Edward Burton, London to William Bower (Treasury official), 14 Sept. 1803 (Reb. papers, 620/11/130/39); Wickham to Carew, 14 Sept., 2 Oct. 1803 (P.R.O., HO 100/113/121; ibid. 100/114/5–7); Wickham to King, 24 Oct. 1803

(P.R.O., HO 100/114/113–6).

23 Enclosure in King to Cooke, 12 Jan. 1798 (Reb. papers, 620/18A/14).

24 Roger Wells, *Insurrection: the British experience 1795–1803* (Gloucester, 1983), p. 242; anonymous information, 17 Aug. 1803 (P.R.O., HO 100/112/299–300).

25 Madden, *United Irishmen*, 3rd ser., iii, 106, 116.

26 Madden, *United Irishmen*, 3rd ser., ii, 212–13.

27 Elliott, *Partners*, p. 310.

28 Byrne, *Memoirs*, i, 352–3.

29 Leon Ó Broin, *The unfortunate Mr Robert Emmet* (Dublin, 1958), p. 55; Elliott, 'Despard conspiracy', pp. 58–9; Hardwicke to Charles Yorke, 20 Sept 1803 (B.L., Hardwicke papers, Add. MS 35703, f. 145); Emmet's speech from the dock, 19 Sept. 1803 (Madden, *United Irishmen*, 3rd ser., iii, 242).

30 McSkimin, 'Insurrection of 1803', p. 551.

31 Anonymous information, *c.* May 1803 (Reb. papers, 620/65/126); Byrne, *Memoirs*, i, 354–5.

32 Madden, *United Irishmen*, 3rd ser., iii, 186; McGucken to Marsden, 31 May 1803 (MacDonagh, *Viceroy's postbag*, 274); Marsden's account of the insurrection of 1803, 15 Nov. 1803 (*Castlereagh corr.*, iv, 327); digest of information on the 1803 insurrection (P.R.O., HO 100/114/178); Wickham's account of the insurrection in Dublin, 5 Dec. 1803 (B.L. Hardwicke papers, Add. MS 35740, f. 202); William Drennan had also heard rumours of his return, June 1803 (Drennan papers, T765/1035).

33 McNally to Marsden, 19 July 1803 (MacDonagh, *Viceroy's postbag*, p. 278); diary of George Knox, May–June 1803 (MacDonagh, *Viceroy's postbag*, pp. 450–1).

34 John Finegan, *Anne Devlin: patriot and heroine* (Dublin, 1992), p. 41.

35 James Hope on the insurrection of 1803 (Hope papers, 7253/1, f. 3)

36 W. J. Fitzpatrick, *The secret service under Pitt* (London, 1892), p. 158.

37 Templeton to Russell, 9 June 1802 (copy) (Madden papers, 873/631); Elliott, *Partners*, p. 238.

38 James Connolly, *Labour in Irish history* (Dublin, 1914), pp. 99, 103.

39 'The provisional government to the people of Ireland', printed proclamation found in the Thomas Street depot, July 1803 (Reb. papers, 620/11/134).

40 James Hope on the insurrection of 1803 (Hope papers, 7253/1, f. 3)

41 Madden, *United Irishmen*, 3rd ser., iii, 292–6; Helen Landreth, *The pursuit of Robert Emmet* (Dublin, 1949), pp. 123–5.

42 Leon Ó Broin, *The unfortunate Mr Robert Emmet* (Dublin, 1958), pp. 61–4; Elliott, *Partners*, p. 319.

43 N.L.I., Luke Cullen papers, MS 9760, ff 268–9; John Finegan, *Anne Devlin: patriot and heroine* (Dublin, 1992), p. 41.

44 Examination of Michael Dwyer, 11 Jan. 1804 (Charles Dickson, *The life of Michael Dwyer* (Dublin, 1944), pp. 253–5).

45 Diary of T. A. Emmet, *c.* 31 May 1803 (*Emmet memoir*, i, 342).

46 T. A. Emmet to Robert Simms, 1 June 1805 (P.R.O.N.I., T/1815/4).

47 See charges against William Farrell (no. 34) in list of Antrim and Down prisoners, 30 Nov. 1803 (Reb. papers, 620/12/142/16) and also the evidence of James Hope in Madden, *United Irishmen*, 3rd ser., i, 281; McGucken to Marsden, 31 May 1803 (MacDonagh, *Viceroy's postbag*, p. 274).

48 Martha McTier to Drennan, 13 June 1803 (*Drennan letters*, p. 324).

49 Information of McGucken, 13 Sept. 1803 (Reb. papers, 620/10/121/15); McGucken to Marsden, 31 May, 4 June 1803 (MacDonagh, *Viceroy's postbag*, pp. 274–5); McGucken to Marsden, 8 July 1803 (MacDonagh, *Viceroy's postbag*, pp. 276–7).

50 Lord Annesley to Marsden, 4 Aug. 1803 (Reb. papers, 620/64/65).
51 Examination of Robert Carty, Aug. 1803 (P.R.O., HO 100/112/363–4); Byrne, *Memoirs*, i, 357, 360–61; Madden, *United Irishmen*, 3rd ser., iii, 102.

CHAPTER FOURTEEN

Raising the North

The attempt to raise the North in 1803 is an obscure episode in Irish history. It produced no battles, or even skirmishes, and there were no casualties in the field; in fact, probably not a single shot was fired in anger. It was, however, a far from insignificant event. The attempted rising produced considerable alarm in loyalist circles, sharpened sectarian tensions and gave rise to a draconian official response that included many arrests, transportations and five executions, including Russell's.

Russell travelled north with Hamilton and Hope in mid-July to make the final preparations for insurrection. On the way the party split up. Hamilton made his way towards counties Cavan and Fermanagh, where he hoped to foment a rising, while Russell and Hope, who were to concentrate their efforts on Down and Antrim, travelled on to Newry. On their arrival in the town there were already worrying signs of the poor communications and planning that would dog their efforts: a party of Down men they had expected as an escort failed to appear. After waiting two nights in Newry, they made their own way to Knockbracken, near Saintfield, Co. Down. There they stayed at the house of the Presbyterian weaver, James Witherspoone, who had been sent some months before as an emissary to Scotland. He later moved on to Belfast where he met various friends, including Mary Ann McCracken and Edward Bunting. He had asked to see the former Catholic activist and United Irishman, Luke Teeling, but Teeling prudently declined. He did meet a number of his old United Irish colleagues, among them William and Robert Simms, to discuss his plans for a rising. According to James Hope's account, 'nothing appeared among them but timidity, and a desire to know only what concerned spies'. The Simms brothers had agreed the previous year not to engage in seditious activity on pain of forfeiting a bond of £8,000, and, not surprisingly, were reluctant to commit themselves. However, some of those who attended claimed they were prepared to act and another meeting was arranged to take place a few days later in Belfast. During the week news came from Emmet that there had been an explosion at one of the arms depots in Dublin on 16 July which had excited some suspicions. To forestall discovery the date of the rising was brought forward from August to Saturday 23 July. Russell sent immediately for Hamilton, with orders to abandon his efforts in Cavan lest the conspiracy be revealed by a premature rising there. Hamilton was now given responsibility for raising Co. Antrim.[1]

Despite this disruption to his planning Russell was still confident of success. According to the information he had gathered since his return from France he estimated that there were no more than 18,000 regular troops in the country. As for the militia and yeomanry, he maintained — despite the clear evidence to the contrary seen in 1798 — that, as Irishmen, they would flock to the United Irish standard once the rebels had won a victory. His confidence was unshakeable: he believed Ulster to be seething with disaffection and that he would light the spark that would ignite a mass rising.[2]

However, as he sought to raise support in his old command of Co. Down, Russell met with a rude awakening. Despite his exhortations to rise, local people proved reluctant to commit themselves, particularly when they learned that there were no arms to be distributed.[3] As in Belfast, middle-class republicans who had lent their support in the 1790s were now unwilling to come forward, but Russell had no qualms about enlisting ordinary working men, like the Downpatrick shoemaker, James Corry, or the horse-dealer, James Drake, to act as his junior officers.

Around 20 July Russell moved on to Co. Antrim, where he hoped for a better response. But here too he met with disappointment. Some weeks later, reporting on the preparations for insurrection in Antrim, the solicitor-general, James McClelland, noted that 'in every instance where Russell endeavoured to collect a numerous meeting of the people or to order them to join him, he has totally failed'. His first attempt to rally support was at Carnmoney, whose inhabitants had earned a notorious reputation for disaffection in the 1790s, but here only a small crowd of about a dozen people gathered to listen to him and these refused to help in any way. He travelled on to Broughshane where he spoke to a larger crowd of about fifty. Dressed in his striking green uniform with large epaulets and embroidered with gold lace, Russell 'urged the people strongly to take up arms, promising them assistance from every part in the king-dom and declaring he was so confident of success that, if five hundred joined him, he would publicly appear with them in arms'. But still the crowd looked on with no more than non-committal curiosity.[4]

With the date set for the rising fast approaching, Russell was running out of time and he spent the last few days desperately trying to organise support. On Thursday 21 July he met those in Belfast who had appeared well disposed towards a rising. Russell was asked for details of his plan of attack but, obsessed with maintaining secrecy, he said he could reveal nothing until men began to turn out. He advised them to stay together for another day and appointed Stephen Wall, who had served with the Tipperary militia, to command the Belfast forces. Russell appointed Hamilton to lead the insurgents in the area around Carrickfergus and assigned James Hope as his lieutenant, giving him what remained of his war-chest — £4. He instructed them that should Belfast fail to rise they were to proceed to Ballymena. He hoped for a determined response in mid-Antrim, since one of the few encouraging meetings he had during the week was with a deputation from Connor and Kells that beseeched him to give them a chance to make amends for their poor showing in 1798.[5]

That night Russell returned to Co. Down to make another effort to rouse the people for the insurrection scheduled to take place the following night. He and James Drake breakfasted in Saintfield, then hired a horse for Russell and travelled on to Annadorn, a village about four miles east of Downpatrick, where Russell summoned a meeting of eight or nine men in James Smith's public house. He announced that there was to be a general insurrection throughout Ireland, that blows would be struck simultaneously at Dublin, Belfast and Downpatrick, and that arms were to be seized from the yeomanry. In addition to the attack on Downpatrick, rebel forces were to march on the villages of Clough and Seaforde, and take leading loyalists as hostages to prevent any outrages being committed by the military. According to prosecution witnesses at Russell's trial, he called on the Catholics to remember their oppression by the Orangemen and to take this opportunity to liberate themselves. Russell was reported as stating that there would be no invasion by the French, but that arms would be landed at Kilkeel and a French army had already invaded Scotland.[6]

As had happened earlier in the week Russell met with a frosty reception. When it was put to a local man, John Keenan, that he should encourage his neighbours to rise, he told Russell that 'they would hit me in the face' if he suggested anything of the sort, while another local, Patrick Doran, maintained that 'none but fools would join them'. Russell responded to this by standing up and saying to Drake: 'James, this will not do'. He then showed them his green general's uniform 'and said there was a large number of those uniforms in Ireland and they would shortly appear, and that there was a store of arms and ammunition underground in Dublin and that the business would be done in one hour all over the kingdom'. He told them that another general was raising Co. Antrim as they spoke, and if there were any objections to his leadership he was willing to surrender command to any man they considered more suitable and fight as a common soldier. But all of this was to no avail: the people still refused to rise.[7]

Later that day Russell and Drake travelled on to Loughinisland. In recent years there had been tensions between local Catholics and Orange societies in the parish, and Russell may have hoped to capitalise on any lingering resentments. However, a number of recent prosecutions of Orangemen by the government had done much to quieten the area.[8] On his arrival in the town Russell met an old acquaintance, Patrick Lynch, who had given him Irish lessons when he was a librarian in Belfast in 1794 and who now lived in Loughinisland. Lynch had intended to go to Belfast but was advised to wait for two or three days. Russell stayed the night in Loughinisland and the following morning he was visited by Lynch, who claimed that on hearing rumours of insurrection he went to dissuade Russell from embarking on any such action. By this stage Russell was exhausted from his constant travelling and exhortation, and was baffled by the reluctance of the people to come forward. When pressed by Lynch for details on the plan of revolt he seemed vague, though this may well have been to preserve secrecy, but he intimated that the main actions would take place at Downpatrick, Killinchy and Loughinisland, and that spades and pitchforks would do for weapons. Later on in the day Patrick Renaghan from Clough arrived. He told Russell that the men of his village wanted nothing to do with any rebellion; the local priests had spoken against it and the people would 'be hanged like dogs' if they turned out. Realising that the rebellion had no chance of success, the inn-keeper, James Fitzpatrick, told a number of people who were waiting about his inn for news that they should return to their homes. Seething with frustration, Russell then left Loughinisland.[9]

He set off towards Downpatrick to meet up with a contingent of rebel forces he hoped would be more ready for action. A hill at Ballyvange just outside Downpatrick had been chosen as the rendezvous for the attack on the town. Earlier in the day, a group of fourteen men, armed only with pitchforks, had formed here under the leadership of James Corry. For several hours they waited for a signal fire to be lit at Seaforde to show that people from the surrounding countryside were marching on Downpatrick. The plan was that they would then proceed to Saintfield and march north to join those in arms in Co. Antrim. But they waited in vain — no fire was seen and the demoralised handful of rebels gradually melted away. Apparently Russell arrived some time later expecting to find a crowd gathered but only three men remained.[10] Since an attack on Downpatrick was now out of the question, Russell decided to return to Loughinisland to make yet another attempt to rally its inhabitants. This he did but they still refused to budge. Corry and another man, John Tate, arrived on the Sunday morning to see Russell but were told that he had left in the early hours of the morning for Co. Antrim. Although angered by the apathy of local people, he was still apparently optimistic. He left his uniform behind, hidden in the church, but told those present that he would return for it with a body of Antrim men.[11]

In Antrim, however, his colleagues were faring no better. On Saturday 23 July Hamilton was bluntly told by Wall in Belfast that 'this town will not act'. Hamilton and Hope then travelled on to Kells, Co. Antrim where some men seemed eager to make a stand, but they were too few to mount any effective action. Moving on to Ballymena they learned that a body of men had assembled, but most of them had returned to their homes when they heard the news that Belfast had not risen. The town's demoralisation was sealed when a false report was circulated that Russell had gone to Dublin to persuade Emmet to call off the entire insurrection. Only Hamilton, Hope and a local leader remained ready to act. The next morning they went to Slemish mountain and met some men from Carnmoney and Templepatrick, but there were too few of them to act on the original plan to march on Belfast or Carrickfergus. In Broughshane, Ballyclare and several other parts of Antrim, small groups gathered but they were either opposed to any action or decided to wait until some favourable news was received. Faced with such a paltry response Hamilton and Hope had no choice but to abandon their efforts and go into hiding. When Russell eventually arrived in the county he was unable to find them.[12] The collapse of rebel efforts in Antrim finally put paid to any hope for a northern insurrection.

The poor response to Russell's call was largely due to the understandable unwillingness of the Ulstermen to sacrifice themselves in what must have seemed a hopeless effort. It was also the case that government agents, notably James McGucken of Belfast, had done much to sow seeds of doubt in their minds and generally frustrate Russell's plans. In early July McGucken was already warning the government of the dangers of insurrection while admitting that most of the people of Antrim and Down 'look upon it as a desperate enterprise'. Still, it appeared that a hardened few, organised on the simplified United Irish plan of 1799, were in favour of a rising. McGucken managed to secure a position of authority among the disaffected in Co. Down which he used to caution local people against any rash acts.[13] He consistently advised the people to await the news from Dublin before coming forward — a step that appeared eminently sensible to most of the northerners. The rumour of Russell's return to Dublin spread at Ballymena indicates that government agents may also have been active in Antrim. When the effective disruption carried out by such agents is added to the rebel weaknesses, there is little wonder that the northern rising turned out to be the shambles it was.

On 24 July, the day that Russell rode into Co. Antrim, a number of printed proclamations exhorting the people to take up arms were posted up in the vicinity of Belfast. By this stage he hoped that Dublin would be in the hands of the insurgents, and the counties around the capital would be in open revolt.[14] He was not to know that the rising had miscarried everywhere. In Dublin preparations had been rushed after the explosion in the arms depot in Patrick Street on 16 July. Time that should have been spent in arranging assembly points and confirming orders for mobilisation was hastily spent in trying to prepare weapons and Emmet's communications largely broke down. He had expected the planned attacks to be spearheaded by 900 veterans of '98 from Kildare, Wicklow and Wexford, but these either did not turn out or arrived in the wrong place or at the wrong time. In the end fewer than 100 reliable men assembled. Some of Emmet's colleagues cautioned him against going ahead, but he insisted on acting, considering himself to be duty bound to support the risings he believed would happen elsewhere.

The intention was to seize strategic buildings such as the Pigeon House, the Artillery Barracks at Islandbridge, the Custom House and most importantly of all — Dublin Castle. Once he had captured the seat of government Emmet believed that the city would effectively be his. A small force of men was to be conveyed into the Castle grounds in covered hackney carriages to achieve complete surprise. But the carriages had a brush with the military on the way to Thomas Street and their frightened drivers fled. When they did not arrive, Emmet decided to attack on foot, but the commotion his followers made in the street alerted the authorities and the Castle gates were closed. With the loss of the element of surprise Emmet recognised that the original plan had been nullified and, having no desire to be responsible for pointless bloodshed, he called off the rising. He and his lieutenants returned to Butterfield Lane and then went into hiding in the Wicklow Mountains. But some of those who had turned out were still prepared to fight and their numbers were swelled by members of the Dublin mob. They were quickly dispersed by troops, but not before they had killed several loyalists who had strayed into their path. Among them were Lord Kilwarden, the attorney general, and his nephew, who were dragged from their carriage in Thomas Street and piked to death.[15]

Elsewhere, there were unsuccessful attacks on Maynooth and Naas, while the rest of the country remained quiet. Given the lack of rebel successes anywhere in the country and the relatively undisturbed state of the North, the proclamation issued from 'Head-quarters' by a 'Member of the Provisional Government and General-in-Chief of the Northern District' rang more than a little hollow. It read:

> Men of Ireland, once more in arms to assert the rights of mankind and liberate your country! You see by the secrecy with which this effort has been conducted, by the multitudes who in all parts of Ireland are engaged in executing these great objects, that your Provisional Government have acted wisely. You will see that in Dublin, in the West, in the North, and in the South, the blow has been struck at the same moment, your enemies can no more withstand than they could foresee, this mighty exertion. This proclamation and regulations will show you that your interest and honour have been considered...The General orders that hostages shall be seized in all quarters, and hereby apprises the English commanders that any outrage contrary to the acknowledged laws of war and morality shall be retaliated in the severest manner. And he further makes known that such Irish as

within ten days…are found in arms against their country shall be treated as rebels, committed for trial and their properties confiscated. But all men behaving peaceably shall be under the protection of the laws. Your valour is well known. Be as just and humane as you are brave, and then rely with confidence that God, with whom is victory, will crown you with success.[16]

The very appearance of these proclamations and reports of bodies of armed men on the move in Antrim and Down were enough to cause considerable alarm among northern loyalists. Thomas Whinnery, the postmaster of Belfast, reported that an army patrol had spotted a body of 3,000 rebels assembled on Cave Hill. He claimed that Belfast was saved from a rebel attack only by the timely receipt of a warning from an anonymous informant, which allowed the rapid mobilisation of the town's garrison.[17] Whinnery had a strong tendency to alarmism and the figure of 3,000 was probably either grossly exaggerated or completely fabricated, for there were no other reports of such a large rebel army gathering in the vicinity of Belfast. A small body of insurgents did turn out near the Malone district of Belfast on the night of 23 July but, lacking any clear instructions and with no signs of rebel activity elsewhere, they dispersed after a few hours. Other reports were received of a group of armed men marching to the tune of a fife in a field near Castlereagh Hill, to the south-east of the town, while an armed gathering at Knockbracken scattered when told that yeomen cavalry were on the way. There was further cause for concern in that some nocturnal searches of homes carried out by the military in the rural hinterland of Belfast found few men at home.[18]

Given these vague rumblings of revolt, General Campbell, the officer commanding Belfast, remained concerned at the state of surrounding counties. Arms had been seized from loyalists and armed parties were reported to be on the move towards Ballymena, which he believed to be the rebel headquarters. A sergeant of the Antrim militia had seen men on the march on Saturday night, 23 July, and heard that the people of Carnmoney were rising and intended to make an attack on Belfast or Carrickfergus. Another soldier reported seeing four or five hundred men armed with muskets and pikes drilling near Comber, in Co. Down. Campbell was taking no chances and called in vulnerable detachments of cavalry from outlying areas, placed the yeomanry on alert, erected military posts on the outskirts of Belfast and imposed a night-time curfew.[19] In swoops against suspected rebels sixty-two people were arrested. A week later, while the general admitted that no overt acts of violence had occurred, he remained concerned that 'the spirit of insurrection is still afloat' in Co. Down, particularly in the areas around Saintfield and Ballynahinch, where nocturnal meetings and drillings had been reported.[20]

Rumour and apprehension excited a far greater degree of panic than the actions of the rebels and the situation remained tense in parts of Antrim and Down for some time. In Belfast, at the first signs of danger, most of the town's loyalists had turned out with any weapons they could lay their hands on. A week later Martha McTier reported another alarm: 'drums beating to order, horsemen galloping through the streets... then returning and ordering all about, cannon drawing etc., everything but a battle, no one able to learn for what nor yet, everything bespeaking alarm and preparation yet no appearance of attack'.[21] In Lisburn most of the inhabitants sat up for several nights with arms at the ready awaiting an assault. The postmaster of Ballymena expected a rebel attack at any moment. Many of the ladies of the town had evacuated themselves to Belfast and he requested a detachment of regular troops to reinforce the local yeomanry. The town of Carrickfergus was reported to be 'in a certain degree of alarm' having received information that it would be attacked and that emissaries were going throughout the surrounding countryside trying to raise the people.[22]

But many loyalists were not unduly worried. The same correspondent who had warned of the impending attack on Carrickfergus wrote to Dublin: 'I cannot bring myself to believe there is anything at this moment to be dreaded in the North of Ireland, except from a small number of disaffected, and that only if an invading army had actually made a descent'. The *Belfast News Letter*, contradicting rumours that an attack had been made on Belfast, reported the surrounding countryside 'to be in a state of perfect tranquillity... No disturbances of any kind have taken place in our vicinity'. The only sign of disaffection was the number of seditious proclamations that had been posted up in the neighbourhood. McGucken had expected a rising to take place in Belfast on 25 or 26 July, but noted that this would depend on the news from Dublin. For the time being, he reported back to the Castle that all was quiet. 'The people in general seem all at a loss. Although in many parts anxious for a rising, yet they can't see how it is to be effected, having no system amongst them. Arms they have but few.'[23]

The assessment of the state of the province by the Revd. Snowden Cupples of Lisburn struck the prevailing note — reasonably confident of Ulster's loyalty yet anxious to maintain a strong degree of vigilance:

> Though it is scarcely to be conceived that Russell would venture here if he had not the strongest expectation of support, yet I do not find that the country is disposed to rise and, if there be not a landing of French troops in considerable force, I am almost persuaded that he will find himself disappointed in his expectations from this part of the country. The people of any property among the Dissenters seem to have changed their sentiments very much since the last rebellion and I think will not be easily induced to engage in another one, and with respect to the Catholics their number is too small to create much apprehension. At the same time however I very much fear that there are among us a number of villains who, having no property, will be ready enough to forward any system of sedition that may be set on foot, if opportunity offers. At present we must be vigilant and wait for events.[24]

Most of the accounts that spoke of the tranquillity of the North, however, contained the important proviso that it would remain so only if the French did not invade. Undoubtedly, far greater numbers would have rallied to Russell's side had he been able to convince them that they would soon be joined by thousands of French troops, but it seems that all he could offer were vague assurances of the landing of arms and of a French invasion of Britain.[25] Moreover, he made no secret of his dislike of Bonaparte, which was hardly likely to inspire confidence in those reluctant to turn out before an invasion. At Russell's trial the judge alleged that he had announced the arrival of thousands of French troops at Ballywalter on the Ards peninsula. He accused Russell of lying deliberately 'for the purpose of deceiving poor ignorant men and inducing them to join in acts of rebellion'. Samuel McSkimin, in his unsympathetic and often unreliable account of the attempted northern rising of 1803, maintained that Russell went to death puzzled by the non-arrival of the French. Marianne Elliott also stressed the reliance of the conspirators of 1803 on French assistance.[26] But though they may have assumed that an invasion was imminent, the evidence suggests that both Emmet and Russell embarked on their decision to rise without any definite assurances that the French would invade. Had they been given such assurances it is almost certain that Russell would have revealed them at the meeting in Butterfield Lane in April, or used them to rally support in the face of mass apathy in Ulster. As it was, Russell's revolutionary proclamation made no mention of foreign assistance while Emmet's explicitly denied that they were acting in concert with the French.[27] Even in their attempts to enlist allies before the rising, they played down the prospects of a French landing: after his discussions with Emmet and Russell, Michael Dwyer emerged under the impression that both harboured a deep distrust of Bonaparte and had no wish to see his troops set foot in Ireland.[28]

Dr Elliott characterises the attitude of the conspirators towards the French as an 'uncomfortable alliance of need and apprehension'[29] — an awareness that French assistance was necessary to secure Irish independence combined with an anxiety that Ireland should not become yet another French puppet. For Russell, however, apprehension outweighed need. Even before his exile in France he regarded Bonaparte as a cynical and duplicitous tyrant, an opinion that his dealings with the French government in 1802–3 abundantly confirmed.[30] James Hope and Mary Ann McCracken denied that Russell had ever claimed that the French had landed in Ulster. Nelly Rabb, at whose home Russell had stayed for some weeks in August 1803, also maintained that he made no such claim. From what he said to her she believed that he had no desire for a French invasion and she had heard him express the opinion that 'Ireland might as well be an English as a French colony'.[31] Given his over-riding desire to effect a revolution, Russell was prepared to accept French aid in some form, but his misgivings about Bonaparte made him very wary indeed of an invasion by a French army, which might remain on Irish soil to assert French interests. His preference seems to have been for a less direct form of assistance that would allow the Irish people to free themselves through their own efforts. As he attempted to rally support in Co. Down he was reported to have claimed that the French would land large quantities of arms and that they had already invaded Britain, while explicitly denying that they would land troops in Ireland. When questioned by a government agent in October 1803, Russell occasionally voiced an expectation that the French would arrive at some stage in the future, but this was a view that was widespread throughout the country at the time. When pressed on this point he proffered the opinion that the French were more likely to land in Britain than Ireland, but he claimed no special knowledge on the subject.[32]

Robert Emmet was also suspicious of Bonaparte. A report attributed to Michael Quigley told of a serious quarrel between Emmet and Arthur O'Connor in Paris in 1802. O'Connor was convinced that nothing could be achieved without a French invasion while Emmet had expressed his 'determination to try the thing alone'.[33] A workman who stumbled into his preparations at one of the Dublin depots and had been made a prisoner by Emmet's men overheard them say that 'they had no idea as to French relief but to make it good themselves'. But although he remained a reluctant solicitor of French aid, Emmet did eventually come to the opinion that some form of assistance was required to effect a successful insurrection. At his trial he admitted that 'connexion with France was, indeed, intended, but only as far as mutual interest would sanction or require'. Significantly, when he sent the emissary Patrick Gallagher to Paris in May he had instructed him to ask for 'money, arms, ammunition and officers', not for large numbers of French troops.[34] However, when the rising in Dublin miscarried so badly, Emmet was left with no other realistic option but to dispatch Miles Byrne to France in August to do all he could to encourage an invasion.[35]

After the failure of all his efforts Russell had little choice but to go into hiding. At first, he stayed in a house in Castlereagh, less than three miles from Belfast. On Wednesday 27 July he was almost taken by a search party led by a local magistrate, but he got wind of their coming and made a narrow escape.[36] The McCrackens then arranged a more secure refuge for him with some friends of theirs, the Rabbs, in a house on the outskirts of Holywood. He remained baffled at the refusal of the people to come forward but was in good spirits and confident that the rebellion would succeed eventually.[37] Martha McTier later heard accounts that during this time Russell was reduced to sleeping in hovels and ditches from where 'he could view the habitations where once he was the most admired — the most loved among the gay, witty and fair'. She had heard that he was forced to beg for sustenance and that on one occasion went to the house of a Mrs Ferguson near Antrim where he asked for a drink, 'but she observing him stagger (perhaps from weakness) told him he had got enough, she thought, already. He replied 'your eye deceives you'.[38]

A week after the date set for insurrection Thomas Whinnery reported that Russell was in the vicinity of Belfast and making strenuous efforts to promote a rising, but as yet without any success. He feared that if he was not apprehended soon 'he will some time or other occasion an insurrection however partial and imbecile [*sic*] it may be'. Whinnery advised the government to put a price of £1,000 on Russell's head which would quickly ensure his apprehension.[39] This sum was duly offered for his capture by the authorities and a further £500 was later subscribed by the citizens of Belfast. The notice for his arrest described him as 'a tall, handsome man, about 5ft 11in high, dark complexion, aquiline nose, large black eyes, with heavy eyebrows... full chested, walks generally fast and has a military appearance... speaks fluently, with a clear distinct voice, and has a good address'. Martha McTier noted that the description 'is nearly just and will gain him female protectors'.[40]

It seems that Russell had indeed still not given up hope of effecting an insurrection. A yeomanry officer reported that Russell had issued a second proclamation in which, despite 'the apparent failure in Dublin, he promises ultimate success to the cause in which his followers are engaged'.[41] A letter written to Francis McCracken at this time confirms that he was still prepared to make a stand if an opportunity presented itself:

> I go this moment for the purpose of, if in my power, rectifying the mistakes that have taken place. Whether I fail or succeed is in the hands of God, but the cause I will never relinquish. He has for the moment stopped our progress no doubt wisely — courage alone was wanting here as far as I can see to render our success not only certain but easy... I am going to join anybody I can find in arms in support of their rights and that of mankind. Let me request of you not... to be dispirited, the cause shall succeed though individuals may fall... I have no doubt committed faults but I acted for the best, and hope I may be able to repay and set all right.[42]

Towards the end of August Russell made one last effort to exhort local people to action, in the hope that once the flame of rebellion was lit it would spread throughout the countryside. Again his appeals were greeted with indifference. Finally, he:

> expressed great indignation that the patriots of the north were so reluctant to take the field, and said that their conduct disgraced themselves and their country. He was extremely anxious that a beginning should be made and said that if fifty or a hundred would assemble, they would increase rapidly; the very fields and hedges as they passed would supply recruits and they would soon number thousands in their ranks... Dublin and the south were completely ready, perfectly

organised, and in force from a hundred thousand upwards which with the assistance of the north, would be sufficient to subdue the kingdom without the assistance of Bonaparte, whom he wished to retain only as an ally, not as a master, because he had often shown the disposition of a despot...Disgusted at the failure of frequent attempts to rouse them he reproached their pusillanimity and want of spirit to support the glorious cause of liberty and equality.[43]

Russell had completely misjudged the mood of the province. The North had completely failed to respond to his entreaties and the events of July 1803 in Ulster do not merit the description of an insurrection. Russell had claimed that he could raise 50,000 men in the North: when the day of the rising came he barely managed to raise fifty.[44] Emmet's verdict on the Dublin insurrection — 'there was failure in all: plan, preparation and men'[45] — applied to an even greater extent to events in Ulster. Although there were sightings of bodies of armed men on the move, there was a marked reluctance in all cases to take on the military and there were no reports of any violent clashes. In his report to London Wickham insisted that he had not heard of a single fatality in the North, or even a case of a military post being fired at.[46] Reviewing the state of the North in the aftermath of Russell's attempt, a government official commented on the placidity of Antrim and Down and observed that the inhabitants of the region 'seem actuated with great zeal in support of His Majesty's government'.[47] Pockets of disaffection remained but these were generally small and lacked any effective system of organisation or communications.[48]

Ulster had undergone many changes since the days when Russell had pounded its roads as a United Irish emissary — changes he failed to appreciate during his long imprisonment and exile. Even before the defeat of 1798 the rise in sectarian tensions and the ruthless military repression of the previous year had done much to weaken the province's attachment to United Irish ideals. The sectarian atrocities that had punctuated the rebellion in the south further eroded the commitment of Ulster republicans to the brotherhood of all Irishmen. This ideal was, however, deeply-rooted enough in parts of the North to produce a respectable turnout of several thousand United Irishmen in Antrim and Down during the '98 insurrection, but many of these bitterly resented their desertion by the movement's leaders and learned a hard lesson as small units of well-armed troops inflicted crushing defeats on much larger bodies of insurgents. A typical response was that of a rebel contingent from Ards, Co. Down, who, after their rout by the military, claimed that never again would they be prevailed upon 'to catch cannon balls on the points of pikes and pitchforks'.[49]

A growing disenchantment with France was also important in causing defections from the republican camp. The republic's tawdry efforts to assist the establishment of Irish independence, its increasingly arrogant conduct towards smaller European neighbours and, most of all, towards the United States of America, had caused many Ulster Presbyterians to rethink the admiration they had once held for the French.[50] A year after the rebellion in the North Castlereagh observed that 'Protestant Dissenters in Ulster have in great degree withdrawn from the union and become Orangemen . . . The province of Ulster comprises at this moment a numerous body of determined loyalists'.[51]

Subsequent events consolidated this movement towards loyalty. Bonaparte's disregard for liberty, and his conclusion of a concordat with the papacy in 1801, meant a further alienation of Ulster Presbyterians from France (and for those inclined to see an Antichrist on the world stage, Bonaparte generally appeared the most likely candidate). Added to this, the abolition of the Irish parliament in 1800, in a sense a radical measure of parliamentary reform, swept away many of the electoral anomalies that had so galled northern Presbyterians in earlier years. Moreover, by giving preferential treatment to the linen industry and providing it with a secure market,[52] the union consolidated the North's growing prosperity and further served to reconcile Ulster Dissenters to the existing regime. By 1803 the heart had gone out of the northern United movement: many of those who had wound the clock of republican separatism in Ulster in the 1790s now had no wish to see it strike.

Russell's old friend, Dr James McDonnell, wrote of this change of mood to Margaret Russell in reply to her enquiry about settling in Belfast. He cautioned her not to expect great friendship or support in the town. Although Russell had been a popular figure in the early 1790s, many of his friends had distanced themselves from him as his politics grew more radical. McDonnell himself, who had always looked on Russell with a mixture of affection and exasperation, had ceased to correspond with him in 1800 while he was imprisoned in Fort George. As for those who shared Russell's political views, some had emigrated or been ruined by prosecutions, while others had completely changed their opinions, severed all links with the United

Irishmen and joined the yeomanry. In fact, the change in attitude to the yeomanry in Belfast was a good indicator of how the wider political situation in the North had changed. Whereas efforts in 1796 to raise a yeomanry corps in the town had to be abandoned, on 5 April 1803 at a well-attended town meeting, the citizens of Belfast proclaimed that should war break out they were ready 'to come forward in arms and oppose the attacks of either the foreign or domestic enemies of their country', and two new corps were raised. The three lieutenants of the Belfast Volunteer Infantry were William Sinclair, Robert Getty and Gilbert McIlveen, all former prominent United Irishmen.[53] McDonnell warned that if Russell was to return to Belfast 'he would find a great difference in this place'.[54] His prophecy was duly borne out in August 1803 when the citizens of the town subscribed £500 to the bounty for Russell's arrest. Even McDonnell contributed fifty guineas. He claimed he did so because he was called from his home to perform an operation at a time when Russell was at large in the North and this cast some suspicion on him. Though he regretted his action soon after, it was a gesture that cost him the friendship of Templeton and the McCrackens for many years.[55] Russell himself finally noted the changes which had come about in the province when after his conviction for high treason in Downpatrick he reminded the local gentlemen that 'he was about to suffer for endeavouring to put into execution the lessons imbibed among them' and he observed that six members of the jury had once been United Irishmen.[56]

After 1798, the increased polarisation between Catholics and Protestants made plans for any broad-based rising very difficult indeed. By this time, even in former United Irish strongholds such as Ballynahinch, yeomanry corps were refusing to admit Catholics into their ranks.[57] The fraternal euphoria of the early 1790s had well and truly evaporated by 1803, and the widespread belief that only 'the lowest orders of the Catholics' had joined Russell was reported as an important factor in discouraging Presbyterian participation.[58]

Bridging the sectarian divide was only one of many obstacles that faced Russell. While Marianne Elliott challenges the traditional image of Emmet and Russell as 'romantic visionaries' and, pointing to Emmet's detailed preparations and his success in maintaining secrecy, makes a persuasive case for the Dublin rising as a serious insurrectionary effort with a real chance of success, it is far more difficult to make a similar case for the attempt in Ulster.[59] Russell believed that 'courage alone was wanting . . . to render our success not only certain but easy',[60] but much more than courage was wanting. The rebels lacked almost everything else required to effect a successful insurrection — popular support, arms, money, an effective system of communications and a realistic plan of action. Russell was convinced that his very presence was itself enough to raise the province and the systematic planning and detailed preparations required for an effective insurrection were almost wholly neglected. His plan of action was rather makeshift: rebel contingents in the hinterlands of Belfast and Downpatrick were to seize the arms of the local yeomanry and then attempt to take the towns. A day before the rising was due to take place Russell did not even have a map of Co. Down.[61] Many of the groups that were spotted drilling on 23 July and subsequent nights may well have been Defenders, but there is no evidence that any concerted effort was made to establish contact with their organisation.[62]

Russell failed completely to establish effective channels of communication between the isolated pockets of disaffection in Ulster. His understandable obsession with secrecy meant that orders could not be conveyed to his lieutenants until the last minute, which resulted in the assembly of poorly organised groups who had no real idea of what action they were to take.[63] Naturally enough these lost heart and soon dispersed when the expected instructions or signals were not received. In the report he made to London on the events in Ulster, Wickham commented on the inefficiency of the rebels' system of communication. He believed that it contrasted poorly with the system set up before 1798 and was 'ill calculated for giving effect to anything but a tumultuous rising, and carries with it a convincing proof that there is a general want of leaders among the disaffected throughout the whole country'.[64] A northern loyalist also commented on the rebels' failure to establish effective communications, with the result that 'to many deemed favourably disposed, their designs were unknown; while, to the mass of the people, even the idea of an insurrection was a complete mystery'.[65]

Russell's military experience in the field was very limited and it had occurred almost twenty years previously. He clearly was no great thinker on the art of war: in his frequent arguments with Tone on military tactics he had always stressed his preference for raw courage over disciplined manoeuvres.[66] In the summer of 1803 his hastily improvised planning showed little expertise or foresight. Moreover, his lieutenants seem to have been of poor quality. Some time before the rising, James Corry had already behaved indiscreetly. In conversation with Andrew Williamson, a smith from Downpatrick, in McCartan's public house in Clough on 3 July he told him that an insurrection would take place in three weeks and that he should begin to manufacture breastplates inscribed with 'Success to Bonaparte'. Williamson claimed that he made it clear that he wanted nothing to do with any such business and that as he left McCartan's, Corry, a glass of beer in his hand, shouted after him: 'Here is Bonaparte's health, and damnation to you and all...against him'. James Drake seems to have been little better. On the 23 July he informed John Roney, a farmer of Drumgooland and a yeoman, of the insurgents' intention to disarm the Seaforde yeomanry. He also attempted to coerce another Drumgooland farmer to join the insurgents by telling him that if he refused to turn out 'it was likely the people would come and force him.[67]

Even had the rising been better led, it is difficult to see how the scattered groups that turned out on 23/24 July could have accomplished much against well-armed regular troops and yeomanry. Had Russell been able to distribute large quantities of arms, point to a French invasion or a successful seizure of the capital, then enough men might have flocked to his standard to mount an insurrection worthy of the name, but without any of these his efforts were doomed.

Loyalists were quick to point out the solid loyalty of the North and to dismiss Russell's failure contemptuously. A town meeting in Belfast announced that Russell and his agents were 'not able, in the whole province of Ulster, even among the very lowest orders of the people, to collect more than a despicable number of insignificant traitors'. At Emmet's trial Russell was dismissed as 'an infuriated zealot...[whose] understanding was lost in his ambition', 'a silly inflated fool...glorying in the empty title of general, and blown up with visionary notions of his own importance'. In Antrim and Down, 'once thought the nursery of sedition, we saw the public mind so entirely altered that the cottager and mechanic, nobly resisting the seduction of the traitor, were ready to answer any overture of disloyalty with an indignant slap in the face'.[68] These sentiments were echoed by the liberal *Dublin Evening Post* :

> Contemptible and desperate, and mean and resourceless as the treason of the capital has proved to be, that which Russell hoped to stir into rebellion appears infinitely more so. After skulking in fear and trembling, and beggarly obscurity, about the counties of Down and

Antrim, after demeaning himself to the basest vices of the vulgar and
in whiskey drinking communications, seeking to draw out all the profligate treason of the country, all the force he could muster was *twelve*
or *fourteen* men, without arms, without system, without correspondence or defined purpose! And how even those few idiots or madmen
were collected is wonderful, when, as is evident from the trial, the
agents, or *recruiting sergeants of General Russell were afraid of being
knocked down if they dared to talk of rebellion to any of their neighbours.*[69]

It is hardly surprising that Russell's efforts to raise Ulster — riding
through Antrim and Down in his general's uniform haranguing the
unwilling inhabitants to take up arms and free their country —
struck most observers as ludicrous. In the face of mass apathy that
would have caused other men to re-think their plans, Russell never
once thought of abandoning his mission. Far from regarding himself
as out of step, on several occasions he expressed his bafflement at
the refusal of the people of Ulster to join him. The picture that
emerges is of a man with a tenuous grip on reality, maintaining a
quixotic confidence in victory in the face of overwhelming evidence
to the contrary. But Russell's unshakeable optimism can only be
understood in the context of his pursuit of the millennium.

Russell's millennialism was the driving force behind his determination to renew the revolutionary struggle after the failure of 1798.
A doctrinaire conviction that he was engaged in fulfilling a divinely-
ordained plan pervades many of his writings and utterances in the
final years of his life. He was certain that, in fighting for liberty and
justice as he saw it, he was doing the work of God. He remained
convinced that, as a Christian, it was his solemn duty to prepare the
way for the millennial utopia.[70] He could simply not bring himself to
believe that the sacrifices made over the last few years, especially the
deaths of close friends such as Tone and McCracken, had all counted
for nothing. Even the complete collapse of the latest attempt at
insurrection failed to dent his confidence. In his attempt to raise
Ulster Russell had, as ever, placed his trust in providence — a
reliance that did not encourage detailed or realistic preparations —
and if providence had chosen to deny him victory on this occasion,
then that need not be the case in the future. As he had written some
years earlier: 'whatever attempts are made ... to extinguish liberty,
or to retard her progress, I have no doubt of her ultimate and speedy
success'.[71] For Russell, rebellion was not simply sanctioned by

scripture, it was *ordained* by it. He believed that the cause of justice and liberty had merely lost a battle in a war in which there could be only one ultimate victor, and that 'failure was alone surprising'.[72] The conviction and zeal that had enabled him to tap into Ulster's popular millennialist expectations in the 1790s had, by 1803, rendered him completely out of touch with the disillusionment that followed the defeat in 1798.[73]

Russell's attempt to raise the North had precisely the effect he would have least desired. Far from assisting the onset of a millennium of Christian harmony it resulted in a sharpening of sectarian tensions. Like Emmet, he had hoped that because the rising was almost entirely led by Protestants, little blame would be attached to the Catholics in the event of failure.[74] They were wrong. Many in authority were quick to characterise the conspiracy as 'clearly of the papist leaven'.[75] The fact that there had been disturbances in the vicinity of Maynooth was seen as suspicious; the government even launched an investigation into the college and made some poorly founded allegations of its complicity in the rising. For some Protestants, recent events merely confirmed their deep-seated mistrust of Catholics and the identification of Catholicism with disloyalty was now closer than ever in the official mind.[76]

Just as Emmet's rising was seen by some members of the ascendancy as an anti-Protestant pogrom,[77] so Russell's call to arms in Ulster aroused traditional fears of Catholics embarking on a spree of massacre and pillage. Although the Catholic response to Russell's call had been negligible, the authorities believed that Russell must have had good reason to concentrate his last-ditch efforts on the Catholics of south Down and that the few who had turned out must have been Catholics.[78] Some observers saw the northern disturbances as primarily the work of the Defenders — an organisation that disaffected Catholics were alleged to have joined *en masse* in recent times — and concluded that Russell had far closer links with the Defenders in Ulster than was really the case.[79] It also seems that in his desperate efforts to recruit support, Russell himself contributed to the sharpening of sectarian tensions by his attempt to play on the anti-Orange sentiments of the Catholics of Annadorn and Loughinisland.[80]

Those suspected of rebel sympathies moved quickly to dissociate themselves from Russell. Patrick MacCartan, the parish priest of Loughinisland, in a declaration to the local landlord on behalf of the Catholic inhabitants of the district, claimed that they had no prior knowledge or suspicion of Russell's plans 'and even then, the mad scheme was communicated to a few individuals, who rejected it with scorn and indignation...We are decidedly of the opinion that any person who would attempt to divide the people...when the entire effort of the whole kingdom is necessary to repel an invading foe must be an enemy to his country'. MacCartan also maintained that his parishioners were willing to prove their loyalty by serving in the local yeomanry corps.[81]

In the highly charged atmosphere after the rising such declarations were often in vain — some Protestants simply interpreted them as further evidence of Catholic duplicity. The Lord Lieutenant, Hardwicke, for example, considered the pastoral letter of the Catholic Archbishop of Dublin, Dr John Troy, condemning the Emmet rebellion as 'the greatest piece of craft, dissimulation and hypocrisy that I have read'. He believed that Troy had advance knowledge of the plot and that his condemnation had been written before the rising.[82] But while distrust of Catholics had increased, considerable reassurance was taken from the inactivity of Ulster Dissenters and there was a general acceptance in government circles that most of the latter and could now be relied on as loyal subjects. Although a rump continued to style themselves United Irishmen, they were now 'so dwindled that they scarcely deserve the name of a body'.[83] The judge who was to pronounce sentence on Russell observed to the lord chancellor that Ulster Presbyterians 'have got it into their heads that the present scheme of rebellion has originated with the papists exclusively, and that idea together with a conviction that, should Bonaparte succeed in his designs, there will be no republic, but on the contrary, despotism and pillage, secures their support in the present crisis'.[84]

Russell's career had come full circle. In his adult life he had found his most congenial home in Belfast and, like Tone, he idealised the town as the cradle of Irish republicanism. It was under the tutelage of the Dissenters of the North that his radicalism had taken shape and it was among the same people that he had striven to transform this organisation into a mass revolutionary movement, and had been arrested as his efforts were bearing fruit. Seven years later, he seems to have believed that he was stepping back into the Ulster of 1796. Though he himself had gone from being a reformer to a revolutionary in a relatively short space of time, he failed to understand that, in the rapidly changing political landscape of the late 1790s and early 1800s, things could just as easily happen in reverse. While the Presbyterians of the North adapted themselves to changed circumstances, Russell held firmly to the vow he had made eight years earlier at the top of McArt's fort never to cease his efforts until he had established Ireland's independence. Now, as he made his last stand in favour of the United Irishmen's ideals, they looked on with apathy, if not downright hostility. The real significance of Russell's failure to raise Ulster in 1803 was that it signalled that the days of mass disaffection of Northern Dissenters were well and truly over.

NOTES

1 Wickham to Abbot, 30 Nov. 1803 (*Colchester corr.*, i, 459); Madden, *United Irishmen*, 3rd ser., ii, 215, 220; list of Antrim and Down prisoners, 30 Nov. 1803 (Reb. papers, 620/12/142/16); information of Lt. Stephenson, 28 July 1803 (S.O.C. papers, 1025/2); Helen Landreth, *The pursuit of Robert Emmet* (Dublin, 1949), p. 178; Wickham's account of the insurrection of 23 July 1803 (*Colchester corr.*, i, 450).

2 Nelly Rabb to Mary Ann McCracken, 18 Nov. 1843 (Madden papers, 873/627); Byrne, *Memoirs*, i, 357; Revd. Snowden Cupples to Revd. Forster Archer, 14 Sept. 1803 (Reb. papers, 620/11/158); examination of Robert Carthy, Aug. 1803 (P.R.O., HO 100/112/363–4).

3 Charles Ruthven (former Crown solicitor, Downpatrick) to Madden, 17 Jan. 1837 (Madden papers, 873/671).

4 McClelland to Wickham, Carrickfergus, 9 Aug. 1803 (B.L., Hardwicke papers, Add. MS 35770, ff 80–1).

5 Madden, *United Irishmen*, 3rd ser., ii, 216; J. A. Russell to Madden, n.d. (Madden papers, 873/674, f. 3v); in his reminiscences to Madden Hope had Russell in Belfast on Friday 22 July, but the evidence of several witnesses place Russell in Loughinisland on the Friday, eg. deposition of William Cosby of Saintfield, 14 Oct. 1803 (*1798 Rebellion in Co. Down*, p. 268).

6 Evidence of John Keenan and Henry Smith of Annadorn at Russell's trial, *Belfast News Letter*, 25 Oct. 1803; Wickham to King, 14 Aug. 1803 (P.R.O., HO 100/112/231–3).

7 Evidence of John Keenan of Annadorn, *Belfast News Letter*, 25 Oct. 1803; deposition of Patrick Doran, 4 Aug. 1803 (*1798 Rebellion in Co. Down*, p. 265).

8 McClelland to Wickham, 13 Oct. 1803 (P.R.O., HO 100/114/66); *Belfast News Letter*, 19 Aug. 1803.

9 Evidence of Patrick Lynch and James Fitzpatrick, Loughinisland, and Patrick Renaghan, Clough, *Belfast News Letter*, 25 Oct. 1803.

10 Evidence of John Tate of Downpatrick at Russell's trial, *Belfast News Letter*, 25 Oct. 1803; deposition of John Tate, a shoemaker, 1803 (*1798 Rebellion in Co. Down*, pp. 265, 270–1); see also Ruthven to Madden, Downpatrick,17 Jan. 1837 (Madden papers, 873/671); Mary Ann McCracken to Madden, 2 July 1844 (Madden papers, 873/155).

11 Evidence of John Tate at James Corry's trial, *Belfast News Letter*, 1 Nov. 1803; deposition of John Tate, 1803 (*1798 Rebellion in Co. Down*, pp. 270–1).

12 Madden, *United Irishmen*, 3rd ser., ii, 217; evidence at trial of Andrew Hunter and William Porter, *Belfast News Letter*, 28 Oct. 1803; McSkimin, 'Insurrection of 1803', pp. 556–7; memories of Mary Ann McCracken, n.d. (Madden papers, 873/672).

278 Soul on fire: a life of Thomas Russell

13 McGucken (aka 'Belfast') to Marsden, 8 July 1803 (MacDonagh, *Viceroy's postbag*, pp. 276–7).
14 Thomas Whinnery to Edward Lees, 25 July 1803 (Reb. papers, 620/67/187); *Belfast News Letter*, 29 July 1803; *Emmet memoir*, i, 368.
15 Elliott, *Partners*, pp. 310–11; 316; 'Account of the late plan of insurrection in Dublin' (B.L., Add. MS 38103, ff 19–25); information of Quigley (B.L., Hardwicke papers, Add. MS 35740, f. 293).
16 Manuscript copy of Russell's proclamation, dated 24 July 1803 (Reb. papers, 620/64/154).
17 Thomas Whinnery to Edward Lees, 24 July 1803 (Reb. papers, 620/67/188); see also John Cleland, Newtownards, to James Clealand [*sic*], Berkshire, 27 July 1803 (P.R.O.N.I., Cleland papers, D714/1/11).
18 McGucken to Marsden, 25 July 1803 (MacDonagh, *Viceroy's postbag*, p. 414); report of Lt. George Stephenson, 28 July 1803 (S.O.C. papers, 1025/2).
19 General Campbell to Wickham, 24 July 1803 (Reb. papers, 620/64/128); George Benn, *History of the town of Belfast* (London, 1877), ii, 41–2.
20 Campbell to Marsden, 31 Aug. 1803 (S.O.C. papers, 1024/4).
21 John Cleland, Newtownards, to James Clealand [*sic*], Berkshire, 27 July 1803 (P.R.O.N.I., Cleland papers, D714/1/11); Martha McTier to Drennan, 2 Aug. 1803 (Drennan papers, T765/1047).
22 Revd. Snowden Cupples to Revd. Foster Archer, Lisburn, 27 July 1803 (Reb. papers, 620/64/154); S. McMaster to John Lees, 27 July 1803 (Reb. papers, 620/66/31); Richard Dobbs to Revd. Forster Archer, Carrickfergus, 30 July 1803 (Reb. papers, 620/64/181).
23 Richard Dobbs to Revd. Forster Archer, Carrickfergus, 30 July 1803 (Reb. papers, 620/64/181); *Belfast News Letter*, 29 July 1803; McGucken to Marsden, 25 July 1803 (MacDonagh, *Viceroy's postbag*, p. 414).
24 Revd. Snowden Cupples to Revd. Forster Archer, Lisburn, 27 July 1803 (Reb. papers, 620/64/154); for a similar view see also Richard Dobbs to Archer, Carrickfergus, 30 July 1803 (Reb. papers, 620/64/181).
25 Russell was reported to have stated that the French would land arms and ammunition at Kilkeel, Wickham to King, 14 Aug. 1803 (P.R.O., HO 100/112/231–3); see also evidence of Henry Smith, *Belfast News Letter*, 25 Oct. 1803.
26 James Clelland (jury member at Russell's trial) to Mary Ann McCracken, 20 Nov. 1843 (Madden papers, 873/626); McSkimin, 'Insurrection of 1803', p. 567; Elliott, *Partners*, p. 315.
27 Russell's proclamation, 24 July 1803 (Reb. papers, 620/64/154); Emmet's proclamation reads 'You are now called upon to show to the world that you are competent to take your place among nations … by the only satisfactory proof you can furnish of your capability of maintaining your independence, your wresting it from England with your own hands … without the hope of foreign assistance' (Reb. papers, 620/11/134).
28 Examination of Michael Dwyer, 11 Jan. 1804 (Charles Dickson, *The life of Michael Dwyer* (Dublin, 1944), p. 255).
29 Elliott, *Partners*, pp. 300, 315.
30 Statement of James Farrell, 24 Oct. 1803 (P.R.O., HO 100//114/23).
31 Mary Ann McCracken to Madden, 2 July 1844 (Madden papers, 873/155).
32 Evidence of John Keenan and Henry Smith, *Belfast News Letter*, 25 Oct. 1803; interviews with Russell, 24, 27 Sept., 5 Oct. 1803 (P.R.O., HO 100/113/195–8, 100/114/11–12, 119–20); Russell to McNally, 24 Sept. 1803, 5 Oct. 1803 (P.R.O., HO 100/113/195–8, 100/114/119).
33 — to King, 13 Oct. 1803 (P.R.O., HO 100/114/56).

34 Evidence of Patrick Farrell in William Ridgeway (ed.), *A report on the proceed-ings of Aug. — Oct. 1803* (Dublin, 1803), ii, 60; Madden, *United Irishmen*, 3rd ser., iii, 240; diary of T. A. Emmet, *c.* 31 May 1803 (*Emmet memoir*, i, 342).

35 Byrne, *Memoirs*, i, 378–9; Wickham to Carew, 25 Sept. 1803 (P.R.O., HO 100/113/199); — to King, 13 Oct. 1803 (P.R.O. HO 100/114/56).

36 Revd. Snowden Cupples to Revd. Forster Archer, Lisburn, 29 July 1803 (Reb. papers, 620/64/154).

37 Nelly Rabb to Mary Ann McCracken, 18 Nov. 1843 (Madden papers, 873/627).

38 Martha McTier to Sarah Drennan, Oct. 1803 (*Drennan letters*, p. 330).

39 Thomas Whinnery to Edward Lees, 31 July 1803 (Reb. papers, 620/67/189).

40 *Belfast News Letter*, 6 Sept. 1803 (notice issued 19 Aug. 1803); Martha McTier to Sarah Drennan, Oct. 1803 (*Drennan letters*, p. 329). This description appears to be taken from the deposition of Hugh Magennis of Ballydougan, 4 Oct. 1803 (*1798 Rebellion in Co. Down*, p. 266)

41 Information of Lt. George Stephenson, 28 July 1803 (S.O.C. papers, 1025/2).

42 Russell to Frank McCracken, *c.* Aug. 1803 [?] (copy) (Madden papers, 873/640). This letter is dated 15 July 1803 but from its content it appears to be written some time after the attempted rising.

43 Revd. Snowden Cupples to Revd. Forster Archer, 14 Sept. 1803 (Reb. papers, 620/11/158).

44 Examination of Robert Carty, Aug. 1803 (P.R.O., HO 100/112/363–4).

45 Robert Emmet to T. A. Emmet, Sept. 1803 (*Colchester corr.*, i, 454).

46 Wickham to Carew, 27 Aug. 1803 (MacDonagh, *Viceroy's postbag*, pp. 327–8).

47 Baron St George Daly to Lord Redesdale, *c.* Oct. 1803 (P.R.O.N.I., Redesdale papers, T3030/9/25).

48 McGucken to Marsden, 25 July 1803 (MacDonagh, *Viceroy's postbag*, p. 414).

49 *Belfast News Letter*, 29 June 1798.

50 Lecky, *Ireland*, iv, 407–16.

51 Castlereagh to Portland, 3 June 1799 (P.R.O., HO 100/87/5–7); on the change in Presbyterian attitudes see A. T. Q. Stewart, 'The transformation of Presbyterian radicalism in the North of Ireland 1792–1825' (MA thesis, Queen's University, Belfast, 1956), pp. 62–77.

52 John J. Monaghan, 'The rise and fall of the Belfast cotton industry' in *I. H. S.*, iii, no. 9, (Mar. 1942), p. 2.

53 George Benn, *History of the town of Belfast* (London, 1817), ii, 28, 40; D. J. Owen, *A history of Belfast* (Belfast, 1921), 187; Henry Joy (ed.), *Historical collections relative to the town of Belfast* (Belfast, 1817), p. xvn.

54 James McDonnell to Margaret Russell, n.d. (Sirr papers, 868/1, ff 256–7); for McDonnell's failure to reply to his letters, see Russell to Templeton, 2 Sept. 1800 (Madden papers, 873/636).

55 Martha McTier to Sarah Drennan, Oct. 1803 (*Drennan letters*, pp. 330–32); James McDonnell to Madden, n.d. (Madden papers, 873/377).

56 *Castlereagh corr.*, iv, 271; James Cleland (a member of the jury at Russell's trial) to Mary Ann McCracken, 20 Nov. 1843 (Madden papers, 873/626).

57 Revd. Snowden Cupples to Revd. Forster Archer, 14 Sept. 1803 (Reb. papers, 620/11/158); for similar opposition to the admission of Catholics into the yeomanry see Baron St George Daly to Lord Redesdale, *c.* Oct. 1803 (P.R.O.N.I., Redesdale papers, T 3030/9/25).

58 Report of the solicitor-general, 9 Aug. 1803 (P.R.O., HO 100/112/202–4).

59 Elliott, *Partners*, pp. 310–18.

60 Russell to Frank McCracken, *c.* Aug. 1803 [?] (copy) (Madden papers, 873/640).

61 Evidence of James Keenan, *Belfast News Letter*, 25 Oct. 1803.

62 Elliott, *Partners*, pp. 312, 321.

63 Revd. Snowden Cupples to Revd. Forster Archer, 14 Sept. 1803 (Reb. papers, 620/11/158).

64 Wickham to Carew, 27 Aug. 1803 (MacDonagh, *Viceroy's postbag*, pp. 327–8).

65 McSkimin, 'Insurrection of 1803', p. 553.

66 Bartlett, *Life of Tone*, p. 520.

67 Depositions of Andrew Williamson, 30 July 1803, John McShean, 18 Oct. 1803, John Roney, 18 Oct. 1803 (*1798 Rebellion in County Down* , pp. 264–5, 270, 269).

68 *Belfast News Letter*, 5 Aug. 1803; speech of Lord Avonmore, Sept. 1803 (*The insurrection of 23rd July 1803 by H.B.C.* [Dublin, 1803], p. 104).

69 *Dublin Evening Post*, 27 Oct. 1803. [Italics as in the original].

70 Russell to Templeton, 5 June 1802 (Madden papers, 873/638); Russell to — , 5 June 1802 (Madden papers, 873/673).

71 Thomas Russell to John Russell, Fort George, 10 Dec. 1800 (copy) (Madden papers, 873/655, f. 1v); Russell to Frank McCracken, Aug. 1803 [?] (copy) (Madden papers, 873/640).

72 Russell to Frank McCracken, Oct. 1803 (copy) (Madden papers, 873/642).

73 John Gray, 'Millennial vision...Thomas Russell re-assessed' in *Linen Hall Review*, vi, no. 1 (spring 1989), p. 9.

74 Reminiscences of James Hope (Hope papers, 7253/1, f. 3).

75 Lord Auckland to John Beresford, 14 Sept. 1803 (*Beresford corr.*, ii, 266).

76 Thomas Bartlett, *The fall and rise of the Irish nation* (Dublin, 1992), pp. 275–6; J. McClelland to —, 28 July 1803 (Reb. papers, 620/66/22); Richard Dobbs to Forster Archer, 30 July 1803 (Reb. papers, 620/64/181); Redesdale to Fingal, 28 Aug., 6 Sept. 1803 (*Castlereagh corr.*, iv, 311–13).

77 Charles Agar (Protestant archbishop of Dublin) to Portland, 25 Aug. 1803 (P.R.O.N.I., T3717/C37/20), cited in Thomas Bartlett, op. cit., p. 275.

78 Auckland to Beresford, 14 Sept. 1803 (*Beresford corr.*, ii, 266); Marsden's account of the insurrection of 1803, 15 Nov. 1803 (*Castlereagh corr.,* iv, 330).

79 John Cleland to James Cleland, 27 July 1803 (P.R.O.N.I., Cleland papers, D714/1/11); information given to Rev. Thomas Beatty, 17 Aug. 1803 (P.R.O., HO 100/112/404–8); Marsden's account of the 1803 insurrection (*Castlereagh corr.*, iv, 330).

80 McClelland to Wickham, 13 Oct. 1803 (P.R.O., HO 100/114/66); evidence of Henry Smith, *Belfast News Letter*, 25 Oct. 1803.

81 Declaration of loyalty by the Roman Catholics of Loughinisland, dated 9 Aug. 1803, *Belfast News Letter*, 19 Aug. 1803.

82 Hardwicke to Yorke, 24 Aug. 1803 (MacDonagh, *Viceroy's postbag*, pp. 325–6).

83 Information given to Revd. Thomas Beatty, 17 Aug. 1803 (P.R.O., HO 100/112/404–8).

84 St George Daly to Lord Redesdale, c. Oct 1803 (P.R.O.N.I., Redesdale papers, T3030/9/25).

CHAPTER FIFTEEN

The Last Days

Towards the end of August Russell learned that Emmet had been arrested; he resolved immediately to go to Dublin to try and rescue him. Mary Ann McCracken provided the funds for the journey. While preparations were being made, he moved to the house of James McCutchen of Craigavad — with a high price on his head it was not safe to remain too long in any one place. A small fishing boat was hired in Bangor to take him south. This brought him to Drogheda where he sought refuge in the house of an acquaintance, a local gentleman named Marky. From Drogheda he made his way to Dublin where, on the evening of 7 September, he rented lodgings on the second floor of the house of Daniel Muley at 28 Parliament Street under the assumed name of Mr Harris.[1] Though Muley later denied that he knew his guest's true identity, he had originally met Russell in Newgate in 1798. A gunsmith by trade, Muley had been employed by Emmet to make weapons for the recent insurrection and was regarded as a suspicious character by the authorities.[2]

While in Dublin Russell ventured out only at night. On several occasions he was stopped by military patrols but managed to deceive them by presenting a counterfeit pass and bluffing his way through.[3] It must soon have become clear to him that there was no realistic prospect of rescuing Emmet from prison and that he would have to leave Dublin as soon as possible. With a price of £1,500 on his head and the city still uneasy after the shock of the recent rebellion, it was extremely dangerous for him to remain in Dublin an hour longer than was necessary. Realising this, he managed to contact some United Irish sympathisers who began to make arrangements for his departure: he was to go to a convent near North King Street, where he would be disguised as a clergyman before embarking for the Isle of Man.[4] But before these arrangements were complete his presence in Parliament Street was discovered.

Friends of Russell later maintained that he chose to stay in

Parliament Street, only a stone's throw from the Castle, so that he could meet with 'persons of distinction' who would have drawn the attention of police agents if they had travelled to out-of-the-way locations. According to Russell's nephew, Henry Grattan was among the distinguished visitors he expected and Russell delayed his departure to meet him. This claim was repeated by Madden who cited James Hope as his source.[5] Since the days in 1793–4 when the United Irishmen and parliamentary opposition had been at daggers drawn, Grattan had edged somewhat closer to the radicals. He had withdrawn from the Irish parliament in 1797 in protest at the government's campaign of coercion and had associated with prominent United Irishmen such as William Sampson and Arthur O'Connor, though he had declined Samuel Neilson's offer to join the society. In the aftermath of the 1798 rebellion, he was denounced by loyalists as a United Irish fellow traveller and dismissed from the Irish privy council. In 1803 the authorities viewed his association with William Dowdall, a former secretary of the Whig Club and one of the leading figures in Emmet's conspiracy, with some suspicion. But Grattan was no radical, still less a revolutionary: he never lost his distaste for violence and was quick to denounce the 'stupidity' and 'barbarity' of Emmet's rising.[6] Moreover, since he generally showed extreme caution in his dealings with the United Irishmen, it is difficult to credit a report that he intended to call on a man who, in recent weeks had been attempting to foment open rebellion, was one of the most wanted fugitives in the land and in the past had been one of his most scathing critics. Not surprisingly, there is no record that any such meeting ever took place and Russell's decision to choose a place of refuge within a hundred yards from Dublin Castle appears as yet another instance of the dubious judgement he showed in these months.

Russell's presence in Parliament Street had been discovered by a young member of the attorneys' yeomanry corps named John Swift Emerson. He had learned that Muley waited on the stranger 'with mysterious respect and attention', brought him his meals himself and took particular care to ensure that his wife never saw him. He immediately informed Major Henry Sirr, Dublin's chief of police, of his suspicions.[7] How Emerson came by this information is unclear. Madden recounts the allegation that he was tipped off by Walter Cox, a former gunsmith who had once been apprenticed to Daniel Muley. Cox, who may already have been in the pay of the government, lived next door to Muley and as he mingled in radical circles he may already have been acquainted with Russell.[8]

At about 9.30 on the night of 9 September Major Sirr, Lieutenant Humphrey Minchin and Emerson, accompanied by a detachment of yeomanry, called at 28 Parliament Street. Emerson stayed below with Mrs Muley while Sirr and Minchin ascended the stairs to question 'Mr Harris'. Apparently, Russell was so absorbed in reading that he did not notice Sirr and Minchin enter his room.[9] Sirr began to question him and during the interrogation took hold of the ends of Russell's neckcloth to see if it was marked by any initials. This was too much for Russell's delicate sense of honour; he exclaimed: 'I will not be treated with indignity' and drew a pistol.[10] It seems that rather than fire immediately, he hesitated, giving the two men time to tackle him. After a fierce struggle he was disarmed and arrested and taken immediately to Dublin Castle. On entering the gates Russell was recognised by George Knox and several other northern gentleman who had been dining with Wickham at the Castle.[11]

The exact circumstances of his seizure were later a matter of bitter dispute: Emerson strongly maintained that he had participated in the disarming of Russell — a claim denied by Sirr and Minchin. Both parties became involved in a prolonged and very public squabble over entitlement to the £1,500 reward.[12]

The authorities were much relieved at Russell's arrest. Wickham, who was still concerned at disaffection in the counties around Dublin, believed that he had come to the capital 'partly in the hope of being able to strike a blow before the trial of Emmet'.[13] Castlereagh noted that the capture of this 'most inveterate traitor' was 'very satisfactory', particularly as his execution under the banishment act would be bound to 'deter his *fellows* from trying their fortune on Irish ground'.[14] Prominent members of the Protestant ascendancy such as John Foster and John Beresford added their voices to the official chorus of approval: the former was delighted to hear that one of 'those rebels whom no leniency could operate on' was finally taken, while the latter was outraged at 'the impudence of the fellow, coming to Dublin and lodging within fifty yards of the Castle'.[15] Russell's arrest even came to the attention of George III, who wrote to the lord lieutenant of his pleasure at his being taken up. Never the clearest of thinkers on events in Ireland, however, he seems to have confused Russell with Emmet, adding that he thought 'his correspondence with the daughter of Mr Curran is certainly *curious*'.[16]

Russell's arrest also pleased northern loyalists and in the next couple of weeks the Castle received several requests, especially from

Belfast and east Down, to be given the privilege of trying and hanging the traitor. They claimed that there would be no difficulty in
securing a conviction from a local jury and the execution of such a
well-known and once popular figure would serve as a warning to
any lingering pockets of disaffection and finally extinguish what
remained of the flame of rebellion in east Ulster.[17]

After a few days Russell was transferred from the Castle to
Kilmainham prison. Here he managed to communicate with Anne
Devlin, who had acted as housekeeper at Butterfield Lane and was
now under arrest. Knowing him to be worried about certain letters
he had left in the house, she managed to put his mind at rest by
telling him that she had destroyed them immediately after the failure
of the rising. Anne's devotion to Robert Emmet is well known but
she was also deeply devoted to Russell, whom she regarded as 'one
of the most gentle and generous beings that ever lived'. Under interrogation she denied all knowledge of him.[18]

The latest insurrection had taken the Irish government completely
by surprise. The fact that it had failed so completely allowed them
to downplay the whole affair, but they were nonetheless deeply
concerned that such potentially dangerous preparations could be
carried out under their noses, and in the weeks that followed they
embarked on a major intelligence gathering operation. In
Kilmainham, and later in Downpatrick, Russell was continually
probed for information. The Castle hoped to use the period before
he was brought to trial to discover what they could on the planning
of the insurrection, the motivation of its leaders and, most importantly, the intentions of the French. Government agents were given
the task of engaging in long conversations with Russell about the
events of recent months and his general political views. Since it was
Wickham's intention to attempt 'to make the leaders contemptible
and to represent them to the people as traitors to the cause and sacrificing the lower orders by their own falsehoods',[19] it was also
probably hoped that Russell would let something slip that government propaganda could exploit.

The two men charged with this task were Dr Edward Trevor,
medical officer and deputy governor of Kilmainham, and a man
skilled at ingratiating himself with prisoners, and the barrister,
Leonard McNally, who, although he had long been in the pay of the
government, was still trusted by most United Irishmen and acted as
defence counsel for Emmet and several of his co-accused.[20] Both men
diligently reported their conversations with Russell to the authorities.

These conversations ranged over a variety of topics, and on one occasion Russell explained his reasons for taking up arms. He claimed that the vast majority of the Irish people were 'bent on a total change of government, by which they expect to obtain a redress of their national and individual grievances', and a visit to the cabin of an Irish cottier would demonstrate to anyone 'that their grievances are not all imaginary'. He challenged the official view that the 'poor of Ireland are devoid of political information', claiming that he had often been surprised at just how well informed they were:

> It is not true that they require the instigations of leaders — they are as ardent as any leaders. The miscarriage of different attempts does not extinguish either the principle or the intention — it serves only to make them more cautious. Nor are these sentiments confined exclusively to the lower orders, they are generally diffused among the rising generation who have grown into manhood within the last five or six years. I am convinced they will always renew the contest whenever they think they can succeed, and equally so that they would join any invading army by whose aid they thought they could establish their independence, for neither they nor their leaders ever dreamed of submitting to any foreign force, and they have perfect confidence in their confidence to maintain their independence if once armed and organised.
>
> Those who have fallen, either in battle or by trial in support of their principle[s], so far from serving as examples to deter, have their memories cherished with fond affection and are considered as martyrs — venerated martyrs — believe me, sir, you cannot be more convinced of the rectitude of your cause than they are.[21]

During these conversations Russell came back to one particular point again and again — that no more blood should be shed than was absolutely necessary and he entreated the government to cease the executions of those involved in the latest rising. By late September Emmet and sixteen of his co-accused had been hanged.[22] Russell made it clear that he was not trying to save his own life: by all means the government could execute the leaders, but they should rest satisfied with this and punish no more of their followers.[23] This, he claimed, was in the interest of the government as well as being dictated by common humanity. He believed that since:

> the intended attack of France will soon take place, its failure or its success must occasion a great change. What I beg to propose and to urge ... is that at least till that great experiment is decided, you will

stop the effusion of blood. If you defeat the French you need not surely dread the Irish — the lives of all those you may think worthy of death will be as much in your power then as now. If, on the contrary, a victorious army arrive at the same time [that] men are executing for their political principles, it will I am convinced lead to a dreadful retaliation. For God's sake...if such a contest is to take place, do not let men come to it in a state of exasperation...Do not be persuaded that acts of lenity are acts of weakness. You state that the leaders of the insurrection in the city have fallen, surely it is useless to proceed further there — I do not speak of moral criminals, if men have murdered unarmed defenceless people let them be punished. For these reasons let me urge you to at least a suspension of execu-tions...Who has been right or wrong an infallible wisdom will ultimately decide. As to myself...if providence permits, and...you should put me to death, let that not invalidate what I have said as to others...The less calamity that is incurred the better. If therefore unfortunately you mean that the sword of your laws should again be bathed in blood, I entreat you, when you sheath it in my heart, there let it remain.[24]

Even before the failure of the rising the desire to minimise bloodshed had been something of an obsession with Russell. While prepara-tions were being made in Dublin he had expressed his fervent hope that the taking of life would be avoided wherever possible. At Loughinisland he expressed similar reservations, hoping that the yeomanry could be disarmed without being put to death.[25] These were not just empty words. Marsden believed Major Sirr owed his life to the fact that he entered the apartment in Parliament Street unarmed and that Russell balked at shooting a defenceless man. This was a viewpoint supported by the account received by William Knox, Bishop of Derry, brother of John and George Knox, which maintained that Russell, 'as a man of humanity,...had the lives of two people in his power but would not make use of pistols against unarmed men'.[26] But although Russell was undoubtedly sincere in his desire to limit killing, he did not shrink from the use of violence in what he saw as a just, indeed a sacred, cause.

During their conversations Russell vehemently denied McNally's assertion that assassination was a United Irish policy, claiming that the movement 'utterly abhorred such practices'. He maintained that in 1798 the people had been 'goaded' into committing sectarian killings and, as for any atrocities carried out in the latest rising, he regretted them — particularly the killing of the respected attorney-general, Lord Kilwarden, who had been dragged from his carriage in Thomas Street on the night of 23 July and piked to death. Russell 'lamented him greatly' and said that Kilwarden 'was a good man, and...if he had commanded that party, he would have put the man to death who would attempt to do that act. He would cut him down.'[27]

Russell discussed several other topics with McNally and Trevor. On the constitutional relationship between Britain and Ireland, he proffered a number of apparently contradictory opinions: on one occasion he claimed that separation was strongly in Ireland's interest; on another that everything should be done to 'assimilate' the two countries as much as possible — 'let them appear as sisters and not allow England to be the oppressor'; on another he spoke of how much better for England it would be to have 'Ireland allied or neutral, than with her hostile'.[28] Like many United Irishmen, Russell was often vague about the precise constitutional arrangement he sought and it is possible that his suspicion of Bonaparte led him to moderate earlier views on separation and to favour some form of link with Britain that would act as a bulwark against French influence. But so long as the present political arrangement remained, Russell advised that the Irish government should rule with clemency and seek to better the lot of the poor, and suggested a plan of social reform to alleviate the grievances of the Irish masses.[29] The government, however, was far more interested in discovering what Russell knew of the intentions of the French than it was in his constitutional theories or blueprints for social justice and McNally frequently tried to raise the subject of invasion. In reply to his queries Russell gave little more than general information: he maintained his belief that the French were more likely to land in Britain than Ireland, but claimed he knew nothing of their invasion plans other than what he had read in the newspapers.[30]

Convinced that Russell was not telling all he knew, the government tried a different tack to elicit the information it sought. They claimed they had evidence which could implicate his sister Margaret and his brother John in his treasonous activities. Margaret, they maintained, knew of her brother's return to Ireland and was therefore an accomplice to a breach of the banishment act; while John had assisted Russell's journey through London and was known to have associated with suspicious persons in London and Paris. The authorities were aware that Russell had no incentive to supply them with any useful information, since he knew that there was no real chance of saving his own life, but they hoped he might make a full disclosure to mitigate any punishment of members of his family. In return, not only would the government decline to press charges against John and Margaret, they would also 'make some provision for them so as to secure them from distress and want'. Wickham was convinced that Russell was:

> the man who had the most direct communication with the French government in the course of last spring, and it is in his power to make on that subject the most important discoveries, and his temper of mind and natural character are such as that nothing would be so likely to induce him to take such a step as kindness shown to his relatives *when you have it in your power to do them mischief*.[31]

Wickham used McNally to broach the subject with Russell, who was visibly shaken by the possibility that members of his family might suffer in some way because of his actions. He strenuously denied that there could be any charge against Margaret and tried to explain away the fact that John was acquainted with so many radicals and conspirators as coincidence.[32] As for John's visit to Paris, he claimed that since he had met his brother after a separation of almost ten years, being deeply fond of each other and with a decade's family business to discuss, it was hardly surprising that they had spent so much time together. He claimed that John had no involvement whatsoever in the planning of the insurrection and he had not given a second thought to the significance of his brother's stay in Paris until the authorities had used the visit to attempt to implicate him in the conspiracy.[33]

Russell was right in thinking that the authorities lacked any real evidence against his sister, and no action was taken against her, but the case against his brother, who, at the very least, had directly assisted known rebels, was a far more serious one. In the weeks before and for some time after Thomas's execution they continued to try to substantiate their allegations against John Russell, though they discovered little that would stand up in court. After prolonged questioning John admitted that his brother had stayed with him in London. He claimed that he had concealed this while Thomas was still alive because 'I shuddered that I might have been the means of accelerating or making sure the stroke of death [of] a brother' whom he loved 'more than life'. He said that Thomas had arrived unexpectedly and told him that he was going to Ireland to marry a young lady of good fortune — apparently the daughter of Hampden Evans, a possibility much talked about among the Irish in Paris during his stay there. The happiness of seeing John and his family made him stay two or three days but 'he yet had too much caution, I may say too much affection, to deposit his political secrets in my breast'. In the end no charges were brought against him.[34]

These attempts by the Castle to implicate members of his family took their toll on Russell. Wickham noted that his 'mind is much agitated and he appears to be by no means so stout-hearted a man as Emmet'.[35] Reporting on Russell at Downpatrick, Trevor claimed that he could observe 'much anxiety about him'.[36] These observations were partly based on the acute concern shown by Russell to the prospect that he might be subjected to any form of undignified treatment. Russell, an extremely proud and sensitive man, often exhibited a pronounced touchiness in relation to his personal honour.

According to Madden's account of his arrest, it was only when he believed that Sirr's behaviour threatened his dignity that he drew his pistol.[37] While at Kilmainham Russell complained of the way in which he was exposed to view but admitted that he was grateful for Wickham's 'gentlemanly conduct' towards him during his imprisonment. On hearing of his impending transfer to Downpatrick he was anxious to convey to the authorities his hope that his treatment there would be marked with 'the same dignity and consideration'.[38] In addition to his sensitivity, Russell's unwavering conviction of the righteousness of his political actions and his religious zeal further contributed to the authorities' impression of his agitated character.

During these days Russell's state of mind appeared to swing between agitation and cheerful stoicism — some reports indicating that he was very much at his ease. Martha McTier in a letter to her sister-in-law claimed that he had 'asked for all his friends, was cheerful and easy, even to gaiety, talked of the news of the day, the politics of Europe, etc. and on some one point (possibly your account of peace) said he supposed they would have his head off before that'. It seems that Russell's charm worked its usual effect even on his captors — McTier noting that 'the officers who guarded him, the man who took him, even Sirr, Osborne, the judge, etc. never tire of his praise'.[39] Similarly, Mary Ann McCracken reported that Russell's 'composure, dignity and firmness' during his last days 'commanded the esteem, admiration and astonishment of all who beheld him ... [They] found themselves attached to him by an extraordinary and irresistible impulse, such as they had never felt for any man before. Even those who had been most active in pursuing him to death now launch out in his praise'.[40]

Nevertheless, for some who had known Russell, his behaviour in the last months of his life, especially his hopeless attempt to raise the North, could only be explained by the fact that he had become mentally unbalanced. Some years later William Sampson accused the government of turning Russell's 'once gentle heart...to desperate madness' by imprisoning him without trial for almost six years. Martha McTier admitted after his death that 'in his late confinement it was not to be wondered at that such a mind as his might have grown even flighty'.[41] But behaviour that appeared redolent of madness to some contemporaries has to be seen in the light of Russell's millennialist expectations, and in the last weeks of Russell's life these were never far from the surface. After Russell had received communion in Kilmainham, 'with apparently great devotion', the clergyman who attended him reported that he had declared:

> In the awful presence of God and at his holy table I acknowledge myself to have been guilty of many immoral acts, many impieties and negligences of sacred duties, but as to political opinions and political actions I have ever been guided by what reason, the result of deep meditation and laboured reflection have shown me to be right. I never intended by what I have politically done other than the advantage of my fellow creatures and even the happiness of my adversaries. Whether the Lord shall be pleased to extend my life for forty years or to cut my thread of existence in an hour I shall not cease from the work I have begun nor give it up but with life itself.'... He then in the cant of the enthusiast began to speak of the kingdom of Jesus, [and] the fulfilling of the prophecies relating to the bringing home of the Jews, which he said was now commencing, that the French arms were the instruments God would use for the purpose. For that nation (as the Romans had done, before Christ's appearance in the flesh finished their conquest of the civilised world) would in like manner subdue the whole earth. He pointed out a mistranslation in the epistle of the Hebrews...objecting to the 'end of the world' and showing from the Greek testament it should be to the 'end of the age'.[42]

While imprisoned in Downpatrick he informed Trevor that 'the present state of Europe, her statesmen admit, is awful and unprecedented... These mighty changes they seek vainly to account for from the policy or power of nations, but they would find them written in the records of heaven'.[43] He was also most anxious to complete and publish a millennialist tract in his last days. When sentenced to death, he requested that he be given three days to complete a work that he believed might be 'of some advantage to the world'. It seems that this was to be a commentary on one of Francis Dobbs's millennialist tracts and he also intended to produce a translation from the Greek of the Book of Revelations to clarify that work's millennial significance.[44]

Russell believed that he had simply played his allotted part in this 'awful and unprecedented' age. He regarded himself as a 'soldier of the Lord Jesus Christ',[45] whose duty it was to promote 'the cause of virtue and liberty'. He believed that this cause would eventually triumph and should he die fighting for it he was certain that God would 'in eternal life reward those who laboured for the welfare and happiness of mankind'.[46] For several years his mind had been gripped by the conviction that his purpose in life was to devote himself to securing his country's liberation and that success or martyrdom would be his reward. An 'enthusiast' he certainly was, and no one can say for certain where fanaticism ends and madness begins, but the statements he prepared for the government, his letters to friends and his replies to McNally's probing do not appear to be those of a madman. Moreover, he did not lapse into messianic fantasies, as sometimes happened to those obsessed by scriptural prophecy; rather he invariably claimed to be no more than a human agent acting in accordance with what he believed was God's will. That said, there seems little doubt that his millennialist zeal had seriously impaired his judgement during the last two or three years of his life. Drennan was probably closest to the mark when in 1802, on hearing that Russell had still not given up hopes of effecting another rebellion, he concluded that 'long imprisonment and perpetual recurrence to the same ideas makes enthusiasm turn into a partial insanity.'[47]

The government decided to set up a special commission to try those arrested in connection with the disturbances in Antrim and Down. Russell could have been tried in Dublin for his breach of the banishment act but the authorities initially decided that since his treasonable activities in the North could be easily proven, it would be better to try him there, and in doing so comply with the wishes of Ulster loyalists to make an example of him. In the unlikely event of his being acquitted in the North, he could then be brought back to

Dublin and tried on the banishment offence.[48] The decision to move him north was given some impetus by the government's discovery that plans were afoot to help him escape from Kilmainham. The ever loyal Mary Ann McCracken, operating through a Dublin contact in the textile trade named James Orr, had passed on to Russell about £200 to bribe his jailer. Orr was hopeful that the attempt would succeed but the jailer notified the authorities and the attempt came to nothing.[49] On 12 October Russell was taken without warning to Downpatrick under a strong military escort and served with his indictment for high treason. The government was taking no chances of any disturbances and a brigade of light infantry under General Archibald Campbell, 600 yeomanry and a troop of regular cavalry were sent to Downpatrick to stand guard during the trial.[50]

Martha McTier still continued to hope that he might be saved and pleaded with her brother to do what he could on his behalf: 'if an eloquent and pathetic pen could secretly affect any one heart that had the power, or could reach those who had, in favour of the unfortunate and accomplished Russell, even to gain transportation, how delightful must the feeling of that man be!' She hoped that one of Russell's influential acquaintances such as the former member of parliament, Francis Dobbs, or one of the Knox family, or a former army colleague, could be persuaded to apply to the authorities to have his sentence mitigated on the grounds of his long imprisonment without trial.[51]

Russell fully expected to be found guilty and executed. Throughout his career the prospect of martyrdom never seems to have been far from his mind. Many years before, in response to Mary Ann McCracken's observation to her brother and Russell that if the United Irishmen failed they would forfeit their lives, Russell had commented 'of what consequence are our lives, or the lives of a few individuals, compared to the liberty and happiness of Ireland'.[52] Some verse he wrote in Fort George in 1800 displayed a similar willingness for self-sacrifice:

> *May the power that rules all grant this ardent request,*
> *May we live our dear country triumphant to see;*
> *Or if this is too great, and it so judges best,*
> *May our deaths, like our lives, serve dear Ireland to free!*[53]

In the final days of his life, he spoke with admiration of Emmet's death, an event he looked on 'with rapture'. He maintained that 'there were as many tears shedding for Emmet as would bathe him

and that he would be considered by the people as a martyr'.[54] Before
his trial he informed friends that he had no intention of offering any
defence of his actions and he refused their offers to pay for legal
representation. He was, however, persuaded that some of his followers awaiting trial might benefit if his case was conducted properly
and he eventually agreed that counsel should be hired and prosecution witnesses cross-examined. Once again, it was Mary Ann
McCracken who raised the required funds. She retained as defence
counsel her cousin Henry Joy and a Counsellor Bell, who demanded
£100 each, and also employed James Ramsay, of the Belfast firm
Ramsay and Garrett, as attorney; Ramsay refused to accept a fee.[55]

Before his trial Russell wrote a letter of thanks to the McCracken
family, probably smuggled out to them by a friend. As well as
expressing his sincere gratitude towards them, he again strongly reiterated his belief that his cause would eventually succeed:

> To the more than friendship I owe to you and your sister it is impos-
> sible to be sufficiently grateful... I would not wish you to make an
> attempt to see me, which would be fruitless and could only serve to
> draw suspicion on you and your family. As to me, I shall only say that
> to the last moment of my liberty I was not thinking for myself or
> acting for myself but for my country, and though what I was engaged
> in with the immortal hero who has fallen is considered as perhaps
> wild, yet I could show and it will be showed that the failure was alone
> surprising. With some of the reasons I am still unacquainted. The
> government have I am sure made a point of my death. If it is to take
> place I wish to make it as useful to the cause that I lived for and your
> brother and so many have died... I perfectly know that not a hair of
> my head is in the power of man without the permission of God and
> am perfectly resigned to his pleasure. He can and perhaps may deliver
> me, but whatever he wills is best... I have no wish to die... but had I
> a thousand lives I would willingly risk or loose them in it and be
> assured liberty will in the midst of these storms be established.[56]

Russell's trial began at 10 a.m. on 20 October and lasted until 8 p.m.
He was charged with high treason, the indictment accusing him of
reading 'compassing and imagining the king's death and conspiring
to levy war against the king'. Though the odds were stacked against
him, Henry Joy made a resourceful and vigorous defence of his
client. He had no sympathy whatsoever with Russell's politics but,
as he came to know him, he claimed that 'he never in his life felt so
interested for any man'.[57] The defence tried to object that the statute

under which Russell was being tried was an English one, passed before the act of union, and therefore was not binding on an Irish subject. Joy also objected that although the prosecution sought to link Russell's activities in Ulster with Emmet's rebellion in Dublin, because the 'overt act' of insurrection had not taken place within Co. Down, then the special commission was exceeding its jurisdiction. Both objections were overruled by the court. There was little else that his counsel could do since Russell refused to allow anyone to be summoned to testify on his behalf. Since he had broken the terms of the banishment act Russell considered himself honour bound not to offer any defence of his actions, especially if it might involve implicating others.[58]

The prosecution produced numerous witnesses to prove that an attempt at insurrection had taken place in Dublin on 23 July and that Russell had done his utmost to incite people in the North to aid it. Most of these appeared willingly but some, such as Patrick Lynch of Loughinisland, his former Irish teacher, testified reluctantly, ending his evidence with the words 'I had a regard for the man; he was my friend'. Several witnesses — James Fitzpatrick of Loughinisland, Patrick Renaghan of Clough, and Patrick Doran, John Keenan and Henry Smith of Annadorn — testified that they had actually been present when Russell was attempting to incite insurrection. The last witness called was Major Sirr who testified that he had arrested Russell as he attempted to pull pistols on him.[59] Given the evidence against him there could only be one outcome. For the sake of decency the jury retired for five minutes and then delivered the verdict of guilty. Russell was then allowed address the court. Joy had seen the original speech that he had prepared and advised him to tone it down, as it was 'too political' and he would never be allowed read it. That which he actually delivered was described as 'eloquent and energetic, though rather unconnected'.[60] It showed him to be unbowed and unrepentant, proud of his political actions and still insisting that government and aristocracy should mend their ways before they were brought to account:

> I look back to the last thirteen years of my life, the period in which I have interfered with the transactions of Ireland, with entire satisfaction, though for my share in them I am now about to die ... My death, perhaps, may be useful in deterring others from following my example. It may serve as a memorial to others and, on trying occasions, it may inspire them with courage. I can now say as far as my

judgement enabled me, I acted for the good of the country and of the world...To me it is plain that all thing are verging towards a change when all shall be of one opinion. In ancient times we read of great empires having their rise and their fall, and yet do the old governments proceed as if they were immortal. From the time I could observe and reflect, I perceived that there were two kinds of laws, the laws of the state and the laws of God, frequently clashing with each other; by the latter I have always endeavoured to regulate my conduct, but that laws of the former kind do exist in Ireland I believe no one who hears me can deny. That such laws have existed, in former times, many and various examples clearly evince. The saviour of the world, Christ, suffered by the Roman laws; by the same [laws] his apostles were put to the torture and deprived of their lives, in his cause.

By my conduct I do not consider that I have incurred any moral guilt. I have committed no moral evil. I do not want the many and bright examples of those who have gone before me, but did I want this encouragement the recent example of a youthful hero, a martyr in the cause of liberty, who had just died for his country, would inspire me...He was surrounded by everything which could endear the world to him, in the bloom of youth, with fond attachments, and with all the fascinating charms of youth and innocence. To his death I look back, even in this state, with rapture.

I have travelled much and seen various parts of the world, and I think the Irish the most virtuous nation on the face of the earth — they are a good and brave people, and had I a thousand lives, I would yield them in their service. If it be the will of God that I suffer for that with which I am charged, I am perfectly resigned to submit to his holy will and dispensation but, I know that unless he wills it, not a hair on my head can be touched. As the soldier of the Lord Jesus Christ I will bow me down to whatever I may be ordained to undergo in this mortal world...

Before I depart from this, for a better world, I wish to address myself to the landed aristocracy of this country...I see around me many who, during the last years of my life, have disseminated principles for which I now am to die. Those gentlemen who have all the wealth and power of the country in their hands, I strongly and earnestly exhort, to pay attention to the poor — by the poor I mean the labouring class of the community, their tenantry and dependants. I advise them, for their good, to look into their grievances, to sympathise in their distress, and to spread comfort and happiness around their dwellings. It is possible that they may not hold their power long, but at all events, to attend to the wants and distresses of the poor is their true interest. If they hold their power they will thus have friends around them, if they lose it, their fall will be gentle, and I am sure unless they act thus, they never can be happy.

I shall now appeal to the right honourable gentleman in whose hands the lives of the other prisoners are and entreat that he will rest satisfied with my death and let that atone for those errors into which I may have been supposed to have deluded others ... [61]

The judge, Baron George, then gave his closing address; he lamented that Russell:

had not been endowed with better principles and a better heart than that which he had lately, as well as on former occasions, manifested; and expressed his most anxious wish that [he] would employ the little time he would have in this world in making his peace with God and in endeavouring to atone for the incalculable miseries his crimes and infatuated conduct had brought, and will yet bring, upon not a few members of that community of which he himself was once a worthy and deservedly esteemed member. [62]

The judge then pronounced sentence. Russell was to be hanged and, in accordance with the penalty for high treason, beheaded. He listened to the passing of sentence with great composure. He had made two requests in his speech from the dock: that he be given three days for the completion of a literary work 'possibly of some advantage to the world', and that his remains should be buried with his parents at the Royal Hospital, Kilmainham. Neither was granted. [63]

The literary work he referred to was a commentary on Francis Dobbs' interpretation of the Book of Revelations. But the authorities were rather more concerned about the second coming of the French than the second coming of Christ and suspected that Russell sought the extra three days only to allow time for a French invasion that might save his life. Apparently the judge dismissed Russell's request for extra time to work on his commentary on Revelations by claiming that if was to allow him enough time to make the Book of Revelations intelligible, then he would probably live as long as anyone else in the courtroom. But the desire to finish this work particularly preoccupied Russell — on the day of his execution he again requested time to compete it, and was again refused. He then entrusted the uncompleted manuscript to Dr Edward Trevor, with instructions that it should be given to his sister, but she never received it. [64]

The execution was set for the following day. Russell's journal entry from 1793 gives some indication as to how he might have viewed his approaching fate. Having heard of the terrified behaviour of the disgraced French general, Custine, approaching the guillotine, he noted that he was 'much shocked at it...a man who braved death in the field to be so timid on the scaffold...I am certainly more affected than by anything I have long heard...Let all men look only hereafter for their rewards and then the guillotine will have no terrors'.[65] On the morning of 21 October 1803 the town sheriff came to his cell in Downpatrick jail to conduct him to the place of execution where a large crowd had gathered. Russell told him 'that he was quite ready. He received the sacrament twice and went with him, bowed to some gentlemen he passed and gave them his good wishes'. He passed through the prison yard where the coffin of brown boards provided by his friends had lain since the previous night. Because the period between the passing and carrying out of the sentence was so short there had only been time to construct a makeshift scaffold — some planks were placed over a couple of barrels at the main gateway of the jail and a crossbeam placed above them. By the gate there was also a sack of sawdust, a block, an axe and a knife. Russell climbed the platform and said loudly to the assembled crowd: 'I forgive my persecutors. I die in peace with all mankind and I hope for mercy through the merits of my redeemer, Jesus Christ'. He turned to those who were attending him and gave them his blessing, and then 'directed the hangman in his office and put the rope round his neck himself'. He was then hanged and after a few minutes cut down and beheaded, and his severed head displayed to the watching crowd. His remains were then taken through a narrow lane between high stone walls connecting the jail with Downpatrick Church of Ireland graveyard and hurriedly buried there.[66]

When she heard the news of Russell's death and of how he had behaved Martha McTier reflected: 'Gordon saw the book and the letter he left for his sister — affectionate and grateful and religious. Enthusiastic he did indeed appear...I rejoice in it — that whatever it was — enthusiasm, fortitude or error — that it bore him up to the last. Few, few have I known like him'.[67] Wickham admitted that Russell had 'behaved with firmness and propriety' at the end. Before his execution he offered to make a full disclosure of his plan of insurrection without implicating any named individuals, if the lives of his followers were spared. But the authorities were in no mood to trade lives for a vague confession and probably now believed that they had been overly lenient to do so in 1798.[68] The special commission went on to secure convictions of high treason against Corry and Drake, Russell's lieutenants in Co. Down, and against Andrew Hunter and William Porter, who had been active in Carnmoney, in Co. Antrim. All four were executed. The authorities were well pleased with their work. 'Our commission has been most effective', wrote the attorney general to Dublin Castle, 'I think I may venture to assure you that a very general and favourable impression has been made upon all ranks of people . . . and that all classes and sects may look with equal confidence to an inflexible and impartial administration of the law'.[69]

There was a sad inevitability about Russell's violent death on the scaffold. He was a man who hated injustice with a consuming passion, whether its victim was the African slave, the Polish patriot, the English factory worker or the Irish peasant. In an age where politics was often characterised by corruption and élitism, he held firmly to the idealistic conviction that its real business should be the happiness and welfare of ordinary people. Not surprisingly, he considered all those political arrangements he came in contact with — in Ireland, in Britain or in France — as variations of tyranny. Even had he lived to see the independence of Ireland established, deep disillusionment would probably have lain in store for him. It is very difficult to see how any government of the day could have satisfied Russell's millennialist expectations: after successful revolutions, few states have shown any inclination to wither away and allow the laws of God to operate in a political vacuum, as Russell would have wished.

His unflinching idealism and millennialist enthusiasm formed a dangerous concoction that was always likely to have fatal consequences for him. Had Russell been at liberty in 1798 then he would almost certainly have shared the fate of Tone and McCracken. As it was, imprisonment and exile merely postponed the day of reckoning. There were many United Irishmen who were prepared to sacrifice their lives, but few embraced their fate as readily as Russell, whose rigid millennialist convictions drove him relentlessly towards martyrdom.

NOTES

1 Nelly Rabb to Mary Ann McCracken, 18 Nov. 1843 (Madden papers, 873/627); Madden, *United Irishmen*, 3rd ser, ii, 218; examinations of Daniel Muley, 10 Sept. 1803 (Reb. papers, 620/11/138/14) and 5 Apr. 1805 (SOC papers, 3632).

2 Examination of Muley, 5 Apr. 1805 (SOC papers, 3632); Helen Landreth, *The pursuit of Robert Emmet* (Dublin, 1949), pp. 308–9; for official suspicions of Muley see Emerson to Sirr, 9 Sept. 1803 (Reb. papers, 620/67/63).
3 Drennan to Martha McTier, 12 Sept. 1803 (*Drennan letters*, p. 328).
4 J. A. Russell to Madden, n.d. (Madden papers, 873/674, f. 5).
5 J. A. Russell to Madden, n.d. (Madden papers, 873/674, f. 5); Madden, *United Irishmen*, 3rd ser., ii, 227.
6 James Kelly, *Henry Grattan* (Dublin, 1993) pp. 35–6; Hardwicke to Pelham, 7 Aug. 1803 (P.R.O., HO 100/112/158–61); Henry Grattan to Revd. Edward Berwick, 25 July 1803 (Henry Grattan jun., *Memoirs of the life and times of the Rt. Hon. Henry Grattan* (London, 1846), v, 223–4).
7 *Dublin Evening Post*, 10 Sept. 1803; Emerson to Sirr, 9 Sept. 1803 (Reb. papers, 620/67/63); *Observations on the arrest of the late General Russell by Verax* (Dublin, 1804), p. 11.
8 Madden, *United Irishmen*, 2nd ser., (2nd edn, Dublin, 1858), pp. 274–5; Helen Landreth, *The pursuit of Robert Emmet* (Dublin, 1949), p. 309; Cox was also an author of a pamphlet on the dispute over the division of the reward money between Sirr and Emerson (Watty Cox, *Remarks by one of the people to whom John Swift Emerson has appealed* (Dublin, 1804)).
9 *Observations on the arrest of the late General Russell by Verax* (Dublin, 1804), p. 11; J. T. Gilbert, *A history of the city of Dublin* (Dublin, 1861), ii, 29–30.
10 Madden, *United Irishmen*, 3rd ser., ii, 232.
11 *Dublin Evening Post*, 10 Sept. 1803.
12 Sirr to Wickham, 8 Nov. 1803, William Smith to Marsden, 24 Oct. 1803 (Reb. papers, 620/67/73; 620/67/79); Wickham to Thomas Kemmis, 28 Oct. 1803 (Frazer MS II/131); *Observations on the arrest of the late General Russell by Verax* (Dublin, 1804); *Remarks by one of the people to whom John Swift Emerson has appealed* (Dublin, 1804); Madden, *United Irishmen*, 3rd ser., ii, 231–7.
13 Wickham to R. P. Carew, 10 Sept. 1803 (P.R.O., HO 100/113/87).
14 Castlereagh to Marsden, 23 Sept. 1803 (Reb. papers, 620/11/160/30).
15 Foster to Marsden, 11 Sept. 1803 (S.O.C. papers, 3521); John Beresford to W. J. Beresford, 14 Sept. 1803 (S.O.C. papers, 1025/75).
16 George III to Harwicke, 14 Sept. 1803 (B.L., Hardwicke papers, Add. MS 35703, f. 125).
17 W. Skeffington, Belfast, to Marsden, 12 Sept. 1803 (Reb. papers, 620/67/74); McGucken to Marsden, 13 Sept. 1803 (Reb. papers, 620/10/121/15); Matthew Forde, Seaforde, to Dublin Castle, 25 Sept. 1803 (Reb. papers, 620/12/141/22).
18 John Finegan, *Anne Devlin: patriot and heroine* (Dublin, 1992), pp. 91–3; Finegan's information is based on the Luke Cullen papers.
19 Wickham to R. P. Carew, 10 Sept. 1803 (P.R.O., HO 100/113/87).
20 MacDonagh, *Viceroy's postbag*, p. 421; for Trevor, see Helen Landreth, *The pursuit of Robert Emmet* (Dublin, 1949), p. 295.
21 Russell's statement to Trevor, 27 Sept. 1803 (P.R.O., HO 100/114/11–12).
22 Hardwicke to Charles Yorke, 11 Oct. 1803 (P.R.O. HO 100/118/57–60); Hardwicke mentions a figure of twenty-two executions; there were five hanged for their part in the northern rebellion.
23 Reported conversation between Russell and McNally, 24 Sept. 1803 (P.R.O., HO 100/113/195–8) and also 6 Oct. 1803 (P.R.O., HO 100/114/121–2).
24 Russell's statement to Trevor, 27 Sept. 1803 (P.R.O., HO 100/114/11–12); for similar views expressed to McNally, see Russell's statement, 5 Oct. 1803 (P.R.O., HO 100/114/119–20).
25 Reminiscences of James Hope (Hope papers, 7253/1, f. 3); evidence of Patrick Lynch, *Belfast News Letter*, 25 Oct. 1803.

26 Marsden to William Smith, 24 Oct. 1803 (Reb. papers, 620/67/79); William Knox to Sirr, 31 May 1804 (Sirr papers 869/2, f. 39). Wickham's account of the arrest made no reference to any hesitation on Russell's behalf, but claimed that he was secured 'under circumstances of great personal danger by the address and intrepidy of Major Sirr. He had a pistol cocked in his right hand which Major Sirr seized; he then pulled out another with his left and was almost in the act of shooting the major with it when it was knocked out of his hand by one of the major's followers'. (Wickham to Carew, 9 Sept. 1803 (P.R.O. HO 100/113/49).

27 Russell to McNally, 24 Sept. 1803 (P.R.O., HO 100/113/195–8).

28 Russell's statement, Downpatrick, 17 Oct. 1803 (MacDonagh, *Viceroy's postbag,* pp. 424–6); Russell to McNally, 5 Oct. 1803 (P.R.O., HO 100/114/119–20); Russell to Trevor, 27 Sept. 1803 (P.R.O., HO 100/114/11–12).

29 Russell's statement, Downpatrick, 17 Oct. 1803 (MacDonagh, *Viceroy's postbag*, pp. 424–6).

30 McNally's report, 24 Sept. 1803 (P.R.O., HO 100/113/195–8).

31 Wickham to King, 25 Sept. 1803 (P.R.O., HO 100/113/191–4); italics as in the original.

32 McNally's report of a conversation with Russell, 24 Sept. 1803 (P.R.O., HO 100/113/195–8).

33 Statement of Thomas Russell, (copy) 2 Oct. 1803 (P.R.O., HO 100/114/9–10).

34 Examination of John Russell, (P.R.O., HO 100/113/143–6); Wickham to Carew, 2 Oct. 1803 (ibid., 100/114/5–7); Wickham to King, 24 Oct. 1803 (ibid., 100/114/113); examination of James Farrell, 24 Oct. 1803 (ibid., 100/114/23); John Russell to Richard Ford, 1 Nov. 1803, Chathham barracks (P.R.O., P.C. 1/3583).

35 Wickham to R. P. Carew, 2 Oct. 1803 (P.R.O., HO 100/114/5–7).

36 Trevor to Wickham, Downpatrick, 18 Oct. 1803 (MacDonagh, *Viceroy's postbag*, pp. 423–4).

37 Madden, *United Irishmen*, 3rd ser., ii, 232.

38 Russell to McNally, 5–6 Oct. 1803 (P.R.O., HO 100//114/119–22).

39 Martha McTier to Mrs Sarah Drennan, c. Oct. 1803 , after 21 Oct. 1803 (*Drennan letters*, pp. 330, 332).

40 Mary Ann McCracken to Margaret Russell, Nov. 1803 [?], (Madden papers, 873/646).

41 *Memoirs of William Sampson* (New York, 1807), p. 359; see also W. C. Taylor, *History of Ireland . . . with additions by William Sampson* (New York, 1833), ii, 325; Martha McTier to Sarah Drennan, Oct. 1803 (*Drennan letters*, p. 331).

42 Revd. Forster Archer to —, Kilmainham, 3 Oct. 1803 (Reb. papers, 620/50/21).

43 Russell's statement to Trevor, 27 Sept. 1803 (P.R.O., HO 100/114/11–12).

44 Russell's speech from the dock, 20 Oct. 1803 (Madden papers, 873/700, f. 3); *Castlereagh corr.*, iv, 271; Marsden's account of the insurrection of 1803 (*Emmet memoir*, ii, 98); Mary Ann McCracken to Madden, 2 July 1844 (Madden papers, 873/155).

45 Russell's trial speech (Madden papers, 873/700, f. 2).

46 Russell to —, 5 June 1802 (Madden papers, 873/673).

47 Drennan to Martha McTier, 26 June 1802 (Drennan papers, T765/986).

48 Hardwicke to Yorke, 21 Sept. 1803 (B.L., Hardwicke papers, Add. MS 35770, f. 120); Hardwicke to Portland, 24 Sept. 1803 (MacDonagh, *Viceroy's postbag*, p. 423); Wickham to R. P. Carew, 2 Oct. 1803 (P.R.O., HO 100/114/5–7).

49 Mary Ann McCracken to Madden, 2 Feb. 1859 (Madden papers, 873/80); see also correspondence between James Orr, Dublin, and Mary Ann McCracken, 1, 8, 13 Oct. 1803 (Madden papers, 873/683–4, 695).

50 *Belfast News Letter*, 14 Oct. 1803; Madden, *United Irishmen*, 3rd ser., ii, 252.
51 Martha McTier to Drennan, 9 Oct. 1803 (Drennan papers, T765/1062).
52 Madden, *United Irishmen*, 3rd ser., ii, 281.
53 R. R. Madden, *Literary remains of the United Irishmen* (Dublin, 1887), p. 284.
54 Russell's trial speech (Madden papers, 873/700); Russell to McNally, 5 Oct. 1803 (P.R.O., HO 100/114/119–20).
55 Mary Ann McCracken to Madden, 2 Feb. 1859 (Madden papers, 873/80); James Ramsay, Downpatrick, to [Mary Ann McCracken], 19 [Oct.] 1803 (Madden papers, 873/696); Mary Ann McCracken's memories of Russell's trial (Madden papers, 873/672); C. E. B. Brett, *Long shadows cast before* (Edinburgh and London, 1978), p. 92.
56 Russell to Frank McCracken, Oct. 1803 (copy) (Madden papers, 873/642).
57 W. M. Medland and Charles Weobly, *A collection of remarkable and interesting criminal trials* (London, 1803), ii, 47; Mary Ann McCracken's memories of Russell's trial (Madden papers, 873/672).
58 Charles Ruthven (Crown solicitor, Downpatrick) to Madden, 17 Jan. 1837 (Madden papers, 873/671); *Dublin Evening Post*, 22 Oct. 1803; Russell's trial speech (Madden papers, 873/700, f. 1).
59 *Belfast News Letter*, 25 Oct. 1803; Cathal O'Byrne, *As I roved out in Belfast and district* (Dublin, 1946), p. 388; *The trial of Thomas Russell, general in the late insurrection* (Dublin, 1803).
60 Madden papers, 873/700, f. 3v; *Dublin Evening Post*, 22 Oct. 1803.
61 Russell's trial speech (Madden papers, 873/700); this version of the speech was taken from notes of Russell's trial found in the papers of James Ramsay of the Belfast solicitors Ramsay and Garrett retained for Russell's defence (Madden, *United Irishmen*, 3rd ser., ii, 260).
62 W. M. Medland and Charles Weobly, *A collection of remarkable and interesting criminal trials* (London, 1803), ii, 47.
63 *Dublin Evening Post*, 22 Oct. 1803; Russell's trial speech (Madden papers, 873/700).
64 Wickham to King, 24 Oct. 1803 (P.R.O., HO 100/114/111); Wickham to Pole Carew, 24 Oct. 1803 (MacDonagh, *Viceroy's postbag*, pp. 426–7). There is some doubt as to what happened to the manuscript: Mary Ann McCracken heard that it had fallen in the hands of John Dubourdieu, rector of Annahil, Co. Down whose father, Saumarez Dubourdieu kept a classical school at Lisburn; James Rose Cleland stated that it was held by James McClelland, solicitor general in 1803 (Madden, *United Irishmen*, 3rd ser., ii, 274).
65 Russell's journal, 9 Sept. 1793 (*Journals*, p. 123).
66 Notes by J. A. Russell (Madden papers, 873/674, ff 3v–4v); Martha McTier to Mrs Sarah Drennan, Oct. 1803 (*Drennan letters*, p. 331); Cathal O'Byrne, *As I roved out in Belfast and district* (Dublin, 1946), pp. 389–90.
67 Martha McTier to Sarah Drennan, Oct. 1803 (*Drennan letters*, p. 331).
68 Wickham to King, 24 Oct. 1803 (P.R.O., HO 100/114/111); Wickham to Pole Carew, 24 Oct. 1803 (MacDonagh, *Viceroy's postbag*, pp. 426–7).
69 *Belfast News Letter*, 28 Oct., 1 Nov. 1803; Standish O'Grady to Wickham, 23 Oct. 1803 (P.R.O., HO 100/118/133).

CHAPTER SIXTEEN

Legacy

Russell was the last well-known United Irishman to be executed in Ireland but he faded rapidly from public memory. For many years after his death there was a reluctance to recall the deeds of such men, and the first account of Russell's life did not appear until 1830. Written by James Morgan and based on materials supplied by Mary Ann McCracken, it claimed that of all the United Irishmen 'the memory of none has suffered more from prejudice and misconception than that of the amiable and unfortunate Russell', and sought to redress the balance by showing him in a sympathetic light. Morgan's account was reasonably accurate but, as R. R. Madden noted, too short to give any real insight into Russell's character.[1]

This was followed six years later by Samuel McSkimin's 'Secret history of the insurrection of 1803', which portrayed Russell as a brooding, unstable zealot, veering between 'the gloomy zeal of the fanatic and the piety of the saint'.[2] One of the few surviving participants in the events of 1803, James Hope, was quick to contradict the details of McSkimin's account and described the entire article as 'a malicious fabrication...calculated to lead the future historian astray'.[3] Captain James A. Russell, son of Thomas's brother John, was another who was highly offended; he wrote to the publication's editor demanding to be allowed publish a refutation.[4] He also began to correspond with Madden and John Gray, editor of the *Freeman's Journal*, to provide them with materials to contradict some of the allegations made. Though much of the McSkimin article was spurious, James Russell, in his zeal to portray his uncle in the best possible light, countered McSkimin's inaccuracies with some of his own. He completely denied Russell's human failings, such as his heavy drinking, claiming that his uncle was 'so opposed to drinking that he used to be teased as a temperance man'. The figure of the dissipated and anguished 'P. P.' recorded in Tone's journals he dismissed as a fabrication and castigated Tone for portraying someone 'proverbial for his very strict religious feelings and sobriety... in the light of a man of loose morals and a habitual drunkard'. He accused Tone of attempting to denigrate the character of his friend so that he could claim complete credit for the founding of the United Irishmen.[5]

Madden duly published his memoir of Russell in 1846, based mainly on material given to him by Mary Ann McCracken, Hope and James Russell.[6] For the most part it accorded Russell the usual hagiographic treatment given by Madden to leading United Irishmen. Russell's dissolute tendencies were whitewashed and certain of his characteristics, which might have supported accusations of fanaticism, were smoothed over. For example, some of the more explicit millennialist references in his trial speech were edited out in the published version.[7] But Madden was not blind to Russell's faults and his overall assessment was judicious in many respects:

> Russell was not a man of transcendent talents; he was not a man calculated to guide, and control, and direct the affairs of a national movement... to a successful issue. Men like Russell, of exalted notions of honour, of purity of principle, of unswerving integrity... of great hopes in the justice of their cause, and of enthusiastic expectations of its success, these are the men whose blood brings forth in due time the buds and blossoms of liberty; they seem ordered to be its martyrs, and not the master spirits who are permitted to lead its followers into the promised land.[8]

Madden's memoir did not herald any great upsurge of interest in Russell, and in the 1840s the Young Irelander Charles Gavan Duffy lamented that most Ulster Presbyterians 'knew no more of Tone and Russell than of the Gracchi'.[9] There was to be no cult surrounding Russell. In many ways this is surprising — he possessed many qualities that would seem to mark him down for inclusion in the pantheon of Irish nationalist saints: his attractive personality, well-attested to by friends and enemies alike; his personal courage and integrity; his hatred of all forms of injustice; his deeply religious nature; his strong pro-Catholic sympathies; his interest in Gaelic culture; his respect and admiration for the Irish common people; and his unswerving devotion to the ideals of the United Irishmen. His career may have ended in fiasco but, as the cult that grew up around Emmet and later nationalist martyrs would show, abject failure could just as easily be a spur to canonisation as an obstacle to it. Then there was the manner in which Russell went to his death:

according to his nephew, on stepping out into the place of execution, Russell uttered the words 'is this the place?'[10] Even on the admission of the authorities, he went to his death with courage and serenity, and readily forgave those who were about to hang him. Attended with these Christ-like resonances, Russell's death would have readily lent itself to the redemption through sacrifice interpretation that was to become part of the nationalist tradition.

Cults, however, need to be fostered. The foundations of the cult of Wolfe Tone were laid in 1826 by his son's publication of Tone's journals, a classic of the genre, and his name was kept in the public eye through the efforts of his strong-minded and dedicated widow until her death in 1849.[11] Russell's fragmentary and near-illegible journals were not to be published until almost two hundred years after his death and, although a valuable historical source, they have little of the flow and panache of Tone's. In the case of Robert Emmet, there was his poignant romance with Sarah Curran and the pen of his friend Thomas Moore to focus public interest on his life. Moreover, both Tone and Emmet lent their names to particular examples of stirring oratory that became enshrined in the nationalist tradition. Tone's 'to substitute the common name of Irishman in place of the denomination of Protestant, Catholic and Dissenter...' and Emmet's eloquent speech from the dock captured the imagination of later Irish nationalists and help ensure their authors' places in posterity. But Russell produced no such memorable statements. Moreover, unlike Tone and Emmet, he lacked an assiduous and discriminating promoter of his memory. His nephew, Captain James Russell, did make some efforts to promote his reputation, but did so by promoting a rather one-dimensional view of this complex man. In any event he died before his efforts had any real chance to bear fruit.

Therefore, although many who had known Russell continued to cherish his memory, his name drifted into obscurity. For many years his only memorial was to be the simple inscribed stone slab laid by his Belfast friends over his grave in Downpatrick churchyard.[12] In 1953 a memorial was raised near his birthplace at Drommahane, Co. Cork, by Eoin O'Mahony, the Cork genealogist and broadcaster. As for literary memorials, he has been the subject of only two poems (as far as I am aware): James Gilland's little-known 'The grave of Russell', written in 1804; and the more popular 'The man from God-knows-where', attributed to an Ulsterwoman, Florence Mary Wilson, and published in a collection in 1918.[13]

Historical cults tend to be self-perpetuating. Once figures emerge from the anonymity of the past they are likely to be the focus of further attention, favourable or otherwise, which can only serve to raise their profile. But if the catalyst that sparks the initial emergence is lacking, then the likelihood is that they will remain in obscurity. This was to be the case with Russell, who did not feature prominently among the nationalist heroes whose reputations were promoted, and ultimately established, by the Young Irelanders. Although Charles Gavan Duffy and a number of colleagues made a pilgrimage to Russell's grave in Downpatrick, even they appear to have known little of the details of his life — describing him as 'the Protestant patriot of '98'.[14] It is ironic indeed that these romantic cultural nationalists neglected the memory of perhaps the most romantically-minded of all the United Irishmen, and one moreover with an interest in Gaelic culture. Similarly, when socially-radical nationalists, such as John Mitchel and Liam Mellows, sought precedents for social revolution, they invoked Tone's 'men of no property' remarks and seem to have been unaware of Russell's more advanced views.[15] Even James Connolly, who lauded the radicalism of United Irishmen such as Napper Tandy, Thomas Addis Emmet and Henry Joy McCracken, and singled out the events of July 1803 as a 'proletarian' rising, omitted to mention the part played in it by Russell, or Russell's desire for radical social change.[16] For most Irish nationalists, the 1803 rising would simply be remembered for the martyrdom of Robert Emmet. As Owen Dudley Edwards has noted, Russell's advocacy of social reform as part of the revolutionary programme of 1803 'has been overshadowed in the popular memory of the Emmet insurrection by the much simpler and more emotionally charged message and image of Emmet himself'.[17]

In terms of twentieth-century historical writing, Russell has fared somewhat better than he has in the popular memory. He featured prominently in a number of works published from the late 1930s to the early 1960s, and was the subject of a scholarly biography written in Irish by Séamus Mac Giolla Easpaig, a Belfast Christian Brother.[18] Mac Giolla Easpaig's work takes a sympathetic view of Russell, is strongly based on primary sources and gives a generally judicious account of his life. However, it largely ignores the importance of millenialism is shaping Russell's career.

Partly due to the painstaking work of Dr Christopher Woods, who has edited and published Russell's journals, making an almost illegible source easily accessible, recent years have seen a strong revival of interest in Russell with the publication of several works which have

raised his historical profile, including the publication of a full length
biography — Denis Carroll's *The man from God knows where*, a
work that provides a useful survey of Russell's life, but does little to
illuminate his complex character and motivation.[19] Other works have
recognised his role as a leading social radical and propagandist
among the United Irishmen and acknowledged the key part he played
in building the underground revolutionary movement in Ulster.[20] It
would seem that Russell is at last receiving the recognition that his
advanced views and active role in the United Irish movement merit.

However, because Russell faded from the popular memory and his
name was so rarely invoked by later nationalists, his contribution to
the Irish nationalist tradition is easy to ignore. Although his ideali-
sation of the Irish people, his pro-Catholic leanings and his interest
in Gaelic culture anticipated the direction of Irish nationalism, his
ideological legacy is a relatively sparse one. He was not a systematic
thinker who left behind lucid and coherent theories or statements
that later nationalists could draw upon. The vagueness of his ideas
on social reform, partly a result of his expectation that all would be
well in the coming millennium, meant that his deeply radical views
had little long-term influence. Russell's dictum that 'property should
be altered in some measure' was one that many nineteenth-century
nationalists would have agreed with, but it was scarcely a slogan to
capture the public imagination. Thus it was that his published writings, though they may have had some impact on contemporaries,
were quickly forgotten. Russell's millennialist motivation may also
have contributed to this neglect. He never published anything on this
subject, and even had he done so, it probably would have been
viewed by later nationalists as an embarrassment or a curiosity.

But Russell's contribution to the Irish nationalist tradition was far
from insignificant. Although his ideological legacy may have been
slight, his pivotal role and almost ceaseless activity in the United
Irish movement made him one of its most important figures. Much
of his contribution stemmed from the influence he had on others.
Besides acting as an inspiration to many minor figures, he exercised
an influence over several prominent United Irishmen, notably Tone,
which was of the utmost importance. It was Russell who introduced
Tone to the Belfast radicals and opened the door for him to play a
part in the founding of the United Irishmen, from which position
Tone was able to pull a number of unformed ideas into shape and
lay a solid foundation for the establishment of the new organisation.[21] Russell appears to have made a significant contribution to *An*

argument on behalf of the Catholics of Ireland — the work that made Tone's reputation as a political journalist, and brought about his appointment as assistant secretary to the Catholic Committee. He can claim considerable responsibility for moderating his friend's early tendencies towards political élitism and his suspicions of the lower orders, and thus contributed to Tone's reputation as a founder of Irish social democracy. He was one of those correspondents who rekindled Tone's revolutionary ardour at a time when it was flagging and encouraged him to leave his new home in America to persuade the French government to mount an invasion of Ireland. And there were others he influenced besides Tone. Russell did much to imbue his friend Henry Joy McCracken with the revolutionary zeal that would make him the dominant leader in the Ulster rebellion of 1798.[22] Similarly with Emmet, Russell's encouragement to the younger man to embark on his ill-fated rising appears to have been a major consideration in his calculations.

Russell also made a notable contribution to the Irish nationalist tradition in his own right. Firstly, he played a central part in founding the United Irishmen, particularly in striving to unite Catholics and Presbyterians. Secondly, he was one of those most active in transforming the society into a popular revolutionary organisation, but because such activities were carried out largely in secret his contribution to this phase of Irish republicanism was until recently largely unacknowledged. Russell was in the forefront of attempts to co-opt Belfast artisans into the United movement and to forge a union between United Irishmen and Defenders; his efforts to transform republicanism from an élitist to a popular ideology remain of lasting significance, though not necessarily in the manner he would have wished. The pluralist republicanism of the United Irish movement did not absorb and tame Defender Catholicism as the organisation's leaders intended, but it did go some way to imbuing it with a new political consciousness, creating a hybrid ideology of sectarianism and republicanism that was to influence strongly the outlook of the Ribbonmen and later physical force movements.[23] Finally, Russell deserves to be remembered for his part in keeping United Irish militancy alive after the defeat of 1798. He was an important figure in encouraging and organising another attempt at revolt, and the only original founding member of the society to play a part in the 1803 insurrection.

Russell therefore is a figure of genuine historical significance because of the importance of his contribution in helping to create, develop and sustain the spirit of militant Irish republicanism. Given the vogue for commemoration that has come about in recent years, it is likely that in the future some will feel the need to acknowledge this contribution. But it is unlikely if any memorial could ever be as fitting as that laid over his grave in the small cemetery of Downpatrick parish church by those who loved him: a plain stone slab with the simple inscription 'The grave of Russell, 1803' that commemorates this complex and enigmatic man with quiet dignity.

NOTES

1 James Morgan, 'Sketch of the life of Thomas Russell' in *Ulster Magazine*, i (1830), pp. 39–60; Madden, *United Irishmen*, 3rd ser., ii, 137.
2 Samuel McSkimin, 'Secret history of the Irish insurrection of 1803' in *Fraser's Magazine* xiv, (July–Dec., 1836), pp. 546–67.
3 Samuel McSkimin to Hope, c. Nov 1836 (Madden papers, 873/652); printed note by Hope on 1803, 8 Jan 1838 (Hope papers, 7253/44); Madden, *United Irishmen*, 3rd ser., ii, 138.
4 J. A. Russell to the editor of *Fraser's Magazine*, 13 Jan. 1837 (Madden papers, 873/649).
5 Notes by J. A. Russell (Madden papers, 873/654); J. A. Russell to John Gray, 22 Apr. 1843 (Madden papers, 873/669).
6 Madden papers, 873/625.
7 Madden, *United Irishmen*, 3rd ser., ii, 148; compare the complete speech in Madden papers, 873/700 with the edited version in *United Irishmen*, 3rd ser., ii, 259–67.
8 Madden, *United Irishmen*, 3rd ser., ii, 281.
9 Charles Gavan Duffy, *My life in two hemispheres* (London, 1898), p. 62.
10 Notes by J. A. Russell (Madden papers, 873/674, f. 4).
11 Elliott, *Tone*, pp. 407, 411.
12 Notes by J. A. Russell (Madden papers, 873/674, f. 4v).
13 *The grave of Russell* (Madden papers, 873/675), for Gilland's authorship see D. J. O'Donoghue (ed.), *The poets of Ireland* (2nd edn, Dublin, 1912), p. 162; Florence Mary Wilson, *The coming of the earls* (Dublin, 1918), pp. 9–12.
14 Charles Gavan Duffy, *My life in two hemispheres* (London, 1898), p. 118.
15 For references by Mitchel and Mellows to Tone see Elliott, *Tone*, pp. 413–14 and Smyth, *Men of no property*, p. ix.
16 James Connolly, *Labour in Irish history* (Dublin, 1914), pp. 92, 96, 98–9.
17 Owen Dudley Edwards, 'Ireland' in Owen Dudley Edwards, Gwyfor Evans, Ioan Rhys and Hugh MacDiarmaid, *Celtic nationalism* (London, 1968), p. 80.
18 Rosamond Jacob, *The rise of the United Irishmen* (London, 1937); Helen Landreth, *The pursuit of Robert Emmet* (Dublin, 1949); Mac Giolla Easpaig, *Ruiséil* (1957); Charles Dickson, *Revolt in the North: Antrim and Down in 1798* (Dublin, 1960); Mary McNeill, *The life and times of Mary Ann McCracken: a Belfast panorama* (Dublin, 1960).
19 Brendan Clifford, *Thomas Russell and Belfast* (Belfast, 1988); John Gray, 'Millennial vision...Thomas Russell re-assessed' in *Linen Hall Review*, vi, no. 1 (spring, 1989); Woods, 'Place of Thomas Russell' (1990); *Journals* (1991);

Denis Carroll, *The man from God knows where: Thomas Russell, 1767–1803* (Dublin, 1995).

20 J. W. Boyle (ed.), *Leaders and workers* (Dublin and Cork, 1978), pp. 87–95; Elliott, *Tone* (1989), pp. 232, 255; Smyth, *Men of no property* (1992), pp. 165–7; L. M. Cullen 'Internal politics of the United Irishmen' in Dickson, Keogh and Whelan (eds), *United Irishmen* (1992), p. 178; Curtin, *United Irishmen* (1994), pp. 181–5; Thuente, *Harp re-strung* (1994), p. 18.

21 Elliott, *Tone*, p. 125.

22 Madden, *Antrim and Down in '98*, p. 9; Mary Ann McCracken to Russell, July 1798 (Reb. papers, 620/16/3).

23 Tom Garvin, 'Defenders, Ribbonmen and others: underground political networks in pre-famine Ireland' in C. H. E. Philpin (ed), *Nationalism and popular protest in pre-Famine Ireland* (Cambridge, 1987), pp. 220, 244; for the sectarian/republican ideology of Ribbonism see M. R. Beames, 'The Ribbon societies: lower-class nationalism in pre-famine Ireland' in ibid., pp. 245–63.

Bibliography

PRIMARY SOURCES: MANUSCRIPTS

British Library, London

Additional MSS 35707–14, 35770–2, Hardwicke papers
Additional MSS 33101–22, Pelham papers

India Office Records, London

Home miscellaneous series, 84

Kent County Record Office, Maidstone

MS U.840 Pratt (Camden) papers

Linen Hall Library, Belfast

Joy MSS
The minute books of the Society for Promoting Knowledge

National Archives of Ireland

Frazer MS
Official papers, OP/
Rebellion papers, 620/
State of the country papers, S.O.C. 1015/1–1017/66; 3521–3632
Westmorland (Fane) correspondence

National Library of Ireland

MS 637 Bennett's notes on Musgrave's Irish rebellions
MS 9760 Luke Cullen papers
MS 22,704 Fallon papers (documents relating to the Emmet Rising)
MS 56 Lake correspondence 1796–99
MS 54A Melville papers
MS 3212 Misc. letters of T. W. Tone

Public Record Office, Kew

Home Office papers: HO 100/31–123; correspondence relating to Ireland, 1791–1804
Privy Council papers: PC 1/3564, 3581–3; information on the Irish insurrection of 1803

Public Record Office, Northern Ireland

T/2541, Abercorn papers
D/714, Cleland papers
D/607, Downshire papers
T/765, Drennan papers
D/272, McCance collection
T/913, Miscellaneous MSS
T/3030, Redesdale papers

Royal Irish Academy

MS 23 K 53, Burrowes MS

Trinity College, Dublin

MSS 7253–6 Hope MS
MS 873 Madden papers
MSS 868–9 Sirr papers
Tone Dickason MS

PRIMARY SOURCES: PRINTED COLLECTIONS OF DOCUMENTS

Bartlett, Thomas. 'Select documents XXXVIII: Defenders and Defenderism in 1795' in *Irish Historical Studies*, xxiv, no. 95 (May 1985), 373–94
Bartlett, Thomas. *Life of Theobald Wolfe Tone* (Dublin, 1998)
Beresford, Rt. Hon. William (ed.), *The correspondence of the Rt. Hon. John Beresford*, 2 vols (London, 1854)
Memoirs and correspondence of Viscount Castlereagh, marquess of Londonderry (ed.), 12 vols (London, 1848–54)
Chart, D. A. (ed.), *The Drennan letters ... 1776–1819* (Belfast, 1931)
H. M. C., *Charlemont MSS. The manuscripts and correspondence of James, first earl of Charlemont*, 2 vols (London, 1891–4)

Colchester, Lord Charles (ed.), *Diary and correspondence of Charles Abbot, Lord Colchester*, 3 vols (London, 1861)

H. M. C., *Dropmore MSS. The manuscripts and correspondence of J. B. Fortesque esq., preserved at Dropmore*, 2 vols (London, 1892–4)

Edwards, R. D. (ed.), 'The minute book of the Catholic Committee, 1772–1792', *Archivium Hibernicum*, ix (1942), 1–172

Gilbert, J. T. (ed.), *Documents relating to Ireland, 1795–1804* (Dublin, 1893)

Hobson, Bulmer (ed.), *The letters of Wolfe Tone* (Dublin, 1921)

Howell, T. B. and T. J. (eds), *A complete collection of state trials*, 34 vols (London, 1811–26)

MacDonagh, Michael (ed.), *The viceroy's postbag* (London, 1904)

McDowell, R. B. 'Select documents, II "United Irish plans of parliamentary reform in 1793" ' in *I. H. S.*, iii, no. 9 (Mar. 1942), pp. 49–51

—, 'The proceedings of the Dublin Society of United Irishmen', *Analecta Hibernia*, no. 17 (1949), pp. 3–143

T. W. Moody, R. B. McDowell and C. J. Woods (eds), *The writings of Theobald Wolfe Tone 1973–98: volume I: Tone's career in Ireland to June 1795* (Oxford, 1998).

Moran, P. F. (ed.), *Spicilegium Ossoriense: being a collection of original letters and papers illustrative of the history of the Irish church from the reformation to the year 1800*, 3 vols (Dublin, 1874–84)

O'Conor Don, C. O. (ed), *The O'Conors of Connaught: an historical memoir* (Dublin, 1891)

O'Faolain, Sean (ed.), *The autobiography of Theobald Wolfe Tone* (London, 1937)

Ross, Charles. *Correspondence of Charles 1st Marquis Cornwallis*, 3 vols (London, 1849)

Thale, Mary (ed.), *Selections from the papers of the London Corresponding Society, 1792–1799* (Cambridge, 1983)

PARLIAMENTARY PROCEEDINGS AND REPORTS

Journals of the House of Commons of the kingdom of Ireland, 21 vols (Dublin, 1796–1802)

The parliamentary history of England...*15 May 1786 to 8 Feb 1788*, xxvi (London, 1816)

The parliamentary register: or history of the proceedings and debates of the House of Commons of Ireland, 1781–97 , 17 vols (Dublin, 1782–1801)

Report from the committee of secrecy of the House of Commons of Ireland (Dublin, 1798); (includes the 1793 and 1797 secret reports)

Report from the committee of secrecy of the House of Lords of Ireland (Dublin, 1798)

NEWSPAPERS AND OTHER PERIODICALS

The Belfast News Letter 1790–1803
Bolg an tSolair [Gaelic Magazine] (Belfast, 1795)
The Courier 1797–8
Dublin Chronicle 1788–91
Dublin Evening Post 1803
Faulkner's Dublin Journal 1795–8, 1803
Hibernian Journal 1798, 1803
Northern Star 1792–7
Saunders' Newsletter, 27 Aug. 1798
The Press 1797–8
Walker's Hibernian Magazine 1792

CONTEMPORARY WORKS AND MEMOIRS

[Bannantine, James]. *Memoirs of the life of Colonel E. M. Despard* (London, 1799)

Barrington, Jonah. *Historical anecdotes and secret memoirs of the legislative union between Great Britain and Ireland* (London, 1809)

—, *Personal sketches and recollections of his own time*, 2 vols (London, 1830)

Birch, Thomas Ledlie. *The obligations upon Christians and especially ministers to be exemplary in their lives, particularly at this important period when the prophecies are seemingly about to be fulfilled in the fall of Antichrist, as an introduction to the flowing in of Jew and Gentile into the Christian church* (Belfast, 1794)

Memoirs of Miles Byrne, ed. by his widow (3 vols, Paris, 1863)

The life of the Reverend James Coigly...as written by himself (London, 1798)

Cox, Walter. *Remarks by one of the people to whom John Swift Emerson has appealed* (Dublin,1804)

Dickson, William Steel. *Three sermons on the subject of scripture politics* (Belfast, 1793)

—, *A narrative of confinement and exile of William Steel Dickson* (Dublin, 1814)

Dobbs, Francis. *Memoirs of Francis Dobbs esq., also genuine reports of his speeches in parliament on the subject of an union and his prediction of the second coming of the messiah with extracts from his poem on the millennium* (Dublin, 1800),

[Dornin, Bernard]. *Sketch of the life of Samuel Neilson of Belfast* (New York, 1804)

Drennan, William. *A protest from one of the people of Ireland against an union with Great Britain* (Dublin, 1800)

Fleming, Robert. *A discourse on the rise and fall of the Antichrist wherein the revolution in France and the downfall of the monarchy in that kingdom are distinctly pointed out* (Belfast, 1795)

Gage, [Catharine]. *A history of the island of Rathlin, 1851* (Coleraine?, 1995)

Gamble, John. *Sketches of history, politics and manners taken in Dublin and the north of Ireland in the autumn of 1810* (London, 1811)

Godwin, William. *Enquiry concerning political justice*, ed. K. Codell Carter (Oxford, 1971)

Goldsmith, Louis. *Secret history of the cabinet of Bonaparte*, 4th edition (London, 1810)

Grimshaw, William. *Incidents recalled or sketches from memory* (Philadelphia, 1848)

[H. B. C.] *The insurrection of the 23rd of July* (Dublin, 1803)

Jackson, William. *Strictures on Paine's age of reason* (Dublin, 1794)

Joy, Henry (ed.), *Belfast politics* (Belfast, 1794)

—, *Historical collections relative to the town of Belfast* (Belfast, 1817)

Lawless, John. *The Belfast politics enlarged: being a compendium of the political history of Ireland for the last forty years* (Belfast, 1818).

MacNeven, William James. *An argument for independence in opposition to a union* (Dublin, 1798)

—, *Pieces of Irish history* (New York, 1807)

McHenry, James. *O'Halloran: or the insurgent chief, an Irish historical tale of 1798*, 2 vols (Philadelphia, 1824)

Medland, W. M. and Weobly, Charles. *A collection of remarkable and interesting criminal trials* (London, 1803)

Musgrave, Richard. *Memoirs of the different rebellions in Ireland*, 2 vols (3rd edn, Dublin, 1802)

Newton, Isaac. *Observations upon the prophecies of Daniel and the apocalypse of St John* (Dublin, 1733)

Paddy's resource: being a select collection of modern and patriotic songs for the use of the people of Ireland (Belfast, 1795 and 1798) and (Dublin, 1803)

Paine, Thomas. (Moncure Daniel Conway, ed.), *The writings of Thomas Paine* (New York, 1967)

—, *The rights of man* (H. Collins, ed.) (Harmondsworth, 1976)

Plowden, Francis. *An historical review of the state of Ireland, from the invasion of that country under Henry II to its union with Great Britain*, 2 vols (London, 1807)

Pope, Alexander. *The works of Alexander Pope, esq.* (London, 1769)

Price, Richard. *Observations on the American revolution* (London, 1784)

Priestley, Joseph. *Letters to the Rt. Hon. Edmund Burke occasioned by his reflections on the revolution in France* (Dublin, 1791)

Richardson, William. *History of the origin of the Irish yeomanry* (Dublin, 1801)

Statement of the origin and progress of the societies of United Irishmen (Dublin, 1798)

Memoirs of William Sampson (New York, 1807).

Stavely, William. *A discourse on the rise and fall of the antichrist wherein the revolution in France and the downfall of the monarchy in that kingdom are distinctly pointed out* (Belfast, 1795)

—, *An appeal to light, or the tenets of the deists examined and disapproved* (Belfast, 1796)

Stokes, Whitley. *A reply to Mr Paine's age of reason* (Dublin, 1795)

Taaffe, Denis. *The probability, causes, and consequences of an union between Great Britain and Ireland* (Dublin, 1798)

Taylor, W. C. *History of Ireland…with additions by William Sampson*, 2 vols (New York, 1833)

Teeling, Charles Hamilton. *Sequel to personal narrative of the 'Irish rebellion' of 1798* (Belfast, 1832)

—, *Personal narrative of the Irish rebellion of 1798* (London, 1928)

Tissot, P. F. *Les trois conjurés irlandais; ou l'ombre d'Emmet* (Paris, 1804)

[T. W. Tone]. *Spanish war: an enquiry how far Ireland is bound, of right, to embark in the impending contest on the side of Great Britain* (Dublin, 1790)

Tone, T. W. *An argument on behalf of the Catholics of Ireland* (Dublin, 1791)

[Tytler, James]. *Paine's age of reason — a vindication of the doctrines of Christianity from the aspersions of that author, by a citizen of the world* (Belfast, 1794)

Tytler, James. *The rising of the sun in the west or the origin and progress of liberty* (Salem, 1795)

The trial of Thomas Russell, general in the late insurrection (Dublin?, 1803)

Verax. *Observations on a pamphlet entitled 'An appeal to the public' by John Swift Emerson on the subject of the arrest of the late General Russell* (Dublin, 1804)

SECONDARY SOURCES

Adams, J. R. R. *The printed word and the common man: popular culture in Ulster* (Belfast, 1987)

Aitken, G. A. *The life and works of John Arbuthnot* (Oxford, 1892)

Anderson, John. *History of the Linen Hall Library* (Belfast, 1888)

Anstey, Roger. *The Atlantic slave trade and British abolition, 1760–1810* (London, 1975)

Bailie, W. D. 'William Steel Dickson D.D. (1744–1824)' in *Irish Booklore* II (1976), pp. 238–67

—, 'Revd. Samuel Barber, 1738–1811, national volunteer and United Irishman' in J. L. M. Haire (ed.), *Challenge and conflict: essays in Presbyterian doctrine* (Antrim, 1981), pp. 72–95

Bartlett, Thomas. 'An end to the "moral economy": the Irish militia disturbances of 1793' in *Past and Present*, no. 99 (May, 1983), pp. 41–64

—, *The fall and rise of the Irish nation* (Dublin, 1992)

Beames, Michael R. 'The Ribbon societies: lower class nationalism in pre-famine Ireland' in C. H. E. Philpin (ed.), *Nationalism and popular protest in pre-famine Ireland* (Cambridge, 1987), pp. 245–63

Beckett, J. C. and Glasscock, R. E. (eds), *Belfast: the origin and growth of an industrial city* (Belfast, 1967)

Benn, George. *History of the town of Belfast,* 2 vols (London, 1877)

Bigger, F. J. 'Queries concerning William Orr, Henry Joy McCracken, Henry Monroe, James Hope, Samuel Neilson and Thomas Russell, leaders of '98' in *Ulster Journal of Archaeology,* ii, xii (Jan., 1906), p. 48

—, 'Note on Russell's Greek testament' in *Irish Book Lover,* xiii (Oct., 1921), p. 37.

—, *Four shots from Down* (Ballynahinch, 1982), p. 47

Blackstock, Allan. *An ascendancy army: the Irish yeomanry 1796–1834* (Dublin, 1998)

Blaugh, Mark. 'The myth of the old poor law and the making of the new' in *Journal of Economic History,* no. 2 (June, 1963), pp. 151–84

Bloch, Ruth. *Visionary republic: millennial themes in American thought 1756–1800* (Cambridge, 1988)

Boyle, J. W. (ed.), *Leaders and workers* (Dublin and Cork, 1978)

Cadell, Patrick. 'Irish soldiers in India' in *Irish Sword,* i (1949–53)

Cameron, Charles A. *History of the Royal College of Surgeons in Ireland* (Dublin, 1886)

Campbell, J. J. *Fifty years of Ulster* (Belfast, 1941)

Cannon, Richard. *Historical record of the thirty-sixth or Herefordshire regiment of foot* (London, 1853)

Carroll, Denis. *The man from God knows where* (Dublin, 1995)

Chase, Malcolm. *'The people's farm': English radical agrarianism 1775–1840* (Oxford, 1988)

Clarkson, J. D. *Labour and nationalism in Ireland* (New York, 1925)

Clifford, Brendan. *Thomas Russell and Belfast* (Belfast, 1988)

Cohn, Norman. *The pursuit of the millennium: revolutionary millenarians and mystical anarchists of the Middle Ages* (revised ed., London, 1970).

Connolly, James. *Labour in Irish history* (Dublin, 1914)

Crawford, W. H. 'The Belfast middle classes in the late eighteenth century' in David Dickson, Dáire Keogh and Kevin Whelan (eds), *The United Irishmen: republicanism, radicalism and rebellion* (Dublin, 1993), pp. 62–73

Cullen, L. M. 'Political structures of the Defenders' in Hugh Gough and David Dickson (eds), *Ireland and the French revolution* (Dublin, 1990), pp. 117–38

—, 'The internal politics of the United Irishmen' in David Dickson, Dáire Keogh and Kevin Whelan (eds), *The United Irishmen:*

republicanism, radicalism and rebellion (Dublin, 1993), pp. 176–96

Curtin, Nancy J. 'The Belfast uniform: Theobald Wolfe Tone' in *Éire\Ireland*, xx, no. 2 (summer, 1985), pp. 40–69

—, 'The transformation of the Society of United Irishmen into a mass-based organisation, 1794–6 ' in *Irish Historical Studies*, xxiv, no. 96 (Nov. 1985), pp. 463–92

—, 'United Irish organisation in Ulster' in David Dickson, Dáire Keogh and Kevin Whelan (eds), *The United Irishmen: republicanism, radicalism and rebellion* (Dublin, 1993), pp. 209–21

—, *The United Irishmen, popular politics in Ulster and Dublin, 1791–8* (Oxford, 1994)

Daly, J. B. (ed.), *Ireland in '98* (London, 1888)

Dickson, Charles. *The life of Michael Dwyer* (Dublin, 1944)

—, *Revolt in the North: Antrim and Down in 1798* (Dublin, 1960)

Dixon, F. E. 'Richard Kirwan, the Dublin philosopher' in *Dublin Historical Record*, xxiv (1971), pp. 52–64

Dodwell, H. H. (ed.), *The Cambridge shorter history of India* (New Delhi, 1979)

Donnelly, James S. 'Propagating the cause of the United Irishmen' in *Studies: an Irish quarterly review*, lxix (1981), pp. 5–23

Donovan, Michael. 'Biographical account of the late Richard Kirwan, esq.' in *Proceedings of the Royal Irish Academy*, iv (1847–50), lxxxi–cxviii

Doorly, Bernadette. 'Newgate prison' in David Dickson (ed.), *The gorgeous mask: Dublin 1700–1850* (Dublin, 1987), pp. 121–31

Duffy, Charles Gavan. *My life in two hemispheres* (London, 1898)

Dunne, Tom. *Wolfe Tone, colonial outsider* (Cork, 1982)

—, 'Popular ballads, revolutionary rhetoric and politicisation' in Hugh Gough and David Dickson (eds), *Ireland and the French revolution* (Dublin, 1990), pp. 139–55

Edwards, Owen Dudley. 'Ireland' in Owen Dudley Edwards, Gwyfor Evans, Ioan Rhys and Hugh MacDiarmaid, *Celtic nationalism* (London, 1968), pp. 1–209

Elliott, Marianne. 'The "Despard conspiracy" reconsidered' in *Past and Present*, 75 (1977), pp. 46–61

—, 'The origins and transformation of early Irish republicanism' in *International Review of Social History*, xxii, pt. 3 (1978), pp. 405–28

—, *Partners in Revolution, the United Irishmen and France* (New Haven and London, 1982)

—, *Wolfe Tone, prophet of Irish independence* (New Haven and London, 1989)

—, 'The Defenders in Ulster' in David Dickson, Dáire Keogh and Kevin Whelan (eds), *The United Irishmen: republicanism, radicalism and rebellion* (Dublin, 1993), pp. 222–33

Emmet, T. A. (ed.) *Ireland under English rule*, 2 vols (New York, 1903)

—, *Memoir of Thomas Addis and Robert Emmet*, 2 vols (New York, 1915)

Finegan, Francis. 'Was John Keogh an informer?' in *Studies: an Irish quarterly review*, 39 (1950), pp. 75–86

Finegan, John. *Anne Devlin: patriot and heroine* (Dublin, 1992)

Fitzhenry, Edna C. *Henry Joy McCracken* (Dublin, 1936)

Fitzpatrick, W. J. *The secret service under Pitt* (London, 1892)

—, *The sham squire* (new edn, Dublin, 1895)

Forrest, Denys. *Tiger of Mysore: the life and death of Tipu Sultan* (London, 1979)

Fortescue, J. W. *History of the British army*, iii (London, 1902)

Foster, R. F. *Modern Ireland 1600–1972* (London, 1988)

Fox, C. M. *Annals of the Irish harpers* (London, 1911)

Froggatt, Peter. 'Dr James McDonnell' in *The Glynns*, ix (1981), pp. 17–31

Fruchtman jun., Jack. 'The apocalyptic politics of Richard Price and Joseph Priestley: a study of late eighteenth century millennialism' in *Transactions of the American Philosophical Society*, lxxiii, pt. 4 (Philadelphia, 1983)

Fuller, J. F. 'The Tones: father and son' in *Journal of the Cork Historical and Archaeological Society*, xxix (1924), pp. 93–101

Garrett, Clark. 'Joseph Priestley, the millennium and the French revolution' in *Journal of the History of Ideas*, no. 34 (1973), pp. 51–66

—, *Respectable folly: millenarians and the French revolution in France and England* (London, 1975)

Garvin, Tom. 'Defenders, Ribbonmen and others: underground networks in pre-famine Ireland' in C. H. E. Philpin (ed.), *Nationalism and popular protest in pre-famine Ireland* (Cambridge, 1987), pp. 219–44

Gaughan, J. A. *The knights of Glin* (Dublin, 1978)

Gibbs, F. W. *Joseph Priestley, adventurer in science and champion of truth* (London, 1965).

Gilbert, J. T. *A history of the city of Dublin* (Dublin, 1861)

Goodwin, Albert. *The friends of liberty: the English democratic movement in the age of the French revolution* (London, 1979)

Grattan, Henry jun. *Memoirs of the life and times of the Rt. Hon. Henry Grattan,* 5 vols (London, 1839–46)

Gray, John. 'Millennial vision…Thomas Russell re-assessed', *The Linen Hall Review,* vi, no. 1 (spring, 1989), pp. 5–9

—, 'Mary Anne McCracken: Belfast revolutionary and pioneer of feminism' in Dáire Keogh and Nicholas Furlong (eds), *The women of 1798* (Dublin, 1998), pp. 47–63

Harrison, J. F. C. *The second coming: popular millenarianism 1780–1850* (London, 1975)

Hill, Myrtle, Turner, Brian and Dawson, Kenneth (eds), *1798 rebellion in County Down* (Newtownards, 1998)

Hone, J. A. *For the cause of truth: radicalism in London, 1796–1821* (Oxford, 1982)

Hutchinson, John. *The dynamics of cultural nationalism* (London, 1954)

Inglis, Brian. *The freedom of the press in Ireland, 1784–1841* (London, 1954)

Jacob, Rosamond. *The rise of the United Irishmen* (London, 1937)

Kavanaugh, Ann C. *John Fitzgibbon, earl of Clare* (Dublin, 1997)

Kelly, Liam. *'A flame now quenched': rebels and Frenchmen in Leitrim 1793–1798* (Dublin, 1998)

Kelly, James. *Henry Grattan* (Dublin, 1993)

Kennedy, David. 'James McDonnell, 1762–1845' in *Capuchin Annual* (1945–6), pp. 353–60

Kennedy, W. B. 'The Irish Jacobins' in *Studia Hibernica*, xiv (1976), pp. 109–21

Keogh, Dáire (ed.), *A patriot priest: the life of Father James Coigly 1761–1798* (Cork, 1998)

Killen, John. *A history of the Linenhall Library, 1788–1988* (Belfast, 1988)

Landreth, Helen. *The pursuit of Robert Emmet* (Dublin, 1949)

Latimer, W. T. *Ulster biographies: relating chiefly to the rebellion of 1798* (Belfast, 1893)

Latocnaye, Jacques Louis Bougrenet, Chevalier de. *A Frenchman's walk through Ireland*, translated by John Stevenson (Belfast, 1917)

Lecky, W. E. H. *A history of Ireland in the eighteenth century*, 5 vols (London, 1892)

MacDermot, Frank. *Theobald Wolfe Tone: a biographical study* (London, 1939)

—, 'Arthur O'Connor' in *Irish Historical Studies*, xv, no. 57 (Mar. 1966), pp. 48–69

Mac Giolla Easpaig, Séamus N. *Tomás Ruiséil* (Dublin, 1957)

McBride, I. R. *Scripture politics: Ulster Presbyterians and Irish radicalism in the late eighteenth century* (Oxford, 1998)

McCalman, Iain. *Radical underworld: prophets, revolutionaries and pornographers in London, 1795–1840* (Cambridge, 1988)

McDonagh, Oliver. *States of mind: a study of Anglo-Irish conflict, 1780–1980* (London, 1983)

McDowell, R. B. 'The personnel of the Dublin Society of United Irishmen, 1791–4' in *Irish Historical Studies*, ii, no. 5 (Mar. 1940), pp. 12–53

—, *Irish public opinion, 1750–1800* (London, 1944)

—, *Ireland in the age of imperialism and revolution, 1760–1801* (Oxford, 1979)

McEvoy, Brendan. 'Father James Quigley' in *Seanchas Ardmhacha*, v (1970), pp. 247–59

—, 'The Peep of Day Boys and Defenders in the County Armagh' in *Seanchas Ardmhacha*, xii, no. 1 (1986), pp. 123–63; xii, no. 2 (1987), pp. 60–127

McLaughlin, P. J. 'Richard Kirwan' in *Studies: an Irish quarterly review*, xxviii (1939), pp. 461–74, 593–605, xxix (1940), pp. 71–83, 281–300

McNeill, Mary. *The life and times of Mary Ann McCracken, 1770–1866: a Belfast panorama* (Dublin, 1960)

McSkimin, Samuel. 'Secret history of the Irish insurrection of 1803' in *Frazer's Magazine*, xiv (July–Dec., 1836), pp. 546–67

—, *Annals of Ulster, 1790–1798* , ed. E. J. Crum (Belfast, 1906)

Madden, R. R. *The United Irishmen, their lives and times*, 3rd ser., 3 vols (Dublin, 1846)

—, *The United Irishmen, their lives and times*, ser. i–iv in 4 vols, 2nd edn (Dublin, 1858)

—, *The United Irishmen, their lives and times*, 4th ser., 2nd edn (Dublin, 1860)

—, *Literary remains of the United Irishmen* (Dublin, 1887)

—, *Antrim and Down in '98* (Glasgow, 1888)

Marshall, J. J. *History of Dungannon* (Dungannon, 1929)

Miller, David W. *Queen's rebels, Ulster loyalism in historical perspective* (Dublin, 1978)

—, 'Presbyterianism and "modernisation" in Ulster' in C.H.E.

Philpin (ed.), *Nationalism and popular protest in pre-Famine Ireland* (Cambridge, 1987), pp. 80–109

Monaghan, John J. 'The rise and fall of the Belfast cotton industry' in *Irish Historical Studies*, iii, no. 9 (Mar. 1942), pp. 1–17

Moody, T. W. 'The political ideas of the United Irishmen' in *Ireland Today*, iii, no.1 (1938), pp. 15–25

Moorsom, W. S. *Historical record of the fifty-second regiment* (2nd ed., London, 1860)

Morgan, James. 'Sketch of the life of Thomas Russell' in *Ulster Magazine*, i (1830), pp. 39–60

Mullan, John. *Sentiment and sociability: the language of feeling in the eighteenth century* (Oxford, 1988)

Mulloy, Sheila. 'James Joseph MacDonnell, "the best known of the United Irish chiefs of the west' in *Cathair na Mart: Journal of the Westport Historical Society* (1985), v, 67–9

Ó Broin, Leon. *The unfortunate Mr Robert Emmet* (Dublin, 1958)

O'Byrne, Cathal. *As I roved out in Belfast and district* (Dublin, 1946)

Ó Casaide, Séamas. *The Irish language in Belfast and Co. Down 1601–1850* (Dublin, 1930)

Ó Cuív, Brian. 'Irish language and literature, 1691–1845' in T. W. Moody and W. E. Vaughan (eds), *A new history of Ireland, iv, eighteenth-century Ireland 1691–1800* (Oxford, 1986), pp. 374–423

O'Farrell, Patrick. 'Millenarianism, messianism, and utopianism in Irish history' in *Anglo-Irish Studies*, ii, (1976), pp. 45–68

O'Flaherty, Eamon. 'The Catholic Convention and Anglo-Irish politics, 1791–3' in *Archivium Hibernicum*, xl (1985), pp. 14–34

O'Toole, Fintan. *A traitor's kiss: the life of Richard Brinsley Sheridan* (London, 1997)

Oliver, W. H. *Prophets and millennialists: the uses of biblical prophecy in England from the 1790s to the 1840s* (Auckland, 1978)

Oman, Charles. *The unfortunate Colonel Despard and other studies* (London, 1922), pp. 1–21

Owen, D. J. *A history of Belfast* (Belfast, 1921)

Pakenham, Thomas. *The year of liberty: the story of the great rebellion of 1798* (London, 1969)

Parsons, L. H. 'The mysterious Mr Digges' in *William and Mary Quarterly*, 3rd ser., xxii (1965), pp. 486–92

Pearse, P. H. *How does she stand?* (2nd edn, Dublin 1915)

Purcell, C. W. 'Thomas Digges and William Pearce: an example of the transit of technology' in *William and Mary Quarterly,* 3rd ser., xxi (Oct., 1964), pp. 551–60

Quinn, James. 'The United Irishmen and social reform' in *Irish Historical Studies*, xxxi, no. 122 (Nov. 1998), pp. 188–201

Robbins, Caroline. *The eighteenth century commonwealthman* (Cambridge, Mass, 1959)

Russell, Conrad. *Science and social change 1700–1900* (London, 1983)

Sadleir, T. U. 'The register of Kilkenny school' in *Journal of the Royal Society of Antiquaries of Ireland*, xiv (1924)

Senior, Hereward. *Orangeism in Ireland and Britain, 1795–1836* (London, 1966)

Sibbett, R. M. *Orangeism in Ireland* 2 vols (Belfast, 1914–15)

Simms, Samuel. *Revd. James O'Coigly, United Irishman* (Belfast, 1937)

Smyth, Jim. *The men of no property: Irish radicals and popular politics in the late eighteenth century* (Dublin, 1992)

St Mark, J. J. 'The Oswald mission to Ireland from America, 20 Feb. — 8 June 1793' in *Éire/Ireland*, xxxiii, no. 2 (summer 1988), pp. 25–38

Stewart, A. T. Q. 'The harp new strung: nationalism, culture and United Irishmen' in Oliver McDonagh and W. F. Mandle (eds), *Ireland and Irish Australia, studies in cultural history* (London, 1986), pp. 258–69

—, *A deeper silence: the hidden roots of the United Irish movement* (London, 1993)

Tesch, Pieter. 'Presbyterian radicalism' in David Dickson, Dáire Keogh and Kevin Whelan (eds), *The United Irishmen: republicanism, radicalism and rebellion* (Dublin, 1993), pp. 33–48

Thompson, E. P. *The making of the English working class*, 2nd ed. (Harmondsworth, 1968)

—, 'The moral economy of the English crowd' in *Past and Present*, no. 50 (1971), pp. 76–136

Thuente, Mary Helen. *The harp re-strung: the United Irishmen and the rise of Irish literary nationalism* (New York, 1994)

Tuveson, E. L. *Redeemer nation: the idea of America's millennial role* (Chicago and London, 1968)

Vance, Norman. 'Celts, Carthaginians and constitutions: Anglo-Irish literary relations 1780–1820' in *Irish Historical Studies*, xxii, no. 87 (Mar. 1981), pp. 216–36

Wall, Maureen. 'The United Irish movement' in *Historical Studies*, v, ed. J. L. McCracken (London, 1965), pp. 122–40

Walsh, J. E. *Ireland ninety years ago* (Dublin, 1876)

Webb, J. J. *Municipal government in Ireland* (Dublin, 1918)

Wells, Roger. *Insurrection: the British experience, 1795–1803* (Gloucester, 1983)

Whelan, Kevin. 'The United Irishmen, the enlightenment and popular culture' in David Dickson, Dáire Keogh and Kevin Whelan (eds), *The United Irishmen: republicanism, radicalism and rebellion* (Dublin, 1993), pp. 297–306

Widdess, J. D. H. 'The Dublin House of Industry (1772–1838)' in William Doolin and Oliver Fitzgerald (eds), *'What's past is prologue': a retrospect of Irish medicine* (Dublin, 1952), pp. 40–55

Wilson, Florence. *The coming of the earls* (Dublin, 1918)

Woods, C. J. 'More on the Kernans of Enniskillen: Randal Kernan (1774–c. 1844) and others' in *Clogher Record*, x, no. 1 (1979), pp. 23–5

—, 'The authorship of a letter reccived by Tone in America in 1795' in *Eighteenth-Century Ireland*, v (1990), pp. 192–4

—, 'The place of Thomas Russell in the United Irish movement' in Hugh Gough and David Dickson (eds), *Ireland and the French revolution* (Dublin, 1990), pp. 83–108

Young, R. M. *Historical notices of old Belfast* (Belfast, 1896)

—, 'Edward Bunting's Irish music and the McCracken family' in *Ulster Journal of Archaeology*, iv, no. 3 (1898), pp. 175–8

Zimmerman, Georges Denis. *Irish political street ballads and rebel songs, 1780–1900* (Geneva, 1966)

DICTIONARIES AND REFERENCE WORKS

Dictionary of national biography, 22 vols (London, 1908–9)

G.E.C., *The complete peerage*, ed. H.A. Doubleday and Howard de Walden, vii (London, 1929)

O' Donoghue, D. J. (ed.), *The poets of Ireland: a biographical and bibliographical dictionary of Irish writers of English verse*, 2nd edn (Dublin, 1912)

UNPUBLISHED THESES

Monaghan, John J. 'A social and economic history of Belfast, 1790–1800' (MA thesis, Queen's University, Belfast, 1936)

Stewart, A. T. Q. 'The transformation of Presbyterian radicalism in the North of Ireland 1792–1825', (MA thesis, Queen's University, Belfast, 1956)

WRITINGS BY THOMAS RUSSELL

Letter signed 'E.', *Northern Star,* 31 Aug. 1793

'On tradesmen's combinations', *Northern Star,* 14 Nov. 1793

[with William Sampson], *The lion of old England or democracy confounded* (Belfast, 1794)

[with William Sampson], 'Chinese journal' in *Northern Star,* 8, 15 Jan.; 5, 26 Feb.; 9 Mar. 1795

A letter to the people of Ireland on the present situation of the country (Belfast, 1796)

Letter by Russell, *Dublin Evening Post,* 22 Dec. 1796

'Mourn lost Hibernia' in *The Press,* 4 Nov. 1797

Statements written for government, Sept.–Oct. 1803 (P.R.O. HO, 100/114/11–12, 119–22)

'On Mrs Emmet's visit to her husband' in R.R. Madden, *Literary remains of the United Irishmen* (Dublin, 1887), p. 284.

'Erin's address to Caledonia' in R.R. Madden, *Literary remains of the United Irishmen* (Dublin, 1887), p. 285–7.

Woods, C. J. (ed.). *Journals and memoirs of Thomas Russell, 1791–5* (Dublin, 1991). (These are based on manuscripts in the National Archives Rebellion papers, 620/15/6/3, 620/20/33, 620/21/23 and T.C.D. Sirr papers MS 868/1 ff 15–20v, 21–3v, 39, 40–3v, 52–3, 100–100v, 184–4v, 207–7v and 326–6v).

Probably by Russell

'A letter to the people', 19 Feb. 1799 (Reb. papers, 620/7/74/12)

Article on the Defenders, *Northern Star,* 18 May 1795

'Enslavement of the Africans' 11 Feb. 1792 (Reb. papers, 620/19/56)

Index